REGIONAL DISPARITIES IN HUMAN DEVELOPMENT

REGIONAL DISPARITIES IN HUMAN DEVELOPMENT
In Haryana
A Spatio-Temporal Analysis

Dr Raj Kumar

KALPAZ

ISBN: 978-93-5128-190-0

Price : 1350

First Published, 2016

Published by

Kalpaz Publications
C-30, Satyawati Nagar,
Delhi-110052
Ph. : 9212142040
E-mail: kalpaz@hotmail.com

Printed at : G. Print Process, Delhi

Cataloging in Publication Data—DK

Courtesy: D.K. Agencies (P) Ltd. <docinfo@dkagencies.com>

Kumar, Raj, 1960- author.
Regional disparities in human development in Haryana : a spatio-temporal analysis: 2001-2011 / Dr Raj Kumar.
pages cm

1. Social indicators—India—Haryana—Regional disparities. 2. Economic indicators—India—Haryana—Regional disparities. 3. Poverty—India—Haryana—Regional disparities. 4. Poverty—India—Haryana—Statistics. 5. Women in economic development—India—Haryana—Regional disparities. 6. Women in economic development—India—Haryana—Statistics. I. Title.

HN690.H37K86 2016 DDC 307.14120954558 23

Contents

Preface

From the second half of the last century, there has been a growing school of thought that human development is not just economic growth but it is also about growth with expansion of choices, access to services and participation of people in the process of development leading to their empowerment. It has been realized that longevity, education and access to resources are the most crucial choices to live a decent life. This is why; the Human Development Index (HDI) developed in UNDP's first Human Development Report (HDR) combines these three essential elements. Since 1990, UNDP has been bringing out global HDRs every year by adding additional criteria for the measurement of human advancement and wellbeing of the people belonging to various nations.

The methodology used by UNDP has undergone a number of changes over time due to geographical conditions of the regions, non availability of data and relevance of index components. Besides, the unit of study has also been changing moving from countries to states and districts to highlight the regional disparities at micro level. India introduced its first National Human Development Report in 2001 by incorporating some changes in methodology used by UNDP.

In Haryana, the idea of human development calls for strenuous endeavour not only to identify and recognise the disparities between regions and genders but also to bring down these disparities to an acceptable level with compliant actions. Addressing relative deprivations amongst regions and people in education, in health, in standard of living, in security, in dignity and in basic human rights, is a serious concern of human development. The present report thrusts on the Spatio-temporal analysis of human development parameters at the district level during 2001-2011 in Haryana. The core of this report is the regional disparities existing in the state in terms of income, education and health dimensions. Whereas Human Development Index focuses on the development perspective, Gender Development Index throws light on the adjusted average achievements to reflect the disparities between males and females in these dimensions. Besides, Human Poverty Index highlights the deprivation aspect of the people in the state. I hope this report shall work as a guiding tool for the state government to concentrate on the grey areas with effective policy measures.

I feel highly beholden to Indian Council of Social Science Research (ICSSR) for providing me an opportunity to take up the research project with hassle free financial support.

I am highly grateful to Professor H. Ramachandran (Former Chairman, Department of Geography, Delhi School of Economics, University of Delhi), my revered teacher for his advice, motivation and intellectual support.

I am profoundly obliged to Sqn. Ldr. Dr. Gurdial Singh (Principal, Govt. College, Hansi) and my Department Colleagues Dr. Indraj Singh and Dr Pardeep Verma for their constant stimulus and extending all support throughout the course of research work.

I extend my warm appreciation to my student Ms. Meenu Kumari (Former Research Associate, Haryana Space Application Centre, Hisar) for providing me priceless technical support in the preparation of maps.

Dr Raj Kumar

1

Geographical Profile of Haryana

Location

Haryana is a landlocked state located between 27°37' north and 30°35' north latitudes and 74°28' east and 77°36' east longitudes. It is one of the twenty eight states of India and is situated in the north-western part of the country. Situated on the doorstep of the national capital Delhi, Haryana is bounded on the north west by the state of Punjab, on the north and north-east by the states of Himachal Pradesh and Uttarakhand, on the east by the state of Uttar Pradesh and the State of Delhi, and on the south and south-west by the state of Rajasthan. Chandigarh, which is located in the north-west of the state, serves as the capital of not only that territory but also of the states of Haryana and Punjab.

Historical Background

Archaeological excavations reveal that Haryana has been one of the cradles of Indian culture and civilisation. It was the home of the legendary *Bharat* dynasty, which has given the name *Bharat* to India. The region has been the scene of many a war as the Gateway to north India. It has witnessed crucial battles with successive streams of Huns, Turks and Afghans.

In the medieval period, Panipat became the ground for two major battles with the Mughals and by 1556 Mughals had established their rule over this region. Towards the middle of the eighteenth century, Marathas had established their influence, but after their defeat in the 3rd battle of Panipat, the Britishers assumed power in this region. Afterwards, the people of Haryana ardently and valiantly took part in the freedom struggle and Haryana remained one of the major sites for the independence struggle.

After independence, Haryana became a part of Punjab province, which had been divided during the partition into East and West Punjab. It was

Table 1.1: Administrative Structure of Haryana

Sr. No.	*Districts*	*Sub-Divisions*	*Tahsils*	*Sub-tahsils*	*Blocks*	*Inhabited Villages†*
1.	Ambala	3	3	4	6	482
2.	Panchkula	2	2	3	4	224
3.	Yamuna Nagar	2	3	3	6	613
4.	Kurukshetra	2	3	3	5	407
5.	Kaithal	2	4	3	6	270
6.	Karnal	3	5	3	6	422
7.	Panipat	2	3	2	5	179
8.	Sonepat	3	4	1	7	323
9.	Rohtak	2	3	1	5	146
10.	Jhajjar	3	4	1	5	247

(Contd.)

(Contd. Table 1.1)

Sr. No.	*Districts*	*Sub-Divisions*	*Tahsils*	*Sub-tahsils*	*Blocks*	*Inhabited Villages†*
11.	Gurgaon	3	5	0	4	694
12.	Faridabad	2	2	1	2	413
13.	Palwal*	3	3	0	4	....
14.	Rewari	2	3	1	5	397
15.	Mahendergarh	2	2	3	5	368
16.	Mewat*	2	4	1	5	....
17.	Hisar	2	4	4	9	272
18.	Fatehabad	3	3	3	6	243
19.	Sirsa	3	4	2	7	321
20.	Jind	3	3	3	7	306
21.	Bhiwani	5	7	2	10	437
Total	**21**	**54**	**74**	**44**	**119**	**6764**

Source: Statistical Abstract Haryana, 2008-09
† As per 2001 Census.
* Villages of Palwal and Mewat are included in Faridabad and Gurgaon districts respectively.

only in 1966 following the Punjab Reorganisation Act that Haryana emerged as a separate entity in the Indian political landscape.

Resources and their Utilisation

Haryana is spread over an area of 44,212 sq. kms. Being a small state it occupies only 1.34 per cent of the total geographical area of the country with 20th rank in twenty eight states. It has two major physiographic regions. First is Alluvial Plains (with the elevation of 210-270 metres) that cover most of the state and the second is Shiwalik Range of Himalayas, a strip of highly dissected topography. The alluvial plains are drained by the only perennial river, the Yamuna that makes eastern boundary of the state. However, many seasonal streams flowing from the Shiwalik range such as Ghaggar, Markanda, Chautang, etc. pass through the area.

The soils of Haryana are generally deep and fertile except for the eroded lands of the hilly terrain in the north-east and the sandy areas of the south-west. Haryana experiences extreme climatic conditions. Summers are quite hot and the winters distinctly cold. Arid to semi-arid conditions prevail in the most of the parts of Haryana with an average annual rainfall of 45 cm.

Agriculturally Haryana is a prosperous state, which witnessed the successful Green Revolution that led to a great deal of prosperity in its rural economy. It contributes a significant quantity of wheat and rice to the central pool. Besides cash crops like cotton, sugar cane, rape and mustard seed etc. are produced here in a large quantity.

As far as manufacturing sector is concerned, Haryana has shown a notable progress especially during the last twenty years. Haryana excels in agriculture based manufacturing industries. Among the most important of such industries are cotton processing, sugar industry and manufacturing

Table 1.2: Divisional Setup of Districts

Sr. No.	*Divisions*	*Included Districts*		
		Number	*% of the Total*	*Name*
1.	Ambala	5	23.8	Ambala, Panchkula, Yamuna Nagar, Kurukshetra, Kaithal
2.	Rohtak	5	23.8	Karnal, Panipat, Sonepat, Rohtak, Jhajjar
3.	Gurgaon	6	28.6	Gurgaon, Faridabad, Palwal, Rewari, Mahendergarh, Mewat,
4.	Hisar	5	23.8	Hisar, Fatehabad, Sirsa, Jind, Bhiwani

Source: Statistical Abstract Haryana, 2008-09.

of farm machinery. Automobile industry is the latest phenomenon of Haryana in this context.

Administrative Setup

For administrative reasons, the state is divided into four divisions namely, Ambala, Rohtak, Gurgaon and Hisar. There are 21 districts, 54 sub-divisions, 74 tahsils, 44 sub-tahsils, 119 blocks and 6764 inhabited villages (Table 1.1 and Table 1.2).

Demographic Characteristics

With 2.09 per cent of India's population as per census of 2011 the state has obtained 16th rank amongst the Indian states. Some of the demographic characteristics have been presented in Table 1.3. Till 2001, Haryana was among the few states that revealed an increase in growth rate while the national growth rate was declining. However, in 2011 census, the state has recorded a notable decline in population growth with decennial growth rate of 19.9 per cent, though it is higher than that of national average of 18.12 per cent.

Apart from a higher population growth rate as compared to the national average, the state has higher population density also. As against an all India density of population of 382, Haryana has a high density of 573 and ranks 11th in terms of density amongst the Indian states and Union Territories in 2011 against 12th rank in 2001. Moreover, as against an all India increase of 57 points in density over the last census, the corresponding increase in Haryana was 95 points, fairly higher than the national increase.

A highly masculine sex ratio has been one of the most striking features of census history of India. As per census 2011, Kerala is the only state in India, which has a sex ratio favouring females (1084) and Puducherry is the only Union Territory, which has a sex ratio above unity (1038). The sex ratio in India is 940 and it has recorded a humble increase of Seven points as compared to the last census. Haryana has the undesirable distinction of ranking at the bottom of the scale amongst the Indian states in respect of sex ratio. Having a sex ratio of 877 in 2011, it ranks 31st and is better positioned only in respect to the National Capital Territory of Delhi (866), the Union Territories of Chandigarh (818), Dadra and Nagar Haveli (775), and Daman & Diu (618). However, Haryana has recorded an appreciable increase of 16 points in sex ratio as compared to the last census.

While the overall sex ratio may be affected by extraneous factors such as migration, it is the sex ratio in the 0-6 age group, which portrays the trend for the future. From its 31st position in respect of sex ratio of the total population, Haryana slides even further down the graph to 35th position (Last Position) amongst the Indian states and Union Territories.

Table 1.3: Growth of Population in Haryana, 1971-2011

Sr. No.	*Year*	*Population*	*Decadal Growth (%)*	*Sex Ratio*	*Density*
1	1971	10036431	-	867	227
2	1981	12922119	28.75	870	292
3	1991	16463648	27.41	865	372
4	2001	21144564	28.43	861	478
5	2011	25353081	19.9	877	573

Source: Directorate of Census Operations, Haryana.

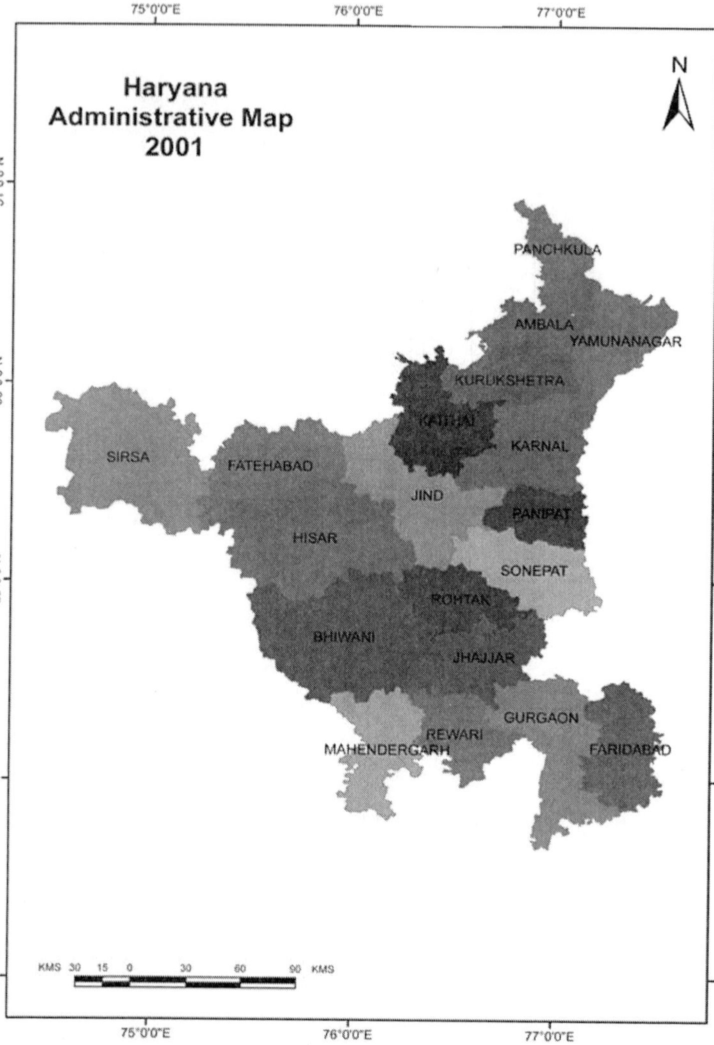

Map 1.1

The 0-6 age group sex ratio of Haryana was merely 830 as compared to 914 of India in 2011 (Table 1.4). However, the satisfactory thing is that Haryana has recorded an increase of modest 10 points in the sex ratio during 2001-2011 in contrast of a sharp decline of 59 points during 1991-2001.

Health Scenario

Haryana has performed well in many health parameters as compared to the national average (Table 1.4). Life expectancy at birth of males is

Table 1.4: Important Health Indicators- Haryana versus India

Sr. No.	Description		Haryana	India
1	Sex Ratio (2011)[1] 0-6 Years Population		830	914
2	Life Expectancy at Birth (2006-11)[2] (Years)	Male	65.5	65.63
		Female	70	67.22
3	Infant Mortality Rate (per 1000 live births)[3] (2010)	Male	46	46
		Female	49	49
		Rural	51	51
		Urban	38	31
4	Death Rate (per 1000) (2010)[3]	Rural	7	7.7
		Urban	5.6	5.8
5	Birth Rate (per 1000) (2010)[3]	Rural	23.3	23.7
		Urban	19.8	18
6	Per cent Villages with Sub-Centre within 3 Km. (2007-08)[4]		77	71.4
7	Per cent Villages with Primary Health Centre within 10 Km. (2007-08)[4]		82.3	71.2
8	Percentage of Live Births by Various Maternal Care Indicators (2007-08)[4]			

(Contd.)

(Contd. Table 1.4)

Sr. No.	Description		Haryana	India
A	Percentage of Mothers who Received any Antenatal Check up	Rural	85.2	70.6
		Urban	93.8	87.1
B	Percentage Receiving Antenatal Care (Full Check up)	Rural	10.2	14.7
		Urban	22.6	29.4
C	Percentage of Birth delivered in Medical Institutions	Rural	42.2	37.9
		Urban	61.4	70.5
D	Percentage of Deliveries Assisted by Health Professional (Safe Deliveries)	Rural	48	43.6
		Urban	69.6	75.9
E	Percentage of Children Age 12-23 Months who Received Full Immunization	Rural	55.9	50.4
		Urban	70.8	63.1
F	Percentage of Boys Married below Age 21	Rural	30.7	28.4
		Urban	17.3	12.6
G	Percentage of Girls Married below Age 18	Rural	18.5	26.9
		Urban	8.2	11
9	Maternal Mortality Rate (2007-09)[5]		13.5	16.3

Source: 1 Census of India, Provisional Population Totals, Paper 1 of 2011
2 Department of Economic and Statistical Analysis, Haryana
3 SRS Bulletin, Registrar General of India, Vol. 46, No. 1, December, 2011
4 District Level Household Survey (DLHS III) 2007-08, RCH, IIPS, Mumbai
5 Special Bulletins on Maternal Mortality in India, 2007-09, SRS, RGI, June, 2011

Note: Figures in Bold Letters indicate better performance of state than the national average.

Table 1.5 (A): Medical Institutions, Beds and Doctors in Haryana

Particulars	*Number*	*Particulars*	*Number*
Hospitals	68	Number of Beds	9986
Community Health Centres (CHC)	84	Number of Doctors (2007) P	1441
Dispensaries	193	Population Served per Bed	2539
Primary Health Centres (PHC)	420	Population Served per Doctor	17594
Total Number of Medical Institutions	3198	Population Served per Medical Institution	7928
Family Welfare Centres	107	Area Covered per Institution (Sq. Km.)	14
		Institution per lakh Population	13
		Beds per Lakh Population	41

Source: Statistical Abstract Haryana, 2008-09. P- Provisional

quite nearer to national average whereas the corresponding Fig.ure for females is considerably higher than the national average. Infant mortality rates (IMR) of the state are largely at par with India except for higher IMR rates in urban areas of Haryana. The state has brought both the

Table 1.5 (B): Achievements of Family Welfare

Programme	*Number*
Sterilisation	87393
IUD Inserted	176684
Oral Pill Users	92553
Conventional Contraceptive Users	388223

Source: Statistical Abstract Haryana, 2008-09.

Table 1.5 (C): Ayurvedic/Unani/Homeopathic Institutions in Haryana (2008-09)

Particulars	*Number*
Hospitals	522
Vaidyas/Hakeems	434
Compounders	411
Patients Treated	3361403

Source: Statistical Abstract Haryana, 2008-09.

birth rates as well as death rates down to the national average, though urban areas of Haryana have recorded higher birth rates.

The development of health infrastructure, in the form of establishment of sub-centres and Primary Health Centres (PHCs), is far better in the state as compared to Indian average. Similarly, majority of the maternal healthcare indicators as well as child healthcare indicators reflect better performance in the state especially in rural areas.

Health is one of the most important human development indicators. Medical and health scenario of the state is depicted in Tables 1.5 (A), (B) and Table 1.5 (C).

Educational Scenario

Education is another important indicator to reflect human development. Table 1.6 (A) represents growth of literacy rates in the state by sex. The overall literacy rate in the state is higher (76.64 per cent) as compared to the national average (74.04 per cent). However, Haryana is at the 15th rank amongst the states in terms of total literacy rate in 2011 and slipped two steps down as compared to 2001 census. Female literacy has been lower as compared to male literacy throughout the census history of India. Gender gap in literacy rates in Haryana indicates that it is declining with time since 1981 and it was the lowest (18.6 per cent) in census 2011. However, the literacy gap in Haryana was higher than national Fig.ure of 16.68 per cent. Like sex ratio, higher literacy gap reflects the poorer living conditions of females in the state.

Table 1.6 (A): Literacy Rates in Haryana (1971-2011)

Year ?	*1971*	*1981*	*1991*	*2001*	*2011*
Total	26.9	36.1	55.9	67.9	76.6
Males	37.3	58.5	69.1	78.5	85.4
Females	14.9	26.9	40.5	55.7	66.8
Gender Gap	22.4	31.6	28.6	22.8	18.6

Source: Census of India, Series 7 and Final Population Totals, Haryana.

Table 1.6 (B): Educational Institutions in Haryana (2007-08)

Institutions	*Number*	*Enrolment*	*Teachers*
High/Senior Secondary/Navoday	6095	2306181	85912
Middle	3196	691258	18514
Primary/Pre Primary	6309	1610721	30124

Source: Statistical Abstract Haryana, 2008-09.

Table 1.6 (B) represents the educational infrastructure available in the state. The highest number of educational institutions belongs to Primary/ Pre Primary education whereas the highest number of students as well teachers belong to the category of High/ Senior Secondary/ Navodaya schools.

Economic Scenario

Table 1.7 depicts economic scenario of the state. The Quick Estimates of the Gross State Domestic Product (GSDP) at factor cost at constant prices (2004-05) worked out to be Rs 151691.82 crore for 2009-10 as against the revised estimates of Rs 137964.81 crore for 2008-09 recording an impressive growth of 9.9 per cent during the year 2009-10. At current prices, the GSDP has been estimated at Rs 216287.26 crore in 2009-10 as compared to the estimates of Rs 182913.97 crore in 2008-09 indicating an appreciable annual growth of 18.2 per cent.

As regard to inter-sector growth of economy, it was 0.7 per cent, 10.3 per cent and 12.9 per cent for primary sector, secondary sector and tertiary sector respectively in 2009-10. Stumpy growth of primary sector is largely due to the discouraging growth of 0.6 per cent in agriculture sector. On the other hand, the encouraging growth of GSDP recorded in secondary sector is exclusively because of the excellent growth of 10.5 per cent each recorded in the manufacturing and construction sectors. Similarly, a heartening growth of tertiary sector was chiefly due to the spectacular growth of 20.1 per cent registered in trade sector.

The per capita income (Per Capita Net State Domestic Product) in real terms at constant (2004-05) prices has been estimated at Rs 55214 during 2009-10 as against Rs 51016 during the previous year showing an annual boost of 8.2 per cent. At current prices the per capita income has been estimated as Rs 78781 in 2009-10 with an annual increase of 16.3 per cent.

The composition of GSDP reveals that the share of primary sector is continuously declining whereas the share of tertiary sector is continuously increasing. In other words, the economy of Haryana reflects a structural shift from primary sector to tertiary sector, which is a sign of healthy economy.

The structural composition of the state economy has witnessed significant changes since the formation of state. Agriculture Sector still continues to occupy a significant position in state's economy, although the share of this sector in the GSDP is declining consistently. The preponderance of agriculture sector is, to a great extent, responsible for instability in the growth rate of economy due to fluctuations in agricultural production. Natural calamities and fluctuations in rainfall often cause

Table 1.7: Economic Scenario of Haryana

Particulars	*Period*	*Unit*	*Value*
Net Area Sown to Total Area	2008-09	%	81.8
Net Irrigated Area to Net Area Sown	2008-09	%	80.5
Average Yield of Wheat	2009-10	Qtl/Hec	42.13
Average Yield of Rice	2009-10	Qtl/Hec	30.08
Consumption of Fertilizers	2009-10	Kg/Hec	210
Per Capita Availability of Milk	2009-10	Gm/Day	673 (P)
Per Capita Income at Constant (2004-05) Prices	2009-10	Rs.	55214 (Q)
Per Capita Income at Current Prices	2009-10	Rs.	78781 (Q)
GSDP at Constant (2004-05) Prices	2009-10	Crore Rs.	151691.82 (Q)
GSDP at Current Prices	2009-10	Crore Rs.	216287.26 (Q)
Index Number of Agriculture (Base Year 1981-82= 100)			
Area	2009-10	Number	120.30 (P)

(Contd.)

(Contd. Table 1.7)

Particulars	*Period*	*Unit*	*Value*
Average Yield	2009-10	Number	217.36 (P)
Production	2009-10	Number	261.48 (P)
Index Number of Industrial Production (Base Year 1999-2000 = 100)			
Mining and Quarrying	2009-10	Number	98.67 (P)
Manufacturing	2009-10	Number	217.98 (P)
Electricity	2009-10	Number	360.22 (P)
General Index	2009-10	Number	223.73 (P)
Total Road Length	2010-11	Km.	26883
Power Availability	2009-10	Million Units	31077.8
Per Capita Consumption of Electricity	2009-10	Units	905
Large and Medium Industrial Units	2010-11	Number	1356
Micro and Small Scale Industrial Units	2010-11	Number	81000

substantial loss in crop production, resulting in fluctuations and instability in growth rate of the state economy. Moreover, rapidly increasing share of services sector in the state GDP adds to the decline in the share of agriculture sector. The share of agriculture and allied sectors has declined from 22 per cent during 2004-05 to 16.1 per cent during 2009-10. The share of secondary and tertiary sectors was 30.5 per cent and 53.4 per cent respectively in 2009-10.

Since Haryana is situated in the most fertile Indo-Gangetic plains, the net sown area of the state was as high as 81.8 per cent to the total area in 2008-09. In this way the cultivable area of the state has already reached at a saturation level and there is little scope to bring more area under cultivation rather it has decreased over the period with the increasing industrialisation and urbanisation. The index number of area under crops has decreased slightly from 120.66 in 2008-09 to 120.30 in 2009-10. Furthermore, the index of agriculture production has decreased from 271.76 to 261.48 and index of average yield decreased from 225.23 to 217.36 during the corresponding period for the obvious reasons that average yield increased at a rapid rate at the onset of Green Revolution in 1970's and 1980's thereafter the existing technology could no longer proved helpful so far.

Industrialisation plays a vital role in the economic development of a region. Haryana has developed a sound industrial base with 1356 Large and Medium scale industries and as much as 81000 Micro and Small Enterprises. Index of industrial production is one of the prime indicators of the economic development for measurement of trend in the industrial production. General index of industrial production has risen up to considerable height of 223.73 points in 2009-10 by registering an annual increase of 10.94 per cent. Likewise, the indices of manufacturing sector (217.98) and electricity sector (360.22) have exhibited a remarkable annual growth of 10.73 per cent and 13.84 per cent respectively. Since the state is devoid of minerals, the index of mining and quarrying has been recorded as low as 98.67, albeit it has registered a humble positive annual growth of 2.80 per cent.

Roads are the basic means of communication not only for the development of economy but also for social development of a region. With the total road length of 26883 km., Haryana has developed a dense road network. In addition to this, some new infrastructure projects such as Kundli Manesar Palwal (KMP) Expressway, Delhi-Mumbai Industrial Corridor (DMIC), Mass Rapid Transport System (MRTS) between Gurgaon and Rewari, etc. are expected to open up new opportunities of investment and growth.

Table 1.8: Annual/ Five Year Plan-wise Outlay and Expenditure of Haryana

Plan Name	Period	Approved Outlay (Crore Rs.)	Total Expenditure	
			Expenditure (Crore Rs.)	% share to Plan Outlay
Annual Plans	1966-69	77.11	94.14	122.09
4th Five Year Plan	1969-74	225.00	358.26	159.23
5th Five Year Plan	1974-79	601.35	677.34	112.64
Annual Plan	1979-80	219.76	202.96	92.36
6th Five Year Plan	1980-85	1800.00	1595.47	88.64
7th Five Year Plan	1985-90	2900.00	2510.64	86.57
Annual Plan	1990-91	700.00	615.02	87.86
Annual Plan	1991-92	765.00	699.39	91.42
8th Five Year Plan	1992-97	5700.00	4899.19	85.95
9th Five Year Plan	1997-02	11600.00	7986.12	68.85
10th Five Year Plan	2002-07	12000.00	12979.64	108.16
11th Five year Plan	2007-12	35000.00	…………	…………

Source: Economic Survey of Haryana, 2010-11.

Table 1.8 represents Plan-wise outlay and expenditure of the state since inception. It is evident from the table that a consistent increase in the approved outlay till the fourth Plan and a sharp increase in the subsequent Plans has been the characteristic feature of the state's outlay history. The size of the 11th Five Year Plan is fixed at Rs 35000 crore.

Table 1.9: Eleventh Five Year Plan Outlay in Different Sectors of Haryana (2010-2011)

Sr. No.	*Sectors*	*Plan Outlay (Crore Rs.)*	*% of the total*
1	Agriculture and Allied Activities	1638.82	4.68
2	Rural Development	1268.42	3.62
3	Social Area Programme	127.40	0.36
4	Irrigation and Flood Control	4165.00	11.90
5	Energy	4713.46	13.47
6	Industries and Minerals	389.52	1.11
7	Transport	4335.35	12.39
8	Science and Technology, Environment	19.88	0.06
9	General Economic Services	90.34	0.26
10	Decentralised Planning	1292.93	3.69
11	Social Services	16697.44	47.71
12	General Services	261.44	0.75

Source: Economic Survey of Haryana, 2010-11.

While allocating plan outlays for the departments, highest priority has been accorded to the social service sector by allocating an outlay of Rs 16697.44 crore for the 11th Plan period which is 47.71 per cent of the total outlay (Table 1.9). Among the social services, due importance has been given to the three basic services-water supply, general education and technical education and healthcare. The second highest priority has been given to the development/improvement of infrastructure of irrigation, energy, roads and road transport sectors by earmarking an outlay of Rs 13213.81 crore which is 37.76 per cent of the total outlay. After reassessing the state's resources, approved outlays have been enhanced from time to time.

District Level Analysis

Since district is the unit of analysis in the present study, it is pertinent to examine all the issues discussed above at district level also. The various aspects pertaining to human development have been examined at length in the succeeding section.

Demographic Attributes

Demographic attributes include various aspects of population-distribution, growth, composition, etc. These aspects not only reflect human development level by themselves but also significantly affect the other human development parameters also.

District-wise distribution of population reveals that Faridabad, with nearly 18 lakh population, is the largest district of Haryana followed by Hisar and Bhiwani (Figure 1.1). The high concentration of population in Faridabad is due to early industrial growth whereas the latter two districts occupy substantially big geographical area. In contrast, Panchkula inhabits less than six lakh people and the district is placed at the bottom rank in population distribution. Rewari and Mahendergarh are other smaller districts in the state.

The population of Haryana is growing at a rate slightly higher than the national average, yet a great regional variation can be observed within the state. The population of Gurgaon district is growing rapidly at galloping pace of more than 70 per cent (Figure 1.2). This is mainly because of influx of people in search of employment as Gurgaon offers favourable environment for fast industrial development due to its location in the vicinity of national capital. The other districts that have recorded steep increase in their population for the similar reasons include Faridabad and Panipat. However, the steep increase in the population of Mewat and Palwal districts is more a function of natural growth (higher birth rate) than the immigration due to industrial development.

On the other hand, the decadal population growth rate has been lower in majority of the districts across the state. Jhajjar district has recorded lowest growth rate and emerged as the solitary district where population growth rate during 2001-2011 has been less than 10 per cent.

Sex ratio, which reflects the gender composition of the population, is the other demographic attribute and throws light on the social set up of the inhabitants. As stated earlier, Haryana has been placed at the bottom amongst the Indian states in respect of the sex ratio. Similar to the Indian states, a considerable variation is noticeable in the district-wise sex ratio of Haryana. Fatehabad and Mewat, the two districts that are lagging behind in the other demographic characteristics, possess appreciably high sex ratio so far as the state is concerned (Figure 1.3). Rewari, Mahendergarh, Kurukshetra and Karnal are among the other districts which have had sex ratio above the state average. Contrary to this, Gurgaon, Sonepat, Jhajjar and Panipat are among the poorest districts with respect to sex ratio.

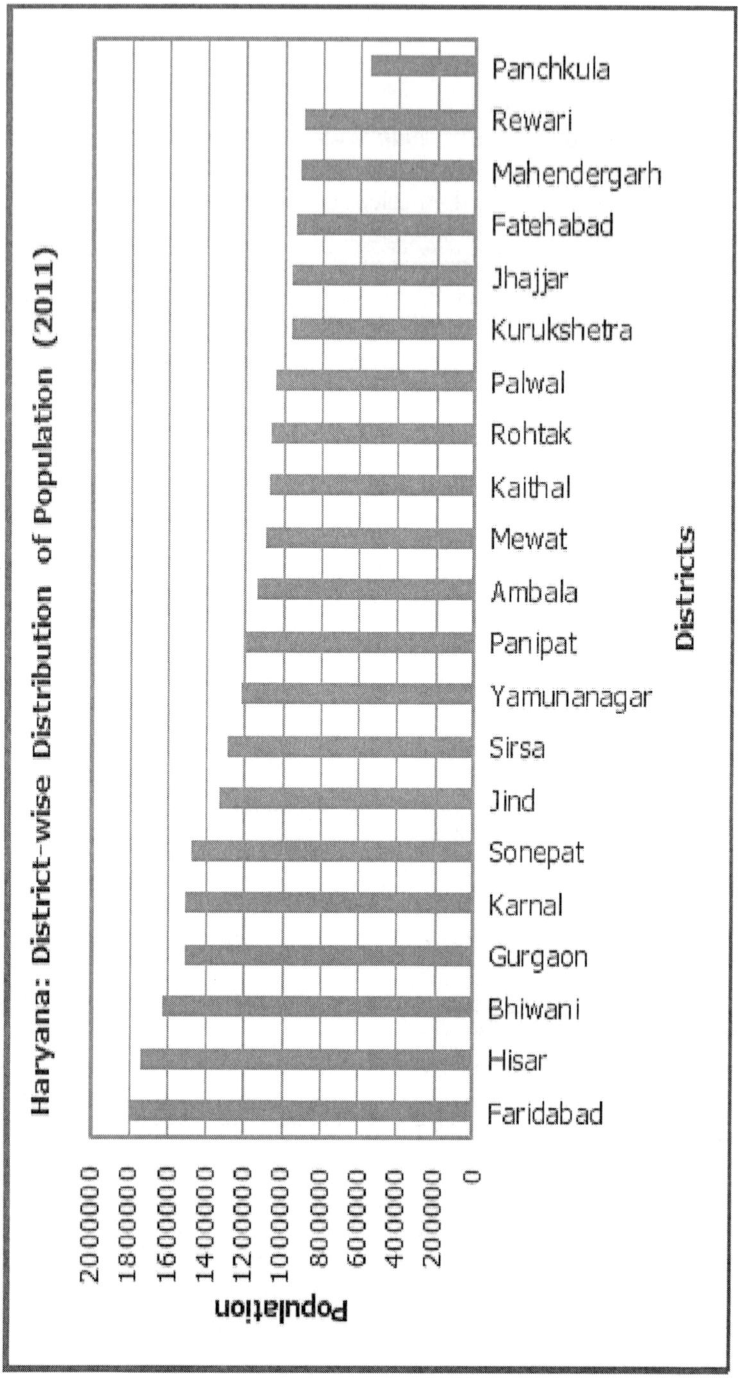
Haryana: District-wise Distribution of Population (2011)
Population
Districts
Panchkula
Rewari
Mahendergarh
Fatehabad
Jhajjar
Kurukshetra
Palwal
Rohtak
Kaithal
Mewat
Ambala
Panipat
Yamunanagar
Sirsa
Jind
Sonepat
Karnal
Gurgaon
Bhiwani
Hisar
Faridabad
0
2000000
4000000
6000000
8000000
10000000
12000000
14000000
16000000
18000000
20000000

Fig. 1.1

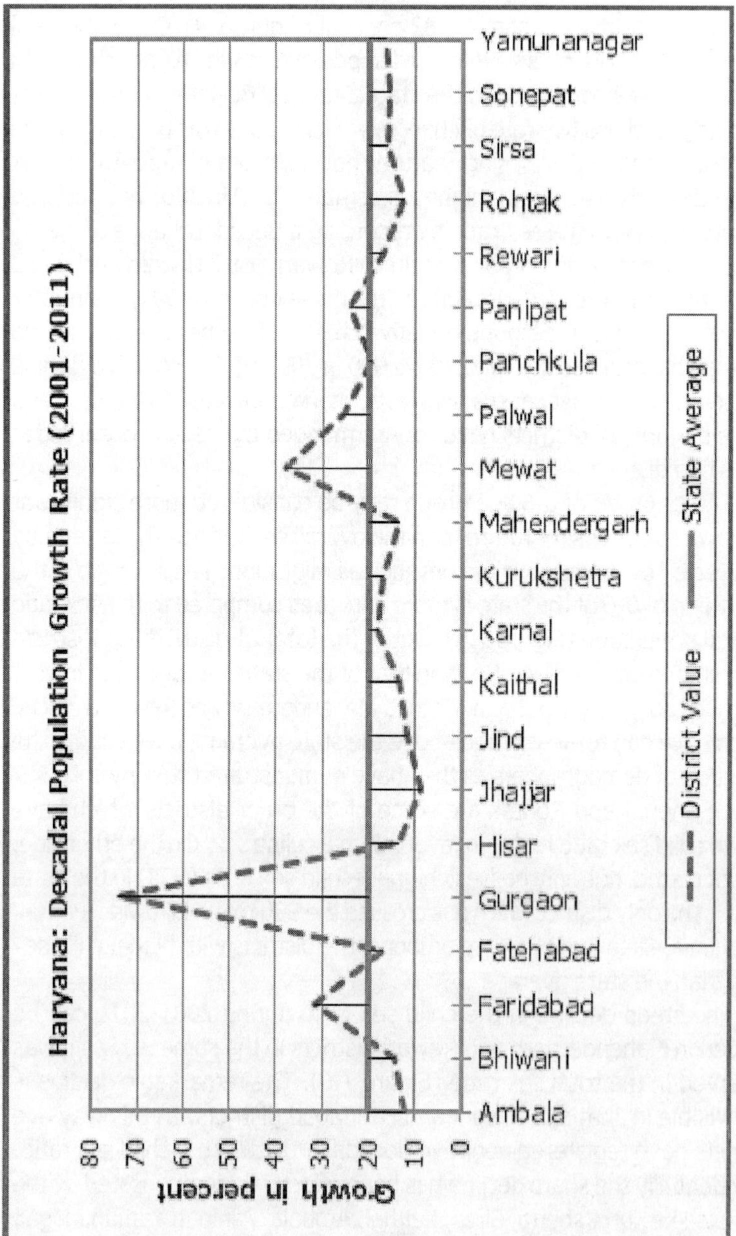
Haryana: Decadal Population Growth Rate (2001-2011)
Growth in percent
80
70
60
50
40
30
20
10
0
Ambala
Bhiwani
Faridabad
Fatehabad
Gurgaon
Hisar
Jhajjar
Jind
Kaithal
Karnal
Kurukshetra
Mahendergarh
Mewat
Palwal
Panchkula
Panipat
Rewari
Rohtak
Sirsa
Sonepat
Yamunanagar
District Value
State Average

Fig. 1.2

The overall sex ratio of the state has increased by 16 points (861 in 2001 and 877 in 2011) during the last decade. In this way the state has recorded a positive change of 1.82 per cent (Figure 1.4). Out of the total 21 districts, 11 districts have recorded positive as well higher change in the sex ratio as compared to the state average. Besides, eight districts have achieved positive rate of change, yet their pace was below the state average. The most alarming feature, noticed from Fig.ure 1.4 is that Mahendergarh district with highest sex ratio of 919 in 2001 has suffered a sharp decline in the sex ratio by recording a decadal change of – 2.65 per cent over the given point of time. Rewari district, which achieved second rank in the state in 2001 with the sex ratio of 901, is another district which has undergone negative change. In other words, the two districts that attained sex ratio above 900 in 2001 have recorded a decline in sex ratio in the last census. However, marked increase in the sex ratio of the majority of districts have countermanded the decline observed in these two districts.

The sex ratio of 0-6 age group may be considered more significant to draw projections for future than the overall sex ratio as the latter may be affected by extreneous factors such as migration. The sex ratio in the age group of 0-6 of the state is more critical as compared to the sex ratio of total population (Figure 1.5). Out of the total 21 districts, 11 districts have shown poorer sex ratio than that of the state average. The lowest sex ratio can be seen in Jhajjar district. Mahendergarh and Rewari districts, which have had total sex ratio above the state average, have caught the attention of demographers as they have demonstrated stumpy child sex ratio. Sonepat and Rohtak are some of the other districts which have shown child sex ratio highly in favour of masculine sex. On the other side, Mewat district not only possess highest child sex ratio (904) in the state but it is the only district which has crossed the 900 mark. Likewise, Palwal, Panchkula, Sirsa and Hisar are amongst the districts with higher child sex ratio than the state average.

The steep decline in the child sex ratio during 2001-2011 can be noticed in Mahendergarh and Rewari districts in the same way as it was observed in the total sex ratio (Figure 1.6). The remarkable decline is also visible in Jhajjar, Bhiwani and Faridabad districts. In this way five districts have registered negative decadal growth in the child sex ratio. Providentially the sharp decline has been effectively compensated by the districts like Kurukshetra, Sirsa, Kaithal, Ambala, Panipat, Yamunanagar, Hisar, Gurgaon and Fatehabad thereby the state as a whole has achieved positive decadal growth of 1.33 per cent in child sex ratio.

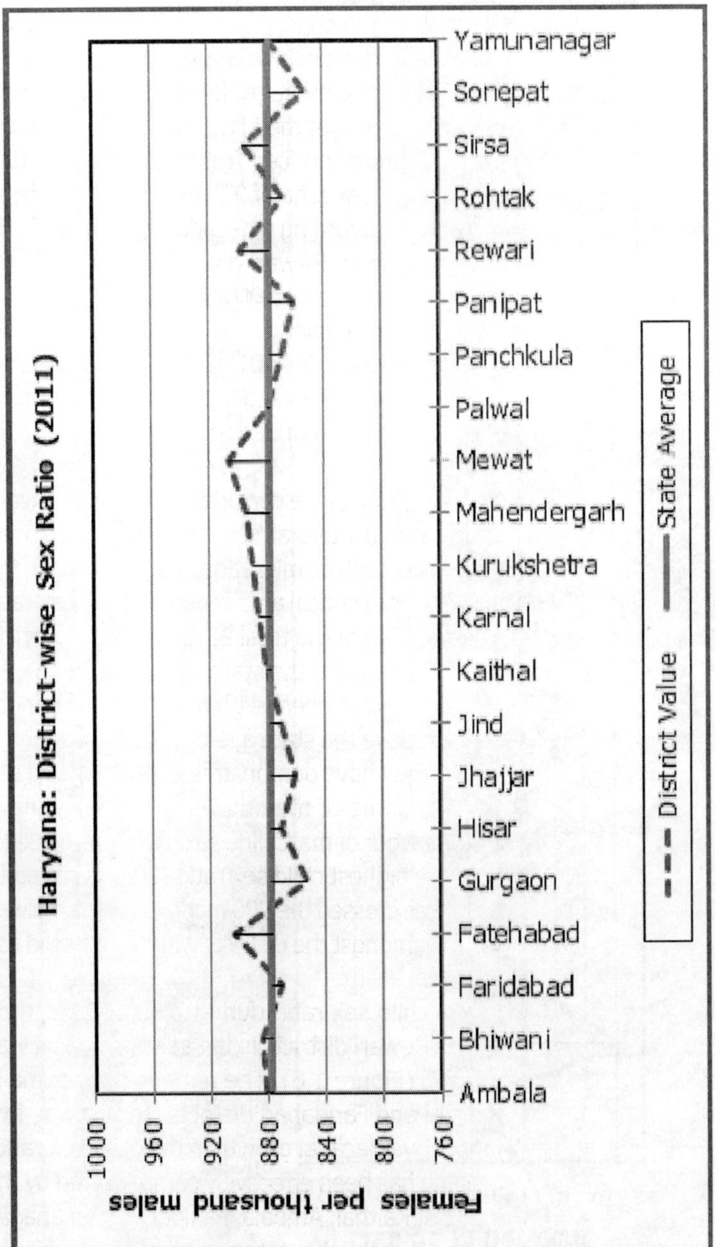
Haryana: District-wise Sex Ratio (2011)
Females per thousand males
1000
960
920
880
840
800
760
Yamunanagar
Sonepat
Sirsa
Rohtak
Rewari
Panipat
Panchkula
Palwal
Mewat
Mahendergarh
Kurukshetra
Karnal
Kaithal
Jind
Jhajjar
Hisar
Gurgaon
Fatehabad
Faridabad
Bhiwani
Ambala
District Value
State Average

Fig. 1.3

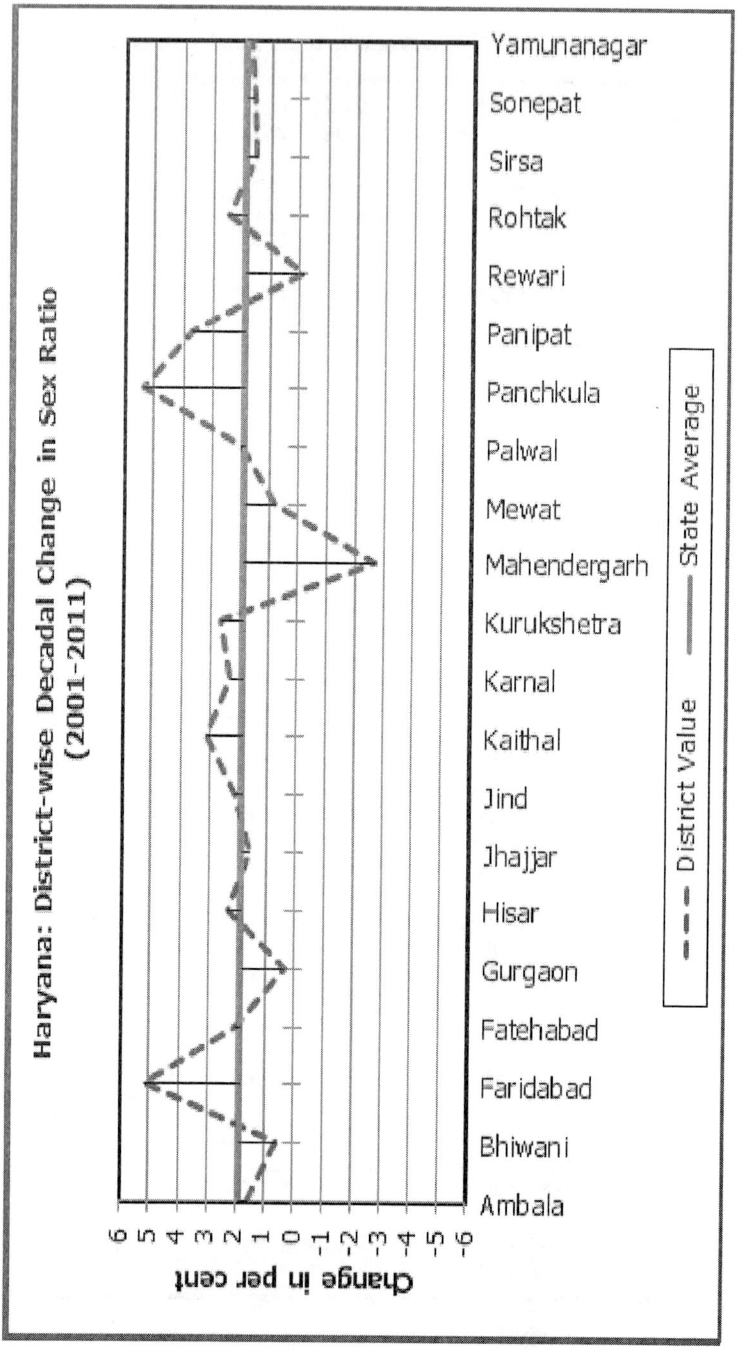
Haryana: District-wise Decadal Change in Sex Ratio (2001-2011)
Change in per cent
6
5
4
3
2
1
0
-1
-2
-3
-4
-5
-6
Ambala
Bhiwani
Faridabad
Fatehabad
Gurgaon
Hisar
Jhajjar
Jind
Kaithal
Karnal
Kurukshetra
Mahendergarh
Mewat
Palwal
Panchkula
Panipat
Rewari
Rohtak
Sirsa
Sonepat
Yamunanagar
District Value
State Average

Fig. 1.4

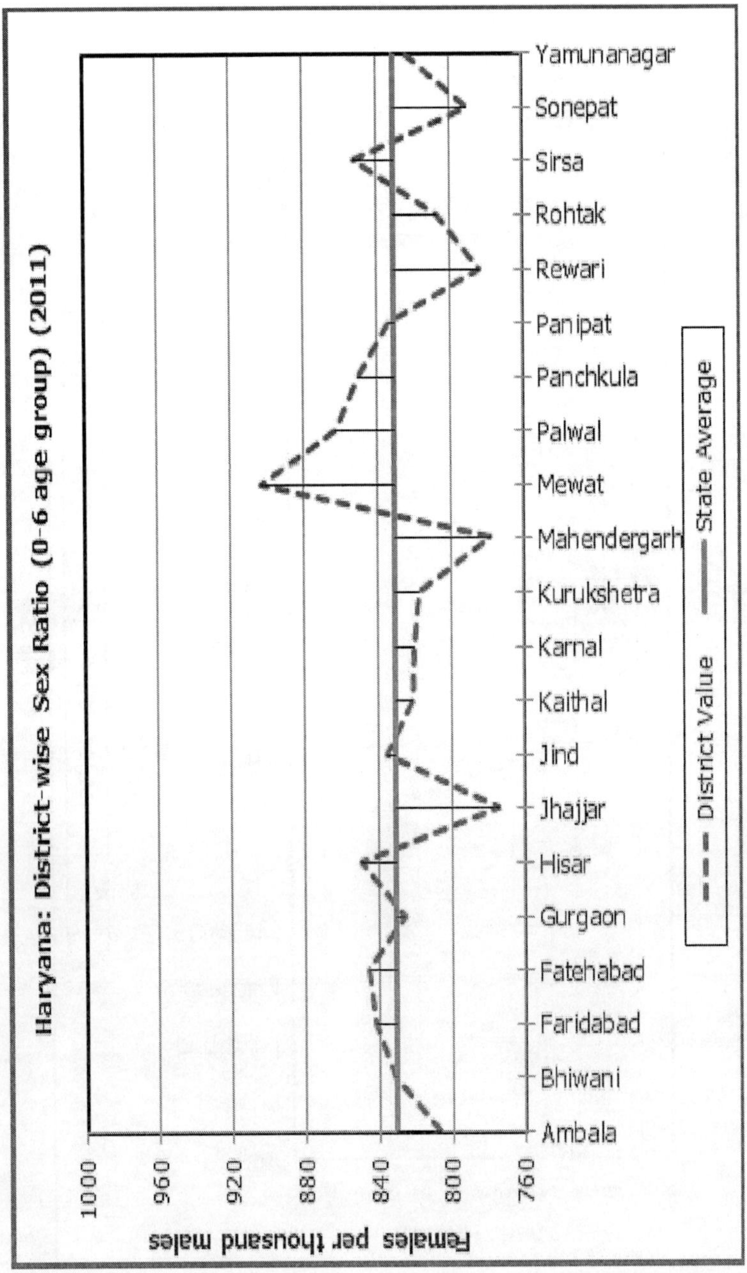
Haryana: District-wise Sex Ratio (0-6 age group) (2011)
Females per thousand males
1000
960
920
880
840
800
760
Yamunanagar
Sonepat
Sirsa
Rohtak
Rewari
Panipat
Panchkula
Palwal
Mewat
Mahendergarh
Kurukshetra
Karnal
Kaithal
Jind
Jhajjar
Hisar
Gurgaon
Fatehabad
Faridabad
Bhiwani
Ambala
District Value
State Average

Fig. 1.5

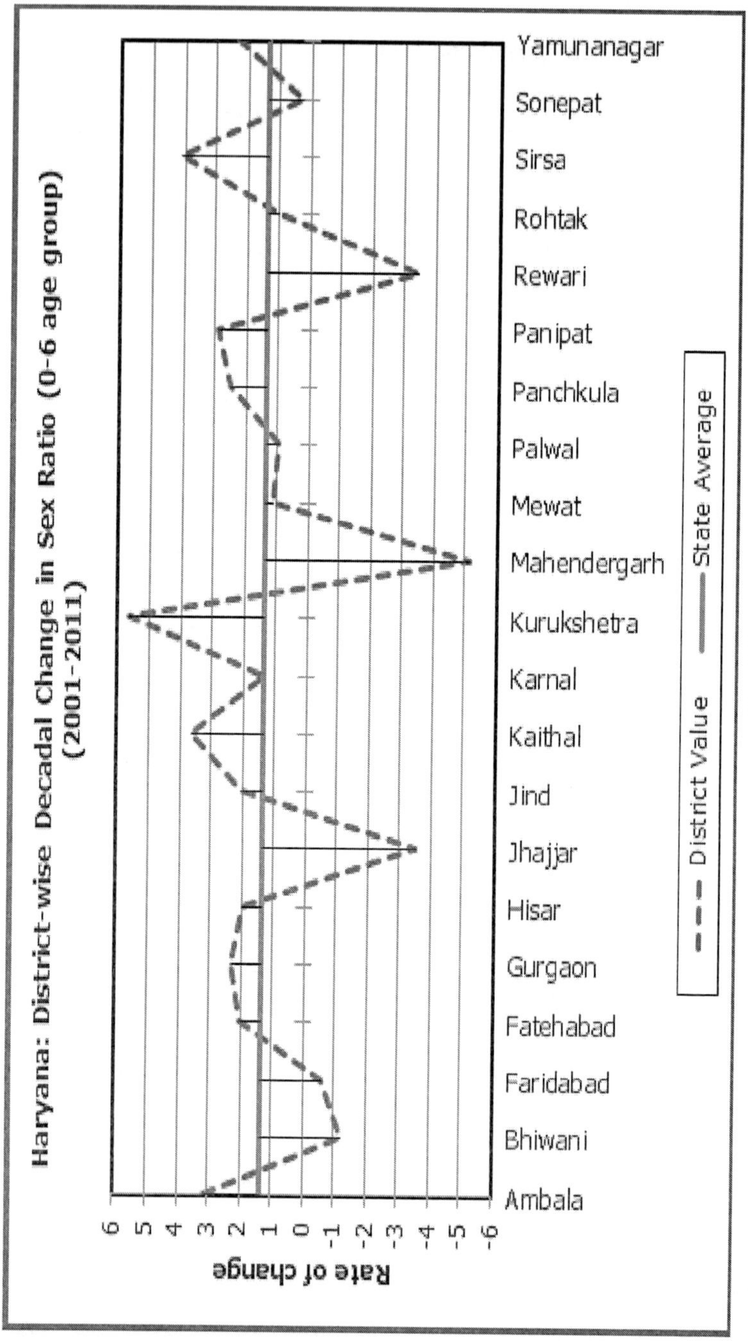
Haryana: District-wise Decadal Change in Sex Ratio (0-6 age group) (2001-2011)
Rate of change
6
5
4
3
2
1
0
-1
-2
-3
-4
-5
-6
Ambala
Bhiwani
Faridabad
Fatehabad
Gurgaon
Hisar
Jhajjar
Jind
Kaithal
Karnal
Kurukshetra
Mahendergarh
Mewat
Palwal
Panchkula
Panipat
Rewari
Rohtak
Sirsa
Sonepat
Yamunanagar
District Value
State Average

Fig. 1.6

Literacy Rate

The literacy rate of Haryana is slightly above the national average. Gurgaon being the district with the highest literacy rate has attained total literacy rate as high as 84.9 per cent. Panchkula and Ambala are the other top ranked districts. Gurgaon has emerged as top ranked district after the most backward part of the state i.e. Mewat has been carved out of Gurgaon. Similarly the high literacy rate of Faridabad is due to the division of its southern part as a new district of Palwal which is comparatively at the rear in terms of literacy rate. Besides Mewat and Palwal, the literacy rate is found below the state average in the districts of Fatehabad, Sirsa, Jind, Kaithal and Hisar (Figure 1.7).

The decadal change in literacy rate reveals that nine districts have recorded better improvement in the literacy rate as compared to the state average (Figure 1.8). Interestingly, highest improvement has been achieved by the districts that are characterised with low literacy rate such as Mewat, Kaithal, Palwal, Jind and Fatehabad. On the contrary, the top ranked district i.e. Gurgaon has recorded the lowest decadal growth rate (compare Figure 1.7 and Figure 1.8). However, three districts with high literacy rate i.e. Bhiwani and Mahendergarh districts in the south and Panchkula district in the north have maintained high (above state average) decadal growth during 2001-2011.

Gender-wise literacy rate of the state is such that it has always been in favour of masculine gender. It can be concluded from figure 1.9 that a considerable number of districts have had insignificant deviation from the state average as regards to male literacy rate except Mewat, Fatehabad, Sirsa (low ranked districts) and Rewari and Mahendergarh (high ranked districts). Secondly, a similar trend in male literacy rate across the districts can be seen as it was observed in total literacy rate with a few exceptions as Kurukshetra and Yamunanagar districts having total literacy rate slightly higher than the state average but lesser in case of male literacy rate (compare Figure 1.7 and Figure 1.9).

As far as the decadal change in male literacy is concerned, all the districts have registered positive decadal change, nevertheless inter district variation is quite high ranging from 2.3 per cent in Gurgaon (the lowest) to 11.8 per cent in Mewat (the highest) as against 6.9 per cent of the state average (Figure 1.10). A comparative analysis of figure 1.9 and figure 1.10 clearly reflects that Rewari, Mahendergarh, Gurgaon, Faridabad, Jhajjar, Sonepat, Ambala and Rohtak districts have attained higher male literacy rate yet they have registered decadal growth below the state average. On the other hand, districts like Karnal, Palwal, Jind, Kaithal, Sirsa, Fatehabad and Mewat have come forward with substantial decadal growth in male literacy rate even though these districts have

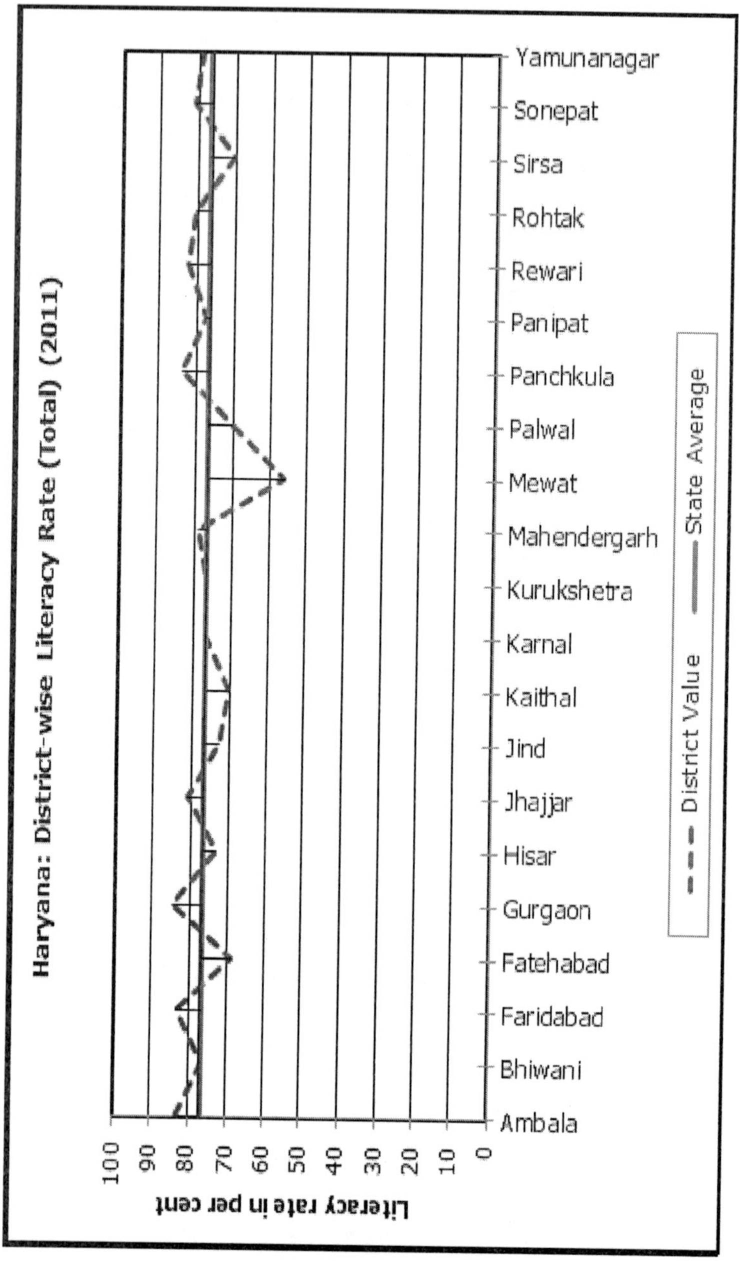
Haryana: District-wise Literacy Rate (Total) (2011)
Literacy rate in per cent
100
90
80
70
60
50
40
30
20
10
0
Ambala
Bhiwani
Faridabad
Fatehabad
Gurgaon
Hisar
Jhajjar
Jind
Kaithal
Karnal
Kurukshetra
Mahendergarh
Mewat
Palwal
Panchkula
Panipat
Rewari
Rohtak
Sirsa
Sonepat
Yamunanagar
District Value
State Average

Fig. 1.7

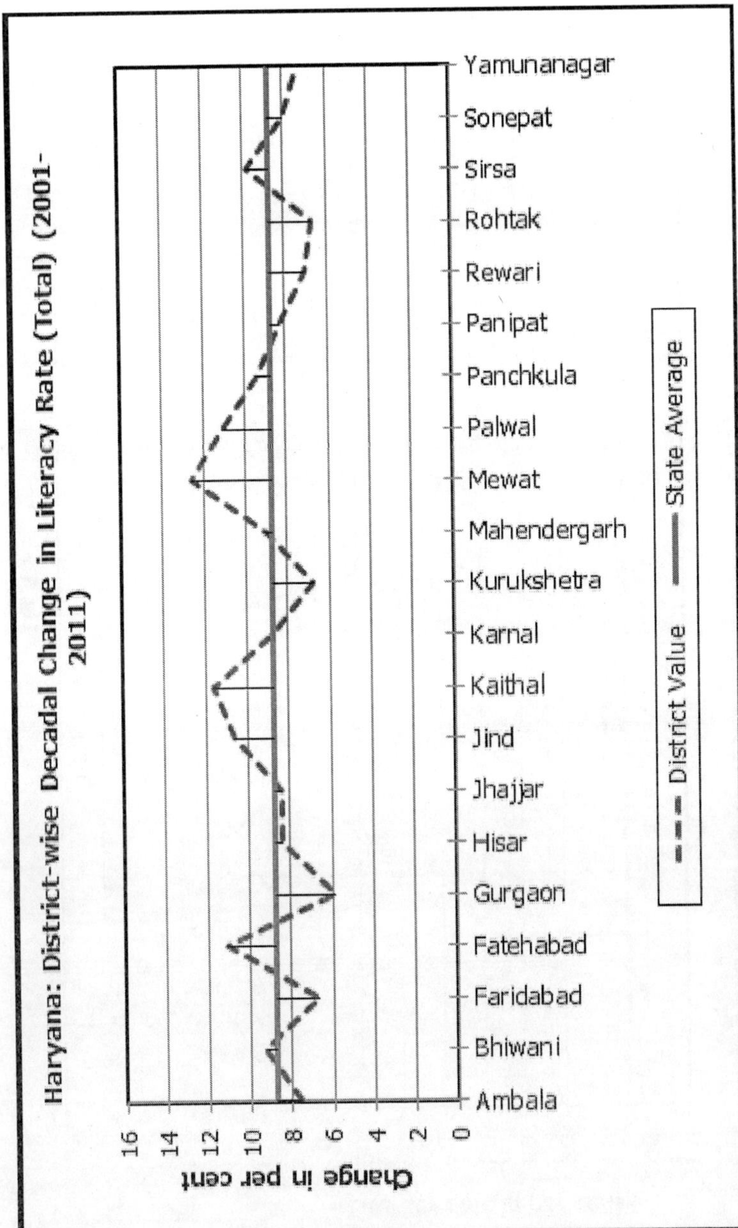
Haryana: District-wise Decadal Change in Literacy Rate (Total) (2001-2011)
Change in per cent
0
2
4
6
8
10
12
14
16
Ambala
Bhiwani
Faridabad
Fatehabad
Gurgaon
Hisar
Jhajjar
Jind
Kaithal
Karnal
Kurukshetra
Mahendergarh
Mewat
Palwal
Panchkula
Panipat
Rewari
Rohtak
Sirsa
Sonepat
Yamunanagar
District Value
State Average

Fig. 1.8

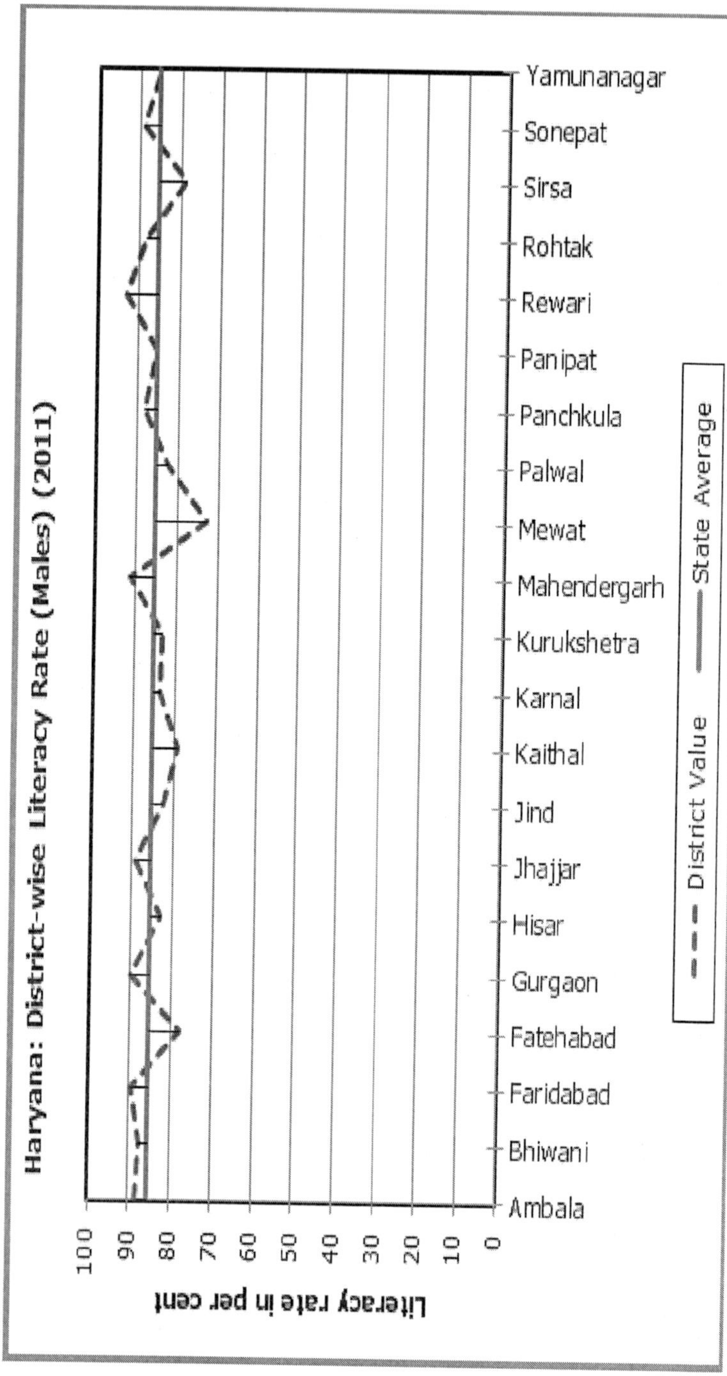
Haryana: District-wise Literacy Rate (Males) (2011)
Literacy rate in per cent
100
90
80
70
60
50
40
30
20
10
0
Ambala
Bhiwani
Faridabad
Fatehabad
Gurgaon
Hisar
Jhajjar
Jind
Kaithal
Karnal
Kurukshetra
Mahendergarh
Mewat
Palwal
Panchkula
Panipat
Rewari
Rohtak
Sirsa
Sonepat
Yamunanagar
District Value
State Average

Fig. 1.9

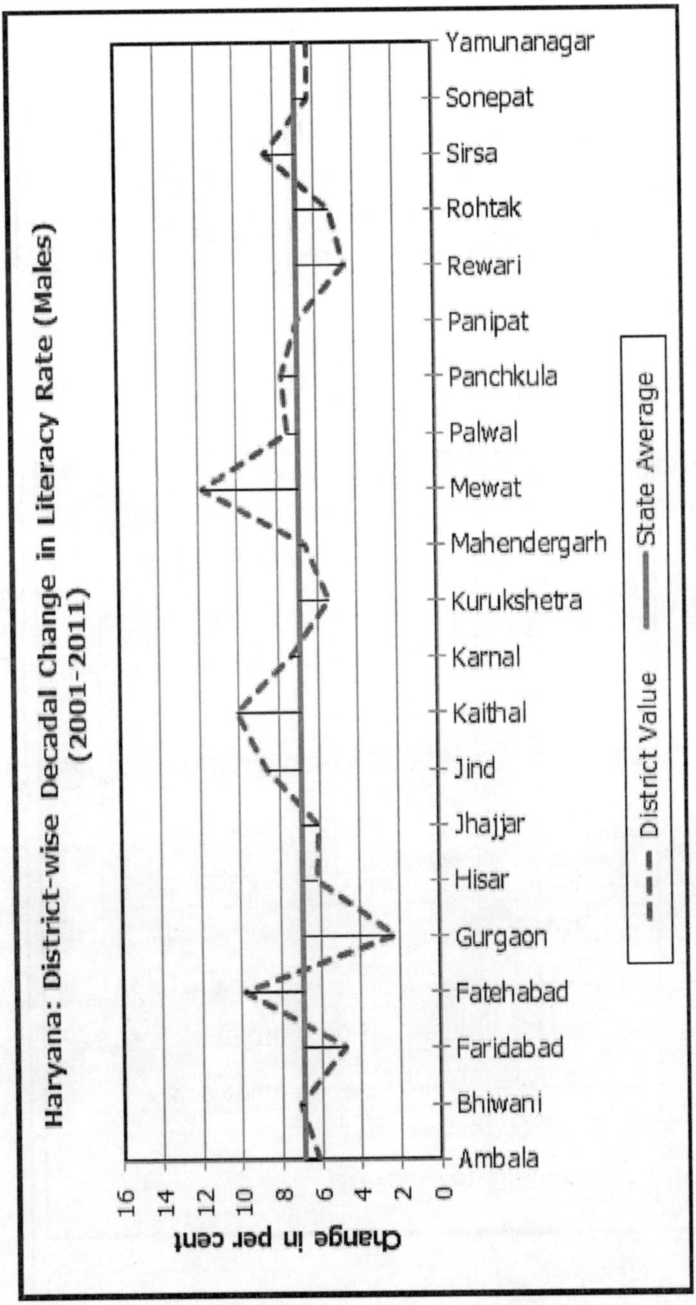
Haryana: District-wise Decadal Change in Literacy Rate (Males)
(2001-2011)
Yamunanagar
Sonepat
Sirsa
Rohtak
Rewari
Panipat
Panchkula
Palwal
Mewat
Mahendergarh
Kurukshetra
Karnal
Kaithal
Jind
Jhajjar
Hisar
Gurgaon
Fatehabad
Faridabad
Bhiwani
Ambala
16
14
12
10
8
6
4
2
0
Change in per cent
District Value
State Average

Fig. 1.10

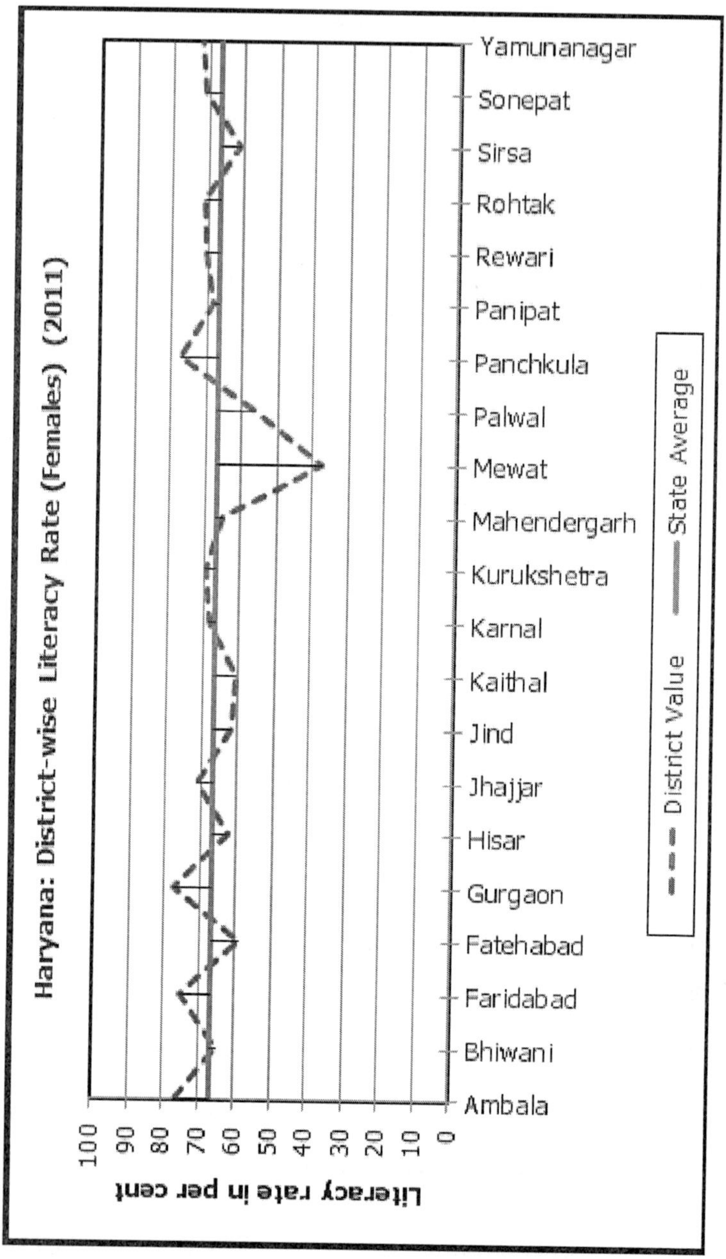
Haryana: District-wise Literacy Rate (Females) (2011)
Literacy rate in per cent
100
90
80
70
60
50
40
30
20
10
0
Ambala
Bhiwani
Faridabad
Fatehabad
Gurgaon
Hisar
Jhajjar
Jind
Kaithal
Karnal
Kurukshetra
Mahendergarh
Mewat
Palwal
Panchkula
Panipat
Rewari
Rohtak
Sirsa
Sonepat
Yamunanagar
District Value
State Average

Fig. 1.11

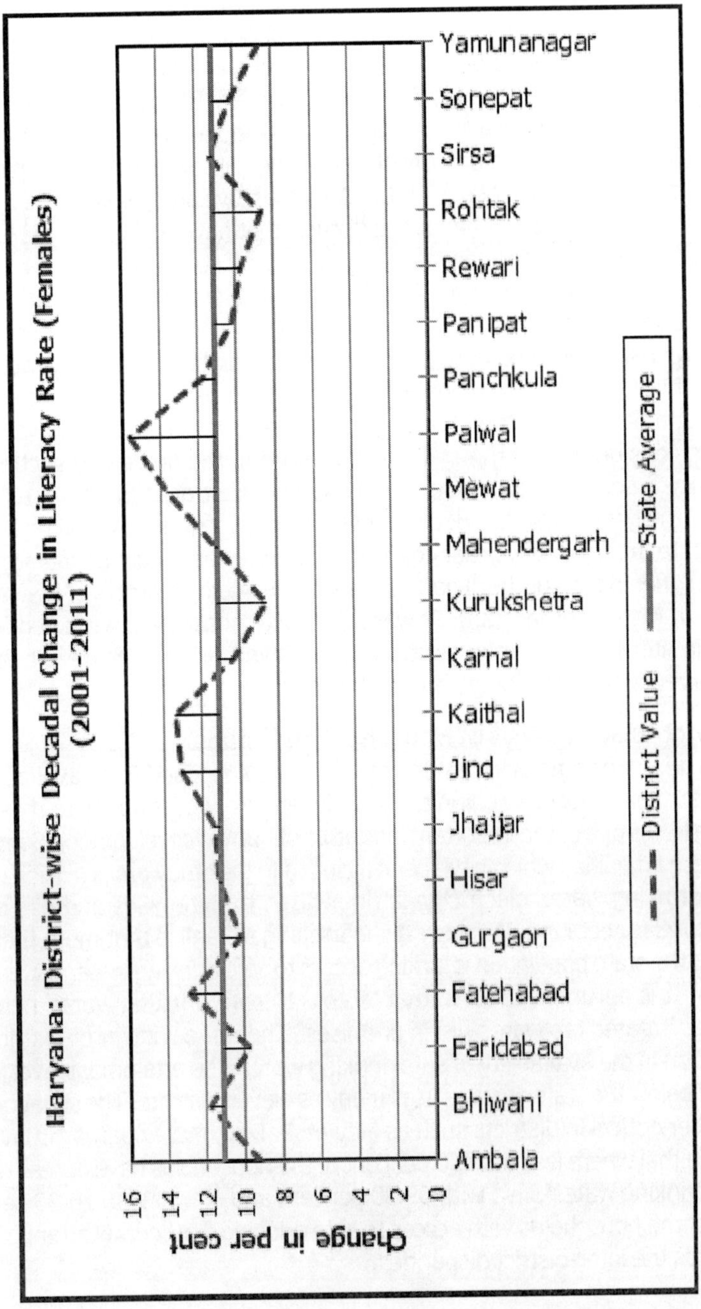
Haryana: District-wise Decadal Change in Literacy Rate (Females)
(2001-2011)
Change in per cent
16
14
12
10
8
6
4
2
0
Ambala
Bhiwani
Faridabad
Fatehabad
Gurgaon
Hisar
Jhajjar
Jind
Kaithal
Karnal
Kurukshetra
Mahendergarh
Mewat
Palwal
Panchkula
Panipat
Rewari
Rohtak
Sirsa
Sonepat
Yamunanagar
District Value
State Average

Fig. 1.12

male literacy rate below the state average. Panchkula district has established a progressive trend by finding a place in the category of 'higher ranked district with higher decadal change'.

A perusal of figure 1.11 reflects that the efforts for the enhancement of female literacy have shown impressive results in districts like Ambala, Faridabad, Gurgaon, Jhajjar, Panchkula, Rewari, Rohtak, Sonepat and Yamunanagar whereas a lot of work has to be done in other parts of the state. The newly formed districts of Mewat and Palwal have to keep up the present pace of growth (Figure 1.12). A comparative analysis of figure 1.11 and figure 1.12 reveals that all the districts that have had female literacy rate above the state average, have recorded lesser decadal growth than the state average and vice versa. However, Panchkula district is an exception.

Gender-wise decadal change as depicted in figure 1.10 and figure 1.12 reveals a pleasing note that improvement in female literacy rate is quite higher than that of male literacy rate across all the districts of Haryana. As a result the gender gap in literacy rate has been lowered down considerably in the state as discussed in the preceding section. District-wise status of gender gap has been illustrated in figure 1.13. While the gender gap has declined over the past decade, it is still high in the state. Interestingly, gender gap in literacy rate has a regional character. It is higher in the southern part of the state including districts of Mewat, Palwal, Mahendergarh and Rewari. Panchkula has the lowest gender gap in literacy rate in the state. No significant differences have been observed in the remaining parts of the state.

District-wise Analysis of Household Amenities

There are some basic amenities which are supposed to be available to the inhabitants of a region to live a decent life. Accessibility to these amenities is one of the important indicators of human development. Some of these amenities which have been included in the study are provision of safe drinking water, electricity, latrine within the premises and use of LPG/PNG for cooking. It is very disheartening to realise that more than half of the state population is lacking access to safe drinking water (Figure 1.14). It is pertinent to learn that 'access to safe drinking water' here implies 'treated tap water within premises'. There is a wide inter-district variation in the availability of safe drinking water. The attainment level is found below the state average in as many as eleven districts. The situation is rather critical in districts such as Mewat, Palwal, Mahendergarh, Jind and Kaithal where less than 30 per cent of the households have access to safe drinking water. Sirsa with 69.30 per cent and Mewat with 10.90 per cent of the households with access to safe drinking water draw attention towards the inter-district disparities.

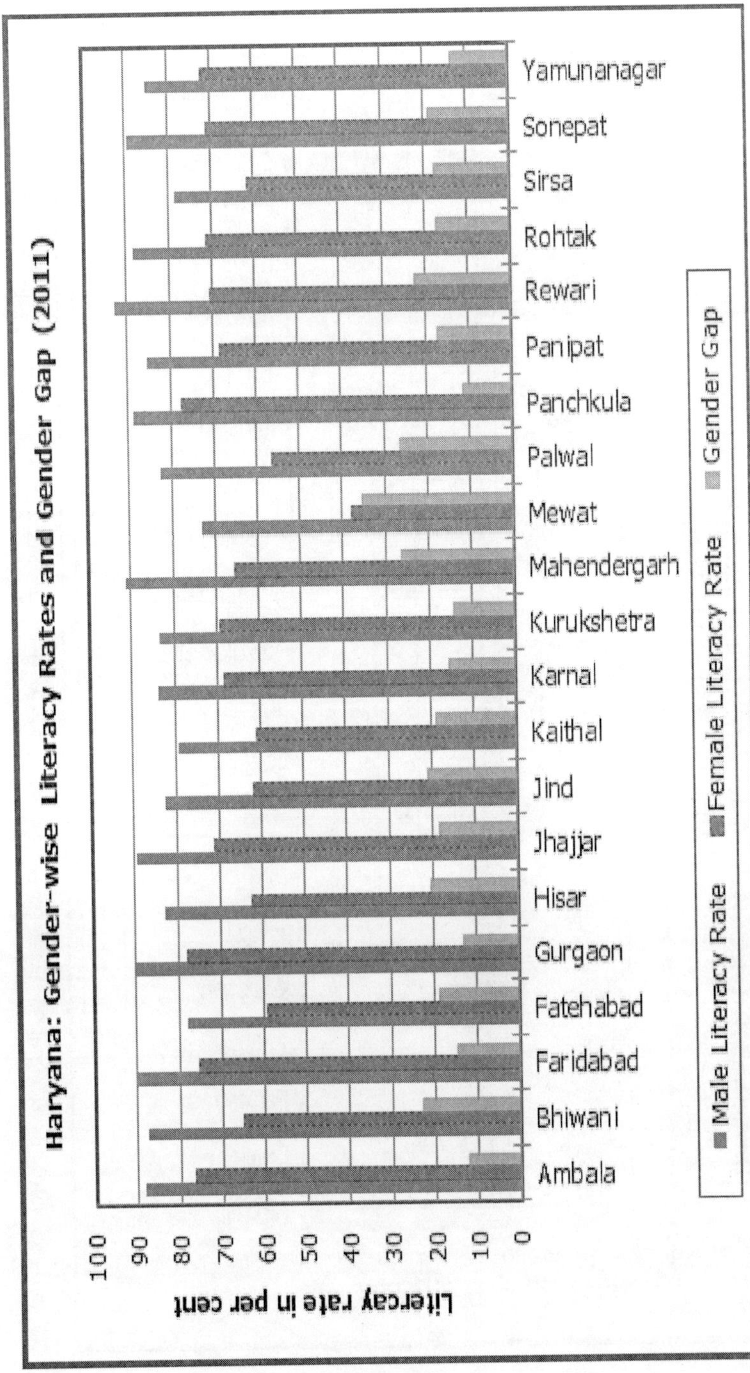
Haryana: Gender-wise Literacy Rates and Gender Gap (2011)
Literacy rate in per cent
100
90
80
70
60
50
40
30
20
10
0
Yamunanagar
Sonepat
Sirsa
Rohtak
Rewari
Panipat
Panchkula
Palwal
Mewat
Mahendergarh
Kurukshetra
Karnal
Kaithal
Jind
Jhajjar
Hisar
Gurgaon
Fatehabad
Faridabad
Bhiwani
Ambala
Male Literacy Rate
Female Literacy Rate
Gender Gap

Fig. 1.13

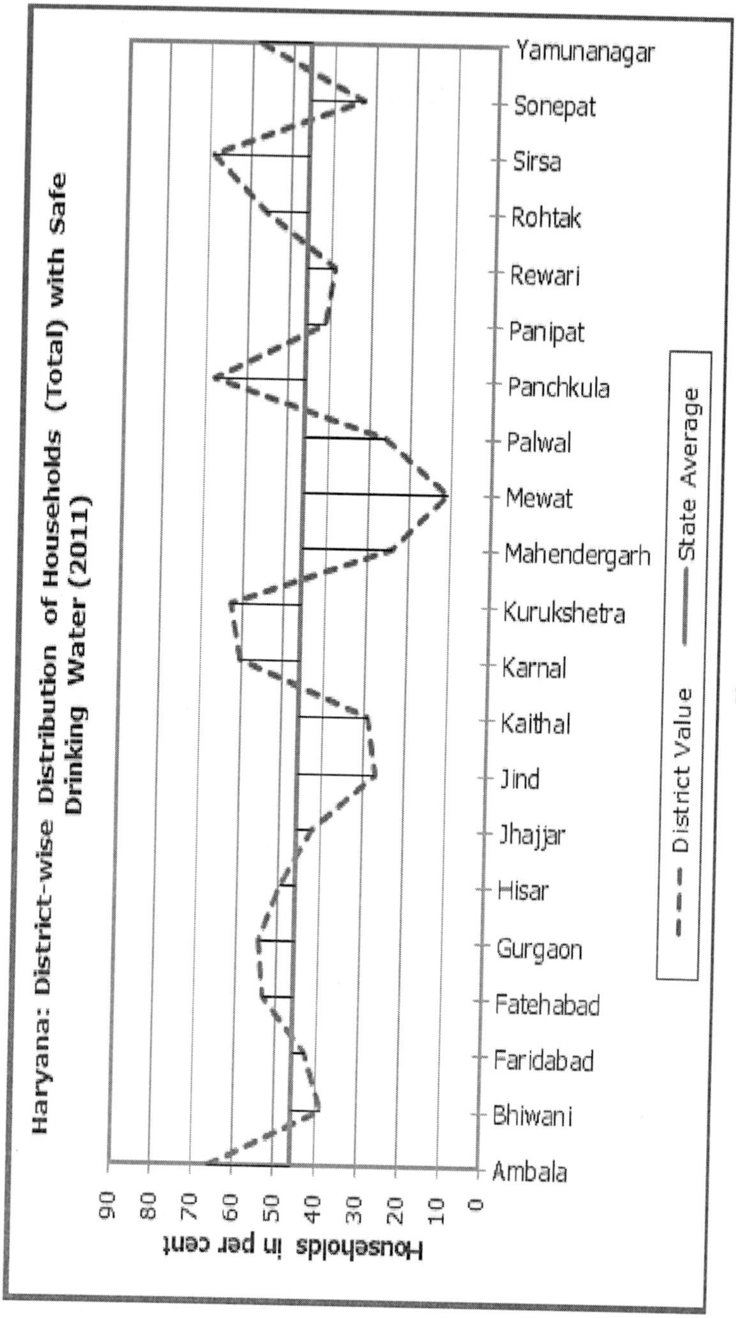
Haryana: District-wise Distribution of Households (Total) with Safe Drinking Water (2011)
Households in per cent
90
80
70
60
50
40
30
20
10
0
Ambala
Bhiwani
Faridabad
Fatehabad
Gurgaon
Hisar
Jhajjar
Jind
Kaithal
Karnal
Kurukshetra
Mahendergarh
Mewat
Palwal
Panchkula
Panipat
Rewari
Rohtak
Sirsa
Sonepat
Yamunanagar
District Value
State Average

Fig. 1.14

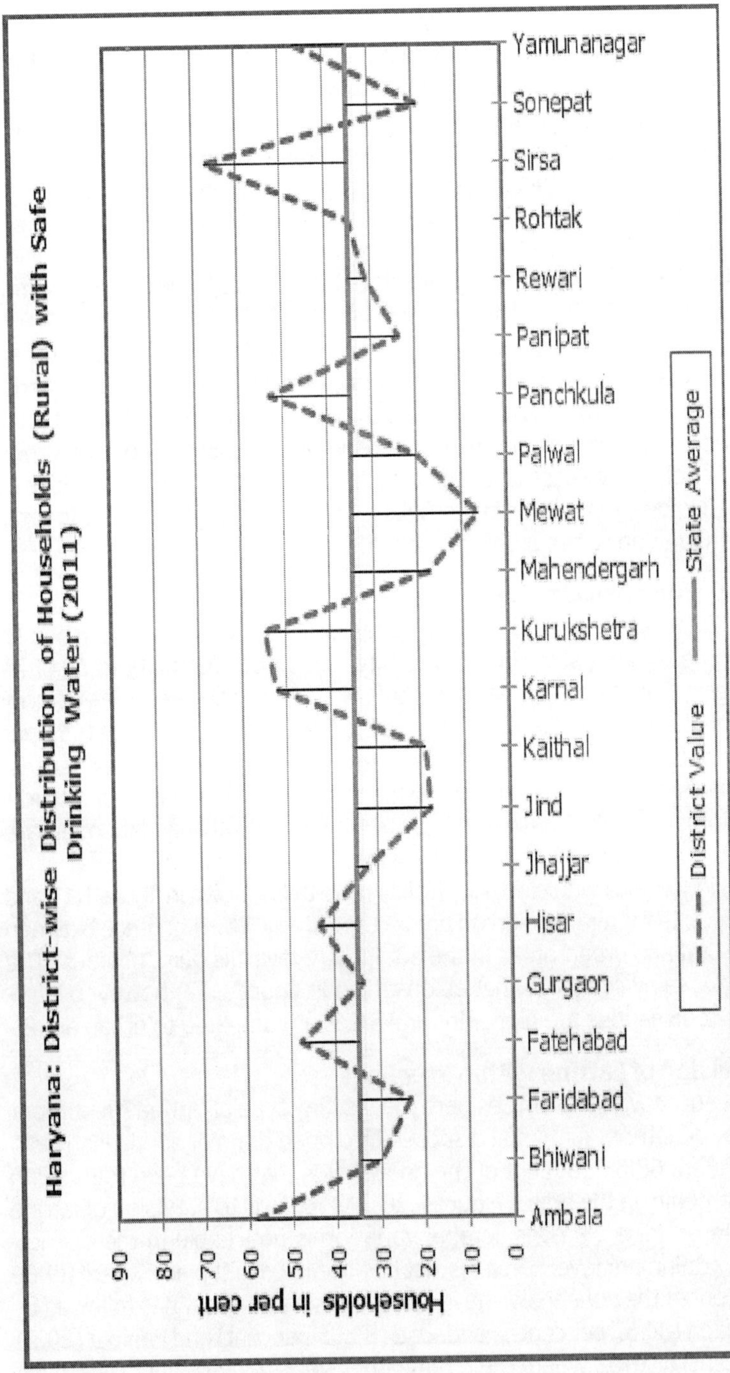
Haryana: District-wise Distribution of Households (Rural) with Safe Drinking Water (2011)
Households in per cent
90
80
70
60
50
40
30
20
10
0
Ambala
Bhiwani
Faridabad
Fatehabad
Gurgaon
Hisar
Jhajjar
Jind
Kaithal
Karnal
Kurukshetra
Mahendergarh
Mewat
Palwal
Panchkula
Panipat
Rewari
Rohtak
Sirsa
Sonepat
Yamunanagar
District Value
State Average

Fig. 1.15

An overview of figure 1.15 reveals that a great deal of the rural households is devoid of safe drinking water and merely one third of them in the state have access to it. Sirsa, again the top ranked district provides safe drinking water to more than two third of its rural inhabitants. Similarly, some other districts like Ambala, Kurukshetra, Panchkula and Karnal have succeeded in providing this basic amenity to more than half of their residents. Mewat again has appeared as the bottom ranked district where a meagre 6.29 per cent of the rural populace have access to safe drinking water. The situation is no better in the districts like Mahendergarh, Jind, Sonepat and Palwal in this regard.

As against the rural areas, a handsome two-third of the urban population of the state has access to safe drinking water, yet inter-district variations are quite high (Figure 1.16). The situation of Rohtak district is found most appreciable in the state where 84.65 per cent of urban households have access to safe drinking water. Paradoxically, Faridabad a well known district for industrialisation has failed to provide this basic amenity to half of its urban households.

Provision of Electricity

Electricity is the other basic amenity. Haryana has a distinction to become the first state in India to have provided electricity to all of its villages. Even then all of the households are not equipped with the electricity connection in their habitats. It is visible from figure 1.17 that 90.51 per cent of the households in the state have electricity at their residences. Inter-district disparities are not so high except for three districts with low attainment levels. These districts are Mewat, Palwal and Mahendergarh located in the southern part of the state.

Households with electricity facility have been shown in figure 1.18 and figure 1.19 for rural and urban areas respectively. The difference between the rural and urban areas in the attainment levels is quite obvious. The trend is fairly similar to that as observed in figure 1.17; however, inter-district disparities are higher in rural areas as compared to urban areas.

Provision of Latrine within Premises

Latrine within premises here means 'any type of latrine (flush/pour flush, pit latrine, night soil disposed into open drain or service latrine)'. There are 68.63 per cent of the households that have been found with this amenity in the state (Figure 1.20). As regards to provision of latrine within premises, a considerable variation is noticeable in the district-wise attainment level. Sirsa district has occupied first place where 89.66 per cent of the households have latrine within premises. It is followed by Gurgaon (84.57 per cent), Faridabad (83.95 per cent) and Panipat (80.21 per cent) districts where the attainment level is above 80 per cent mark.

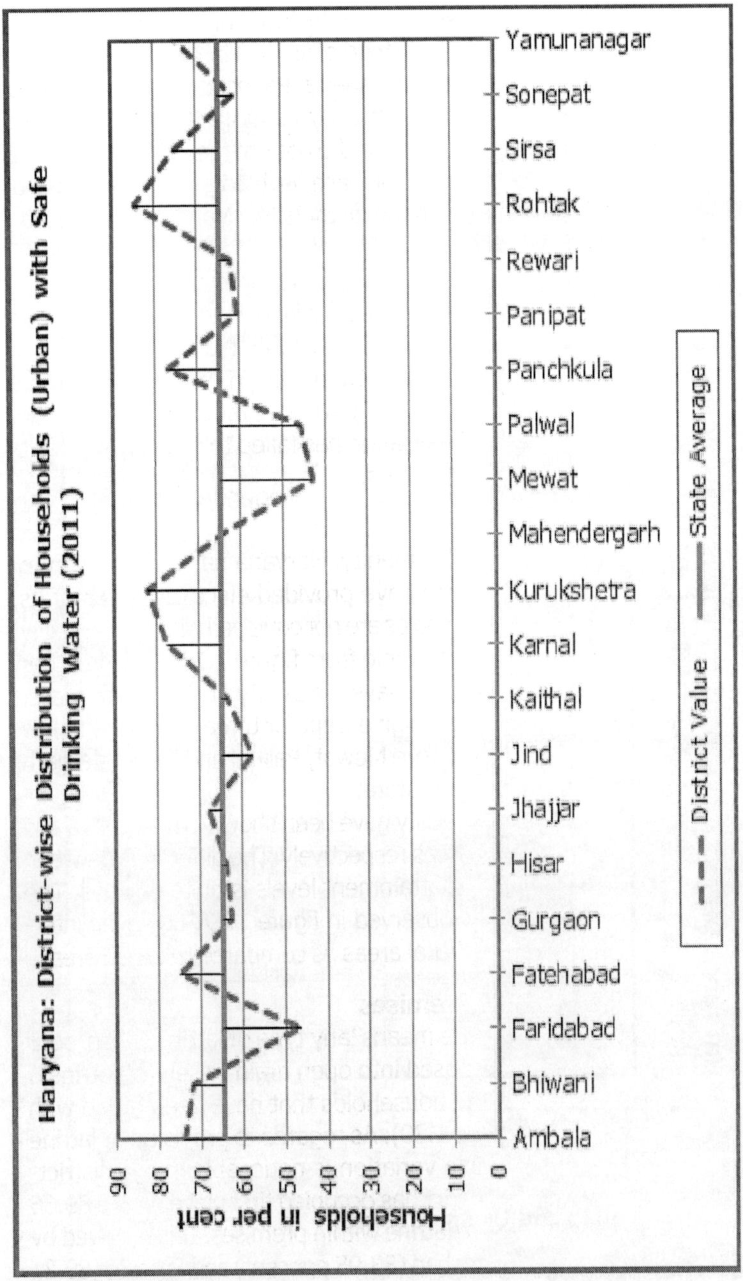
Haryana: District-wise Distribution of Households (Urban) with Safe Drinking Water (2011)
Households in per cent
0
10
20
30
40
50
60
70
80
90
Ambala
Bhiwani
Faridabad
Fatehabad
Gurgaon
Hisar
Jhajjar
Jind
Kaithal
Karnal
Kurukshetra
Mahendergarh
Mewat
Palwal
Panchkula
Panipat
Rewari
Rohtak
Sirsa
Sonepat
Yamunanagar
District Value
State Average

Fig. 1.16

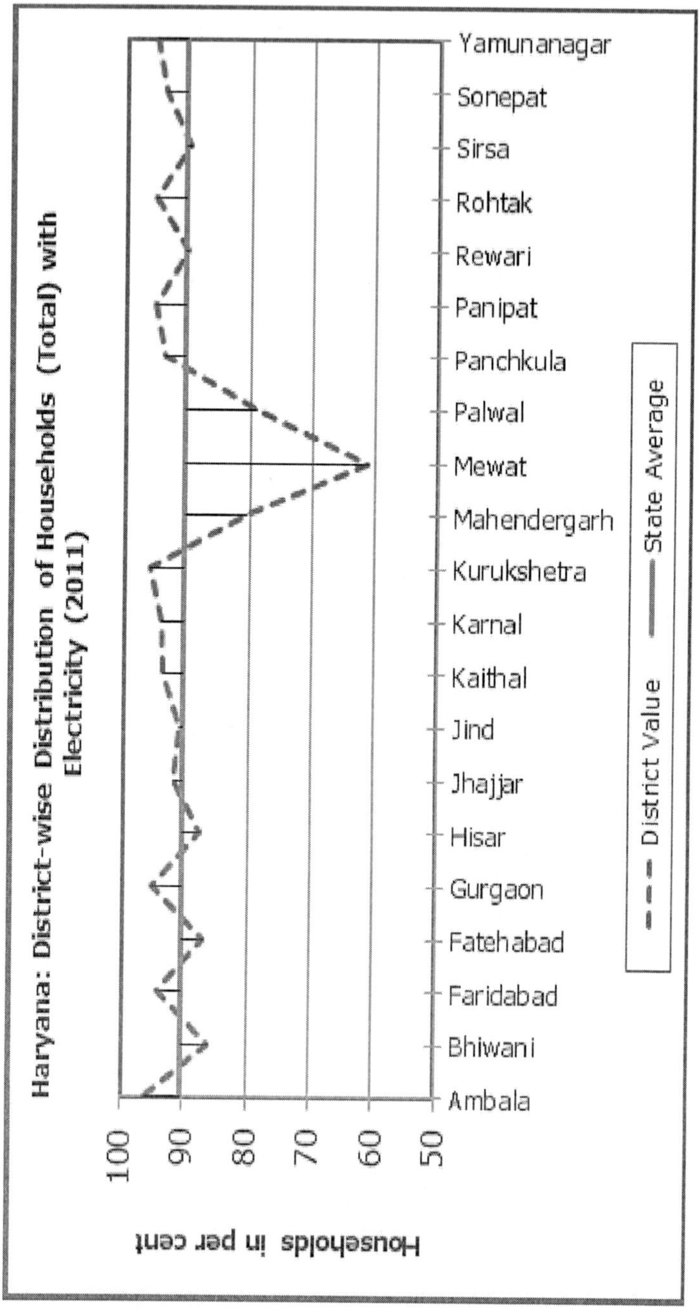
Haryana: District-wise Distribution of Households (Total) with Electricity (2011)
Households in per cent
100
90
80
70
60
50
Ambala
Bhiwani
Faridabad
Fatehabad
Gurgaon
Hisar
Jhajjar
Jind
Kaithal
Karnal
Kurukshetra
Mahendergarh
Mewat
Palwal
Panchkula
Panipat
Rewari
Rohtak
Sirsa
Sonepat
Yamunanagar
District Value
State Average

Fig. 1.17

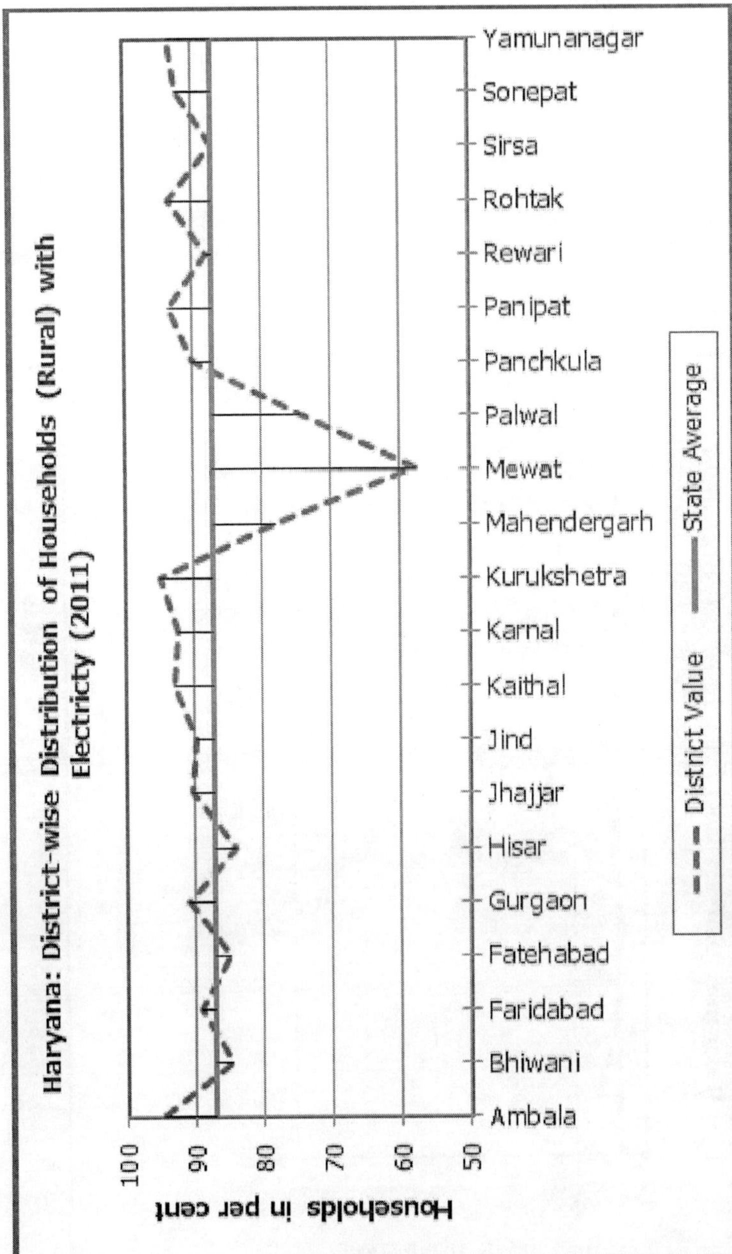
Haryana: District-wise Distribution of Households (Rural) with Electricty (2011)
Households in per cent
100
90
80
70
60
50
Ambala
Bhiwani
Faridabad
Fatehabad
Gurgaon
Hisar
Jhajjar
Jind
Kaithal
Karnal
Kurukshetra
Mahendergarh
Mewat
Palwal
Panchkula
Panipat
Rewari
Rohtak
Sirsa
Sonepat
Yamunanagar
District Value
State Average

Fig. 1.18

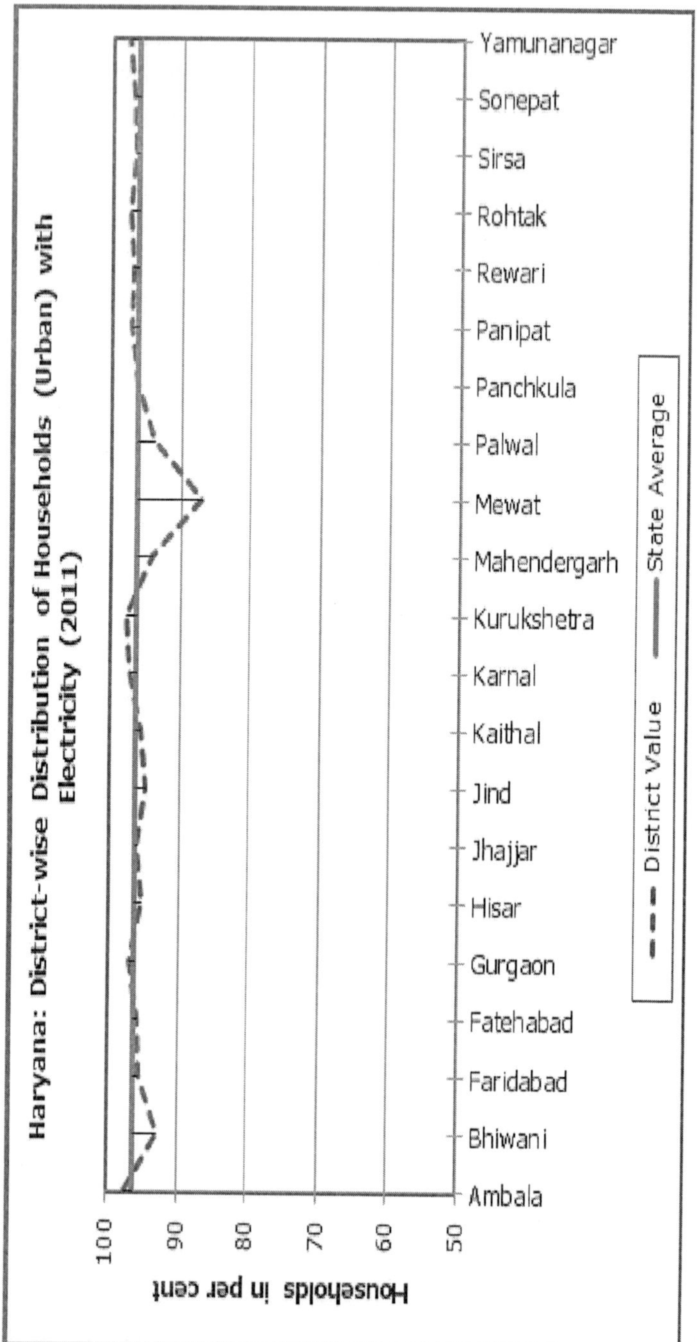
Haryana: District-wise Distribution of Households (Urban) with Electricity (2011)
Households in per cent
100
90
80
70
60
50
Ambala
Bhiwani
Faridabad
Fatehabad
Gurgaon
Hisar
Jhajjar
Jind
Kaithal
Karnal
Kurukshetra
Mahendergarh
Mewat
Palwal
Panchkula
Panipat
Rewari
Rohtak
Sirsa
Sonepat
Yamunanagar
District Value
State Average

Fig. 1.19

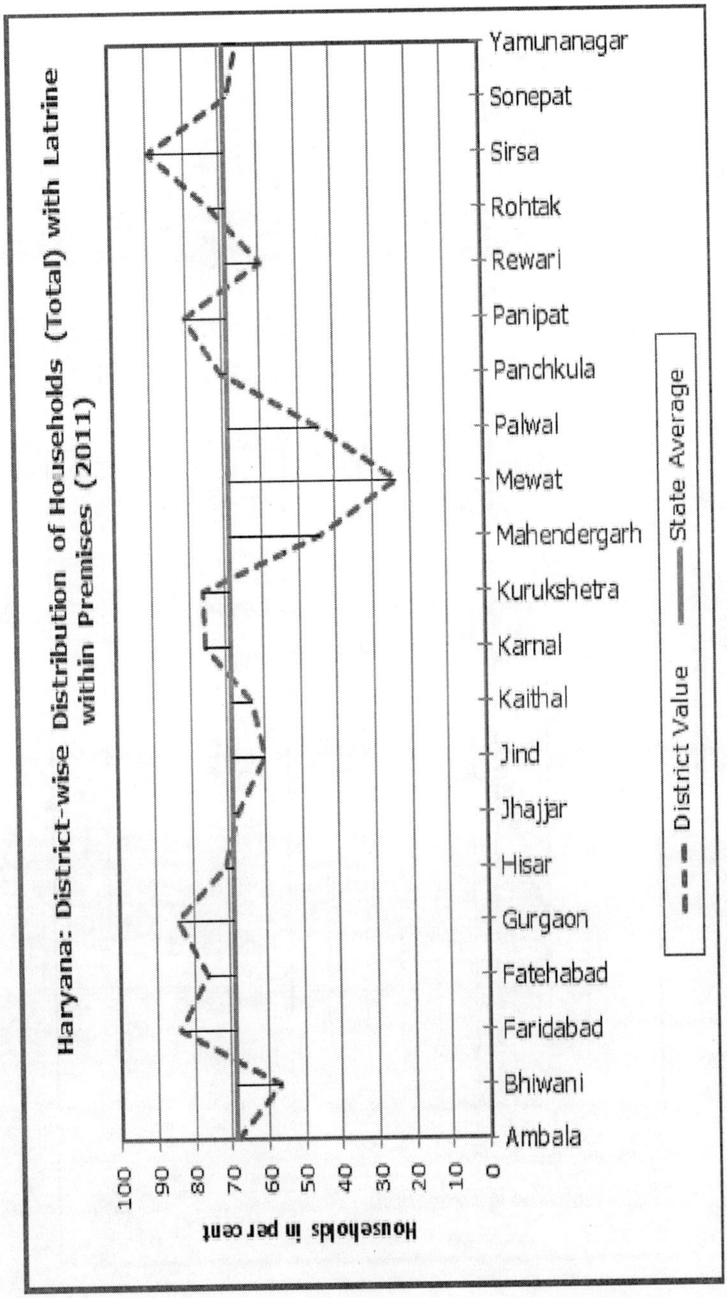
Haryana: District-wise Distribution of Households (Total) with Latrine within Premises (2011)
Households in per cent
100
90
80
70
60
50
40
30
20
10
0
Ambala
Bhiwani
Faridabad
Fatehabad
Gurgaon
Hisar
Jhajjar
Jind
Kaithal
Karnal
Kurukshetra
Mahendergarh
Mewat
Palwal
Panchkula
Panipat
Rewari
Rohtak
Sirsa
Sonepat
Yamunanagar
District Value
State Average

Fig. 1.20

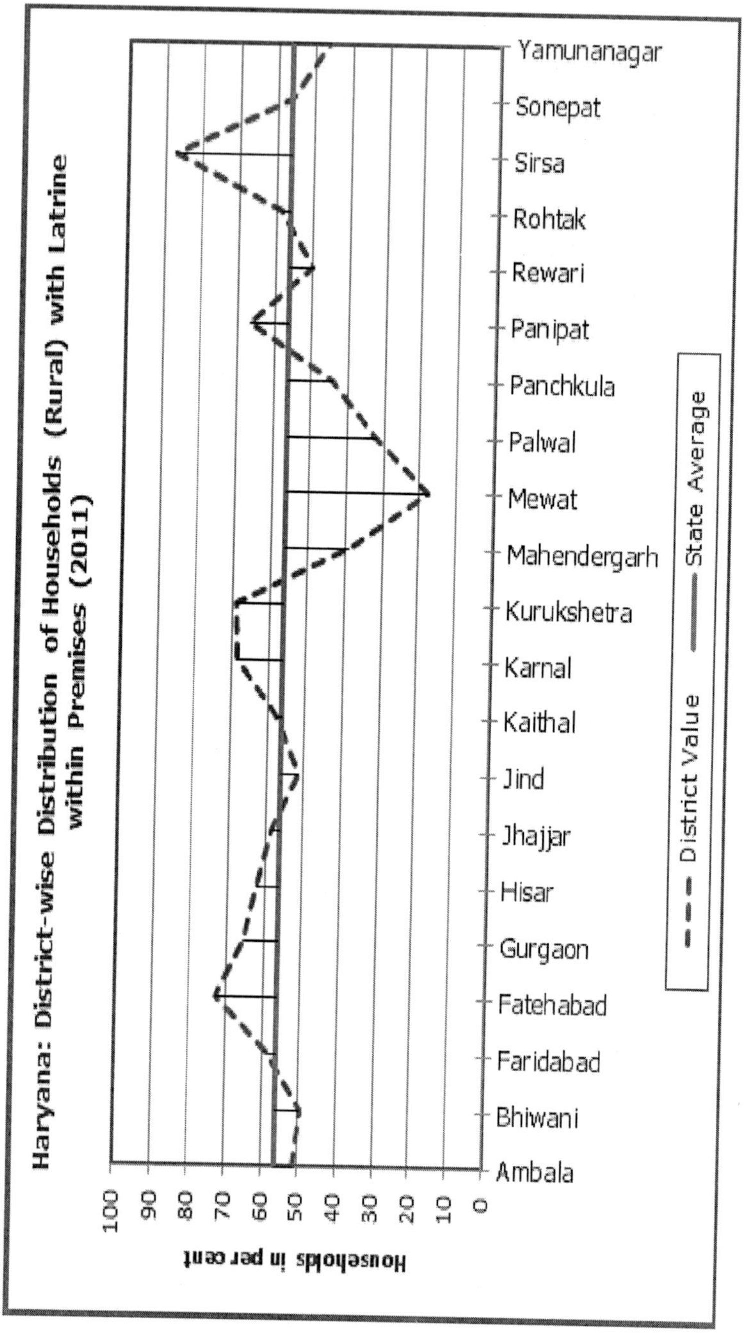
Haryana: District-wise Distribution of Households (Rural) with Latrine within Premises (2011)
Households in per cent
100
90
80
70
60
50
40
30
20
10
0
Ambala
Bhiwani
Faridabad
Fatehabad
Gurgaon
Hisar
Jhajjar
Jind
Kaithal
Karnal
Kurukshetra
Mahendergarh
Mewat
Palwal
Panchkula
Panipat
Rewari
Rohtak
Sirsa
Sonepat
Yamunanagar
District Value
State Average

Fig. 1.21

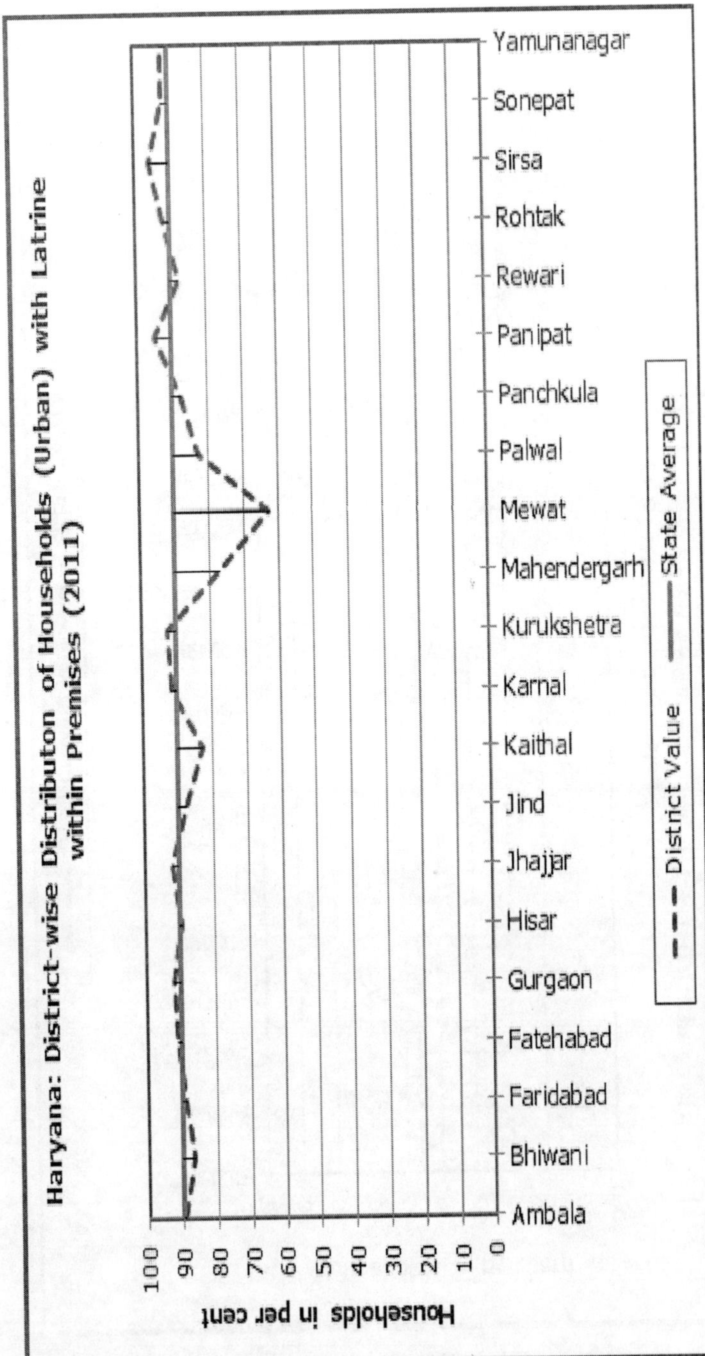
Haryana: District-wise Distributon of Households (Urban) with Latrine within Premises (2011)
Households in per cent
100
90
80
70
60
50
40
30
20
10
0
Ambala
Bhiwani
Faridabad
Fatehabad
Gurgaon
Hisar
Jhajjar
Jind
Kaithal
Karnal
Kurukshetra
Mahendergarh
Mewat
Palwal
Panchkula
Panipat
Rewari
Rohtak
Sirsa
Sonepat
Yamunanagar
District Value
State Average

Fig. 1.22

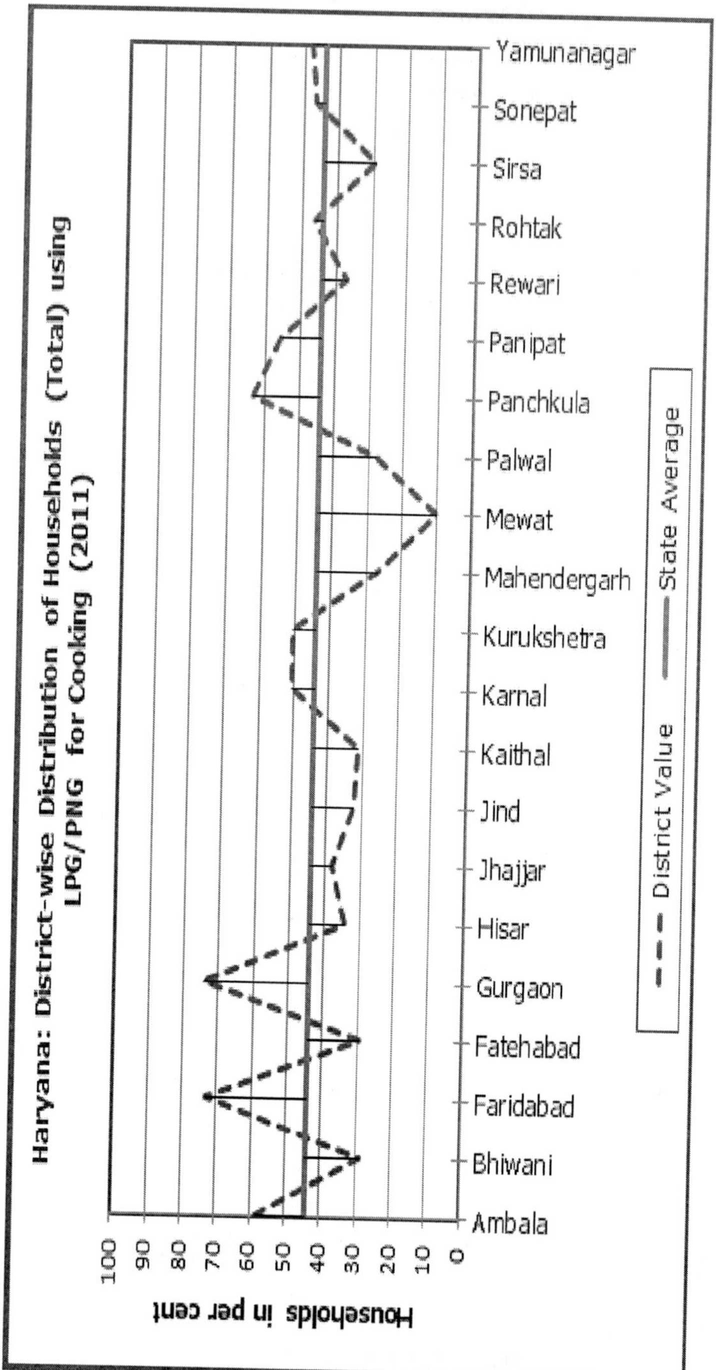
Haryana: District-wise Distribution of Households (Total) using LPG/PNG for Cooking (2011)
Households in per cent
100
90
80
70
60
50
40
30
20
10
0
Ambala
Bhiwani
Faridabad
Fatehabad
Gurgaon
Hisar
Jhajjar
Jind
Kaithal
Karnal
Kurukshetra
Mahendergarh
Mewat
Palwal
Panchkula
Panipat
Rewari
Rohtak
Sirsa
Sonepat
Yamunanagar
District Value
State Average

Fig. 1.23

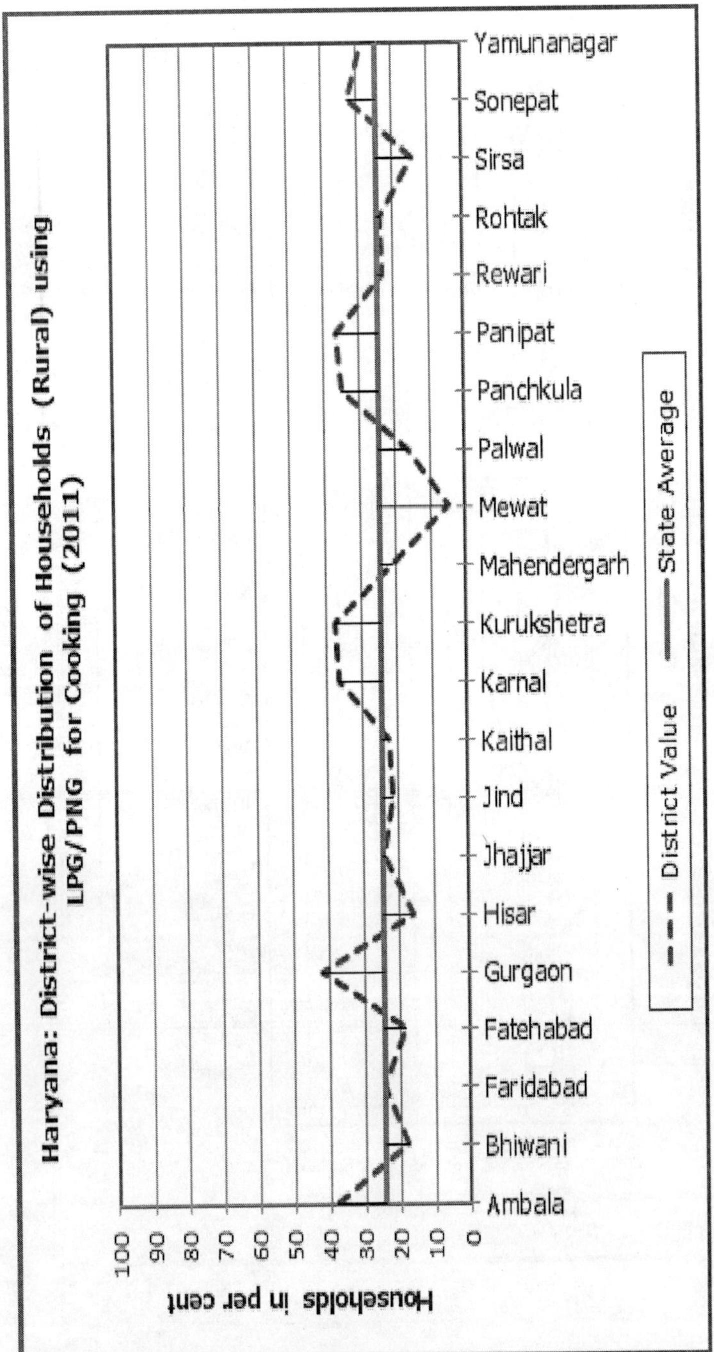
Haryana: District-wise Distribution of Households (Rural) using LPG/PNG for Cooking (2011)
Households in per cent
100
90
80
70
60
50
40
30
20
10
0
Ambala
Bhiwani
Faridabad
Fatehabad
Gurgaon
Hisar
Jhajjar
Jind
Kaithal
Karnal
Kurukshetra
Mahendergarh
Mewat
Palwal
Panchkula
Panipat
Rewari
Rohtak
Sirsa
Sonepat
Yamunanagar
District Value
State Average

Fig. 1.24

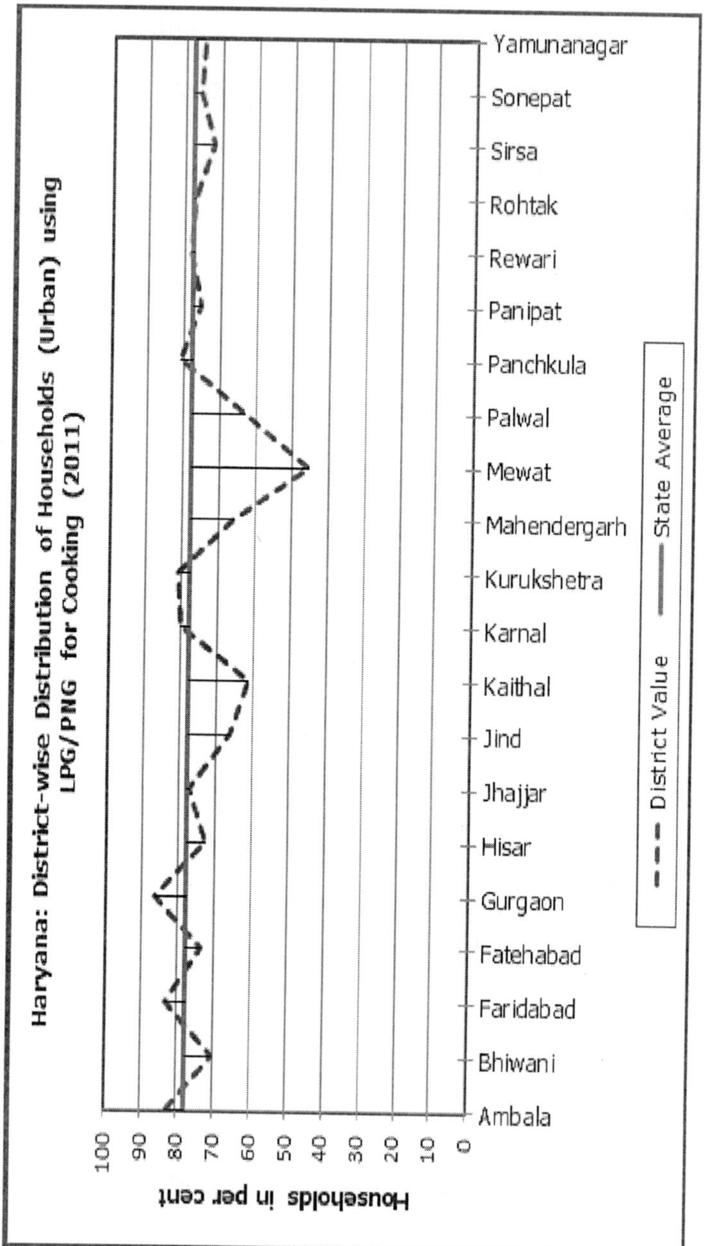
Haryana: District-wise Distribution of Households (Urban) using LPG/PNG for Cooking (2011)
Households in per cent
100
90
80
70
60
50
40
30
20
10
0
Ambala
Bhiwani
Faridabad
Fatehabad
Gurgaon
Hisar
Jhajjar
Jind
Kaithal
Karnal
Kurukshetra
Mahendergarh
Mewat
Palwal
Panchkula
Panipat
Rewari
Rohtak
Sirsa
Sonepat
Yamunanagar
District Value
State Average

Fig. 1.25

On the other hand, Mewat district has appeared as most backward district where merely 23.44 per cent of the households have latrine facility within premises. Mewat is well accompanied by the districts like Mahendergarh (44.27 per cent) and Palwal (44.41 per cent) in this category.

As far as the availability of latrine in rural areas is concerned, it is possessed by nearly 56 per cent households. District-wise trend is almost similar in rural and urban areas, though the attainment level is quite high in urban areas. Besides, inter-district variations are considerably high in rural areas (compare figure 1.21 and figure 1.22).

Households using LPG/PNG for Cooking

Variety of fuel has been used by the people for cooking their food. It ranges from fire-wood, crop residue, cow dung cake, coal, charcoal, kerosene, electricity, biogas to Liquefied Petroleum Gas (LPG). Among these fuels, LPG has been considered as most viable, efficient and clean source of energy for cooking. Hence, use of LPG/PNG is taken as basic household amenity in the study. Figure 1.23 reflects that more than half of the state's households cook their food without using LPG/PNG. The situation is quite dismal in Mewat, Palwal, Mahendergarh, Bhiwani, Fatehabad and Sirsa districts where less than 30 per cent households use LPG/PNG in their kitchen. However, Gurgaon and Faridabad districts have registered their entry in the other extreme where more than 70 per cent households use LPG/PNG for cooking. In this way the districts located in the southern part of the state have demonstrated highest inter-district disparities in this respect.

In rural Haryana, use of traditional fuel for cooking is still fairly popular. This is why; LPG is used by a handful of 24.15 per cent households (Figure 1.24). Gurgaon district with 42.5 per cent mark tops the tally while Mewat is lingering at the bottom with a meagre 4.85 per cent figure. On the other hand, LPG/PNG has acquired a prominent place in the kitchen of urban dwellers and as much as 77.61 per cent households use LPG/PNG for cooking (Figure 1.25). The figure is highest in Gurgaon (86.55 per cent) followed by Faridabad (83.21 per cent), Panchkula (80.96 per cent) and Karnal (80.09 per cent). In other words, at least four out of every five of the urban households in these districts use LPG/PNG for cooking. The lowest extreme is again represented by the trio of Mewat (45.17 per cent), Palwal (63.32 per cent) and Mahendergarh (65.78 per cent) districts. Kaithal has also joined the trio by recording second lowest figure of 61.44 per cent.

Rural-Urban Gap in Household Amenities

Rural-urban gap has been carried out for the four household amenities discussed above. The higher the rural-urban gap in the accessibility of

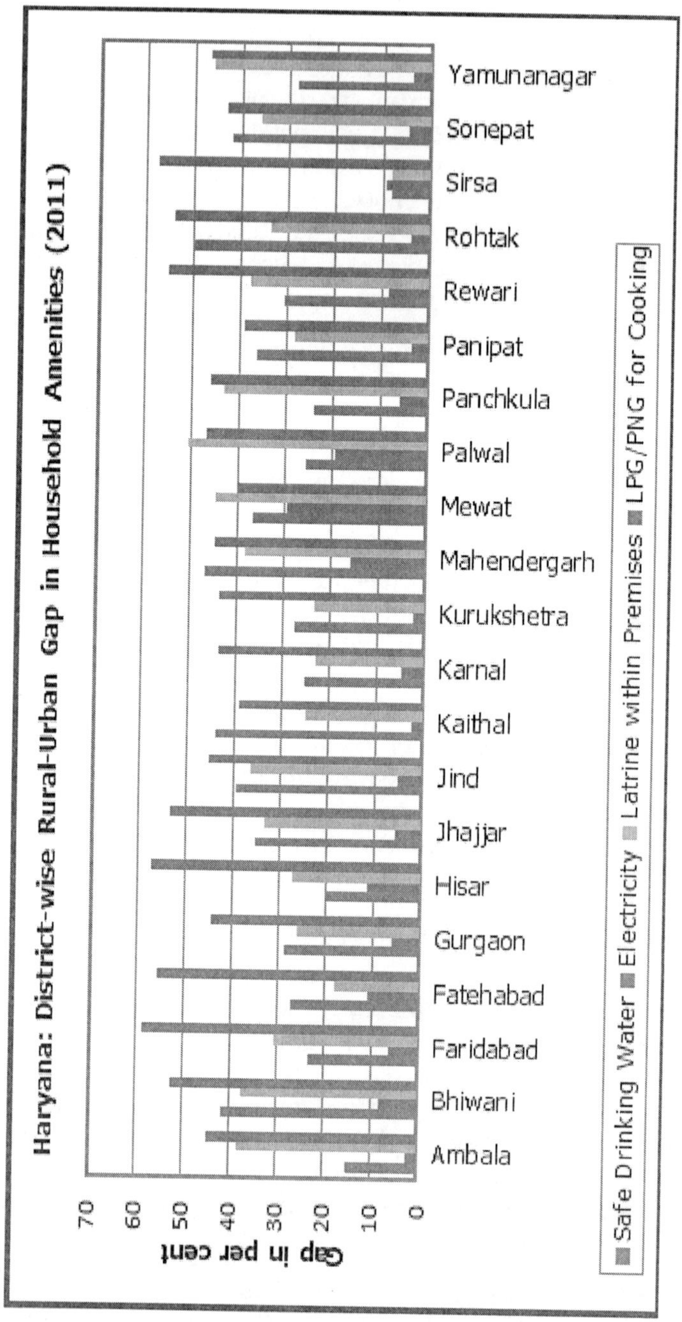
Haryana: District-wise Rural-Urban Gap in Household Amenities (2011)
Gap in per cent
0
10
20
30
40
50
60
70
Yamunanagar
Sonepat
Sirsa
Rohtak
Rewari
Panipat
Panchkula
Palwal
Mewat
Mahendergarh
Kurukshetra
Karnal
Kaithal
Jind
Jhajjar
Hisar
Gurgaon
Fatehabad
Faridabad
Bhiwani
Ambala
Safe Drinking Water
Electricity
Latrine within Premises
LPG/PNG for Cooking

Fig. 1.26

basic amenities more would be the disparity between the living standards of the two communities, which is not desirable in a healthy society. The highest gap is observed in the 'use of LPG/PNG for cooking' (53.46 per cent) followed by 'latrine within premises' (33.82 per cent) and 'access to safe drinking water' (29.77 per cent). On the contrary, the amenity of 'electricity' has come into view with the lowest rural-urban gap of 9.01 per cent in the state. The district wise rural-urban gap is demonstrated in figure 1.26. The highest rural-urban gap with regard to 'access to safe drinking water' is found in Rohtak (49.76 per cent) whereas the lowest gap can be seen in Sirsa (8.25 per cent) district. The corresponding positions of districts for the other three amenities of electricity, latrine within premises and use of LPG/PNG for cooking are Mewat (29.41 per cent) and Kurukshetra (2.48 per cent); Palwal (50.69 per cent) and Sirsa (8.35 per cent); and Faridabad (58.62 per cent) and Kaithal (39.08 per cent).

Correlates of Demographic Attributes and Household Amenities

Firstly, Pearson's correlation coefficient has been carried out to establish relationship between the various demographic attributes. The following conclusions can be drawn on the basis of correlation matrix constructed in Table 1.10:

- Population size has low and negative correlation (-0.31) with sex ratio. It means sex ratio is found poorer in the districts with larger size of population and vice versa. Growth in literacy rate has also been adversely affected to some extent in districts with larger size of population.
- Higher decadal growth of population is positively associated with the child sex ratio but inversely related with the total sex ratio. Moreover, the higher growth rate of population has inversely affected the growth of male literacy rate.
- The negative correlation between the sex ratio and literacy rate indicates that sex ratio is higher in the districts which are lagging in literacy rate, yet they have recorded higher decadal improvement in literacy. Besides, a good number of districts which have registered high decadal change in sex ratio are those where overall sex ratio is lesser.
- A moderate correlation of 0.53 between decadal change in sex ratio and decadal change in 0-6 age sex ratio here implies that the trend of change is in the similar direction.
- Unfortunately a high negative correlation has been noticed between the child sex ratio and all the three indicators of literacy. However, the satisfactory note is that child sex ratio is positively associated with all the indicators showing decadal change whether it is sex ratio or it is literacy rate.

Table 1.10: Correlation Matrix of Demographic Attributes of Haryana (2011)

Demographic Attributes	*Population Size*	*Population Growth 2001-11*	*Sex Ratio*	*Decadal Change in Sex Ratio, 2001-2011*	*Sex Ratio 0-6 age*	*Decadal Change in Sex Ratio, 0-6 age*	*Total Literacy Rate*	*Decadal Change in Total Literacy Rate 2001-2011*	*Male Literacy Rate*	*Decadal Change in Male Literacy Rate 2001-2011*	*Female Literacy Rate*	*Decadal Change in Female Literacy Rate 2001-2011*
Population Size	1.00	0.24	-0.31	0.05	0.14	0.05	0.04	-0.24	0.02	-0.25	0.05	-0.16
Population Growth 2001-11		1.00	-0.22	-0.06	0.34	0.13	0.03	-0.19	0.03	-0.31	0.03	0.02
Sex Ratio			1.00	-0.34	0.28	-0.04	-0.58	0.46	-0.49	0.53	-0.58	0.24
Decadal Change in Sex Ratio, 2001-2011				1.00	0.36	0.53	0.10	-0.02	-0.14	0.09	0.23	-0.03
Sex Ratio 0-6 age					1.00	0.49	-0.69	0.55	-0.74	0.54	-0.61	0.51

(Contd.)

(Contd. Table 1.10)

Demographic Attributes	Population Size	Population Growth 2001-11	Sex Ratio	Decadal Change in Sex Ratio, 2001-2011	Sex Ratio 0-6 age	Decadal Change in Sex Ratio, 0-6 age	Total Literacy Rate	Decadal Change in Total Literacy Rate 2001-2011	Male Literacy Rate	Decadal Change in Male Literacy Rate 2001-2011	Female Literacy Rate	Decadal Change in Female Literacy Rate 2001-2011
Decadal Change in Sex Ratio, 0-6 age, 2011						1.00	-0.24	0.09	-0.54	0.21	-0.04	-0.05
Total Literacy Rate							1.00	-0.83	0.93	-0.84	0.97	-0.67
Decadal Change in Total Literacy Rate 2001-2011								1.00	-0.76	0.94	-0.82	0.89

(Contd.)

(Contd. Table 1.10)

Demographic Attributes	Population Size	Population Growth 2001-11	Sex Ratio	Decadal Change in Sex Ratio, 2001-2011	Sex Ratio 0-6 age	Decadal Change in Sex Ratio, 0-6 age	Total Literacy Rate	Decadal Change in Total Literacy Rate 2001-2011	Male Literacy Rate	Decadal Change in Male Literacy Rate 2001-2011	Female Literacy Rate	Decadal Change in Female Literacy Rate 2001-2011
Male Literacy Rate									1.00	-0.82	0.82	-0.55
Decadal Change in Male Literacy Rate 2001-2011										1.00	-0.78	0.68
Female Literacy Rate											1.00	-0.70
Decadal Change in												1.00

(Contd. Table 1.10)

Demographic Attributes	*Population Size*	*Population Growth 2001-11*	*Sex Ratio*	*Decadal Change in Sex Ratio, 2001-2011*	*Sex Ratio 0-6 age*	*Decadal Change in Sex Ratio, 0-6 age*	*Total Literacy Rate*	*Decadal Change in Total Literacy Rate 2001-2011*	*Male Literacy Rate*	*Decadal Change in Male Literacy Rate 2001-2011*	*Female Literacy Rate*	*Decadal Change in Female Literacy Rate 2001-2011*
Decadal Change in Sex Ratio, 0-6 age, 2011						1.00	-0.24	0.09	-0.54	0.21	-0.04	-0.05
Total Literacy Rate							1.00	-0.83	0.93	-0.84	0.97	-0.67
Decadal Change in Total Literacy Rate 2001-2011								1.00	-0.76	0.94	-0.82	0.89

(Contd.)

(Contd. Table 1.10)

Demographic Attributes	Population Size	Population Growth 2001-11	Sex Ratio	Decadal Change in Sex Ratio, 2001-2011	Sex Ratio 0-6 age	Decadal Change in Sex Ratio, 0-6 age	Total Literacy Rate	Decadal Change in Total Literacy Rate 2001-2011	Male Literacy Rate	Decadal Change in Male Literacy Rate 2001-2011	Female Literacy Rate	Decadal Change in Female Literacy Rate 2001-2011
Male Literacy Rate									1.00	-0.82	0.82	-0.55
Decadal Change in Male Literacy Rate 2001-2011										1.00	-0.78	0.68
Female Literacy Rate											1.00	-0.70
Decadal Change in												1.00

Table 1.11: Correlation Matrix of Selected Demographic Attributes and Household Amenities (2011)

Indicators	*Population Size*	*Sex Ratio*	*Total Literacy Rate*	*Total Households with Safe Drinking Water*	*Total Households with Electricity*	*Total Households with Latrine within Premises*	*Total Households using LPG/PNG for Cooking*
Population Size	1.00	-0.31	0.04	-0.04	0.12	0.28	0.19
Sex Ratio		1.00	-0.58	-0.10	-0.56	-0.40	-0.61
Total Literacy Rate			1.00	0.47	0.77	0.52	0.79
Total Households with Safe Drinking Water				1.00	0.66	0.76	0.57
Total Households with Electricity					1.00	0.82	0.74
Total Households with Latrine within Premises						1.00	0.68
Total Households using LPG/PNG for Cooking							1.00

- A moderate but negative correlation (-0.54) between decadal change in child sex ratio and male literacy rate reflects that high decadal change does not take place in the districts with high male literacy rate. In other words higher decadal change in sex ratio is more prevalent in the districts with poor male literacy rate.
- A very high positive association of total literacy rate with both the variables showing gender-wise literacy rate is quite obvious. But it is inversely associated with the variable showing decadal change in literacy rate. In other words, the districts with high literacy rate do not show high decadal change in literacy rate; and high decadal change in literacy rate is restricted to the districts which are lagging in total literacy rate and vice versa. Similar trend can be noticed in the case of gender-wise literacy rate.

Relationship between the selected demographic attributes and household amenities has also been worked out. The results have been presented in Table 1.11. The following inferences can be drawn on the basis of correlation coefficients:

- Population size of the districts is not significantly associated with any of the variable except for a modest but negative correlation with sex ratio.
- Sex ratio is negatively associated not only with the literacy rate but with the variables showing household amenities, though the relationship is insignificant with 'households with safe drinking water'. Sex ratio is found to be higher in the districts with low literacy rate and poor household amenities.
- Contrary to sex ratio, literacy rate is positively associated with all the variables showing household amenities. It means higher the literacy rates in a district higher would be the level of household amenities in that district. This is more so in the case of amenities like electricity and LPG/PNG.
- All the variables related to household amenities are highly associated with each other in a positive way. It implies that a district which is doing better in any household amenity will perform better in other household amenities also and vice versa.

Sum up

Haryana is amongst the smaller states of India as regards to population as well as geographical area. It is not only a densely populated state but the decennial growth of population is also higher. As far as the literacy rate is concerned, it is slightly higher in the state as compared to the national average. The state has been placed at the 15th rank on the state-wise tally of total literacy rate in census 2011. The state has an edge over the national average as regards to gender-wise literacy rates also. Besides, the state has developed impressive educational infrastructure not only to provide elementary education but also for higher and technical education especially during the last decade. The state has an undesirable distinction of ranking at the bottom of the scale amongst the Indian states as regards to sex ratio. However, the latest trend of change is encouraging. The state has performed better in a number of health parameters as compared to the country. However, it has shown weakness in the other aspects. The economic development in the state is rather remarkable. It has witnessed phenomenal growth in secondary and tertiary sectors of economy. However, fluctuations in agricultural production cause instability in the growth rate of economy from time to time. Moreover, rapidly increasing share of services sector in the state GDP adds to the decline in the share of agriculture sector. As far as district-wise analysis of demographic attributes and household amenities are concerned, the most striking feature which is noticed from the preceding analysis is the prevalence of inter-district, rural-urban and gender disparities.

2

Data Base and Methodology

Concept of Human Development

From the second half of the last century, there has been a growing school of thought that economic development alone does not necessarily amount to overall equitable growth as it did not on its own reduce poverty levels, improve health or end gender and social discrimination. In 1990, the United Nations Development Programme (UNDP) brought out the first global Human Development Report (HDR) under the leadership of Mahbub-ul-Haq with the key statement "People are the real wealth of a nation. The basic objective of development is to create an enabling environment for people to enjoy long, healthy and creative lives...... the process of human development must transmit itself, essentially by means of enlarging the choices of all persons concerned........". Since then, UNDP has been bringing out HDRs regularly which attracted global attention towards the concept of human development. Thus, a "people-centred" human development concept became the point of debate.

Human development is not just economic growth but it is also about growth with expansion of choices, access to services and participation of people in the process of development leading to their empowerment. It has been realised that longevity, education and access to resources are the most crucial choices to live a decent life. That is why; the indicators that have been considered to measure the human development level are quality of health, extent of education, level of employment and real income levels.

Human Development Index

The Human Development Index (HDI), developed in UNDP's first Human Development Report, combines three essential elements of a

Table 2.1: Human Development Index Trends of India

Year	*1980*	*1985*	*1990*	*1995*	*2000*	*2005*	*2006*	*2007*	*Long term 1980-2007*	*Medium term 1990-2007*	*Short term 2000-2007*
Index	0.427	0.453	0.489	0.511	0.556	0.596	0.604	0.612	1.33	1.32	1.36

Source: UNDP Human Development Report, 2009.

decent life. These include – life expectancy at birth representing attainment in the health sector, literacy rate and combined gross enrolment in the primary, secondary and tertiary education indicating attainment in the domain of knowledge and gross domestic product indicating attainment in the income sector. Equal weight has been given to the three indicators and thus relative Human Development Index (HDI) of administrative units is calculated. Since 1990, UNDP has been bringing out HDRs every year by adding additional criteria for the measurement of human advancement and wellbeing of the people belonging to various nations. In 1997, it introduced Human Poverty Index (HPI), which is a multi-dimensional measure of human deprivation. Likewise other indicators such as Gender-related Development Index (GDI) and Gender Empowerment Measure (GEM) were also introduced and countries were ranked on these bases. In 2007, India with HDI value of 0.612 was ranked 134th amongst 182 countries (UNDP, HDR, 2009) and placed in the category of 'Medium Human Development'. Human Development Index trends of India are tabulated here:

The methodology used by UNDP has undergone a number of changes over time due to geographical conditions of the regions, non-availability of data and relevance of index components. Besides, the unit of study has also been changing moving from countries to states and districts to improve the methodology. India introduced its first National Human Development Report in 2001 by incorporating some changes in methodology.

It is being gradually recognised that socio-economic issues of importance at macro, meso and micro level could be effectively addressed by human development profile of spatial units such as district. At the state level, a number of states like Rajasthan, Madhya Pradesh, Punjab, Karnataka, Haryana, etc., have published their HDRs by modifying the UNDP's methodology to some extent as various geographical factors such as physical, economic, political, social, technological, etc., affect human development of a region.

Haryana, the state known for its agricultural production is located strategically close to Delhi and one-third of its area falls within the National Capital Region. This region represents one of the biggest trade and consumption centres in the country. Between 1994 and 2003, the economy of Haryana grew at an average rate of 6.5 per cent per annum. Haryana has the fourth highest per capita income in India. The state offers significant potential for agro-based industries, property development and retailing. But it is disheartening to note that the industrial development is restricted to a few districts located in the radius of 60 kilometres from Delhi and the other districts are far behind in the race. As a result, the

rank achieved by the state with respect to Human Development is quite disappointing (Table 2.2).

Table 2.2: Rank of Haryana in Human Development Dimensions in India

Year	*HDI Rank*	*GDI Rank*	*HPI Rank*
1981	15	24	13
1991	16	17	10

Source: National Human Development Report, 2001.

The first and only Human Development Report of Haryana was prepared by the Haryana Institute of Public Administration (HIPA), Government of Haryana in 2005. The report was based on the two sets of indicators- the indicators used by the UNDP and the indicators used by Planning Commission of India. Since then a little work on the various issues of human development has been carried out by any agency or individual in the state.

Thus, in Haryana the idea of human development calls for a concerted effort to identify, recognise and then to remove with affirmative action, disparities between regions and communities. Addressing relative deprivations amongst regions and people in education, in health, in standard of living, in security, in dignity and in basic human rights, is a serious concern of human development.

In the light of above observations it becomes imperative to study all the development parameters that affect human development in the Spatio-temporal context and to highlight the regional disparities in the human development in the state. For this, district seems a proper unit of study as it is recognised as a unit of micro/ meso level planning in India.

Review of Literature

The first human development report brought out by UNDP in 1990 started with a simple but far reaching statement: "People are the real wealth of the nation. The basic objective of development is to create an enabling environment for people to enjoy long, healthy and creative lives. Human development is a process of enlarging people's choices." Since then UNDP has been bringing out a human development report by adding additional criteria for the measurement of human progress and highlighting different human development issues each year. Human Rights (2000), Millennium Development Goals (2003), Beyond Scarcity (2006), Fighting Climate Change (2007), and Human Mobility (2009) are some of the themes emphasised by UNDP in its HDRs.

On the lines of UNDP, the Planning Commission of India brought out its first HDR in 2001.This Report breaks fresh ground in quite a few areas in presenting the status of human development at state level in India. It has, for the first time, put together an extensive database for at least two and in some cases three points of time since 1980, covering nearly 70 distinct social indicators on various aspects of the quality of life and wellbeing of the people. The report highlights the inequalities in the attainment levels of people depending on their place of residence, whether rural or urban areas, and on the sex of the person.

The Himachal Pradesh HDR (2002) attempts to assess and explain the status of human development in the state and articulates policy implications. Gender studies and people's participation are the cross-cutting themes of the report, which focuses on health, education, natural resources and poverty. The analysis, moving from the state to the district level, helps to highlight the existence of regional imbalances within the state.

The Maharashtra Human Development Report (2002) analyses the issues related to population, poverty, education, health, nutrition and gender. While highlighting the State's achievements, the report recommends interventions for sustainable human development. In particular, the report calls for better management of water resources, stabilisation of income potential from agriculture operations, empowerment of women, compulsory elementary education for all children and improved healthcare.

The Rajasthan HDR (2002) is a frank assessment of the status of human development in the state. It highlights the issues of income and employment generation, reduction in poverty and regional disparities, provision of basic minimum services, people's participation, and development of human capabilities, especially that of the income poor. The Report flags the critical importance of ensuring sustainable livelihoods and minimising the impact of drought through appropriate, community centred strategies such as rainwater harvesting and watershed management.

The Andhra Pradesh HDR (2007) provides a comprehensive picture of the status of human development at the district level to serve as a baseline for evaluating the trends that will emerge in future. It compares disparities in levels of human development across sub-population groups identified by their socioeconomic (gender, caste, poverty, occupation etc.,) and geographical (region, district, location: rural-urban) characteristics. It identifies problems specific to the state, region and district. Ultimately it focuses on the way towards the progress of human development in the state and relevant policy measures for addressing the emerging areas of concern.

Similarly some other states like Punjab, Madhya Pradesh, Orissa, Nagaland, etc have also published the state level HDRs assessing and explaining the identical issues pertaining to human development following, more or less, the same methodology.

Aims and objectives of the study

The present study aims at bringing out regional disparities in the various aspects of human development in Haryana. The objectives can be stated as under:

(a) To carry out the Human Development Index (HDI) of Haryana at district level for 2001 and 2011 and to underline the inter-district disparities in the level of human development.
(b) To study changing relative status of districts regarding HDI.
(c) To study changing relative status of districts regarding Human Poverty Index (HPI) and Gender Development Index (GDI).
(d) To highlight the factors responsible for the regional disparities in human development.
(e) To suggest policy measures to bring down the regional disparities at an acceptable level.

Hypotheses

The following hypotheses have been tested in the study:

(a) Inter-district disparities in the level of human development are quite high in Haryana and these are intensifying with time.
(b) The level of human development in Haryana is positively associated with the proximity of National Capital.
(c) The more the rail/ road density in a region, the higher is the level of human development.

The Study Area

The present research work deals with Haryana state. The unit of study is district.

Sources of Data

The study is based on secondary data that are available from the following sources:

(1) Census of India, State Volumes of 2001 and 2011.
(2) Statistical Abstract, Haryana.
(3) District Census Handbooks (all districts), Haryana.
(4) Directorate of Economics and Statistics, Government of Haryana.
(5) Directorate of Census Operations, Haryana.
(6) Department of Health, Government of Haryana.
(7) Directorate of Elementary and Secondary Education, Government of Haryana.

(8) National Sample Survey Organisation (NSSO).
(9) Sample Registration Scheme of the Registrar General of India.
(10) Reproductive and Child Health: District Level Household Survey, International Institute of Population Sciences, Mumbai.

Research Methodology

The methodology which is adopted in the present research work is basically UNDP's methodology. However, few modifications have been made due to geographical set up of the state, objectives of the study and data constraints. Human Development Index (HDI), Human Poverty Index (HPI) and Gender Development Index (GDI) have been calculated at district level separately for 2001 and 2011. The results have been mapped and tabulated to highlight the trends of human development parameters and the regional disparities.

I. Human Development Index (HDI): Description of the Variables Used

HDI is a summery measure of human development that determines the average achievements of a state/ district on three basic dimensions of human development. The detail of these three dimensions is discussed below:

(a) A Decent Standard of Living- The UNDP has used per capita Gross Domestic Product (PPP US$) and carried out GDP index to appraise the decent standard of living. The same variable is used in the present study to carry out income index.

(b) Knowledge- The UNDP has used two variables to determine the knowledge level of the people- adult literacy rate (with two-third weight) and the combined primary, secondary and tertiary gross enrolment ratio (with one-third weight). On the lines of UNDP, education index comprising Adult Literacy Rate (2/3 weight) and School Attendance/ Enrolment Ratio (1/3 weight) was initially proposed to be carried out. Adult literacy rate, here, implies for the proportion of literate population above the age of 14 and School Attendance/ Enrolment Ratio means proportion of population in the age group '6+ to 14' attending educational institutes. Census of India generates the relevant data. But the age data pertaining to literacy rates had not been released by the institution for 2011 till the end of 2013. Hence literacy rates have been taken into account to determine the knowledge level of the people in the present study. Since the study focuses on the decadal changes, the data of same nature has been used for 2001 to make the comparative analysis meaningful even though the age data of literacy rate is available for 2001.

(c) A Long and Healthy Life- Life Expectancy at Birth (LEB) has been considered by the UNDP to judge the health status of the population.

The district level data pertaining to life expectancy at birth is not available in India. Infant Mortality Rate (IMR) is another significant indicator to reflect the health status of people. Institute of Economic Growth, New Delhi has calculated district level IMR for Haryana for 2001. But the district level IMR data for 2011 is not available. Since the present study focuses on the Spatio-temporal analysis of 2001 and 2011, the IMR data, which is available for 2001 only, could not be used. International Institute of Population Sciences (IIPS) Mumbai conduct District Level Household Survey (DLHS) on regular intervals that covers various aspects of child and women health. Using the IIPS data, five variables have been used in the present study to determine the health index. These variables are- proportion of villages with any government health facility (includes sub-centre, primary health centre, community health centre or referral hospital, government hospital and government dispensary within a village); proportion of villages with doctor (either private or visiting doctor); proportion of children age 12-35 months fully vaccinated (BCG, three injections of DPT, three doses of Polio and measles); proportion of women that received full ante-natal check-ups (at least three visits for ante-natal check-ups, at least one TT injection received and adequate amount of IFA) and proportion of women who had institutional deliveries. All the five variables have been given equal weight to calculate health index.

The human development index is a simple average of the above three indices.

II. Human Poverty Index (HPI): Description of the Variables Used

HPI is a measure of capability deprivation popularised by UNDP as an alternative to income poverty. It recognises that human deprivation is multi-faceted and seeks to measure the levels of deprivation in a society with respect to health, education and basic material needs. The UNDP has devised separate HPI for two sets of countries i.e. HPI_1 for developing countries and HPI_2 for Organisation for Economic Co-operation and Development (OECD) countries. In the calculation of HPI_1, they have considered three dimensions i.e. deprived of a long and healthy life (vulnerability to death at a relatively early age), deprived of knowledge (exclusion from the world of reading and communications) and deprived of a decent standard of living (lack of access to overall economic provisioning) whereas in the calculation of HPI_2 diverse criteria has been used to determine the three dimensions. Besides, an additional dimension i.e. social exclusion has also been considered. Here, three dimensions as used by the UNDP in the calculation of HPI_1 are taken into consideration. The description of variables used by the UNDP vis-à-vis in the present study is discussed below:

(a) Deprived of decent standard of living- The dimension has been measured by the UNDP considering the un-weighted average of two indicators- the percentage of population without sustainable access to an improved water source and the percentage of children under weight for age. Here, only one variable i.e. proportion of population living below poverty line has been considered as the data regarding the variables used by the UNDP is not available at district level.

(b) Deprived of knowledge- Only one variable i.e. adult illiteracy rate has been considered by the UNDP to measure the deprivation of knowledge. On the lines of UNDP, the single variable 'Illiteracy Rate' has been used in the present analysis as 'Adult illiteracy Rate' could not be estimated in the non-availability of age data as mentioned in the preceding section.

(c) Deprived of long and healthy life- The UNDP has measured the dimension by the probability at birth of not surviving to age 40. Such data is not available in India at district level. Hence, a combined indicator of five variables-proportion of villages without any government health facility; proportion of villages without doctor; proportion of children age 12-35 months not fully vaccinated; proportion of women that did not receive full ante-natal check-ups and proportion of women who had non-institutional deliveries has been used in the study by giving equal weight to each variable.

III. Gender Development Index (GDI): Description of the Variables Used

While the HDI measures average achievements of a society in respect of the three basic dimensions of human development, the GDI adjusts the average achievements to reflect the disparities between men and women in these dimensions. The gender wise data of the same variables has been used by the UNDP to calculate GDI as used in the measurement of HDI. Due to data constraints, the variables used in the present study for the three dimensions are listed below:

(a) Income- Apportioned income for males and females, based on the shares of male and female workers in total workforce and the ratio of average male wage rate to average female wage rate. The ratio of the average female wage to the average male wage is not available for any region in India. Hence, the ratio is assumed to be the average ratio for the agricultural sector, which has been assumed as 66.67 per cent based upon some recently conducted poverty assessment surveys.

(b) Education- Gender-wise literacy rates have been taken into consideration.

(c) Health- Gender-wise proportion of marriages above the legal age of marriage.

For each dimension, an Equally Distributed Index (EDI) has been calculated taking into account the gender disparities.

Computing Human Development Index

The methodology adopted here for computing the HDI for the districts is generally the same as the one devised by the UNDP. As stated earlier, HDI is a simple average of three dimensions- decent standard of life, education and healthy life. In other words equal weight has been assigned to each of the three dimensions as each of the components contributes equally for the well-being of people. In this way the HDI reflects how far a district has travelled on the path of development and also how far still it has to travel. The computation of HDI may be defined as:

$$HDI_j = \frac{1}{3}\sum I_{ij}$$

Where HDI_j is Human Development Index of jth district and I_{ij} is normalised dimension index for the ith indicator in j[th] district.

The normalised dimension index I_{ij} refers to income index, health index and education attainment index.

Goalposts for determination of HDI

Goalposts are the minimum and maximum values of variables that reflect the lowest level of human development and the highest level of human development respectively. In fact, the maximum value is a target fixed for a region to achieve the highest level of human development. In

Table 2.3: Goalposts for calculating the district level HDI, 2001 and 2011

Sr. No.	*Variables*	*Minimum value*	*Maximum value*
1	Income index Per capita GDP (PPP$) (as per UNDP HDR 2003)	100	40,000
2	Education index Literacy rate	0	100
	Health index		
3	% villages with any government health facility	0	100
4	% villages with doctor	0	100
5	% children age 12-35 months fully vaccinated	0	100
6	% women that received full ante-natal checkups	0	100
7	% women who had institutional deliveries	0	100

scaling the diverse variables, the main consideration has been to make attainments on each of them comparable and at the same time ensuring that the selection of goal posts for each variable are such that they support temporal comparisons for a reasonable period of time. The goalposts, which have been fixed for the determination of HDI, are described in Table 2.3.

1. Computing Income Index

Income serves as an alternate for all the dimensions of human development not reflected in a long and healthy life and in knowledge. The UNDP HDI uses 'adjusted per capita income for countries' to compute the income index because achieving a respectable level of human development does not require unlimited income. Earlier *Aitkinson's* formula, based on the marginal utility of incomes was used by the UNDP to adjust incomes. This adjustment reduced the impact of very high incomes in some regions; however, it discounted incomes above a threshold level quite drastically. Hence, they now use a different method of adjusting income using algorithm of income. The formula used in the present study does not discount income as sharply as it was observed in the *Aitkinson's* formula whereas it discounts all income, not just the income above the threshold level. The formula is:

$$\textbf{Income Index}(I_{ij}) = \left[\frac{\log(\textbf{actual value}) - \log(\textbf{minimum value})}{\log(\textbf{maximum value}) - \log(\textbf{minimum value})}\right]$$

For the computation of the income index for the districts, per capita district GDP has been converted into its PPP$ equivalent by taking the ratio of per capita district GDP to that of India in rupees and multiplying this by the per capita GDP of India in PPP$. The method is illustrated as under:

Per capita GDP for India in 2000-2001 at constant prices (1999-2000) = Rs. 16,133

Per capita GDP for India in PPP$ (UNDP HDR, 2003) = $2840

$$\textit{Real district PC GDP\$} = \frac{\textit{District PC GDP in Rs.}}{\textit{PC GDP of India in Rs.}} X \textit{PC GDP for India in PPP\$}$$

Then income index has been computed as below:

$$\textit{Income Index of a district} = \left[\frac{\log(\textit{Real District PC GDP}) - \log 100}{\log 40,000 - \log 100}\right]$$

Illustration: Income Index of Ambala district, 2001

Per capita GDP of Ambala = Rs. 30,065

Per capita GDP of India = Rs, 16,133

Per capita GDP for India in PPP$ = $2840

$$\textbf{Real district PC GDP\$ of Ambala} = \frac{2,840}{16,133} X30,065 = 5293$$

$$\textbf{Income Index} = \left[\frac{\log 5293 - \log 100}{\log 40,000 - \log 100}\right] = 0.66$$

2. Computing Education Index

Education index has been carried out using single variable i.e. literacy rate. Formula to calculate education index:

$$\textbf{Education Index} = \left[\frac{\text{actual value of a district} - \text{minimum value}}{\text{maximum value} - \text{minimum value}}\right]$$

Illustration: Education Index of Ambala district, 2001

Literacy Rate = 75.31

$$\textbf{Education Index} = \left[\frac{75.31-0}{100-0}\right] = 0.75$$

3. Computing Health Index

Life expectancy at birth (LEB) has been used by the UNDP to signify long and healthy life. Due to non-availability of district level LEB data and IMR data, a composite indicator of five health variables has been devised. First the index is obtained from each indicator and the health index is calculated by combining these indicators in the following manner:

$$Index_{1,2,...5} = \left[\frac{\text{actual value of indicator}_{1,2,....5} - \text{minimum value}}{\text{maximum value} - \text{minimum value}}\right]$$

$$\textbf{Health Index} = \frac{\textbf{Index}_1 + \textbf{Index}_1 + \textbf{Index}_1 + \textbf{Index}_1 + \textbf{Index}_1}{5}$$

Illustration: Health Index of Ambala district, 2001

Proportion of villages with any govt. health facility = 44.3

$$Index_1 = \frac{44.3-0}{100-0} = 0.44$$

% villages with doctor = 18.0

$$Index_2 = \frac{18.0-0}{100-0} = 0.18$$

% children age 12-35 months fully vaccinated = 92.9

$$Index_3 = \frac{92.9-0}{100-0} = 0.93$$

% women that received full ante-natal check-ups = 19.2

$$Index_4 = \frac{19.2-0}{100-0} = 0.19$$

% women who had institutional deliveries = 61.8

$$Index_5 = \frac{61.8-0}{100-0} = 0.62$$

$$\textbf{Health Index}\left(I_{ij}\right) = \frac{0.44+0.18+0.93+0.19+0.62}{5} = 0.47$$

4. Computing Human Development Index

As stated earlier, HDI is an un-weighted average of the above three dimensions. Hence, its calculation is straightforward as discussed below:

$$HDI_j = \frac{1}{3}\sum I_{ij}$$

Illustration: Human Development Index of Ambala district, 2001

Income index = 0.66
Education index = 0.75
Health index = 0.47

$$\textbf{Human Development Index} = \frac{0.66+0.75+0.47}{3} = 0.63$$

Computing Human Poverty Index (HPI)

This is an index of deprivation with respect to the three dimensions – economic, education and health. The Indexes of Deprivation (IODs) of the three dimensions have been worked out in percentage terms. Equal weights have been assigned to each of the three dimensions as each variable is equally important. Human Poverty Index then calculated using the following formula:

$$\textbf{Human Poverty Index} = \left[\tfrac{1}{3}\left(P_1^3 + P_2^3 + P_3^3\right)\right]^{1/3}$$

Where P_1 = IOD income, P_2 = IOD education, P_3 = IOD health
Illustration: Human Poverty Index of Ambala district, 2001
% population below poverty line = 5.83
Index of deprivation in income = 5.83
Literacy rate (%) = 75.31

$$\textit{Index of deprivation in education} = 100 - \textit{Literacy Rate}$$

Index of deprivation in education $= 100 - 75.31 = 24.69$

% villages without any govt. health facility = 55.7

% villages without doctor = 82.0

% children age 12-35 months not fully vaccinated = 7.1

% women that do not receive full ante-natal check-ups = 80.8

% women who had non-institutional deliveries = 38.2

$$\textit{Index of deprivation in health} = \frac{55.7 + 82.0 + 7.1 + 80.8 + 38.2}{5} = 52.76$$

$$\textit{Human Poverty Index} = [\frac{1}{3}(5.83^3 + 24.69^3 + 52.76^3)]^{1/3} = 37.81$$

Computing Gender Development Index (GDI)

The GDI uses the same variables as used in the HDI; however the average achievement of each dimension has been adjusted for gender inequality. The process involves three steps. First, gender-wise indices have been carried out for each dimension by adopting the same methodology as used in the calculation of the HDI. Second, adjustment is done with respect to aversion to gender inequality. Equally distributed indices (EDIs) have been calculated by combining gender-wise dimension indices in such a way that differences in the achievements between both the sexes may be reprimanded. The formula for the calculation of equally distributed indices may be stated as:

$$EDI_{ij} = [\{SFP \times (FI_{ji})^{1-[}\} + \{SMP \times (MI_{ji})^{1-[}\}]^{1-[}$$

Where

i = i[th] indicator, j = j[th] district, SFP = share of female population, FI = female index, SMP = share of male population, MI = male index, [(epsilon) = harmonic mean, which takes the value of 2 in the construction of the GDI.

Third, the GDI is obtained by combining the three equally distributed indices in an un-weighted average.

Illustration: Gender Development Index of Ambala district, 2001

(i) Computing the Equally Distributed Income Index (EDII)

Computation of EDII is quite intricate. Values of real per capita GDP (PPP$) for males and females are calculated out of their respective shares of earned income.

Total population

Male (N_m) = 542977 Female (N_f) = 471434 Total (N) = 1014411

Population share

Male: 0.535..... Female: 0.464.......

% share of population

Male: 53.53 Female: 46.47

Share of economically active population

Male (ea_m): 85.24 Female (ea_f): 14.76 Real Per capita GDP (PPP$) = 5293

Ratio of female wage (w_f) to male wage (w_m) = 0.67

$$\text{Female share of wage bill } (s_f) = \frac{(w_f / w_m) \times ea_f}{\left[(w_f / w_m) \times ea_f\right] + ea_m}$$

$$= \frac{(0.67) \times 14.76}{\left[(0.67) \times 14.76\right] + 85.24} = 0.103468855$$

Total district GDP (y) = ***Real PC GDP X Total population***

$$= 5293 \, x \, 1014411 = 5369277423$$

$$\text{Real PC GDP female } (y_f) = \frac{s_f \times y}{N_f}$$

$$= \frac{0.103468855 \times 5369277423}{471434} = 1178.43$$

$$\text{Real PC GDP male } (y_m) = \frac{(1 - s_f) \times y}{N_m}$$

$$= \frac{0.8965 \ldots\ldots \times 5369277423}{542977} = 8865.43$$

Treating income in the same way in the calculation of the HDI, the adjusted income for females W (y_f) is given by:

$$W(y_f) = \left[\frac{Log\, y_f - Log_{min}}{Log_{max} - Log_{min}}\right]$$

$$= \left[\frac{Log\, 1178.43 - Log\, 100}{Log\, 40000 - Log\, 100}\right] = 0.411\ldots\ldots$$

Similarly, the adjusted income for males W (y_m) is given by:

$$W(y_m) = \left[\frac{Log\ m - Log_{min}}{Log_{max} - Log_{min}}\right]$$

$$= \left[\frac{Log\,8865.43 - Log\,100}{Log\,40000 - Log\,100}\right] = 0.748......$$

Now the EDII is computed as below:

$$EDII = \begin{bmatrix} (\text{female population share})\,X\,(\text{adjusted income for females})^{1-\epsilon} \\ +(\text{male population share})\,X\,(\text{adjusted income for males})^{1-\epsilon} \end{bmatrix}^{1-\epsilon}$$

$$EDII = \begin{bmatrix} (0.464...)\,X\,(0.411...)^{-1} \\ +(0.535...)\,X\,(0.748...)^{-1} \end{bmatrix}^{-1} = 0.54$$

(ii) Computing the Equally Distributed Education Index (EDEI)

Literacy rate

Male: 82.31 Female: 67.39

$$Literacy\ index\,(males) = \frac{(82.31 - 0)}{(100 - 0)} = 0.8231$$

$$Literacy\ index\,(females) = \frac{(67.39 - 0)}{(100 - 0)} = 0.6739$$

Now the EDEI is given by:

$$EDEI = \begin{bmatrix} (\text{female population share})\,X\,(\text{literacy index of females})^{1-\epsilon} \\ +(\text{male population share})\,X\,(\text{literacy index of males})^{1-\epsilon} \end{bmatrix}^{1-\epsilon}$$

$$EDEI = \begin{bmatrix} (0.464...)\,X\,(0.673...)^{-1} \\ +(0.535...)\,X\,(0.823...)^{-1} \end{bmatrix}^{-1}$$

(iii) Computing the Equally Distributed Health Index (EDHI)

% marriages above the legal age at marriage

Male: 87.80 Female: 98.40

(Goalpost for this indicator is fixed as- maximum: 100, minimum: 0)

$$Health\ index\,(males) = \frac{(87.80 - 0)}{(100 - 0)} = 0.878$$

$$\textit{Health index}\left(\textit{females}\right)=\frac{(98.40-0)}{(100-0)}=0.984$$

Now the equally distributed health index (EDEI) is given by:

$$\textbf{EDHI}=\begin{bmatrix}(\textbf{female population share})X(\textbf{health index of females})^{1-\epsilon}\\+(\textbf{male population share})X(\textbf{health index of males})^{1-\epsilon}\end{bmatrix}^{1-\epsilon}$$

$$EDHI=\begin{bmatrix}(0.464\ldots)X(0.984)^{-1}\\+(0.535\ldots)X(0.878)^{-1}\end{bmatrix}^{-1}=0.924\ldots$$

Hence, the GDI will be as follows:

$$\textbf{Gender Development Index}=\frac{1}{3}(\textbf{EDII}+\textbf{EDEI}+\textbf{EDHI})$$

$$\textbf{Gender Development Index}=\frac{1}{3}(0.54\ldots+0.74\ldots+0.92\ldots)=0.737$$

Data gaps (Limitations of the study)

As stated in the preceding section, the study is by and large based on the methodology adopted by the UNDP in the preparation of HDRs of various regions. In this context, difficulties that had to be faced during the preparation of research report are discussed below:

- Instead of using two variables 'Adult Literacy Rate' and 'Gross Enrolment Ratio (GER)' to measure education index as used in UNDP HDR, only one variable i.e. 'Literacy Rate' is finally used in the present study. At the initial stage it was proposed to use two variables i.e. 'Adult Literacy Rate' and 'Proportion of Population age 6-14 Attending Educational Institutions' by giving two-third and one third weight respectively. But the age data is available for 2001 only and the data pertaining to 2011 is still (till December 2013) not released by the Census of India.
- As a measure of long and healthy life, UNDP has used Life Expectancy at Birth (LEB). The LEB data at district level has not been estimated all over India. The infant mortality rate is a consistent alternate of LEB, which is used in the preparation of state level HDRs in India. But the IMR data, too, is not generated regularly by any agency at district level. The data pertaining to various health aspects like maternal and child health, family planning and other reproductive health services is generated by the IIPS, Mumbai. Here, as many as five variables (the detail of which is given in the preceding section) have been

considered to carry out health index. In the measurement of health dimension of GDI, gender wise data pertaining to proportion of marriages above the legal age at marriage has been used in place of gender-wise LEB data used by UNDP for the same reason discussed above.

- The data pertaining to health aspects, which has been taken from District Level Household Survey (DLHS) conducted by IIPS during its two rounds i.e. during 2002-04 (2nd round) and during 2007-08 (3rd round). Since the present study focuses on two time periods i.e. 2001 and 2011, 2nd round DLHS data represents 2001 and 3rd round data represents 2011.

3

Human Development Index, 2001

Broadly there are three dimensions of human development- income, education and health. All of these have been discussed separately in this chapter and finally human development index has been carried out based on these dimensions. Maps have been prepared to analyse the results effectively as they have added advantage by focussing on the districts with moderate performance which may be ignored on account of average performance. The districts are classified into four categories viz. districts with high attainment level, upper moderate attainment level, lower moderate attainment level, and low attainment level. It must be kept in mind that this classification is done only to highlight the inter-district disparities and it does not serve any other purpose.

Income Dimension

Income dimension represents the economic development of the state reflected in real per capita gross domestic product. On the basis of real per capita GDP (PPP$) income index has been worked out and districts have been classified into four categories (Map 3.1). Besides, district-wise rankings have been given in Table 3.1. The state income index during 2001 has been 0.64. Gurgaon district has outpaced all the districts and captured first rank with an impressive index value of 0.74. Credit goes to the galloping pace of industrial development in the district especially during the last two decades.

The districts i.e. Panipat (0.69) and Faridabad (0.68) which are given second and third ranks respectively are far behind Gurgaon district. Out of the five districts that have been placed in the first two categories of income index are either bordering New Delhi (Gurgaon and Faridabad) or Chandigarh (Ambala and Panchkula). On the other hand, Mahendergarh

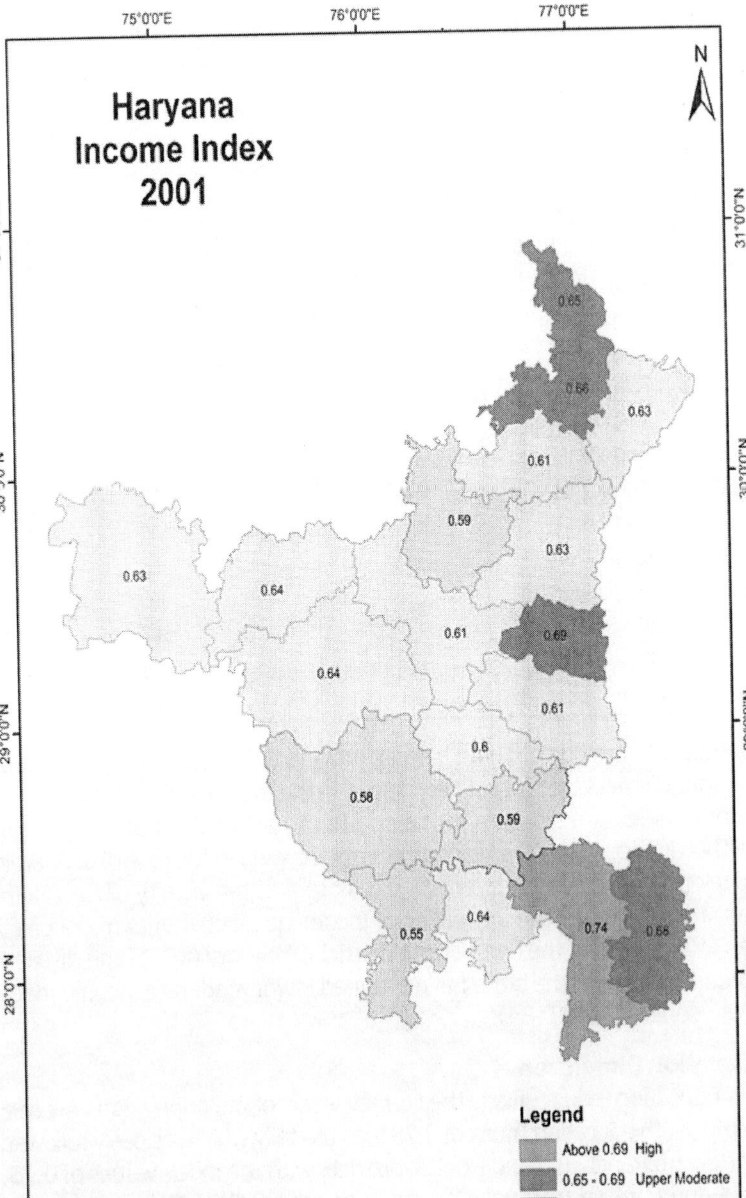
75°0'0"E
76°0'0"E
77°0'0"E
31°0'0"N
30°0'0"N
29°0'0"N
28°0'0"N
27°0'0"N
N
Haryana
Income Index
2001
0.65
0.66
0.63
0.61
0.59
0.63
0.63
0.64
0.61
0.69
0.64
0.61
0.6
0.58
0.59
0.64
0.55
0.74
0.68
Legend
Above 0.69 High
0.65 - 0.69 Upper Moderate
0.60 - 0.64 Lower Moderate
Below 0.60 Low
30 15 0 30 60 90
Kms

Map 3.1

Table 3.1: Income Index

Districts	*Rankings*
Gurgaon	1
Panipat	2
Faridabad	3
Ambala	4
Panchkula	5
Rewari	6
Hisar	7
Fatehabad	8
Sirsa	9
Karnal	10
Yamunanagar	11
Sonepat	12
Kurukshetra	13
Jind	14
Rohtak	15
Jhajjar	16
Kaithal	17
Bhiwani	18
Mahendergarh	19

district is at the bottom with a meek income index of 0.55. Three out of the four districts that have been placed in the fourth and last category of income index are situated in the southern part of the state. However, Kaithal district in the Ghaggar basin is also lagging in the race of economic development. It is quite interesting to note that the vicinity of New Delhi has little impact on the up scaling of income level of Jhajjar district as it has found place in the five bottom districts. Majority (10) of the districts spreading all over the state have attained lower moderate income index (between 0.60 and 0.64).

Education Dimension

Education index reflects the literacy levels of the population. Ambala district, with education Index of 0.75 tops the tally which is closely followed by Rewari, Panchkula and Rohtak districts with the index values of 0.75, 0.74 and 0.74 respectively. As many as seven districts have acquired education Index above 0.71 and have been placed in the first category of high attainment level. A considerable number (6) of districts has acquired upper moderate attainment level. On the other side, three districts i.e.

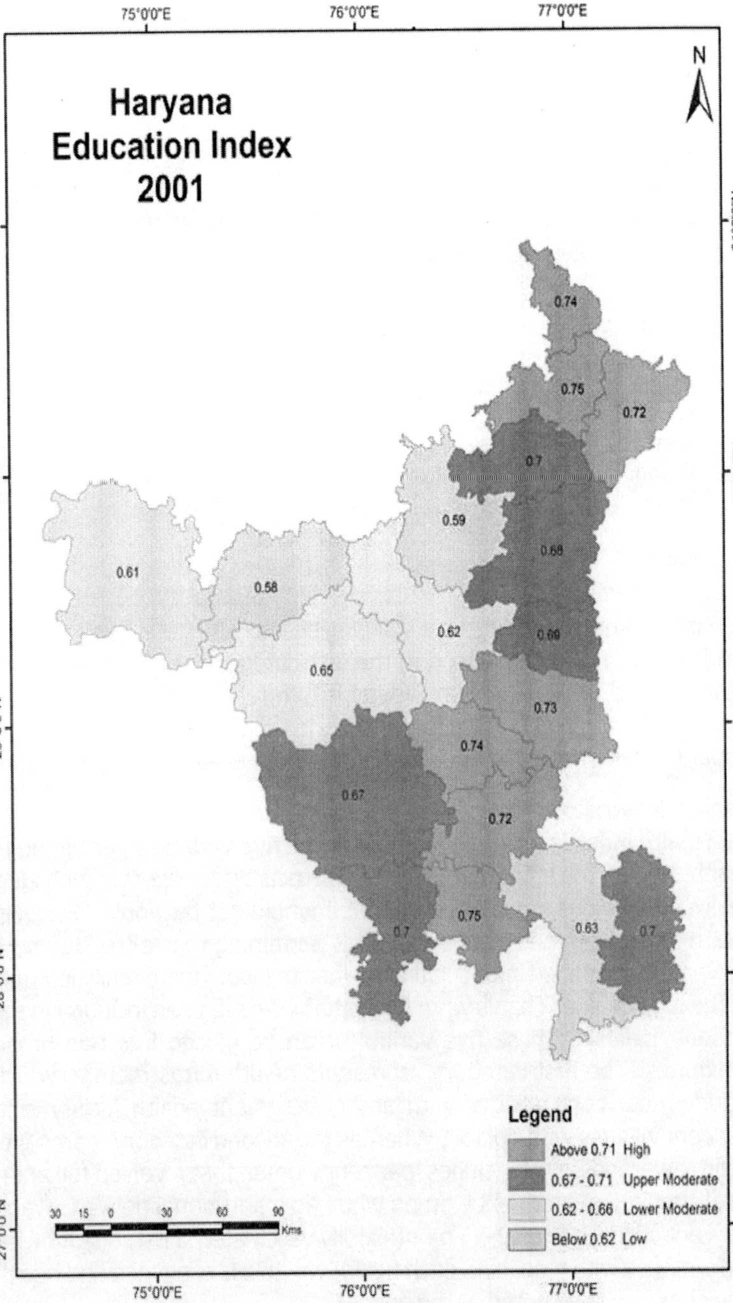

Haryana
Education Index
2001
N
75°0'0"E
76°0'0"E
77°0'0"E
31°0'0"N
30°0'0"N
29°0'0"N
28°0'0"N
27°0'0"N
0.74
0.75
0.72
0.7
0.59
0.68
0.61
0.58
0.62
0.69
0.65
0.73
0.74
0.67
0.72
0.75
0.7
0.63
0.7
Legend
Above 0.71 High
0.67 - 0.71 Upper Moderate
0.62 - 0.66 Lower Moderate
Below 0.62 Low
30 15 0 30 60 90
Kms

Map 3.2

Table 3.2: Education Index

Districts	*Rankings*
Ambala	1
Rewari	2
Panchkula	3
Rohtak	4
Sonepat	5
Jhajjar	6
Yamunanagar	7
Faridabad	8
Mahendergarh	9
Kurukshetra	10
Panipat	11
Karnal	12
Bhiwani	13
Hisar	14
Gurgaon	15
Jind	16
Sirsa	17
Kaithal	18
Fatehabad	19

Fatehabad, Kaithal and Sirsa are standing behind with the education Index below 0.62 and hence placed in the last category of attainment level (Map 3.2 and Table 3.2). A considerable difference of 0.17 index points between the top and bottom ranked districts indicates high inter-district disparities with regard to education attainment level.

Health Dimension

Health index is a simple average of the five variables pertaining to health. In fact, the attainment levels of districts with respect to individual health dimensions are so diverse that it would not be viable to extract health index from one or two variables pertaining to health. The more the variables included in calculating the health index; more realistic would be the index value. That is why; five variables have been included in the present analysis. These five variables can be placed into two broad categories. The first category represents health infrastructure, which includes 'per cent villages with any government health facility' and 'per cent villages with doctor'. Whereas the second category represents health awareness that includes 'per cent women that received full ante-natal check-ups', 'per cent women who had institutional deliveries' and 'per cent children age 12-35 months fully vaccinated'. First, district wise performance with respect to each health variable is examined and health index has been discussed at the end.

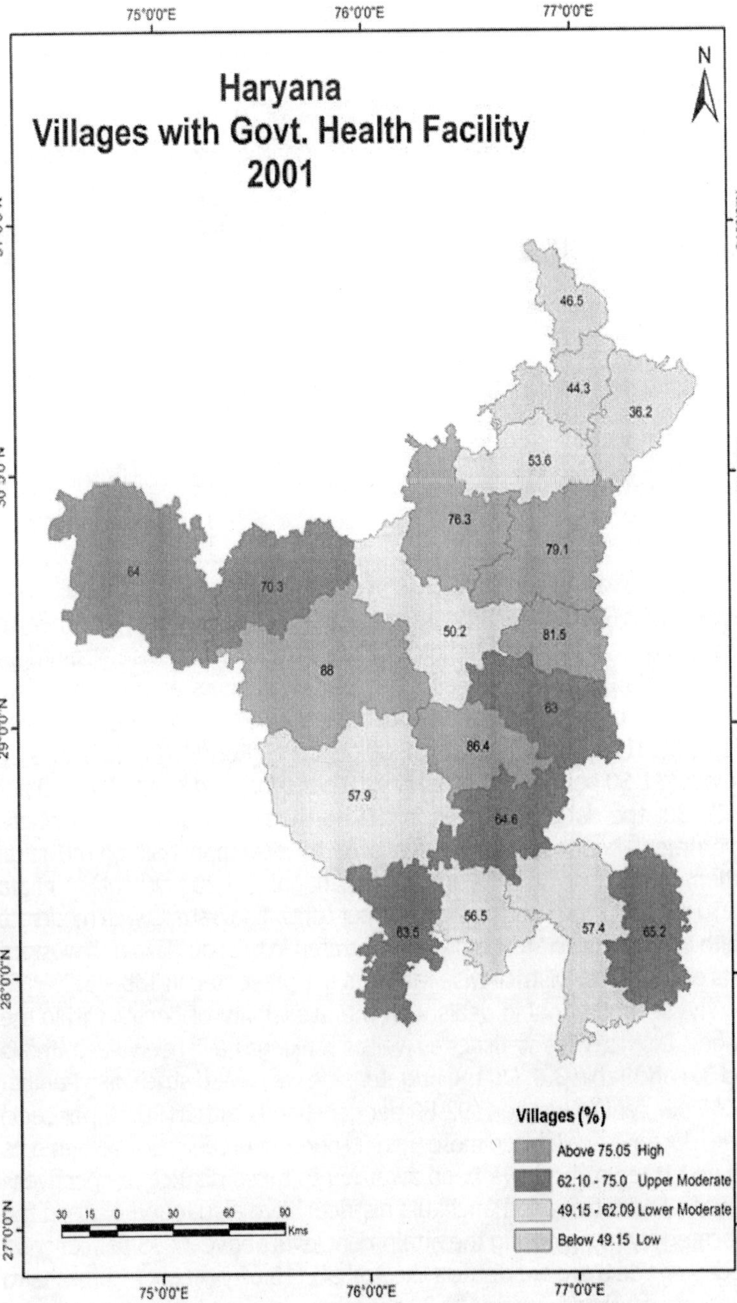
75°0'0"E
76°0'0"E
77°0'0"E
Haryana
Villages with Govt. Health Facility
2001
N
31°0'0"N
30°0'0"N
29°0'0"N
28°0'0"N
27°0'0"N
46.5
44.3
36.2
53.6
76.3
79.1
64
70.3
50.2
81.5
88
63
86.4
57.9
64.6
56.5
63.5
57.4
65.2
Villages (%)
Above 75.05 High
62.10 - 75.0 Upper Moderate
49.15 - 62.09 Lower Moderate
Below 49.15 Low
30 15 0 30 60 90
Kms

Map 3.3

Table 3.3: Villages with Government Health Facility (2001)

Districts	*Rankings*
Hisar	1
Rohtak	2
Panipat	3
Karnal	4
Kaithal	5
Fatehabad	6
Faridabad	7
Jhajjar	8
Sirsa	9
Mahendergarh	10
Sonepat	11
Bhiwani	12
Gurgaon	13
Rewari	14
Kurukshetra	15
Jind	16
Panchkula	17
Ambala	18
Yamunanagar	19

The first variable included in the analysis 'per cent villages with any government health facility' represents the accessibility of health infrastructure to rural households of the state. District-wise attainment level reflects that there are as many as five districts where more than three-fourth of the rural settlements are equipped with the health facility (Map 3.3). These include Hisar (88.00 per cent), Rohtak (86.40 per cent), Panipat (81.50 per cent), Karnal (79.10 per cent) and Kaithal (76.30 per cent). But the darker side lies in the northern part of Haryana where government health facility is available to less than half of the rural settlements. These districts are- Yamunanagar (36.20 per cent), Ambala (44.30 per cent) and Panchkula (46.50 per cent). The districts with moderate health infrastructure are mainly concentrated in the southern and western parts of the state. District-wise rankings are presented in Table 3.3.

The second variable deals with the availability of doctor within the villages. District-wise statistics as well as rankings have been illustrated in Map 3.4 and Table 3.4. On the brighter side we have districts like Panipat (97.40 per cent), Gurgaon (92.80 per cent) and Kaithal (90.10 per cent) where doctor is available in more than 90 per cent of their rural settlements and first three ranks have been awarded to these districts respectively. Bhiwani, Faridabad and Panchkula districts have also found place in the first category by recording the attainment level above 77.55 per cent. On the darker side there are districts like Ambala (18.00 per cent), Kurukshetra (19.80 per cent) and Rewari (29.30 per cent) where majority of the villages

Table 3.4: Villages with Doctor (2001)

Districts	*Rankings*
Panipat	1
Gurgaon	2
Kaithal	3
Bhiwani	4
Faridabad	5
Panchkula	6
Yamunanagar	7
Sonepat	8
Jind	9
Karnal	10
Rohtak	11
Sirsa	12
Mahendergarh	13
Jhajjar	14
Fatehabad	15
Hisar	16
Rewari	17
Kurukshetra	18
Ambala	19

are devoid of any doctor. This is why these districts have been put together in the category of low attainment.

A comparative analysis of Table 3.3 and Table 3.4 clearly reflects that the district-wise attainment level with regard to the two health variables differ considerably. The districts with first and second rank in govt. health facility are far behind with 16th and 11th rank respectively as regards to the availability of doctor. Opposite is the situation in districts like Gurgaon and Panchkula where the performance of these districts is fairly better and they have captured second and sixth rank respectively with regard to the availability of doctor, but the corresponding ranks are 13th and 17th as regards to the availability of health facility. Some other districts like Karnal, Fatehabad, Jhajjar, Bhiwani, Jind, etc. have also shown such inconsistency in the possession of these two health facilities.

The other three variables focus on the health awareness of the households. One of them shows the proportion of women who received full ante-natal check-ups. The district wise attainment level has been presented in Map 3.5 and Table 3.5. So far as the reception of ante-natal check-ups is concerned, the attainment level all over the state is fairly low. Even in the top ranked district Panchkula, there are only 20.80 per cent women who have received full ante-natal check-ups. However, the better performing districts are concentrated in the extreme north whereas the district with worst performance i.e. Faridabad (6.50 per cent) is located in

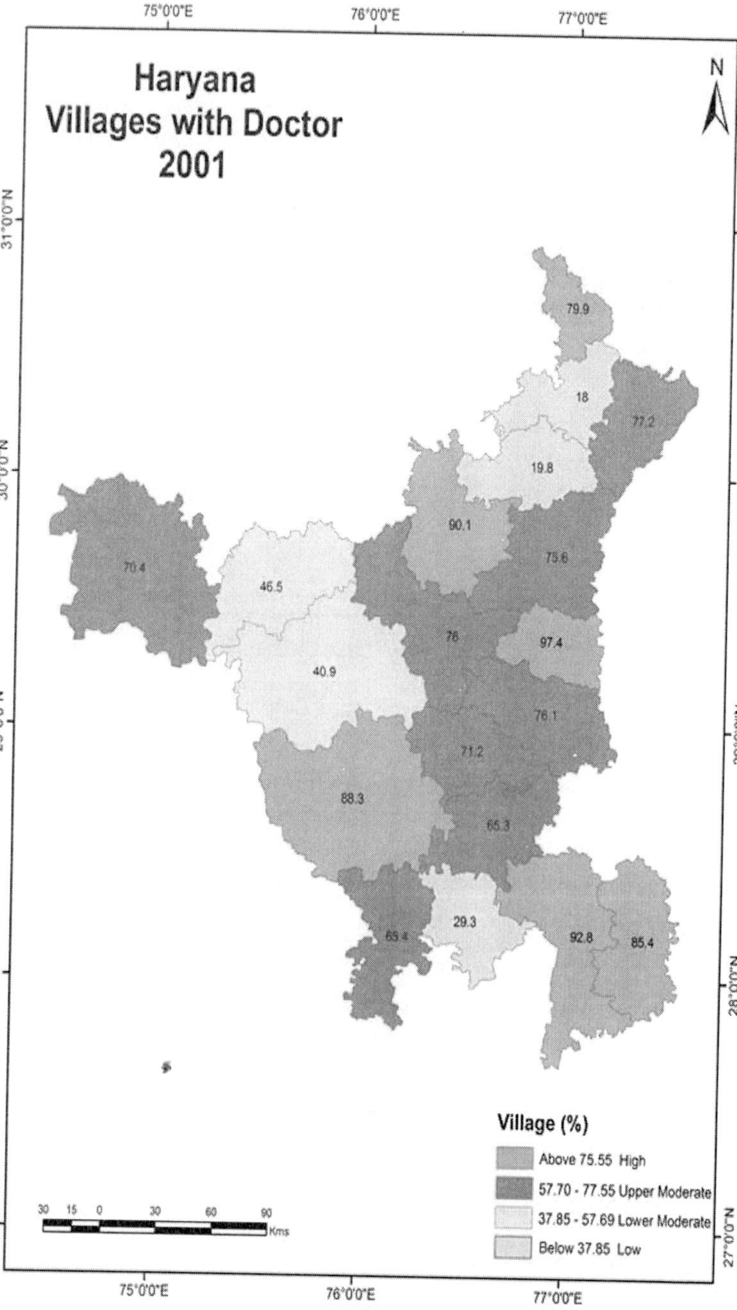
Haryana
Villages with Doctor
2001
N
75°0'0"E
76°0'0"E
77°0'0"E
31°0'0"N
30°0'0"N
29°0'0"N
28°0'0"N
27°0'0"N
79.9
18
77.2
19.8
90.1
75.6
70.4
46.5
76
97.4
40.9
76.1
71.2
88.3
65.3
29.3
65.4
92.8
85.4
Village (%)
Above 75.55 High
57.70 - 77.55 Upper Moderate
37.85 - 57.69 Lower Moderate
Below 37.85 Low
30 15 0 30 60 90
Kms

Map 3.4

Table 3.5: Women Received Full Ante-natal check ups (2001)

Districts	*Rankings*
Panchkula	1
Kurukshetra	2
Ambala	3
Rohtak	4
Bhiwani	5
Jhajjar	6
Hisar	7
Panipat	8
Karnal	9
Kaithal	10
Rewari	11
Yamunanagar	12
Gurgaon	13
Sonepat	14
Fatehabad	15
Sirsa	16
Mahendergarh	17
Jind	18
Faridabad	19

the south. The performance of Jind, Mahendergarh, Sirsa and Fatehabad districts is also quite miserable. Out of the seven districts that have been placed in the category of low attainment level, six districts have been found with the attainment level well below 10 per cent.

Again the district-wise trend of women that received full ante-natal check-ups has little association with the attainment levels of the two variables of health infrastructure discussed above. In other words, a district showing high attainment level as regards to health infrastructure variables not necessarily perform better in the terms of health awareness and vice versa. Consider the case of Panchkula district that has attained top position as regards to women that received full ante-natal check-ups but it has slipped to 17th place in govt. health facility and to sixth place as regards to the facility of doctor. Similarly the corresponding figures for the second ranked district of Kurukshetra are 15th and 18th; and third ranked district of Ambala are 18th and 19th (Compare Tables 3.3, 3.4 and 3.5)

The status of the second health variable in health awareness category i.e. proportion of women who had institutional deliveries has been illustrated in Map 3.6 and Table 3.6. Importance of this variable lies in the fact that institutional deliveries not only reduce the maternal mortality rate but effectively check the infant mortality rates as well. The present statistics reveals that institutional deliveries are not very much prevalent

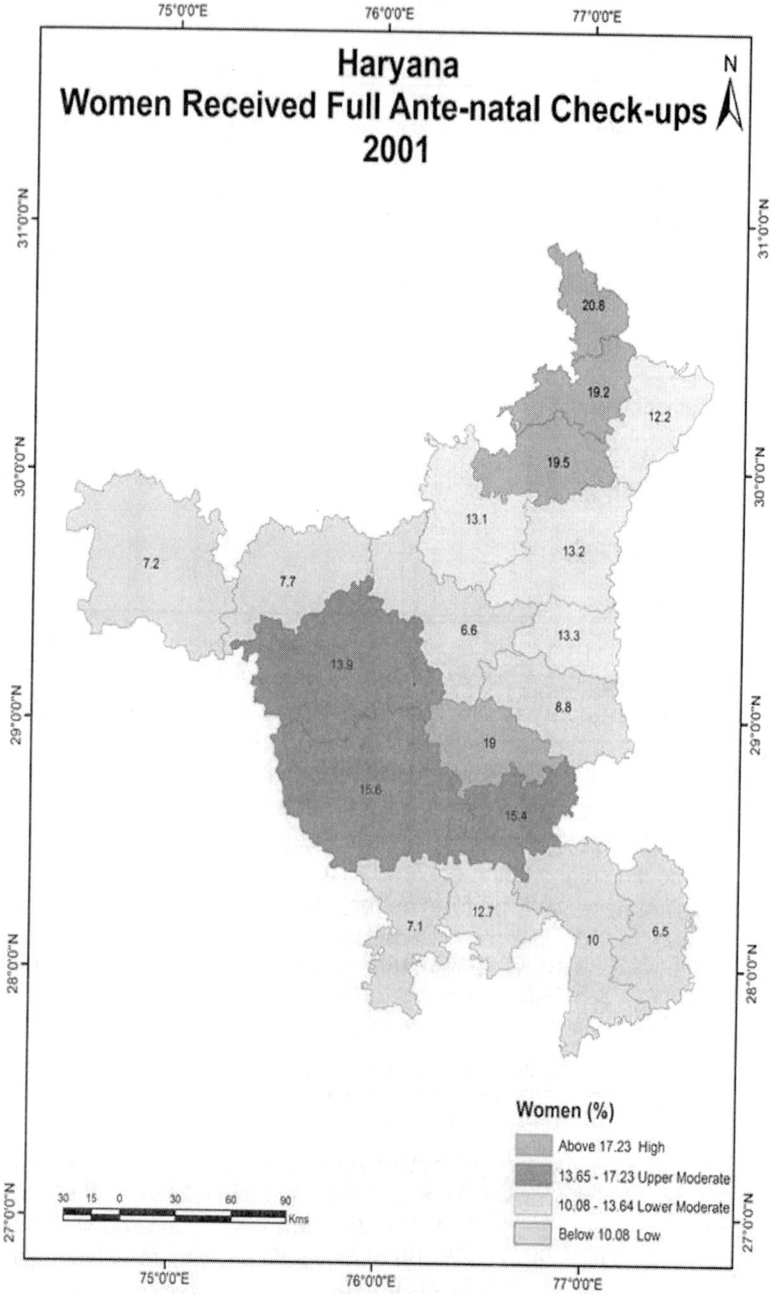
Haryana
Women Received Full Ante-natal Check-ups
2001
N
75°0'0"E
76°0'0"E
77°0'0"E
31°0'0"N
30°0'0"N
29°0'0"N
28°0'0"N
27°0'0"N
20.8
19.2
12.2
19.5
13.1
13.2
7.2
7.7
6.6
13.3
13.9
8.8
19
15.6
15.4
7.1
12.7
10
6.5
Women (%)
Above 17.23 High
13.65 - 17.23 Upper Moderate
10.08 - 13.64 Lower Moderate
Below 10.08 Low
30 15 0 30 60 90
Kms

Map 3.5

Table 3.6: Institutional Deliveries (2001)

Districts	*Rankings*
Ambala	1
Kurukshetra	2
Jhajjar	3
Rewari	4
Panchkula	5
Rohtak	6
Sonepat	7
Fatehabad	8
Mahendergarh	9
Bhiwani	10
Panipat	11
Karnal	12
Sirsa	13
Hisar	14
Yamunanagar	15
Faridabad	16
Kaithal	17
Jind	18
Gurgaon	19

in the state as Ambala; the top ranked district has merely 61.80 per cent women who had institutional deliveries. The second ranked district Kurukshetra (50.30 per cent) is fairly behind Ambala. Gurgaon district, with a depressing figure of 20.40 per cent is at the bottom which is immediately preceded by Jind (27.10 per cent) and Kaithal districts (28.40 per cent). No regional pattern on the basis of attainment level can be seen in the state.

The third and final variable pertaining to health awareness focuses on the incidence of vaccination. Like institutional deliveries, vaccination is an effective measure to bring down infant mortality rate and to improve the child health. The data reveals that attainment levels are quite high in four districts viz. Ambala (92.70 per cent), Panchkula (85.70 per cent), Kurukshetra (81.70 per cent) and Rohtak (81.00 per cent). As a result these districts have been placed in the category of high attainment level. On the other hand, three districts have been placed in the category of lowest attainment level. In this category, the most pathetic performance can be seen in Gurgaon (32.90 per cent) district. The performance of districts like Kaithal (41.40 per cent) and Bhiwani (47.80 per cent) are also no better (see Map 3.7 and Table 3.7). Distribution pattern of the districts suggests that the best performing districts are concentrated in the northern part whereas the districts belong to other categories are

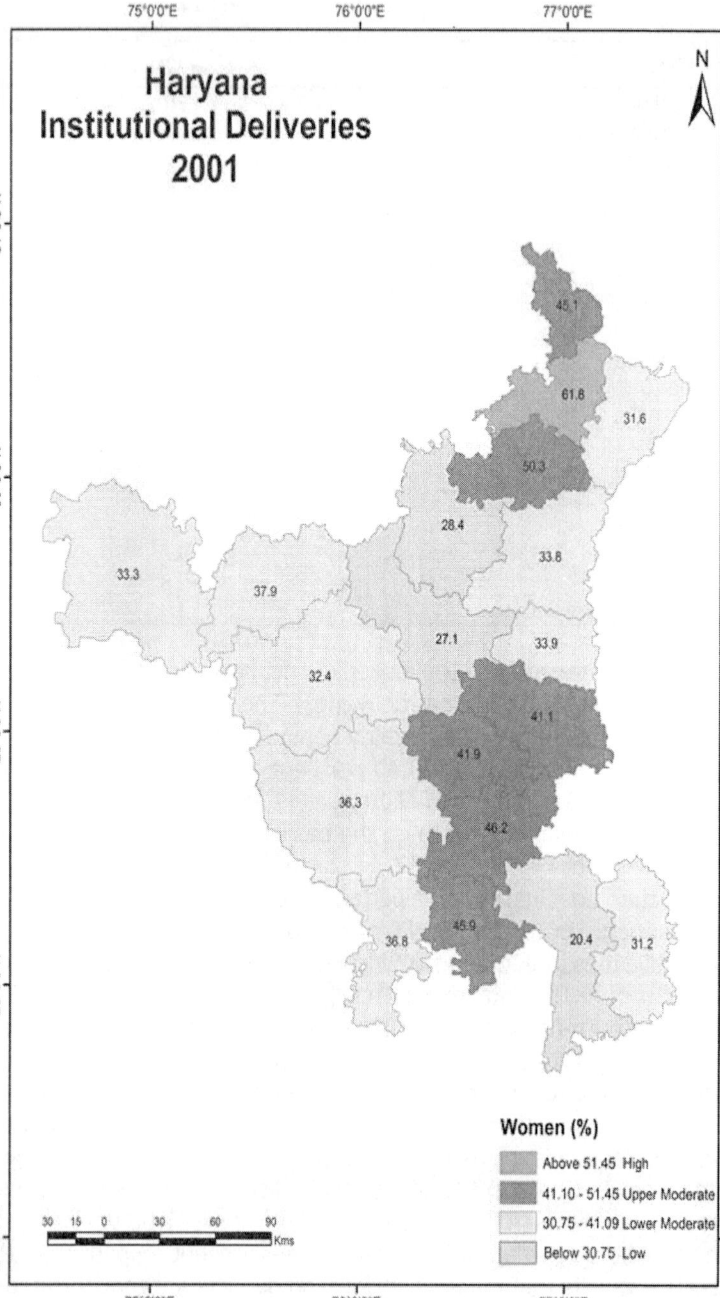
75°0'0"E
76°0'0"E
77°0'0"E
31°0'0"N
30°0'0"N
29°0'0"N
28°0'0"N
27°0'0"N
Haryana
Institutional Deliveries
2001
N
45.1
61.8
31.6
50.3
28.4
33.8
33.3
37.9
27.1
33.9
32.4
41.1
41.9
36.3
46.2
45.9
36.8
20.4
31.2
Women (%)
Above 51.45 High
41.10 - 51.45 Upper Moderate
30.75 - 41.09 Lower Moderate
Below 30.75 Low
30 15 0 30 60 90
Kms

Map 3.6

Table 3.7: Children Age 12-35 Months Fully Vaccinated (2001)

Districts	*Rankings*
Ambala	1
Panchkula	2
Kurukshetra	3
Rohtak	4
Karnal	5
Yamunanagar	6
Jhajjar	7
Rewari	8
Fatehabad	9
Panipat	10
Hisar	11
Jind	12
Sonepat	13
Faridabad	14
Mahendergarh	15
Sirsa	16
Bhiwani	17
Kaithal	18
Gurgaon	19

dispersed all over the state without showing any specific concentration pattern.

Health index is demonstrated in Map 3.8 and Table 3.8. Rohtak district tops the tally by scoring an index value of 0.60. It is quite interesting to note that Rohtak district does not appear at 1st rank in any of the five health dimensions, but the performance of the district was consistently good in four of the five dimensions and it has obtained a moderate rank in the second variable of health infrastructure. Likewise, the second rank captured by Panipat with the index value of 0.58 is largely due to first rank in one of the five variables and consistently satisfactory performance in other variables. However, Panchkula district succeed to be placed on the third rank with an index value of 0.56 by virtue of very good performance in all the health awareness variables and in one of the health infrastructure variables. A single pitiable performance in the first variable of health infrastructure has pushed the district two places back. Furthermore, Ambala district has become the victim of its underprivileged health infrastructure and despite of its unparallel attainment level in health awareness it is slipped to a modest 11th place on health index. It is worthwhile to mention the situation of Panipat district, which has excelled in health infrastructure and occupies second rank on health index albeit its modest performance in health awareness programmes.

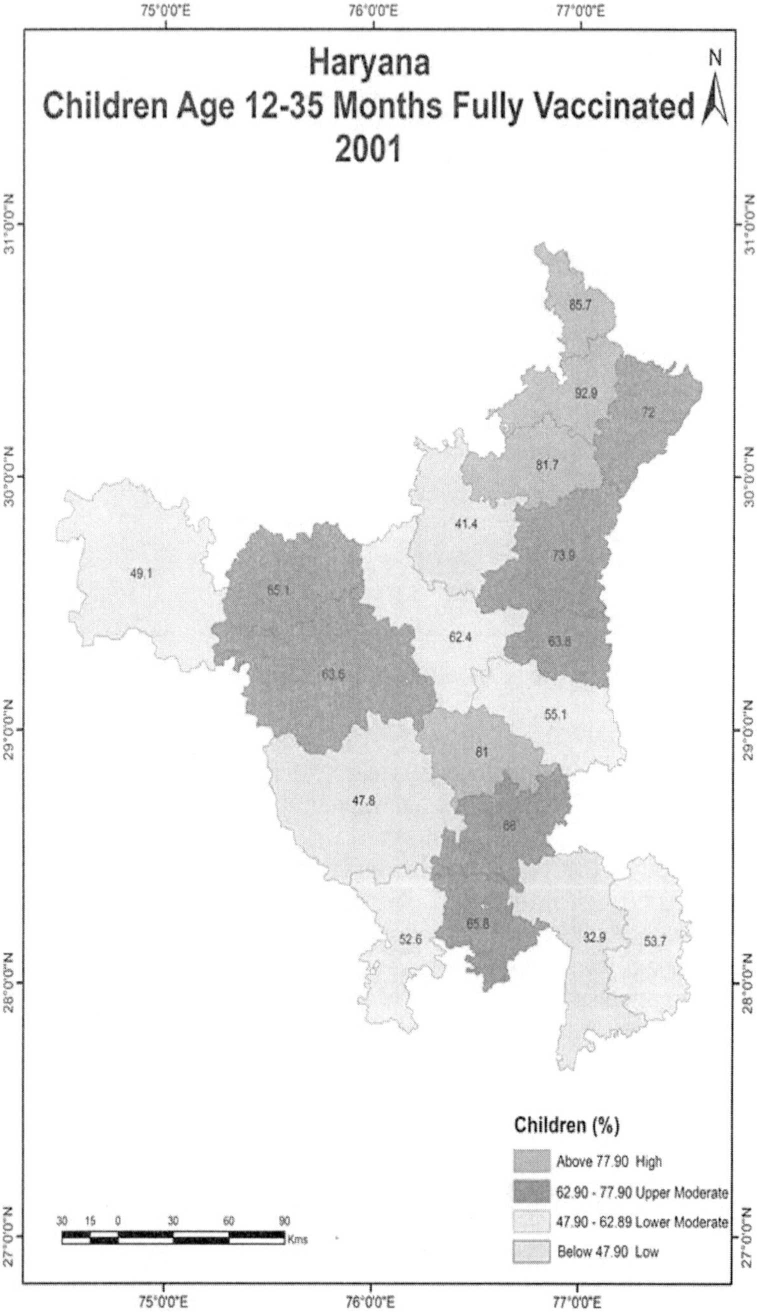
Haryana
Children Age 12-35 Months Fully Vaccinated
2001
N
75°0'0"E
76°0'0"E
77°0'0"E
31°0'0"N
30°0'0"N
29°0'0"N
28°0'0"N
27°0'0"N
85.7
92.9
72
81.7
41.4
73.9
49.1
65.1
62.4
63.8
63.6
55.1
81
47.8
68
65.8
52.6
32.9
53.7
Children (%)
Above 77.90 High
62.90 - 77.90 Upper Moderate
47.90 - 62.89 Lower Moderate
Below 47.90 Low
30 15 0 30 60 90
Kms

Map 3.7

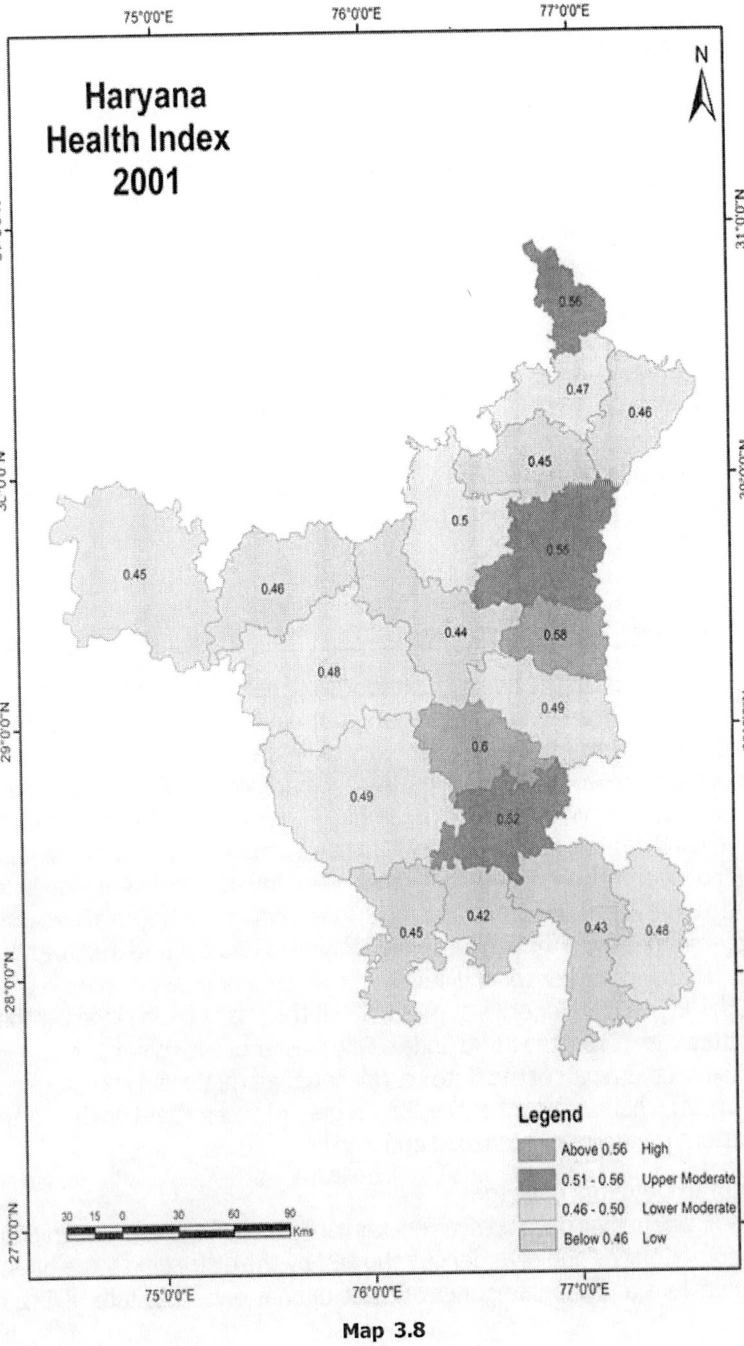
Haryana
Health Index
2001
N
75°0'0"E
76°0'0"E
77°0'0"E
31°0'0"N
30°0'0"N
29°0'0"N
28°0'0"N
27°0'0"N
0.56
0.47
0.46
0.45
0.5
0.55
0.45
0.46
0.44
0.58
0.48
0.49
0.6
0.49
0.52
0.42
0.45
0.43
0.48
Legend
Above 0.56 High
0.51 - 0.56 Upper Moderate
0.46 - 0.50 Lower Moderate
Below 0.46 Low
30 15 0 30 60 90
Kms

Map 3.8

Table 3.8: Health Index (2001)

Districts	*Rankings*
Rohtak	1
Panipat	2
Panchkula	3
Karnal	4
Jhajjar	5
Kaithal	6
Bhiwani	7
Sonepat	8
Faridabad	9
Hisar	10
Ambala	11
Yamunanagar	12
Fatehabad	13
Mahendergarh	14
Kurukshetra	15
Sirsa	16
Jind	17
Gurgaon	18
Rewari	19

As regards to the two sub-categories of health dimension, it can be noticed from the trend of inter-district attainment levels that a district performing better in the first category of health infrastructure does not necessarily perform better in the second category pertaining to health awareness and vice versa. For example, Panipat, Kaithal and Faridabad districts that have had better health infrastructure are sitting at the rear seat of health awareness programmes. Similarly the districts like Ambala and Kurukshetra have shown exemplary performance in health awareness programmes even though these are lagging in health infrastructure.

There is another set of districts with modest or poor performance in both the health categories and as a result they have been placed at the bottom with respect to health index. One cluster of such districts is found in the southern part of the state i.e. (Mahendergarh, Rewari and Gurgaon districts) whereas the other is visible in the districts located on the north western part (Sirsa, Fatehabad and Jind).

Human Development Index

Finally human development index is carried out after due consideration of consistencies and divergences showed by the districts in three basic dimensions and sub-categories of these dimensions. The state HDI has

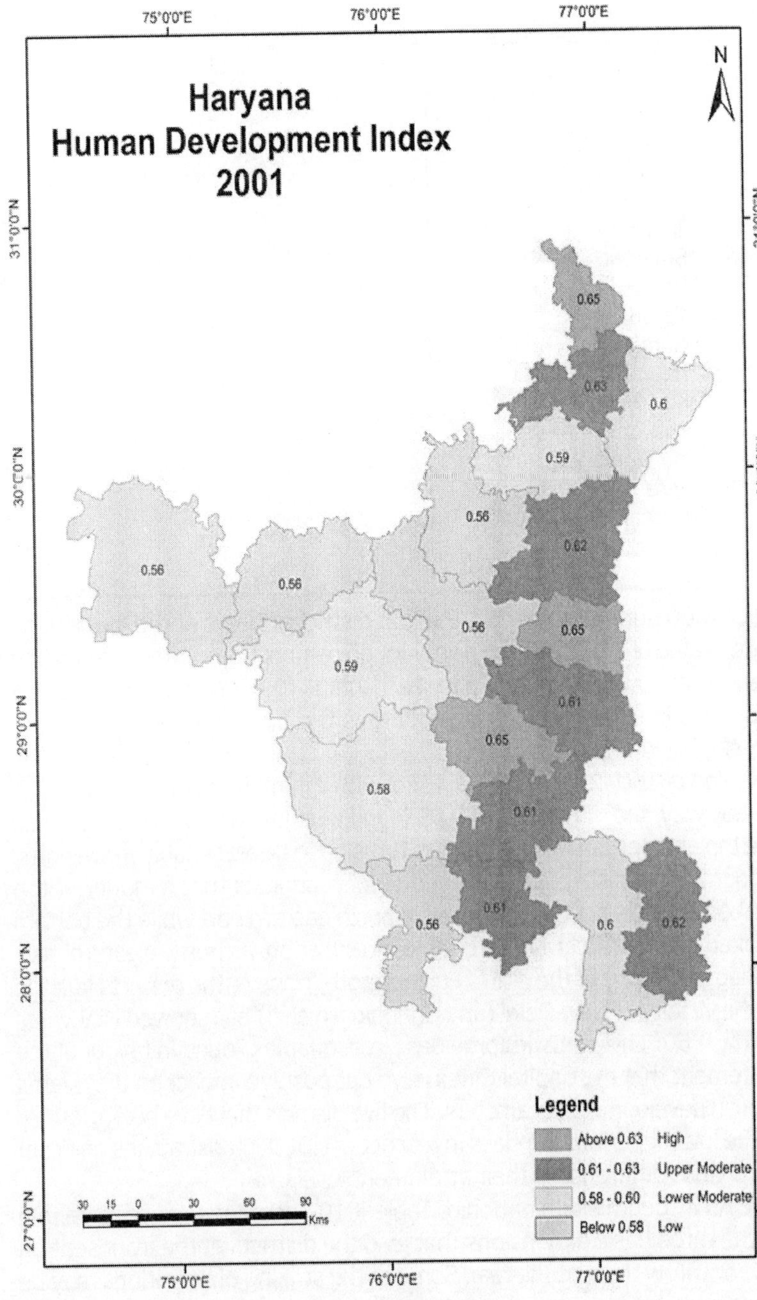
Haryana
Human Development Index
2001
N
0.65
0.63
0.6
0.59
0.56
0.62
0.56
0.56
0.56
0.65
0.59
0.61
0.65
0.58
0.61
0.61
0.56
0.6
0.62
Legend
Above 0.63 High
0.61 - 0.63 Upper Moderate
0.58 - 0.60 Lower Moderate
Below 0.58 Low
30 15 0 30 60 90
Kms
75°0'0"E
76°0'0"E
77°0'0"E
31°0'0"N
30°0'0"N
29°0'0"N
28°0'0"N
27°0'0"N

Map 3.9

Table 3.9: Human Development Index (2001)

Districts	Rankings
Panipat	1
Panchkula	2
Rohtak	3
Ambala	4
Faridabad	5
Karnal	6
Jhajjar	7
Sonepat	8
Rewari	9
Yamunanagar	10
Gurgaon	11
Hisar	12
Kurukshetra	13
Bhiwani	14
Mahendergarh	15
Sirsa	16
Kaithal	17
Fatehabad	18
Jind	19

been 0.60 during the period. Panipat district appears at the top with an index value of 0.6527 facing a very tough competition with second ranked Panchkula (0.6484) and third ranked Rohtak (0.6466) districts. The HDI statistics is shown in Map 3.9 whereas the district-wise rankings are presented in Table 3.9.

Jind district occupies the last seat with a humble HDI value of 0.5573. In this way, the difference of 0.0954 index points of HDI value between the top and bottom ranked districts turns up to be reasonably meaningful. Geographical distribution of the districts suggests that majority of top ranked districts are concentrated in north eastern part while the bottom ranked five districts show their concentration in north-western part (Ghaggar Basin) of the state. Furthermore, none of the districts located in the vicinity of New Delhi (and Chandigarh also) has showed HDI value below 0.60. This statistics provides a reasonable ground in favour of the statement that the Capital Cities have put positive impact on the overall human development parameters. The five districts that have been grouped in the lowest performing class in respect of HDI demonstrate insignificant intra-class difference in their attainment levels.

An in-depth examination of Table 3.10 underlines the decisive role of the three basic dimensions that lead the districts at the front seat on HDI or throw them at the rear. Some of the striking observations may be listed as below:

Table 3.10: Construction of Human Development Index (2001)

Districts	*Income Index*	*Education Index*	*Health Index*	*Human Development Index*
Panipat	2	11	2	1
Panchkula	5	3	3	2
Rohtak	15	4	1	3
Ambala	4	1	11	4
Faridabad	3	8	9	5
Karnal	10	12	4	6
Jhajjar	16	6	5	7
Sonepat	12	5	8	8
Rewari	6	2	19	9
Yamunanagar	11	7	12	10
Gurgaon	1	15	18	11
Hisar	7	14	10	12
Kurukshetra	13	10	15	13
Bhiwani	18	13	7	14
Mahendergarh	19	9	14	15
Sirsa	9	17	16	16
Kaithal	17	18	6	17
Fatehabad	8	19	13	18
Jind	14	16	17	19
Correlation of individual dimension with HDI	0.46	0.74	0.61	

- The second position both in income and health dimension leads Panipat district on the front seat of HDI even after a humble 11th rank in education dimension. Similarly Panchkula district occupies a respectable second place on HDI by virtue of third rank both in education and health dimension and a slightly lesser fifth rank in income dimension.
- Not only is the rank, the magnitude of index value is equally important. Considering the example of Rohtak and Ambala districts where the former has achieved third HDI rank (15th rank on income index with index value 0.60, fourth rank on education index with index value 0.74 and first rank on health index with index value 0.60 thereby reaches the total index value of 1.94) and the latter is standing at fourth HDI rank (fourth rank on income index with index value 0.66, first rank on education index with index value 0.75 and 11th rank on health index with index value 0.47 thereby reaches the total index value of 1.88 which is less than the total index value of Rohtak district). For the same reason Mahendergarh district outpaces Fatehabad district where the former compensates effectively the weakness of its income dimension by recording appreciable performance in education dimension but the latter fails to compensate its weakness of education dimension as it could get effective edge neither in income dimension nor in health.

By virtue of impressive industrialisation, Gurgaon district has achieved a very high index value in income dimension and succeed to retain itself in 'Districts with Lower Moderate HDI' albeit its pathetic performance in education and health dimensions.

- The case of Rewari district is rather attention-grabbing as the notable performances on the income and education dimensions fail to put forth the district in top five districts with respect to HDI. This happens largely due to the poorest performance of the district on health dimension.
- The importance of income is beyond any debate for achieving higher standards of living as it gives ability to buy goods and services and widens the range of consumption options. Nonetheless, high literacy and better health can be achieved even with low per capita income. Consider the case of Rohtak district which has attained high standards of education (fourth rank) and health (first rank) in spite of poor income (15th rank). Jhajjar district, too, has shown the similar spirit. The districts like Karnal, Sonepat, Mahendergarh, Yamunanagar, Bhiwani and Mahendergarh have performed better either in education or in health dimension without having higher income level.
- One more striking feature which can be noticed from Table 3.4 is that none of the districts is perfectly consistent in the attainment

level of all the three dimensions, whether it is on the upper end or on the lower end of the scale. On one hand, the most advanced districts have shown weakness in one or another dimension while on the other hand; the most backward districts have shown a ray of hope in one or another dimension of human development.

- The correlation coefficients explain that education dimension has put most significant impact on construction of the HDI, though the role of health dimension cannot be underrated. On the other hand, the income dimension is far less influential as it has a moderate (0.46) correlation with the HDI.

Sum up

As a whole the state is characterised with a moderate level of human development. Panipat district appears at the top whereas Jind district occupies the last seat. Geographical distribution of the districts suggests that majority of top ranked districts are concentrated in north eastern part while the bottom ranked five districts show their concentration in north western part of the state. Delhi and Chandigarh have put positive impact on the human development parameters of the neighbouring districts. One of the most striking features which have been noticed in the analysis is that education and health dimensions cannot be overlooked in order to achieve high level of human development.

4

Gender Development Index, 2001

The high economic development is meaningless in a society characterised with gender discrimination and inequality. The UNDP Human Development Report (1995) rightly quotes "Human development is a process of enlarging the choices for all people, not just one part of the society. Such a process becomes unjust and discriminatory if most women are excluded from its benefits. And the continuing exclusion of women from many economic and political opportunities is a continuing indictment of modern progress".

Despite the firm constitutional provisions, development in India has not been equitable and gender biasness is clearly visible in social, economic and political fronts as well. The National Human Development Report (2001) concludes "women were better off in the Southern Indian states than in the Indo-Gangetic plains. States like Andhra Pradesh and Tamil Nadu in the south and Haryana and Jammu & Kashmir in the north have made considerable progress in improving the status of women vis-à-vis men on the human development indicators. States that have done well in improving their female literacy levels are also the ones that have substantially improved their gender equality. On the whole gender disparities across the states have declined over the period".

To be more specific, it is worthwhile to quote Jean Dreze and Amartya Sen "The north-western states, for instance, are notorious for highly unequal gender relations, some symptoms of which include the continued practice of female seclusion, very low labour participation rates, a large gap in literacy rates, extremely restricted property rights, strong boy preference in fertility decisions, widespread neglect of female children and drastic separation of a married from her natal family". Pam Rajput observes that "women in Haryana continue to be subordinated, subjugated and deprived, as evidenced in the extremely low sex ratio, high level of anaemia among women and children and prevalent violence against women".

Keeping in mind the importance of gender equality in a society, UNDP introduced Gender Development Index (GDI) in 1995 which measures the inequality in attainments on selected human development indicators between men and women. GDI adjusts the average achievement of each district in income, education and health dimensions. In this way GDI demonstrates the status of women as a ratio of attainments for females to that of males. Generally, the index value lies between zero and one. A district with higher gender disparity would be penalised more and vice versa. The higher the penalty, higher would be gender disparity or gap in gender development level. An index value of unity would reflect an absolute equality in the respective attainments of males and females.

Like HDI, GDI is a composite measure consisting of three dimension indices- Equally Distributed Income Index (EDII), Equally Distributed Education Index (EDEI) and Equally Distributed Health Index (EDHI) reflecting the attainment level of females on various composite variables as a proportion to that of males. In the case of income and education dimensions, the same set of variables has been used as has been used for the calculation of HDI. In the case of health dimension, the variable 'proportion of males and females married above the legal age at marriage' has been used due to non-availability of gender-wise data on health infrastructure and health awareness as used in the calculation of HDI. The findings have been discussed in the succeeding section.

Income Dimension

At the beginning gender-wise status of Economically Active Population (EAP) has been examined. Although 'working population above the age of 15' seems more effective measure to estimate economically active population yet the data pertaining to age and sex (2011) was not published till the completion of report. Moreover, the study focuses on the decadal changes; it is pertinent to take the data sets of similar nature for both the time periods. This is why, economically active population irrespective of age is considered for this purpose.

It becomes pertinent here to explain the term 'Economically Active Population (EAP)' which refers to the proportionate values of two components i.e. males and females that takes the total at 100 percentage points. A district showing higher rankings in economically active population with respect to males does not necessarily be advanced on economic front; it is just showing the higher proportion of males (and lower

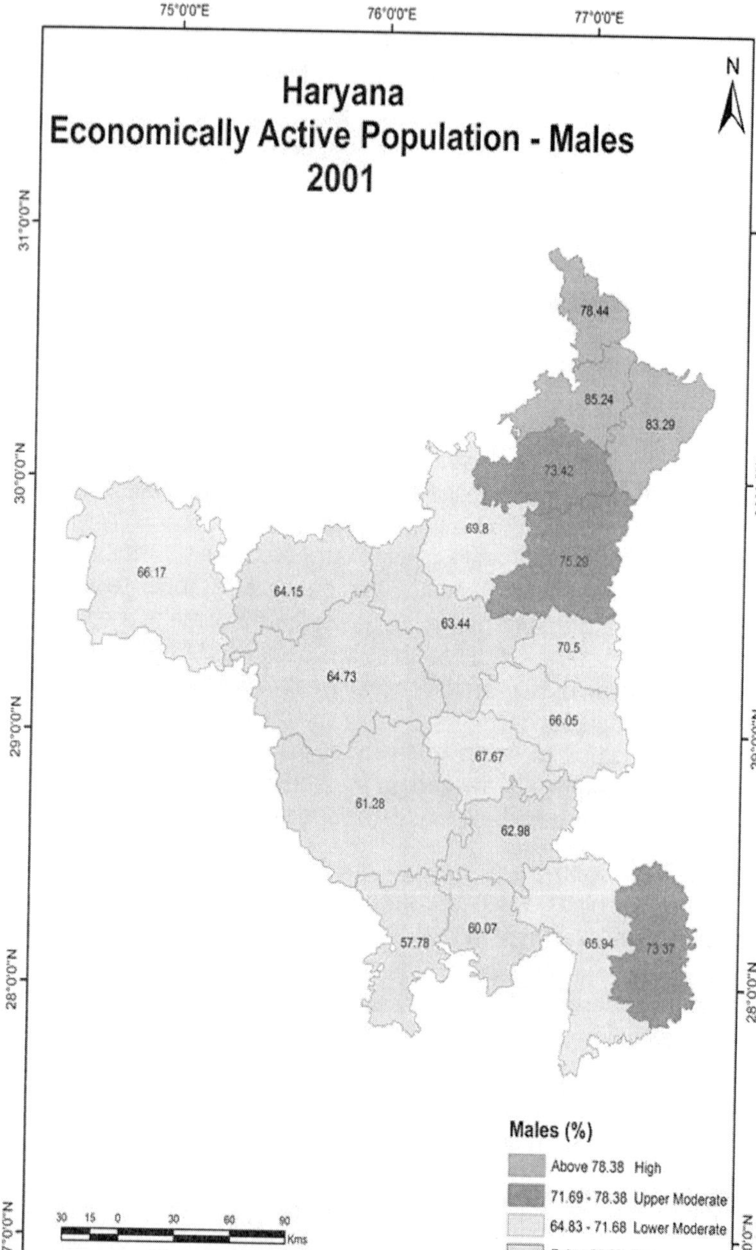
Haryana
Economically Active Population - Males
2001
N
75°0'0"E
76°0'0"E
77°0'0"E
31°0'0"N
30°0'0"N
29°0'0"N
28°0'0"N
27°0'0"N
78.44
85.24
83.29
73.42
69.8
75.29
66.17
64.15
63.44
70.5
64.73
66.05
67.67
61.28
62.98
60.07
57.78
65.94
73.37
Males (%)
Above 78.38 High
71.69 - 78.38 Upper Moderate
64.83 - 71.68 Lower Moderate
Below 64.83 Low
30 15 0 30 60 90
Kms

Map 4.1

Table 4.1: Economically Active Population – Males (2001)

Districts	*Rankings*
Ambala	1
Yamunanagar	2
Panchkula	3
Karnal	4
Kurukshetra	5
Faridabad	6
Panipat	7
Kaithal	8
Rohtak	9
Sirsa	10
Sonepat	11
Gurgaon	12
Hisar	13
Fatehabad	14
Jind	15
Jhajjar	16
Bhiwani	17
Rewari	18
Mahendergarh	19

proportion of females). In other words, the higher the proportion of economically active male population in a district, lower would be the proportion of economically active female population and vice versa. In this way the term 'Economically Active Population' differs totally from the term 'Work Participation Rates', where the latter measures the gender-wise proportion of workforce out of the total population in the corresponding gender. Hence the sum of gender-wise work participation rates may be less than 100 percentage points or equal to 100 percentage points or may be more than that depending on the factors like employment rate, demographic composition of a region, etc.

On an average 68.22 per cent of the population engaged in economic activities in the state belongs to masculine gender. Map 4.1 illustrates the distribution of districts into four development categories whereas district-wise rankings have been presented in Table 4.1.

Reasonable inter-district disparities can be noticed in this respect. There is a difference of 27.46 percentage points between the top ranked Ambala (85.24%) district and bottom ranked Mahendergarh (57.78%) district. The first category that represents the higher ranked districts includes the districts where the figure of EAP-male is more than 78.38 per cent. The three northernmost districts i.e. Ambala, Yamunanagar and Panchkula have found place in this category with the top three ranks

Table 4.2: Economically Active Population – Females (2001)

Districts	*Rankings*
Mahendergarh	1
Rewari	2
Bhiwani	3
Jhajjar	4
Jind	5
Fatehabad	6
Hisar	7
Gurgaon	8
Sonepat	9
Sirsa	10
Rohtak	11
Kaithal	12
Panipat	13
Faridabad	14
Kurukshetra	15
Karnal	16
Panchkula	17
Yamunanagar	18
Ambala	19

respectively. On the contrary, the last category, showing the lowest proportion (less than 64.83 per cent) of EAP-males incorporates south-western districts like Mahendergarh, Rewari, Bhiwani, Jhajjar, Jind, Fatehabad and Hisar.

It is disheartening to realise that the females constitute only 31.78 per cent of the total economically active population of the state as against the 50 per cent mark to achieve gender equality. So far as the district-wise trend is concerned, it is characterised with high inter-district disparities. On the one hand there are top ranked districts located in the southern part of the state like Mahendergarh, Rewari, Bhiwani and Jhajjar that have extended firm steps towards gender equality by achieving more than 35.36 per cent contribution of females in economically active population (Map 4.2 and Table 4.2) thereby placed in the category of high development. On the other end of the scale there are northern districts like Ambala, Yamunanagar and Panchkula that have shown a little hope of gender equality on economic front with corresponding figure of less than 21.62 per cent and these districts have been awarded lowest ranks. The districts located in the central part of the state have shown moderate response in this respect.

Figure 4.1 illustrates gender gap in economically active population. At the state level it accounts for 36.45 per cent. Gender gap is found more than the state average in as many as eight districts (Figure 4.1).

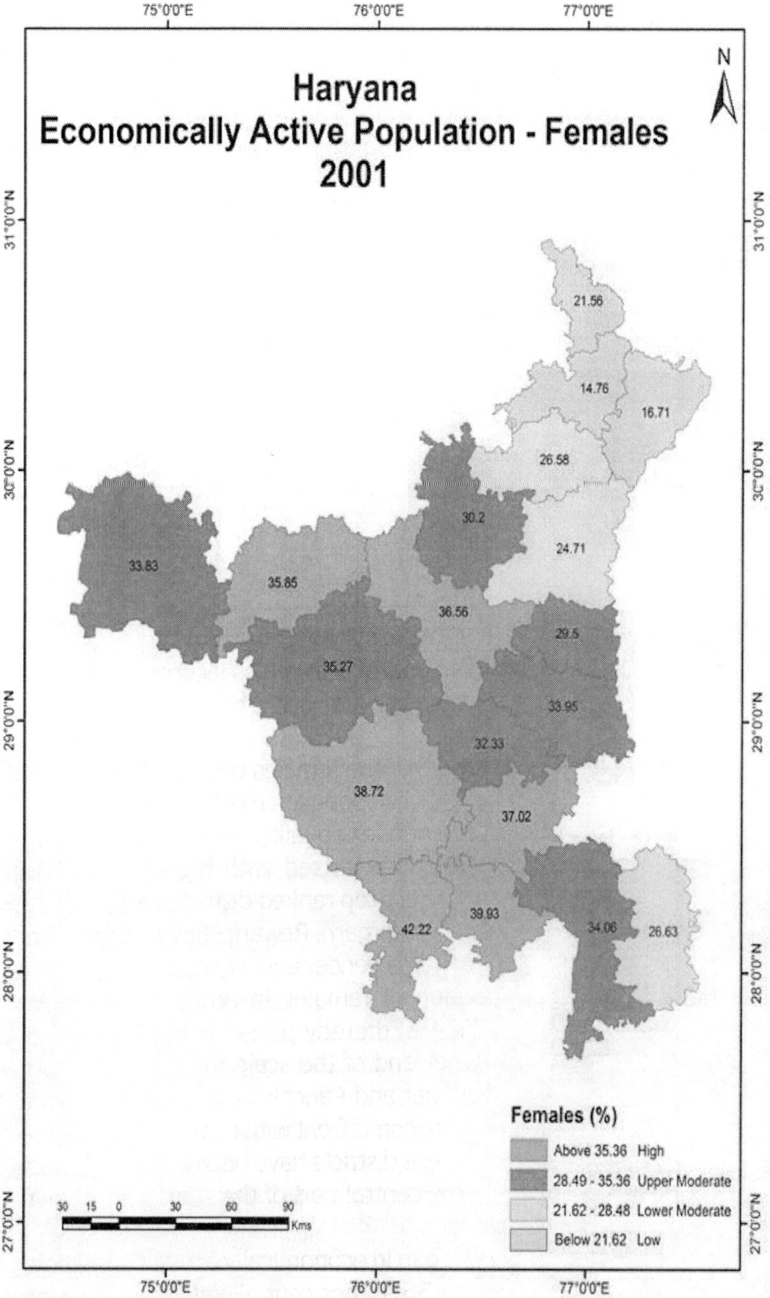
Haryana
Economically Active Population - Females
2001
N
75°0'0"E
76°0'0"E
77°0'0"E
31°0'0"N
30°0'0"N
29°0'0"N
28°0'0"N
27°0'0"N
21.56
14.76
16.71
26.58
30.2
24.71
33.83
35.85
36.56
29.5
35.27
33.95
32.33
38.72
37.02
39.93
42.22
34.06
26.63
Females (%)
Above 35.36 High
28.49 - 35.36 Upper Moderate
21.62 - 28.48 Lower Moderate
Below 21.62 Low
30 15 0 30 60 90
Kms

Map 4.2

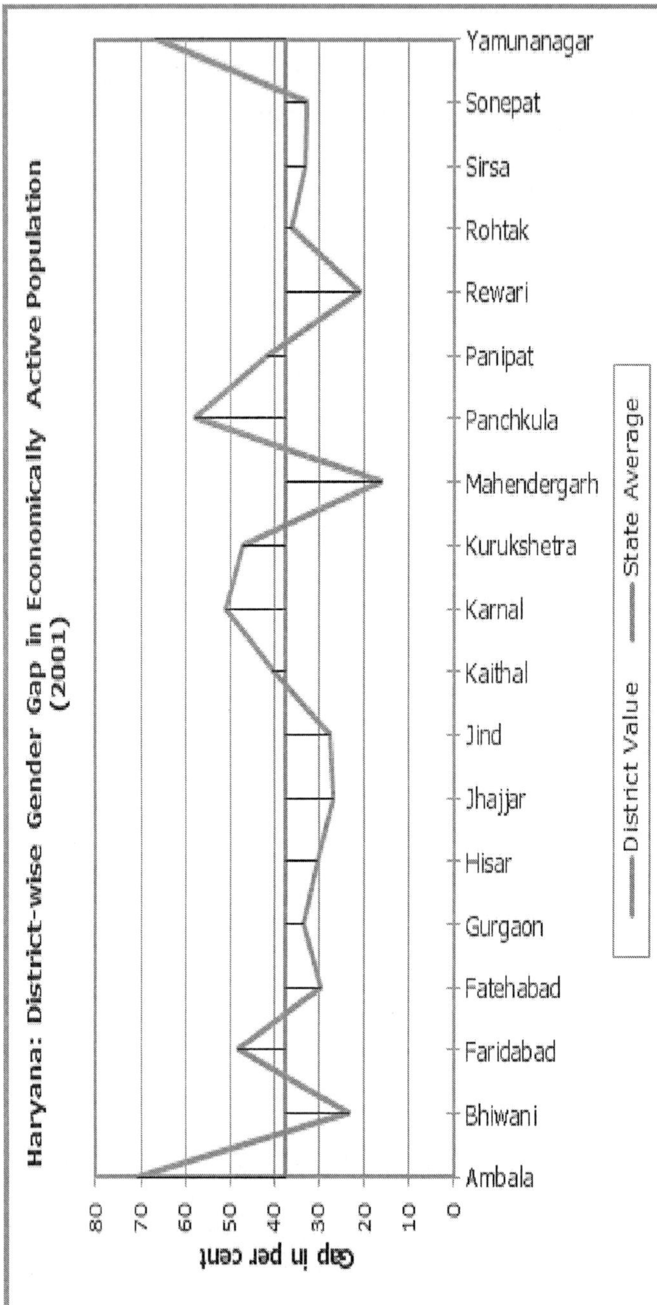

Fig. 4.1

Note: Gender gap here implies female values deducted from male vales. Hence higher and positive value of gender gap shows higher attainment level of males as compared to females and vice versa.

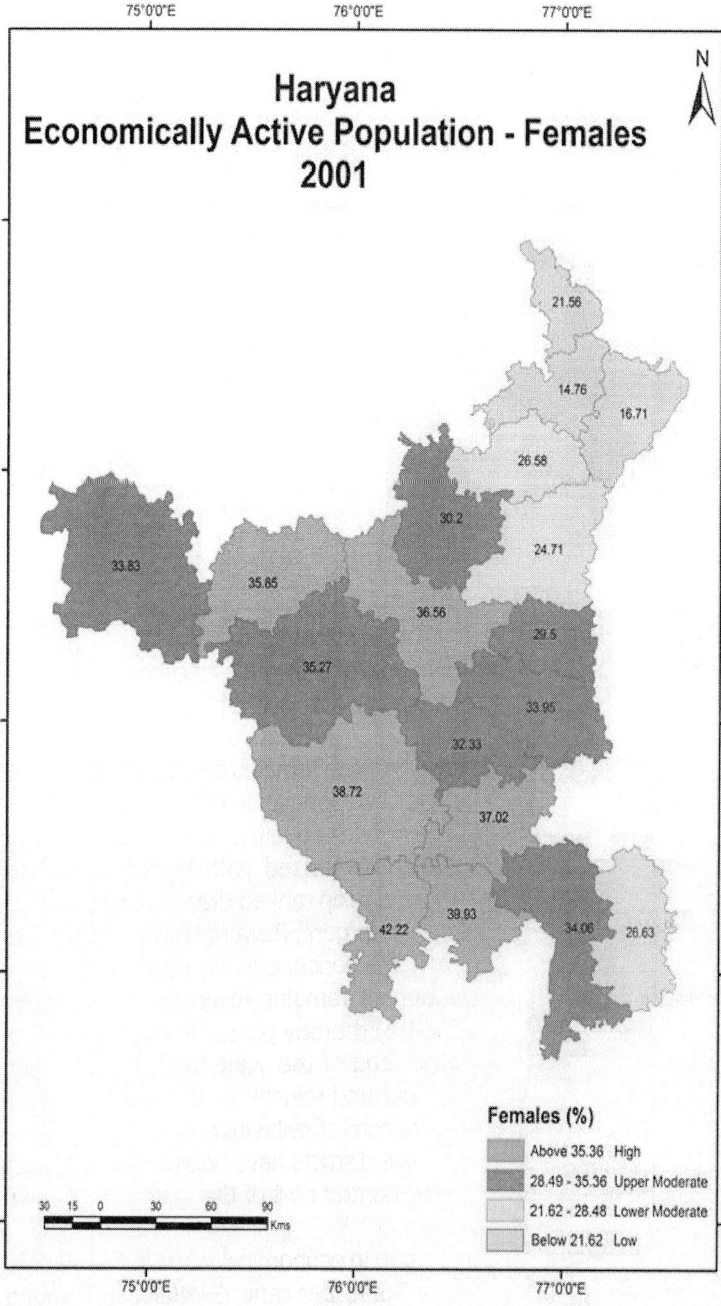

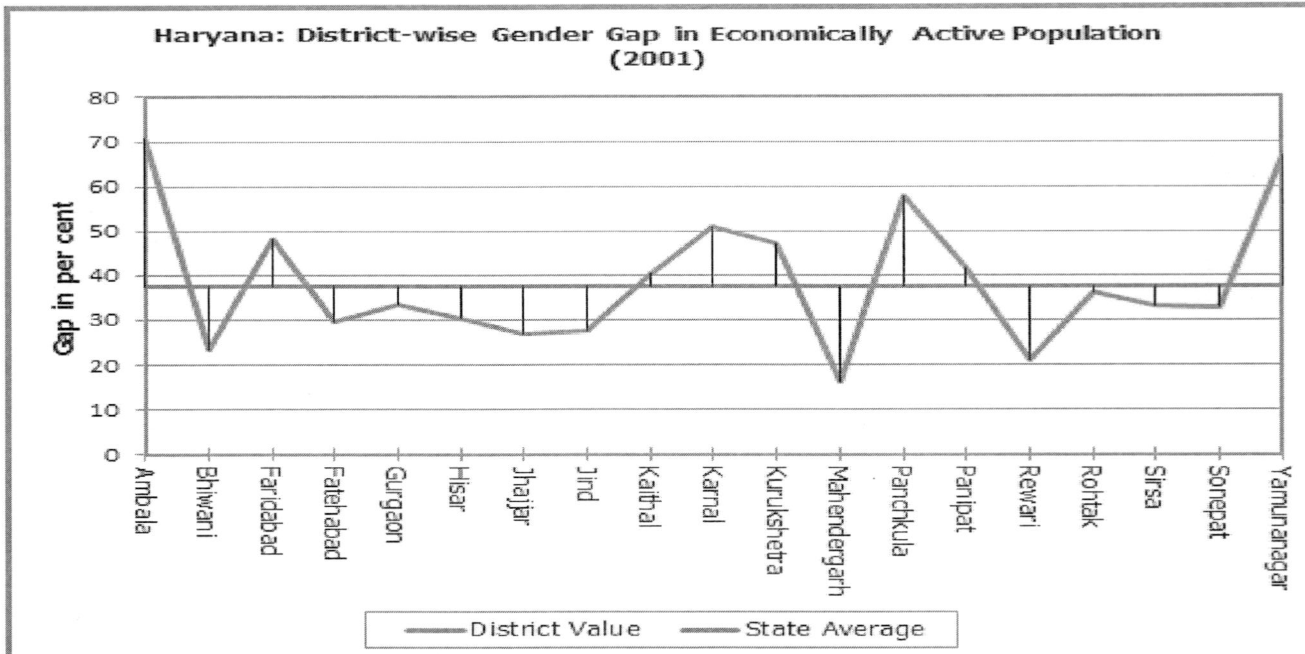

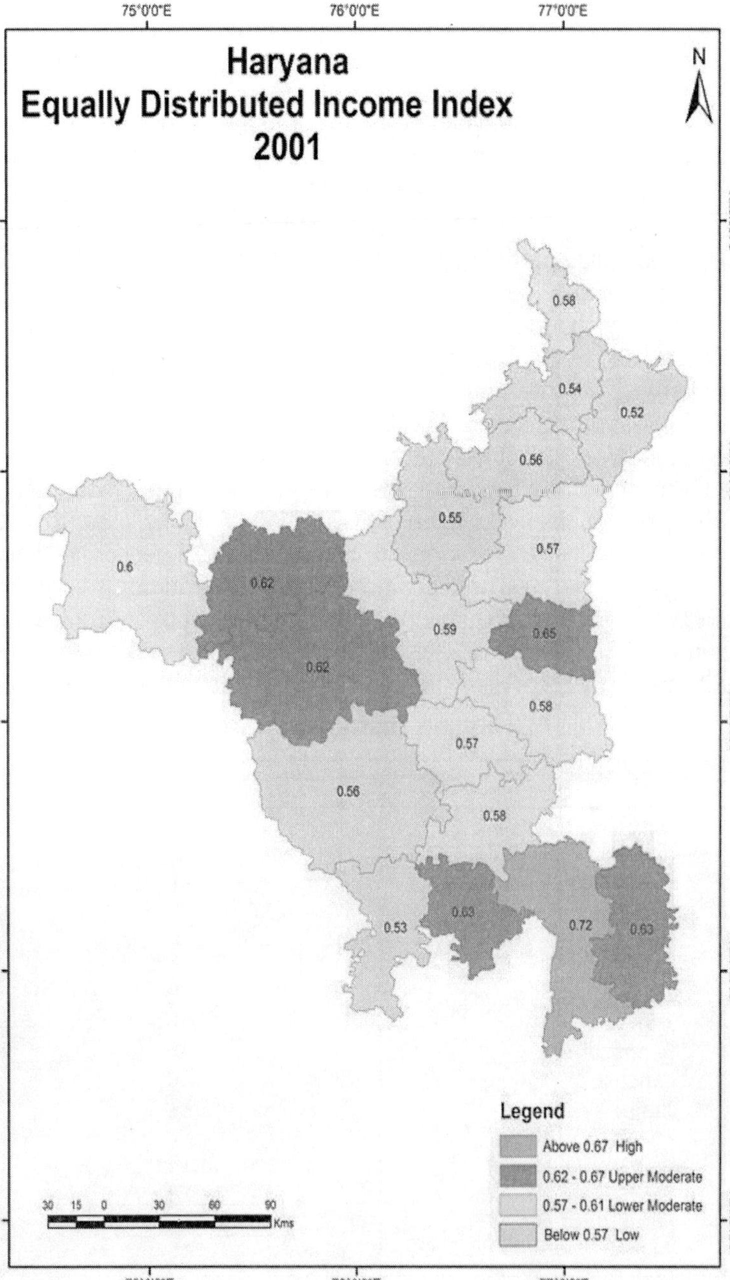
Haryana
Equally Distributed Income Index
2001
N
75°0'0"E
76°0'0"E
77°0'0"E
31°0'0"N
30°0'0"N
29°0'0"N
28°0'0"N
27°0'0"N
0.58
0.54
0.52
0.56
0.55
0.57
0.6
0.62
0.59
0.65
0.62
0.58
0.57
0.56
0.58
0.63
0.53
0.72
0.63
Legend
Above 0.67 High
0.62 - 0.67 Upper Moderate
0.57 - 0.61 Lower Moderate
Below 0.57 Low
30 15 0 30 60 90
Kms

Map 4.3

Ambala district has appeared with the highest gender gap (70.49 per cent) in the EAP followed by Yamunanagar (66.57 per cent), Panchkula (56.87 per cent) and Karnal (50.58 per cent). In this way gender gap is found above 50 percent in these districts. On the contrary, Mahendergarh has appeared as a district with the lowest gender gap amounting to as low as 15.56 per cent. The other districts with reasonably low gender gap include Rewari (20.14 per cent), Bhiwani (22.56 per cent), Jhajjar (25.96 per cent), Jind (26.89 per cent) and Fatehabad (28.31 per cent). In the remaining part of the state gender gap has been found between 30 per cent and 50 per cent.

Following the same methodology as adopted in extracting the income index for HDI, equally distributed income index has been carried out giving gender-wise weights. The results are depicted in Map 4.3 and Table 4.3.

Gurgaon district maintains its top rank on EDII similar to the top rank in income index of HDI. It has outpaced all the other districts of the state in such a manner that it appears as the solitary district in the category of high EDII. However, the index value of EDII (0.72) is slightly lesser than the index value of the income index (0.74) on account of gender inequality. Similarly Panipat (second position) district in addition to the two neighbouring districts of Gurgaon i.e. Faridabad (third position) and Rewari (fourth position) districts have also achieved a handsome index value above 0.62. Two districts i.e. Hisar (fifth position) and Fatehabad (sixth position)

Table 4.3: Equally Distributed Income Index

Districts	*Rankings*
Gurgaon	1
Panipat	2
Faridabad	3
Rewari	4
Hisar	5
Fatehabad	6
Sirsa	7
Jind	8
Sonepat	9
Panchkula	10
Jhajjar	11
Rohtak	12
Karnal	13
Bhiwani	14
Kurukshetra	15
Kaithal	16
Ambala	17
Mahendergarh	18
Yamunanagar	19

situated in the western part of the state have also joined these districts in the category of 'upper moderate level'. Yamunanagar (19th position), Mahendergarh (18th position), Ambala (17th position), Kaithal (16th position), Kurukshetra (15th position) and Bhiwani (14th position) districts find place in the lowest category of EDII with index value below 0.57 for diverse reasons. The reason behind the low attainment level of Bhiwani and Mahendergarh districts lies in the fact that these districts have had lower per capita GDP whereas the low attainment level noticed in Ambala and Yamunanagar districts is mainly due to a very high gender inequality. However, Panchkula district succeeds to find place in the lower moderate EDII category by virtue of neutralising the adverse impact of gender inequality by high per capita GDP. The lower index values of the four categories of EDII as compared to the corresponding values of HDI income index reveals that gender inequality is prevalent (in different magnitude) across all the districts of Haryana.

Whatever the official data speaks about the pitiable situation of females on economic front, the hard fact is that the contribution of the women of Haryana is no less than the contribution of females from southern states of India. In rural areas of the state, not only most of the animal husbandry chores are performed by the women but they toil a lot in the fields also. Inclusion of such activities in 'economic activities' can turn the situation drastically in favour of females in the state.

Education Dimension

In the beginning, gender-wise education attainment levels have been carried out for each district. Then Equally Distributed Education Index (EDEI) has been constructed by combining these two aspects. Map 4.4 reveals distribution of districts in different attainment categories whereas district-wise rankings have been presented in Table 4.4.

Only two districts (Rewari with first position and Mahendergarh with second position) situated in the southern part of the state succeed to find place in the category of top attainment level by achieving EI-males above 0.83. Majority (10) of the districts have been placed in the category of upper moderate attainment level. These districts are spread all over the state except for western part. The districts located in the western part of the state have shown lowest attainment levels. Fatehabad district is at the bottom with a modest index value of 0.68. The other two districts (Kaithal with 18th position and Sirsa with 17th position) have joined it in the category of low attainment level. The difference of a huge index value of 0.20 points between the top ranked and bottom ranked districts underlines the fact that there exist great inter-district disparities in the education attainment levels of males. A perusal of map 4.4 affirms the

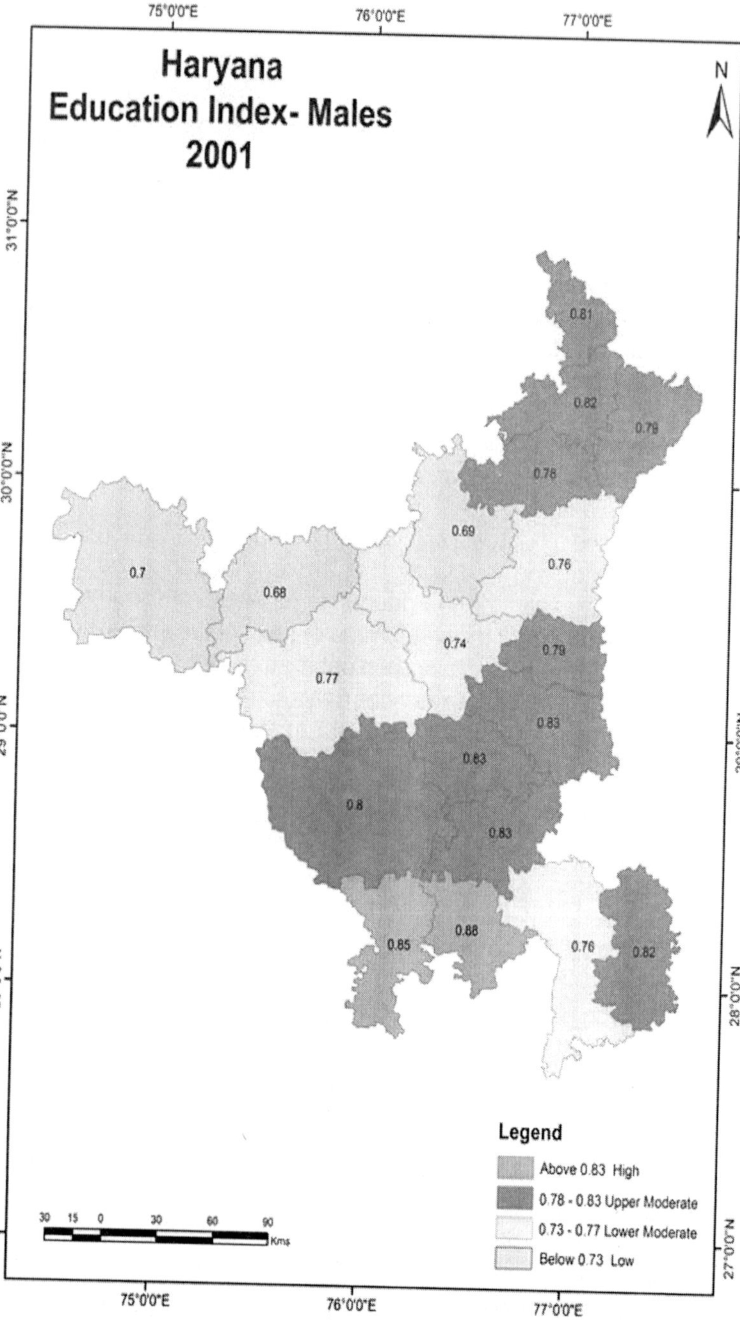
Haryana
Education Index- Males
2001
N
75°0'0"E
76°0'0"E
77°0'0"E
31°0'0"N
30°0'0"N
29°0'0"N
28°0'0"N
27°0'0"N
0.81
0.82
0.79
0.78
0.69
0.76
0.7
0.68
0.74
0.79
0.77
0.83
0.83
0.8
0.83
0.88
0.85
0.76
0.82
Legend
Above 0.83 High
0.78 - 0.83 Upper Moderate
0.73 - 0.77 Lower Moderate
Below 0.73 Low
30 15 0 30 60 90
Kms

Map 4.4

Table 4.4: Education Index-Males (2001)

Districts	*Rankings*
Rewari	1
Mahendergarh	2
Jhajjar	3
Rohtak	4
Sonepat	5
Ambala	6
Faridabad	7
Panchkula	8
Bhiwani	9
Yamunanagar	10
Panipat	11
Kurukshetra	12
Hisar	13
Karnal	14
Gurgaon	15
Jind	16
Sirsa	17
Kaithal	18
Fatehabad	19

statement that the districts located in the south-eastern part of the state have clear edge over the districts located in the north-west as regards to education attainment levels of males.

The picture is considerably different of EI-females from the one that has been observed of EI-males. This difference is not only pervasive in the distribution pattern of the districts but is also reflected in the magnitude of index value and inter-district disparities as well (Table 4.5 and Map 4.5). In this case, the top ranked districts belong to the northern part of the state. The top three districts in descending order are- Ambala (0.67), Panchkula (0.66) and Yamunanagar (0.63). Fatehabad district again records its presence at the last rank with an index value of 0.47 which is immediately preceded by Kaithal (0.47) district. However, Gurgaon district has made it to find place in the category of lower moderate attainment level by recording EI-females marginally above Kaithal district.

Considering education indexes of both the sexes Fatehabad district is consistently at the bottom (Compare Table 4.4 and Table 4.5). Similarly Kaithal and Jind districts have also not shown any improvement and remained at 18th and 16th positions respectively. Mahendergarh district has obtained respectable second rank on EI- males but it is far behind at 12th place on EI- females thereby shown greater gender disparities in education attainment level. Ambala district has shown appreciable improvement of five points to reach the top rank on EI-females and it has interchanged its ranks with Rewari district. Unlike male education level,

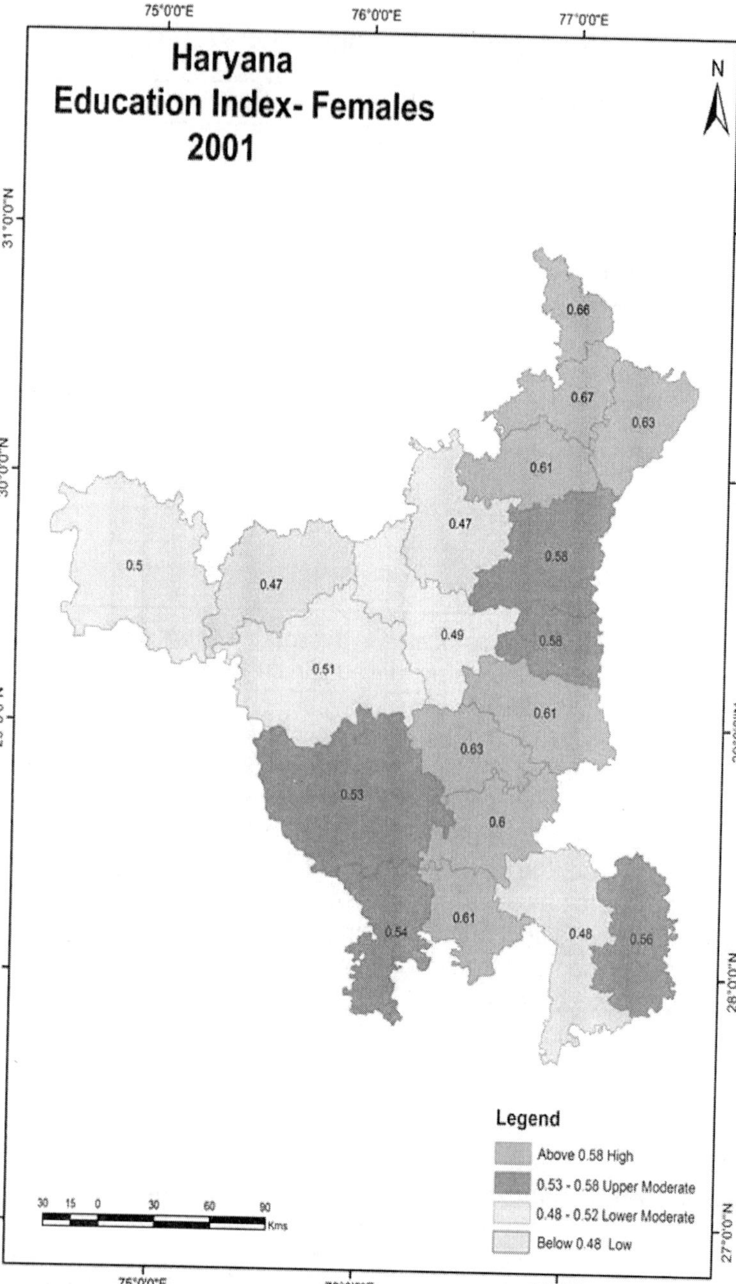
75°0'0"E
76°0'0"E
77°0'0"E
Haryana
Education Index- Females
2001
N
31°0'0"N
30°0'0"N
29°0'0"N
28°0'0"N
27°0'0"N
0.66
0.67
0.63
0.61
0.47
0.58
0.5
0.47
0.49
0.58
0.51
0.61
0.63
0.53
0.6
0.61
0.54
0.48
0.56
Legend
Above 0.58 High
0.53 - 0.58 Upper Moderate
0.48 - 0.52 Lower Moderate
Below 0.48 Low
30 15 0 30 60 90
Kms

Map 4.5

Table 4.5: Education Index-Females (2001)

Districts	*Rankings*
Ambala	1
Panchkula	2
Yamunanagar	3
Rohtak	4
Rewari	5
Sonepat	6
Kurukshetra	7
Jhajjar	8
Karnal	9
Panipat	10
Faridabad	11
Mahendergarh	12
Bhiwani	13
Hisar	14
Sirsa	15
Jind	16
Gurgaon	17
Kaithal	18
Fatehabad	19

females have found more respectable position in north Haryana, but pathetic in comparatively larger western tracts of the state. Unfortunately the index value of the state EI-females (0.56) is fairly lesser than its counterpart (0.78).

Figure 4.2 clearly indicates that there exists a huge gender gap as far as the education attainment in the state are concerned. On the state average male education attainment level is higher by 22.76 percentage points than that of the females, which reflects quite discriminatory aspect of development. Mahendergarh with a figure of 30.64 percentage points appears as the district where highest gender gap is noticed. It is the only district where the figure is above 30 per cent mark. Whereas Ambala district represents the other end with gender gap as low as 14.92 percentage points. A general trend of gender gap in education attainment level is such that it is lower in the districts located in the northern part such as Ambala (14.92 per cent), Panchkula (15.22 per cent), Yamunanagar (15.43 per cent), Kurukshetra (17.45 per cent), Karnal (18.32 per cent), etc. whereas it is higher in the districts located in the southern part viz. Mahendergarh (30.64 per cent), Bhiwani (27.26 per cent), Faridabad (25.21 per cent), Rewari (27.62 per cent), Gurgaon (28.39 per cent), etc. As a whole eight districts have recorded gender gap above the state average.

By combining education indexes of both the genders, Equally Distributed Education Index (EDEI) has been computed. The results have

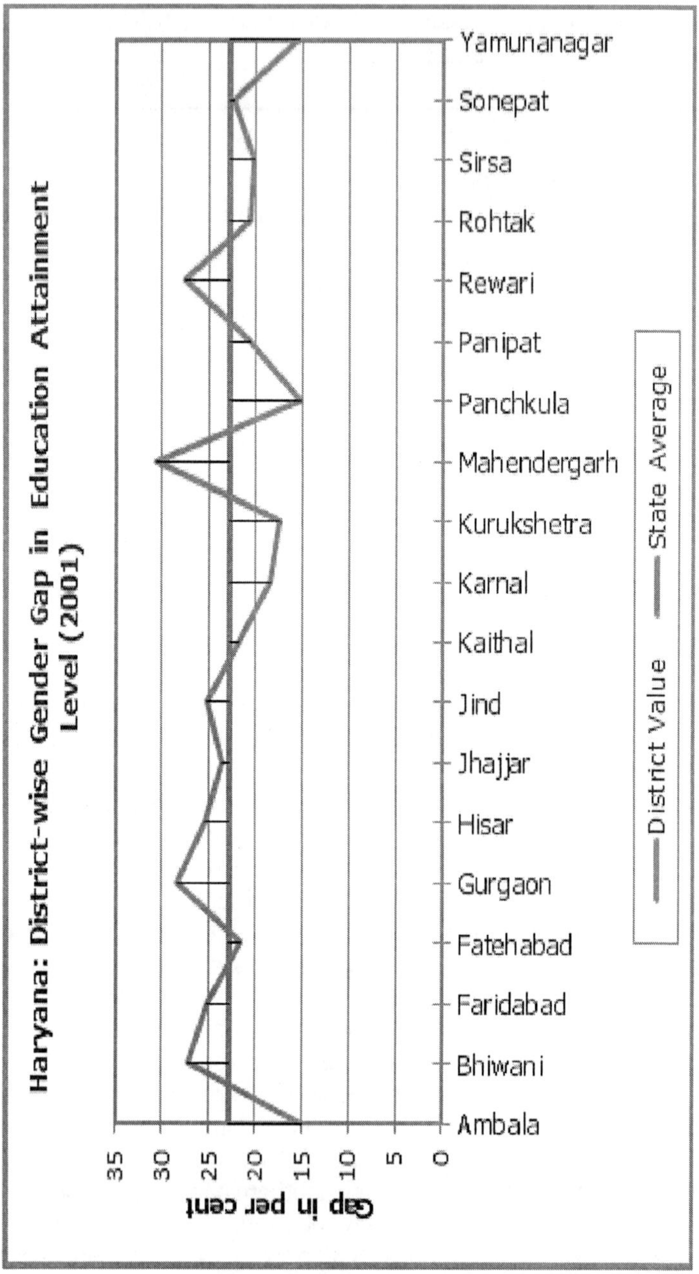
Haryana: District-wise Gender Gap in Education Attainment Level (2001)
Gap in per cent
35
30
25
20
15
10
5
0
Ambala
Bhiwani
Faridabad
Fatehabad
Gurgaon
Hisar
Jhajjar
Jind
Kaithal
Karnal
Kurukshetra
Mahendergarh
Panchkula
Panipat
Rewari
Rohtak
Sirsa
Sonepat
Yamunanagar
District Value
State Average

Fig. 4.2

been portrayed in Map 4.6 and the district-wise rankings are tabulated in Table 4.6. Six districts i.e. Ambala (0.75), Panchkula (0.73), Rewari (0.73), Rohtak (0.72), Sonepat (0.71) and Yamunanagar (0.71) districts have found place in the category of high attainment level thereby occupied the top six ranks respectively. All of them have obtained index value above 0.70. Equal number of districts have found place in the category of upper moderate attainment level ranging from 0.66 to 0.70. Most of these districts are spread over the eastern part of the state beginning from Karnal in the north-east to Faridabad in the south-east. Only two districts namely, Bhiwani and Hisar that have come up with lower moderate attainment level (between 0.61 and 0.65) constitute the west-central quadrant. The lowest attainment level as regards to EDEI can be seen in five districts viz. Fatehabad, Kaithal, Sirsa, Jind and Gurgaon as all these have attained EDEI below 0.62.

A cross examination of Tables 4.4, 4.5 and 4.6 reveals that the districts that have performed better in the case of feminine gender have obtained clear edge in the EDEI even after a moderate performance in the case of masculine gender. On the contrary, the districts which have performed very well in the case of masculine gender but failed to maintain the attainment level in the case of feminine gender are penalised for the

Table 4.6: Equally Distributed Education Index (2001)

Districts	*Rankings*
Ambala	1
Panchkula	2
Rewari	3
Rohtak	4
Sonepat	5
Yamunanagar	6
Jhajjar	7
Kurukshetra	8
Faridabad	9
Panipat	10
Mahendergarh	11
Karnal	12
Bhiwani	13
Hisar	14
Gurgaon	15
Jind	16
Sirsa	17
Kaithal	18
Fatehabad	19

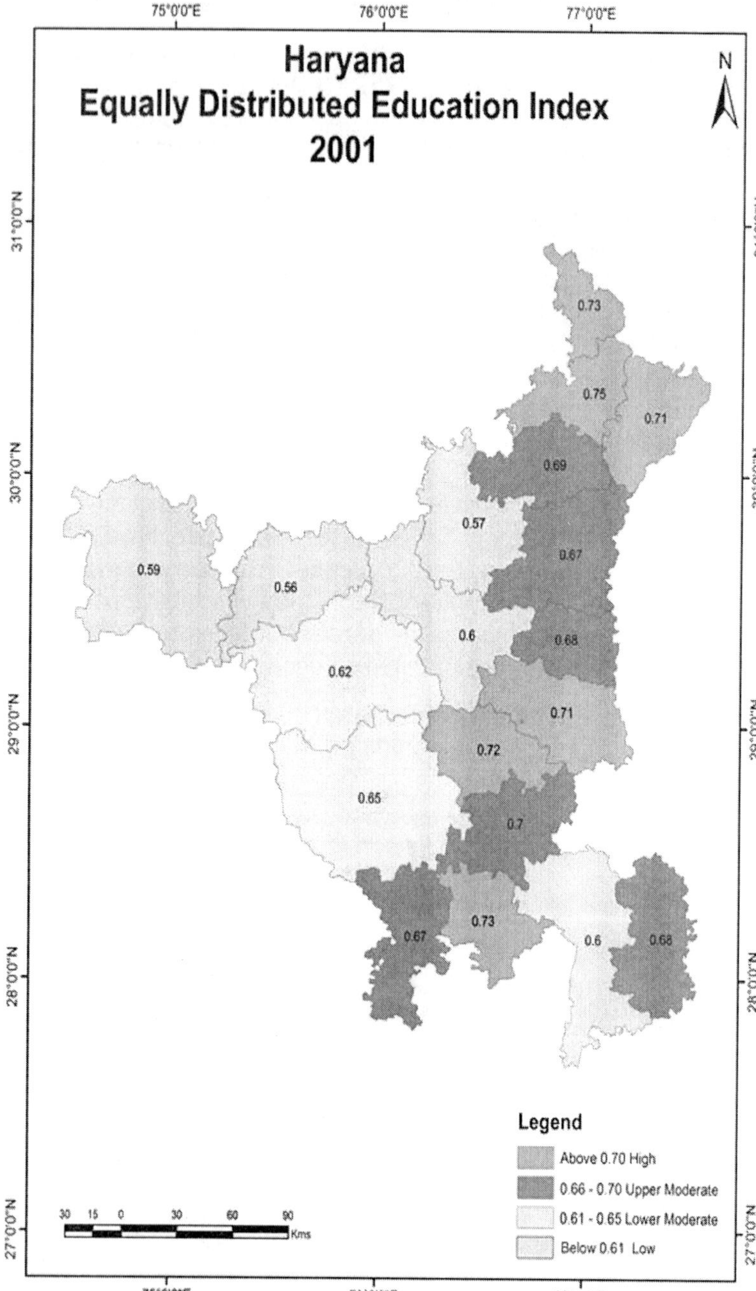
Haryana
Equally Distributed Education Index
2001
N
75°0'0"E
76°0'0"E
77°0'0"E
31°0'0"N
30°0'0"N
29°0'0"N
28°0'0"N
27°0'0"N
0.73
0.75
0.71
0.69
0.57
0.67
0.59
0.56
0.6
0.68
0.62
0.71
0.72
0.65
0.7
0.73
0.67
0.6
0.68
Legend
Above 0.70 High
0.66 - 0.70 Upper Moderate
0.61 - 0.65 Lower Moderate
Below 0.61 Low
30 15 0 30 60 90
Kms

Map 4.6

discriminatory development against the latter and hence failed to capture a respectable rank on EDEI. Consider the case of Ambala district which has succeeded in achieving top rank of EDEI by virtue of top rank in EI-females even though it has a moderate sixth rank in the case of EI-males. Similar is the situation of Panchkula district. The case of Rewari district is rather attention-grabbing. It is placed at third rank on EDEI after Ambala and Panchkula, even though it has obtained top rank in EI-males but lagged a little behind at fifth rank in EI-females and as a result it is penalised due to inequitable development against the females or in favour of males. Let us consider the case of Mahendergarh also. It has performed consistently well by achieving second rank in EI-males but placed on a moderate 11th rank on EDEI on account of poor performance in EI-females.

Health Dimension

Gender-wise health index has been calculated to reach the Equally Distributed Health Index (EDHI). Health index is represented by the attainment level in terms of marriages above the legal age of marriage. The significance of this variable in determining health lies in the fact that child marriage not only deteriorates the physical and mental health of the people but it puts adverse effect on the health of offspring also. Hence, lower the incidence of child marriage (or higher the incidence of marriage above the legal age at marriage); better would be the health status of population.

Table 4.7: Health Index-Males (2001)

Districts	*Rankings*
Ambala	1
Panchkula	2
Rohtak	3
Jhajjar	4
Yamunanagar	5
Kurukshetra	6
Sonepat	7
Rewari	8
Hisar	9
Karnal	10
Panipat	11
Fatehabad	12
Bhiwani	13
Kaithal	14
Sirsa	15
Jind	16
Mahendergarh	17
Faridabad	18
Gurgaon	19

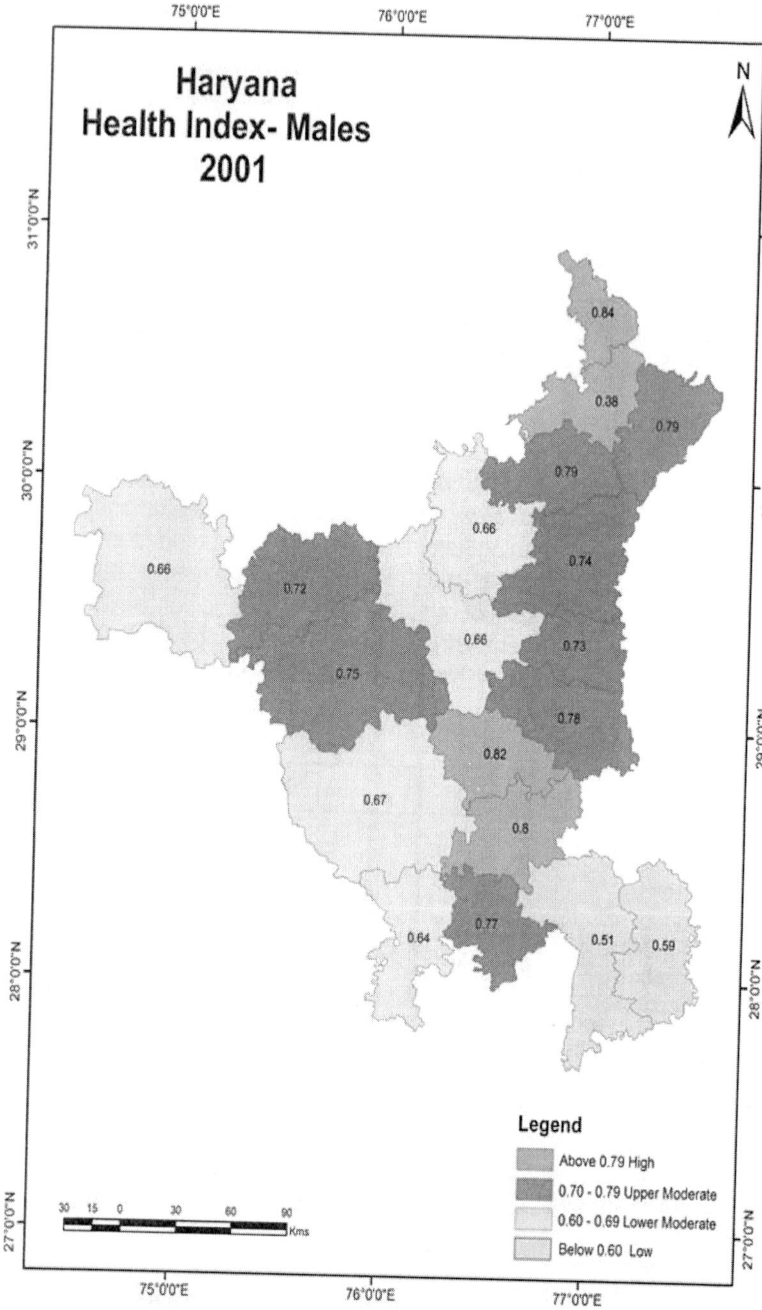
Haryana
Health Index- Males
2001
N
75°0'0"E
76°0'0"E
77°0'0"E
31°0'0"N
30°0'0"N
29°0'0"N
28°0'0"N
27°0'0"N
0.84
0.38
0.79
0.79
0.66
0.74
0.66
0.72
0.66
0.73
0.75
0.78
0.82
0.67
0.8
0.77
0.64
0.51
0.59
Legend
Above 0.79 High
0.70 - 0.79 Upper Moderate
0.60 - 0.69 Lower Moderate
Below 0.60 Low
30 15 0 30 60 90
Kms

Map 4.7

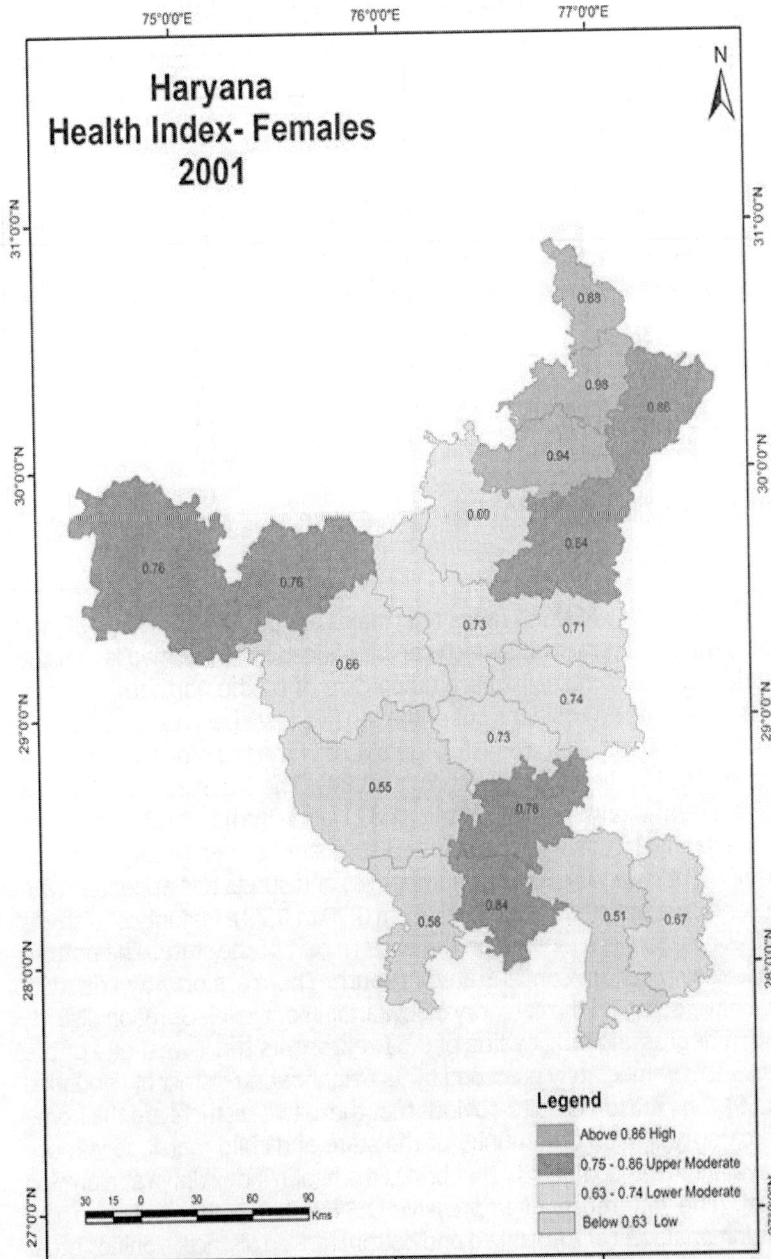
Haryana
Health Index- Females
2001
N
75°0'0"E
76°0'0"E
77°0'0"E
31°0'0"N
30°0'0"N
29°0'0"N
28°0'0"N
27°0'0"N
0.94
0.76
0.76
0.73
0.71
0.66
0.74
0.73
0.55
0.78
0.84
0.58
0.51
0.67
Legend
Above 0.86 High
0.75 - 0.86 Upper Moderate
0.63 - 0.74 Lower Moderate
Below 0.63 Low
30 15 0 30 60 90
Kms

Map 4.8

Table 4.8: Health Index- Females (2001)

Districts	Rankings
Ambala	1
Kurukshetra	2
Panchkula	3
Yamunanagar	4
Karnal	5
Rewari	6
Jhajjar	7
Fatehabad	8
Sirsa	9
Sonepat	10
Jind	11
Rohtak	12
Panipat	13
Kaithal	14
Faridabad	15
Hisar	16
Mahendergarh	17
Bhiwani	18
Gurgaon	19

The results of Health Index (HI) males are portrayed in Map 4.7 and Table 4.7. A general trend which can be noticed from the map is that the health aspect of males is more taken care of by the northern districts. This is why; three positions out of the top five have been captured by the northern districts. Ambala district gets hold of the top rank with an index value of 0.88 followed by Panchkula (0.84). The third and fourth ranks have been attained by Rohtak (0.82) and Jhajjar (0.80) districts respectively. In this way these four districts have been grouped in high attainment category. Highest number (8) of districts has appeared with upper moderate attainment level (from 0.70 to 0.79). Majority of districts in this category are located on the eastern part of the state. The bottom ranked districts are concentrated in south. There are only two districts that have occupied the category of low attainment level. Gurgaon district, with a depressing index value of 0.51 represents the lowest end of the scale. It is immediately preceded by its neighbouring district of Faridabad (0.59). The reason is quite obvious that these two districts are the home of majority of *Meo* Community of the state and child marriage is more prevalent in this community that brings the health index down at alarming level. The difference of impressive 0.37 index points between the attainment levels of top ranked and bottom ranked districts signifies great deal of inter-district disparities.

Surprisingly, the statistics reveals that health status of females is better than their counterparts in the state. This is the only dimension where females have shown an edge over males. The state HI-females accounts for 0.72, which is higher, though slightly, than the HI-males (0.71). Ambala district maintains its first rank by gaining a handsome index value of 0.98 (Map 4.8 and Table 4.8).

The second rank has been captured by Kurukshetra (0.94) district while Panchkula (0.88) is at the third place. In this way these three districts have found place in the category of high attainment level. On the contrary, Gurgaon district is again lingering at the last place with a pitiable index value of 0.51 without enhancing its standing. Bhiwani (0.55) and Mahendergarh (0.58) districts have joined Gurgaon in the category of lowest performance. The difference of 0.47 index points between the index values of districts with extreme performances reflects marked inter-district disparities in the health attainment level of females.

A comparative analysis of health attainment status of both the genders brings out some striking inferences (Compare Map 4.7 and Map 4.8). First, Ambala district has attained top rank both in males and females. But the index value in the case of females (0.98) is fairly higher than the index value of males (0.88) which suggests that incidence of child marriage with respect to females is almost absent in the district whereas it still exists in the case of males. Second, high attainment level of females is restricted to a few northern districts whereas in the case of males it is found in greater number of districts with larger spatial expansion. Kurukshetra, Yamunanagar, Rewari, Karnal, Fatehabad, Sirsa, Jind and Faridabad are amongst the districts that upscale their ranks with respect to females as compared to males (Compare Table 4.7 and Table 4.8). On the contrary, Panchkula, Jhajjar, Rohtak, Sonepat, Panipat, Hisar and Bhiwani districts relegate their ranks in this context. Except Jhajjar, all these districts have experienced lower health status of females as that of males. The remaining districts maintain their status on HI-females whatever rank they have been awarded on HI-males.

Map 4.9 demonstrates the spatial distribution of districts in different classes of EDHI whereas the rankings have been tabulated in Table 4.9.

Ambala district has obtained first rank on EDHI with an index value of 0.92. The second rank is captured by Panchkula (0.86) district albeit its third rank on HI-females. Consider the case of Kurukshetra district that has slipped to third rank on EDHI even after a better (second) rank on HI-females. In fact, Kurukshetra district fails to take the advantage on account of poor performance on HI-males (sixth rank) and Panchkula district, on the other hand, takes the benefit of this situation as it has achieved a better second rank on HI-males (Compare Tables 4.7, 4.8 and 4.9). As many as eight districts have recorded upper moderate EDHI (0.72-0.82). Unique pattern of these districts can be seen along with Yamuna River. However, Rohtak, Jhajjar, Rewari and Fatehabad districts have also

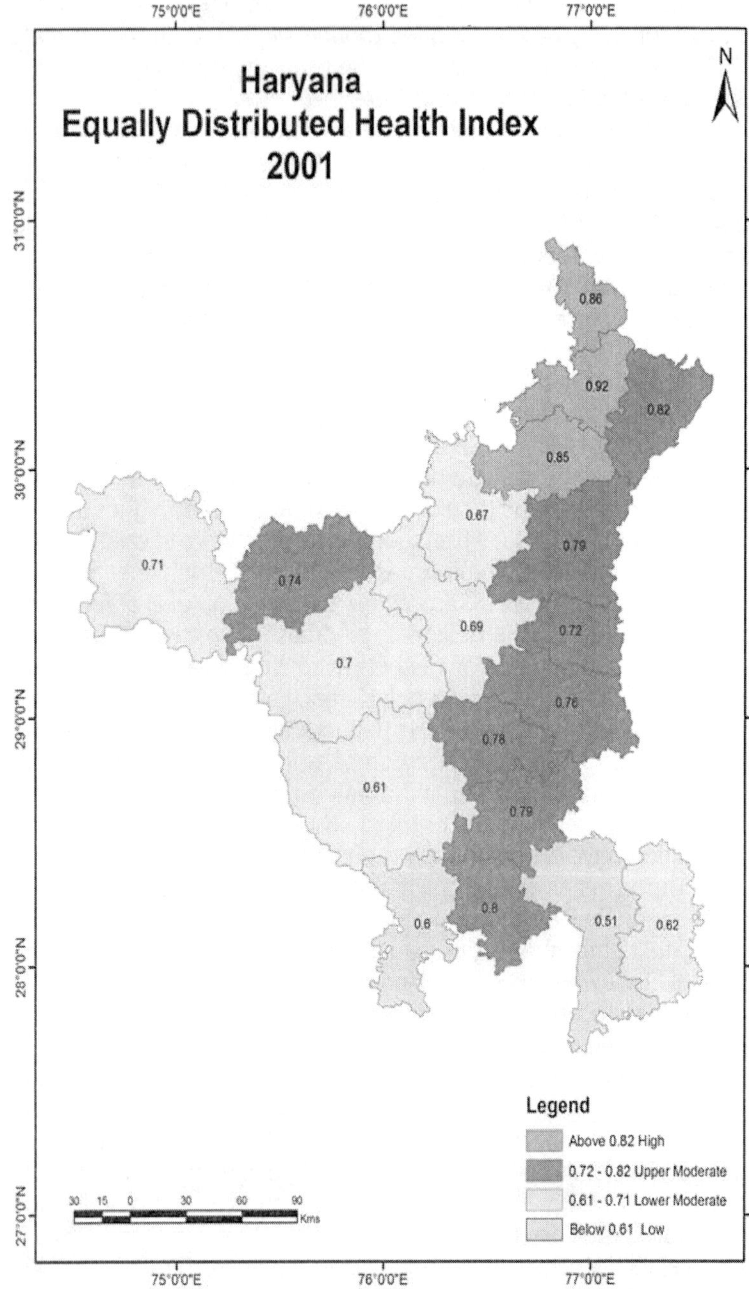
75°0'0"E
76°0'0"E
77°0'0"E
Haryana
Equally Distributed Health Index
2001
N
31°0'0"N
30°0'0"N
29°0'0"N
28°0'0"N
27°0'0"N
0.86
0.92
0.82
0.85
0.67
0.79
0.71
0.74
0.69
0.72
0.7
0.76
0.78
0.61
0.79
0.8
0.6
0.51
0.62
Legend
Above 0.82 High
0.72 - 0.82 Upper Moderate
0.61 - 0.71 Lower Moderate
Below 0.61 Low
30 15 0 30 60 90
Kms

Map 4.9

Table 4.9: Equally Distributed Health Index (2001)

Districts	*Rankings*
Ambala	1
Panchkula	2
Kurukshetra	3
Yamunanagar	4
Rewari	5
Jhajjar	6
Karnal	7
Rohtak	8
Sonepat	9
Fatehabad	10
Panipat	11
Sirsa	12
Hisar	13
Jind	14
Kaithal	15
Faridabad	16
Bhiwani	17
Mahendergarh	18
Gurgaon	19

joined this class. Sirsa, Hisar, Kaithal, Jind, Bhiwani and Faridabad are amongst the districts that have achieved low (0.61- 0.71) EDHI. The two districts i.e. Gurgaon (0.51) and Mahendergarh (0.60), located on the southern border, have performed quite below the desired level by placing themselves in the most minuscule category of EDHI below 0.61.

Like the other dimensions of development, reasonable gender gap is perceptible in health attainment levels also. But this time it is found in the favour of feminine gender. Negative index value of gender gap indicates better attainment level of females as compared to males. The gender gap at the state level (-0.012) is slightly in favour of females (Figure 4.3). The fluctuating trend line shows that there persists a great deal of inter-district disparities in this regard. The district-wise trend of gender gap indicates that it is in favour of females in the north and eastern part whereas it is against the females in south and western part of the state. However, districts like Faridabad, Fatehabad, Rewari and Sirsa do not support this generalisation. Kurukshetra (-0.150) district has shown highest discrimination in favour of females as regards to health attainment level whereas the district of Bhiwani (0.125) is standing antipodal of Kurukshetra. Health attainment status of females is found better in as many as eleven districts out of the total nineteen districts.

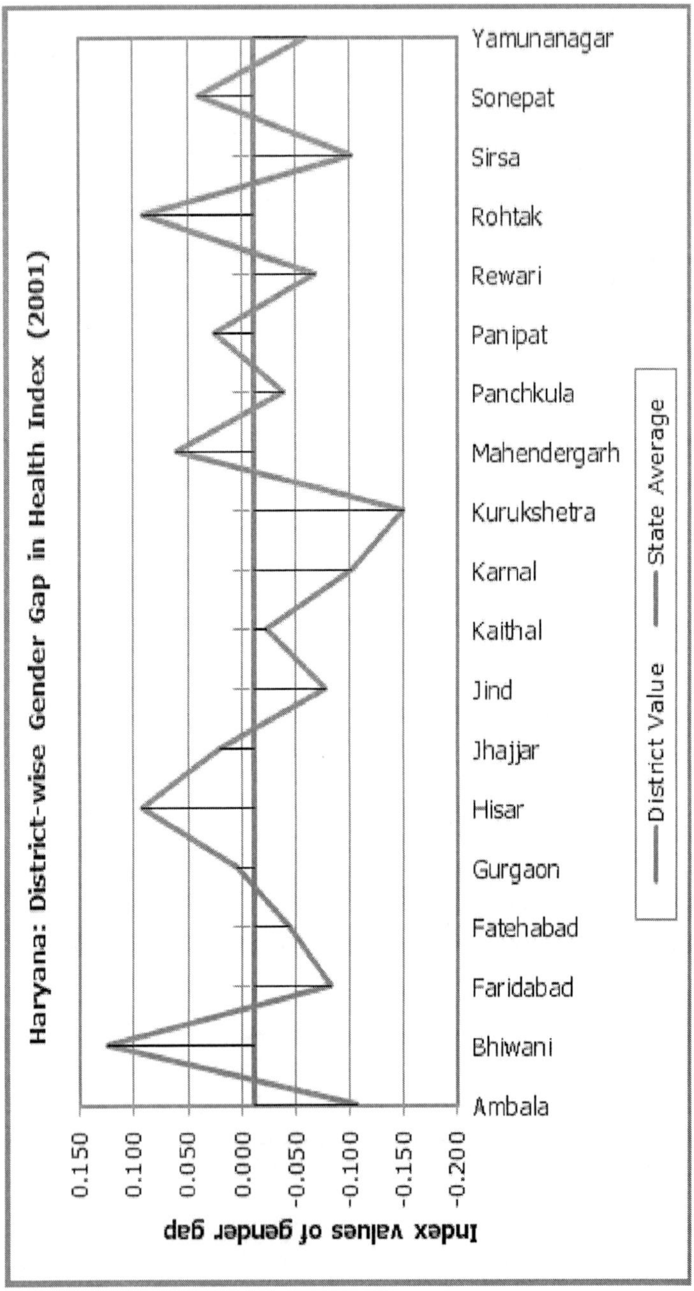
Haryana: District-wise Gender Gap in Health Index (2001)
Index values of gender gap
0.150
0.100
0.050
0.000
-0.050
-0.100
-0.150
-0.200
Ambala
Bhiwani
Faridabad
Fatehabad
Gurgaon
Hisar
Jhajjar
Jind
Kaithal
Karnal
Kurukshetra
Mahendergarh
Panchkula
Panipat
Rewari
Rohtak
Sirsa
Sonepat
Yamunanagar
District Value
State Average

Fig. 4.3

Gender Development Index

Gender Development Index (GDI) has now been obtained by computing the simple average of the equally distributed indexes pertaining to three dimensions- income, education and health. Map 4.10 demonstrates district-wise pattern of GDI whereas district-wise rankings have been presented in the last column of Table 4.10. All the three districts i.e. Ambala (0.74), Panchkula (0.72) and Rewari (0.72) that find place in the first category of high development have been awarded top three ranks respectively. The seven districts which are characterised with the upper moderate development (0.67 to 0.71) form a unique pattern in the eastern part of the state. In north-south order, these districts are Yamunanagar (0.68), Kurukshetra (0.70), Karnal (0.67), Panipat (0.68), Sonepat (0.69), Rohtak (0.69) and Jhajjar (0.69). The GDI is found lower moderate (0.63 to 0.66) in the districts such as Hisar (0.65), Faridabad (0.64) and Fatehabad (0.64). However, the attainment level is found lowest (below 0.63) in as many as five districts dispersed all over the state. Kaithal (0.60) district is at the bottom which is preceded by Mahendergarh (0.60), Bhiwani (0.61), Gurgaon (0.61) and Jind (0.62) districts.

The cross examination of Table 4.10 brings out some interesting inferences regarding the GDI rankings.

- Ambala and Panchkula districts that have attained top two positions have shown admirable performance as regards to education and health dimensions but none of them perform up to the mark in income dimension. But their poor performance in the income dimension is well compensated by the other two.
- Only three districts all over the state have shown consistent performance in all the three dimensions. By virtue of good consistent performance, Rewari district has been placed at third position on GDI. On the contrary, Kaithal and Bhiwani districts have been placed at 19th and 16th rank respectively as these districts have performed consistently poor in all the three dimensions.
- Gurgaon district has failed to recover from its pitiable position in respect of education and health, even though it has outraced all the districts in income dimension and it has finally been placed at 16th position on GDI.
- A high positive correlation can be seen between the rankings of two dimensions i.e. education and health with the GDI. A district performing well in one dimension is also performing well in the other dimension or vice versa.
- Income dimension has insignificant negative correlation (-0.09) with the GDI. Hence, a district performing well as regards to income dimension shows poor performance in remaining two dimensions

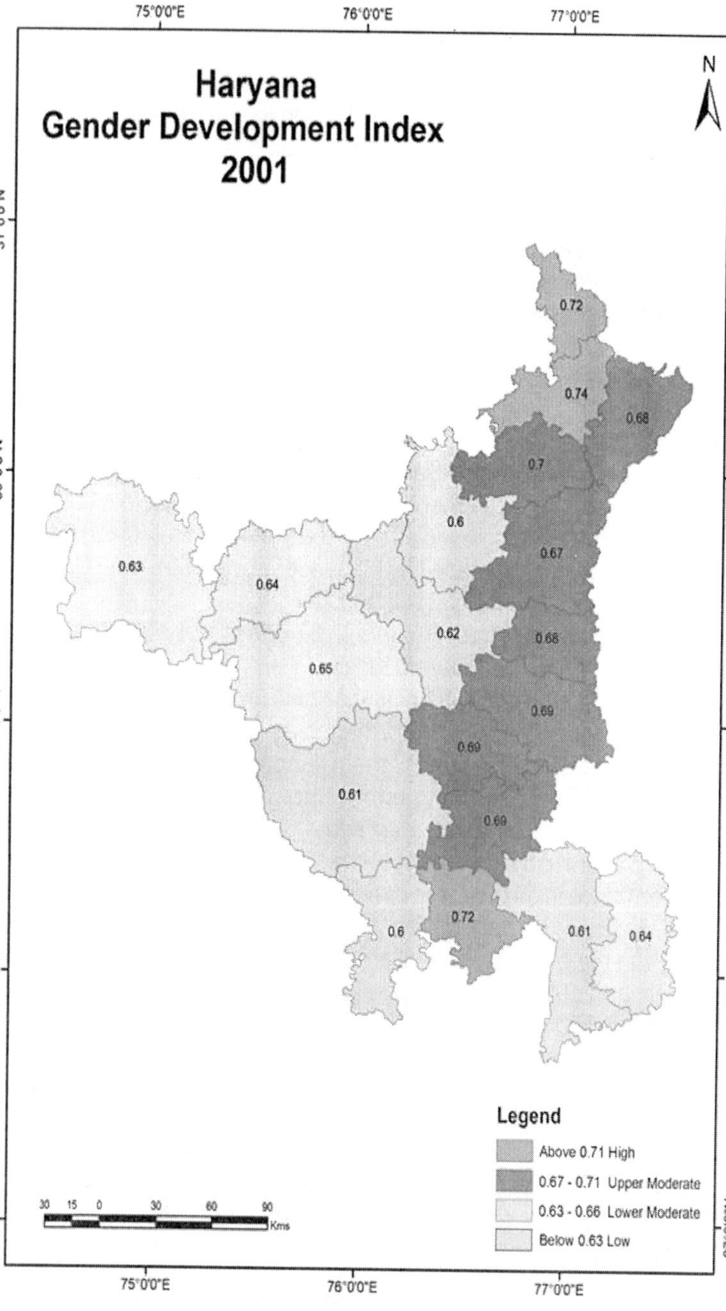
Haryana
Gender Development Index
2001
N
75°0'0"E
76°0'0"E
77°0'0"E
31°0'0"N
30°0'0"N
29°0'0"N
28°0'0"N
27°0'0"N
0.72
0.74
0.68
0.7
0.6
0.67
0.63
0.64
0.62
0.68
0.65
0.69
0.69
0.61
0.69
0.72
0.6
0.61
0.64
Legend
Above 0.71 High
0.67 - 0.71 Upper Moderate
0.63 - 0.66 Lower Moderate
Below 0.63 Low
30 15 0 30 60 90
Kms

Map 4.10

Table 4.10: Gender Development Index: District-wise Rankings (2001)

Districts	*Equally Distributed Income Index*	*Equally Distributed Education Index*	*Equally Distributed Health Index*	*Gender Development Index*
Ambala	17	1	1	1
Panchkula	10	2	2	2
Rewari	4	3	5	3
Kurukshetra	15	8	3	4
Rohtak	12	4	8	5
Jhajjar	11	7	6	6
Sonepat	9	5	9	7
Yamunanagar	19	6	4	8
Panipat	2	10	11	9
Karnal	13	12	7	10
Hisar	5	14	13	11
Faridabad	3	9	16	12
Fatehabad	6	19	10	13
Sirsa	7	17	12	14
Jind	8	16	14	15
Gurgaon	1	15	19	16
Bhiwani	14	13	17	17
Mahendergarh	18	11	18	18
Kaithal	16	18	15	19
Correlation between the ranks of individual dimensions with the GDI	-0.06	0.86	0.91	

i.e. education and health. This is why; the better performing districts in income dimension could not succeed in attaining better GDI rank. Gurgaon, Panipat, Faridabad, etc. are amongst such districts. However, Rewari district is an exception.

Sum up

The gist of the above analysis is that the districts located in the north-eastern part have shown higher attainment level while poor attainment level is visible in the south-western part of the state. However, Rewari district in the southern part has exceptionally come up with high attainment level. Only three districts all over the state have shown consistent performance in all the three dimensions. By virtue of it, Rewari district has been placed higher on GDI tally whereas Kaithal and Bhiwani districts have been placed at bottom as these districts have performed consistently poor in all the three dimensions. Ambala and Panchkula districts that have attained top two positions have shown admirable performance as regards to education and health dimensions but none of them perform up to the mark in income dimension. But their poor performance in the income dimension is well compensated by the other two. On the other hand, Gurgaon district has failed to recover from its pitiable position in respect of education and health, even though it has outraced all the districts in income dimension. Education and health dimensions are significantly associated with the GDI while income dimension has shown insignificant association with it.

5

Human Poverty Index, 2001

Poverty is another critical issue which requires attention. It is a state of deprivation which reflects the inability of an individual to secure a normative minimum level of living. In the present study, the Human Poverty Index (HPI) has been estimated to reflect the depressing perspective on development (deprivation aspect) on the basis of multiple variables. Like HDI, these variables of deprivation can be put in three broad groups- Income Deprivation, Educational Deprivation and Health Deprivation. All these variables have been examined separately in the succeeding section and HPI is explained at the end. The HPI value ranges from '0 to 100' as against '0 to 1' in respect of HDI and GDI. Furthermore, the scoring pattern of the HPI is such that a higher deprivation for a district means a value closer to 100. The index value of 100 implies that the entire population of the district is deprived of minimum attainment level. On the other hand, the index value closer to zero for a dimension shows lower deprivation or higher attainment level in that dimension. The higher is the rank obtained by a district on the HPI; higher would be the deprivation level in that district. The districts have been classified into four categories on the scale of deprivation- high deprivation, upper moderate deprivation, lower moderate deprivation and low deprivation.

Income Deprivation

The HPI seeks to measure the income deprivation on the basis of a single parameter i.e. proportion of population living below poverty line. Though the reliability of data is also an issue of debate as misleading information is supplied by the respondent households to avail the benefit of government welfare schemes which are meant for the BPL population. Nonetheless this is the most appropriate variable which can be used to

Table 5.1: Index of Deprivation in Income (2001)

District	*Rankings*
Jind	1
Bhiwani	2
Sirsa	3
Kurukshetra	4
Karnal	5
Hisar	6
Yamunanagar	7
Kaithal	8
Fatehabad	9
Rewari	10
Gurgaon	11
Rohtak	12
Panchkula	13
Faridabad	14
Jhajjar	15
Sonepat	16
Panipat	17
Mahendergarh	18
Ambala	19

reflect income deprivation. At the state level 10.21 per cent of the population was deprived of satisfying its minimum level of living due to income poverty. Geographical distribution of districts with different magnitude of IOD-income is given in Map 5.1 whereas district-wise rankings are presented in Table 5.1.

Income deprivation is found highest in Jind where 14.26 per cent population has been struggling for normative living. As a result, it has been awarded top rank in this regard. Bhiwani and Sirsa districts follow closely Jind district on IOD-income by having 13.61 per cent and 13.47 per cent BPL population and obtained second and third ranks respectively. All the three districts that have been placed in the category of high deprivation are characterised with low level of industrial development.

In contrast, Ambala district has set the best example of inclusive economic growth by having minimum (5.83 per cent) population below poverty line and as a result it has been placed at the last position on IOD-income. The similar spirit has been shown by the districts like Mahendergarh (6.51 per cent), Panipat (6.95 per cent) and Sonepat (7.89 per cent) as all of these districts have BPL population less than 7.94 per cent thereby placed in the category of lowest deprivation level. Surprisingly Gurgaon district, characterised with the highest level of industrial development, could not find place in this category. This may be because the benefits of industrial development are restricted to limited strata of

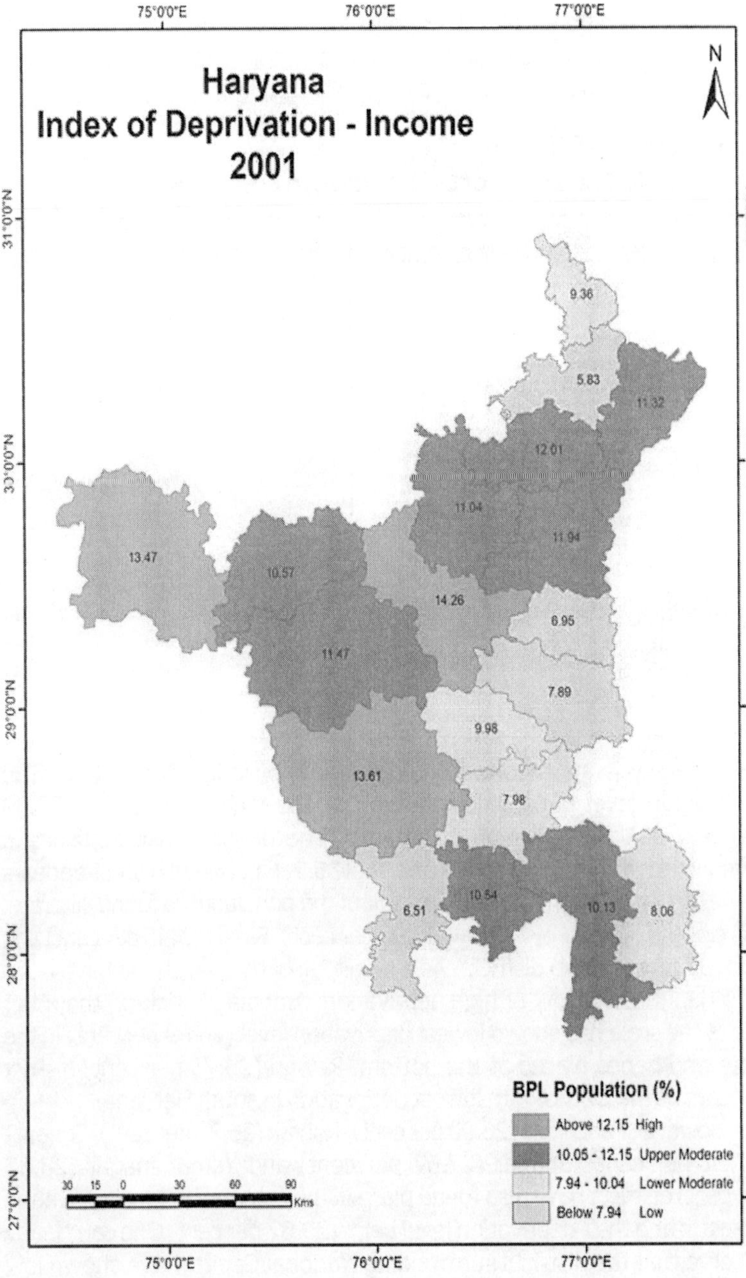
Haryana
Index of Deprivation - Income
2001
N
75°0'0"E
76°0'0"E
77°0'0"E
31°0'0"N
30°0'0"N
29°0'0"N
28°0'0"N
27°0'0"N
9.36
5.83
11.32
12.01
11.04
11.94
13.47
10.57
14.26
6.95
11.47
7.89
9.98
13.61
7.98
10.54
6.51
10.13
8.06
BPL Population (%)
Above 12.15 High
10.05 - 12.15 Upper Moderate
7.94 - 10.04 Lower Moderate
Below 7.94 Low
30 15 0 30 60 90
Kms

Map 5.1

population. Majority of districts spread all over the state have shown moderate deprivation level by recording IOD-income between 7.94 per cent and 12.15 per cent. The difference of 8.43 percentage points between the top and bottom ranked districts underlines the fact that inter-district disparities as regards to BPL population are reasonably at the higher level.

Educational Deprivation

Table 5.2: Index of Deprivation in Education (2001)

District	*Rankings*
Fatehabad	1
Kaithal	2
Sirsa	3
Jind	4
Gurgaon	5
Hisar	6
Bhiwani	7
Karnal	8
Panipat	9
Kurukshetra	10
Mahendergarh	11
Faridabad	12
Yamunanagar	13
Jhajjar	14
Sonepat	15
Rohtak	16
Panchkula	17
Rewari	18
Ambala	19

Illiteracy is an important indicator of knowledge deprivation. The deprivation level is convincingly high at the state level where 32.09 per cent of the population is illiterate. The district- wise statistics is demonstrated through Map 5.2 and Table 5.2. Fatehabad district appears at the top where more than 42 per cent of the population is found illiterate. It is closely followed by Kaithal (40.98 per cent), Sirsa (39.45 per cent) and Jind (37.88 per cent) districts. As a result, all of these districts have been placed in the category of high deprivation. Ambala district, on the other end of the scale has shown lowest deprivation level (24.69 per cent) in the state and hence placed at the bottom. Rewari (24.75 per cent) district appears as the district with lowest deprivation in south Haryana.

However, Panchkula (26.00 per cent), Rohtak (26.28 per cent), Sonepat (27.21 per cent), Jhajjar (27.62 per cent) and Yamunanagar (28.37 per cent) districts have also found place in the category of low deprivation by restricting their deprivation level below 29.02 per cent. One can clearly observe that the districts surrounding National Capital have shown low deprivation, however, Gurgaon is an exception. A reasonable gap of

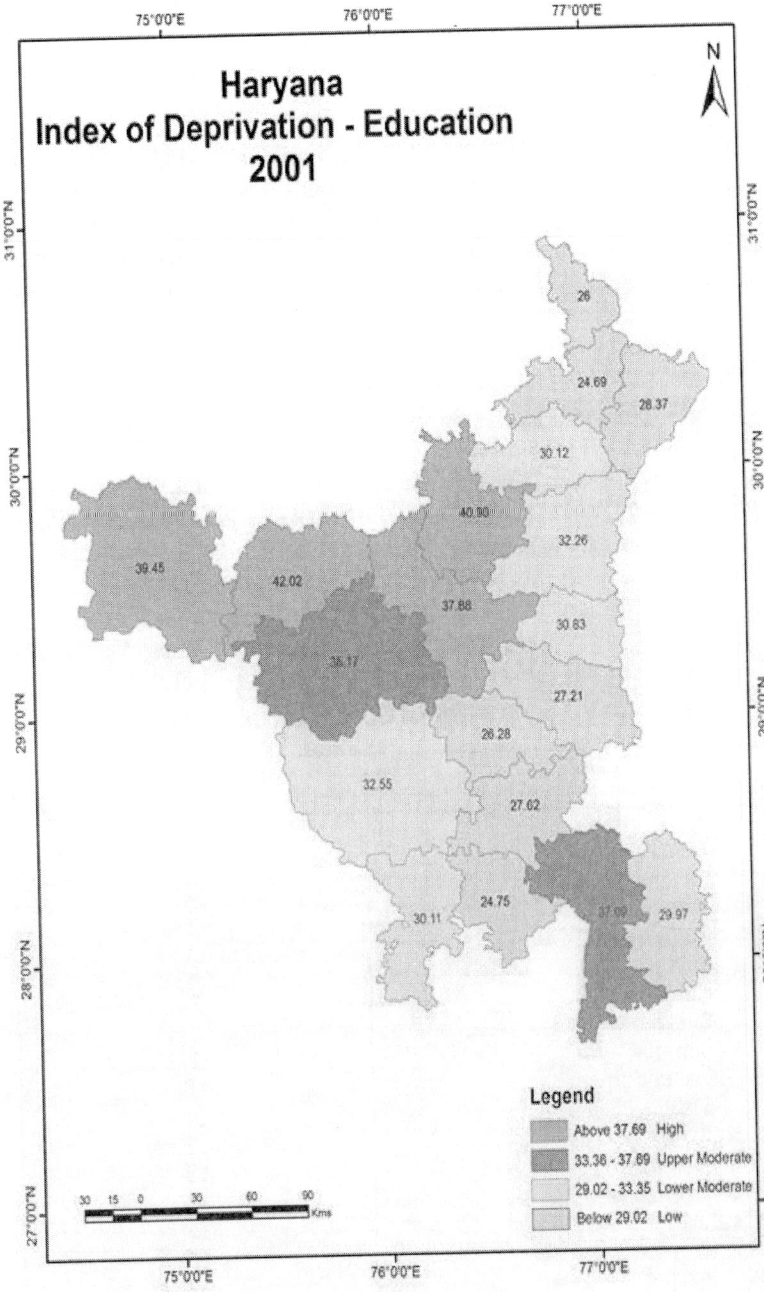
Haryana
Index of Deprivation - Education
2001
N
75°0'0"E
76°0'0"E
77°0'0"E
31°0'0"N
30°0'0"N
29°0'0"N
28°0'0"N
27°0'0"N
26
24.69
28.37
30.12
40.90
32.26
39.45
42.02
37.88
30.83
35.17
27.21
26.28
32.55
27.62
24.75
30.11
37.09
29.97
Legend
Above 37.69 High
33.36 - 37.69 Upper Moderate
29.02 - 33.35 Lower Moderate
Below 29.02 Low
30 15 0 30 60 90
Kms

Map 5.2

17.33 percentage points between the districts with extreme deprivation level again draws the attention of the regional planners.

Health Deprivation

IOD-health is the third and final broad dimension which encompasses five basic dimensions- two of them showing deprivation on account of health infrastructure (population without any government health facility and population without doctor) whereas the other three representing deprivation with respect to health awareness (women do not receive full ante-natal check-ups, non-institutional deliveries and children age 12-35 months not fully vaccinated). As far as the magnitude of deprivation at the state level is concerned, 36 per cent of the villages are devoid of govt. health facility. The geographical distribution of districts with diverse deprivation level on govt. health facility is shown in Map 5.3 whereas their rankings are presented in Table 5.3.

Surprisingly the three districts of northern Haryana (Yamunanagar, Panchkula and Ambala) that have come up with the highest deprivation level in terms of govt. health facility are those that have performed appreciably well in the human development parameters. It is a demoralising fact that as much as 63.80 per cent of the rural settlements of Yamunanagar district are devoid of any type of govt. health facility. The situation of second ranked Ambala (55.70 per cent) and third ranked

Table 5.3: Villages without Govt. Health Facility (2001)

District	*Rankings*
Yamunanagar	1
Ambala	2
Panchkula	3
Jind	4
Kurukshetra	5
Rewari	6
Gurgaon	7
Bhiwani	8
Sonepat	9
Mahendergarh	10
Sirsa	11
Jhajjar	12
Faridabad	13
Fatehabad	14
Kaithal	15
Karnal	16
Panipat	17
Rohtak	18
Hisar	19

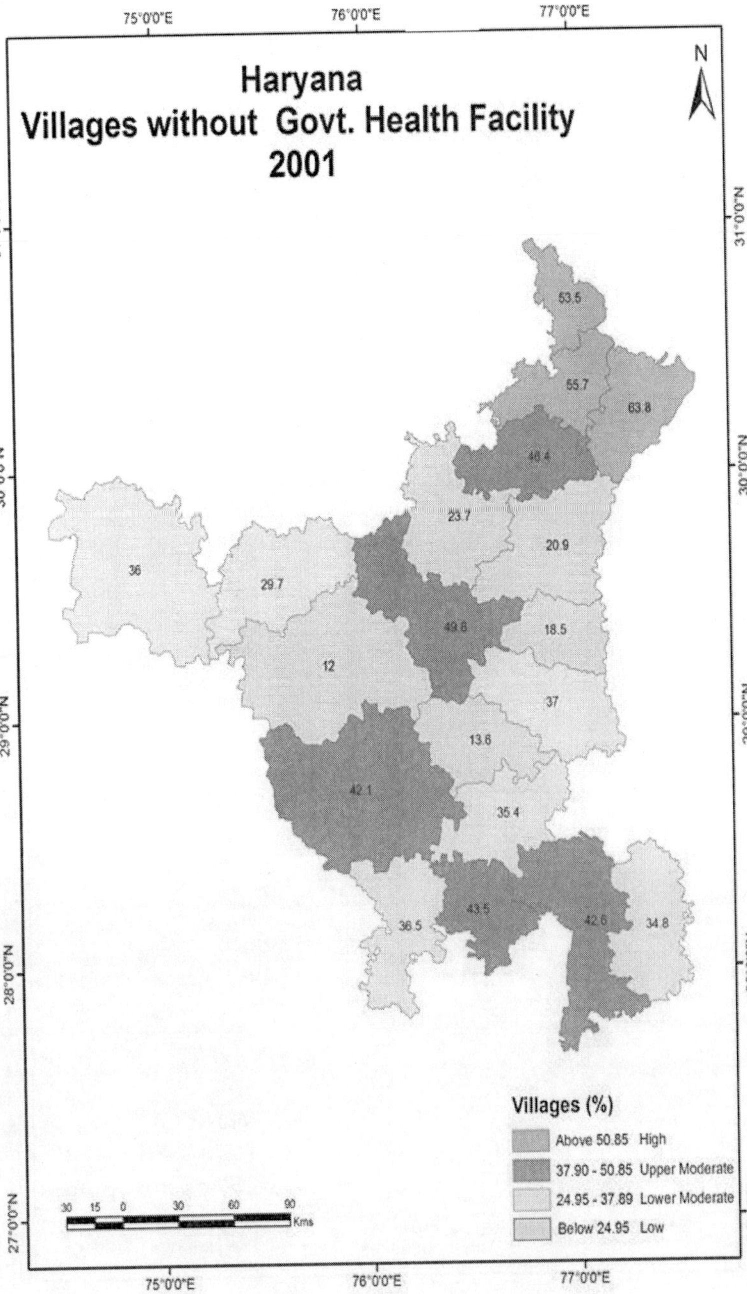
Haryana
Villages without Govt. Health Facility
2001
N
75°0'0"E
76°0'0"E
77°0'0"E
31°0'0"N
30°0'0"N
29°0'0"N
28°0'0"N
27°0'0"N
53.5
55.7
63.8
46.4
23.7
20.9
36
29.7
49.8
18.5
12
37
13.6
42.1
35.4
43.5
36.5
42.6
34.8
Villages (%)
Above 50.85 High
37.90 - 50.85 Upper Moderate
24.95 - 37.89 Lower Moderate
Below 24.95 Low
30 15 0 30 60 90
Kms

Map 5.3

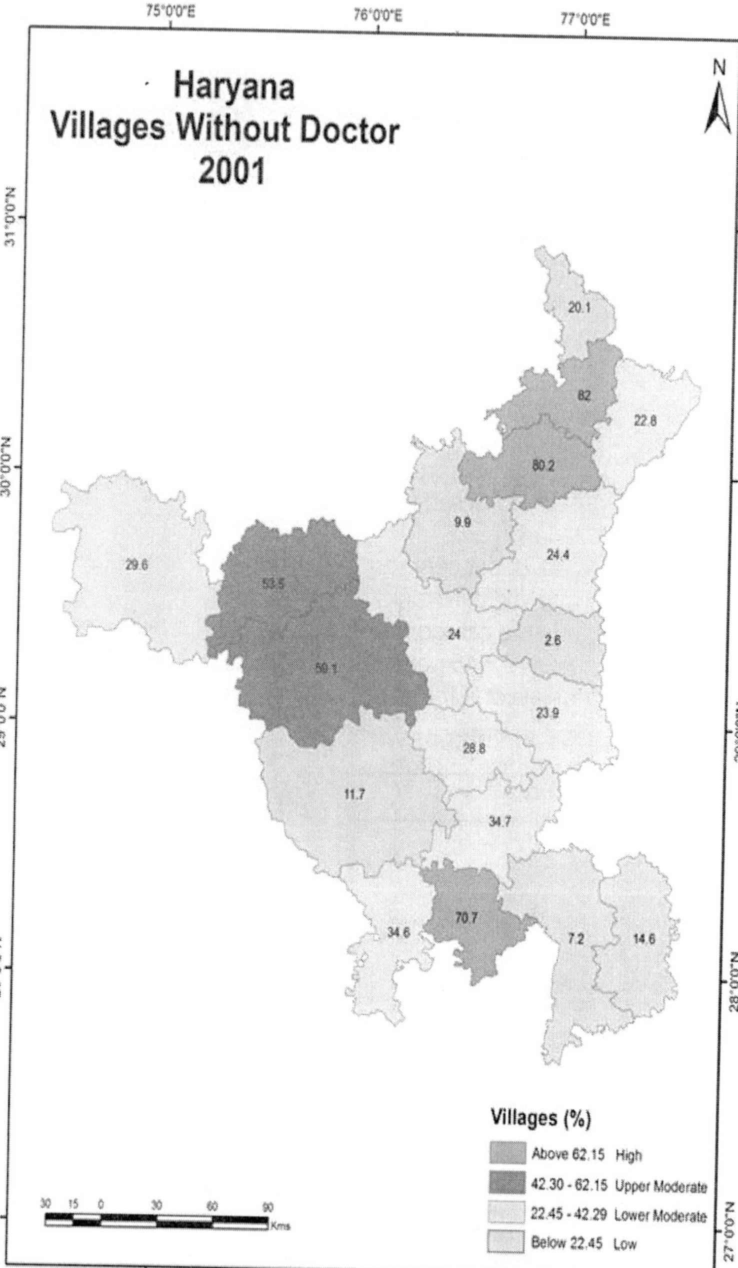
Haryana
Villages Without Doctor
2001
N
75°0'0"E
76°0'0"E
77°0'0"E
31°0'0"N
30°0'0"N
29°0'0"N
28°0'0"N
27°0'0"N
20.1
62
22.8
60.2
9.9
24.4
29.6
53.5
24
2.6
59.1
23.9
28.8
11.7
34.7
70.7
34.6
7.2
14.6
30 15 0 30 60 90
Kms
Villages (%)
Above 62.15 High
42.30 - 62.15 Upper Moderate
22.45 - 42.29 Lower Moderate
Below 22.45 Low

Map 5.4

Panchkula (53.50 per cent) is equally worse. On the other end of the deprivation scale there are five districts that have restricted their deprivation level below 24.95 per cent. Hisar district is at the bottom with deprivation level as low as 12.00 per cent. The other districts that find place in this category are Rohtak (13.60 per cent), Panipat (18.50 per cent), Karnal (20.90 per cent) and Kaithal (23.70 per cent). These districts are chiefly concentrated in the central part of the state. The districts situated in the south and western parts of the state have kept their deprivation level between 24.95 per cent and 50.85 per cent thereby these are placed in the categories of moderate deprivation. Striking regional disparities are evident in Haryana as the availability of government health centres is not a regular phenomenon across the districts.

More than 70 per cent rural settlements of Ambala, Kurukshetra and Rewari districts are deprived of doctor facility. Hence, these districts have been placed into high deprivation category. Ambala district is most deprived as 82.00 per cent of the rural settlements are found without doctor facility (Map 5.4 and Table 5.4).

Kurukshetra (80.20 per cent) and Rewari (70.70 per cent) districts have obtained second and third ranks respectively. On the other extreme, six districts appear in the category of low deprivation by containing the deprivation level below 22.45 per cent. The availability of doctors in the villages of Panipat district is found appreciably high as the deprivation

Table 5.4: Villages without Doctor (2001)

District	*Rankings*
Ambala	1
Kurukshetra	2
Rewari	3
Hisar	4
Fatehabad	5
Jhajjar	6
Mahendergarh	7
Sirsa	8
Rohtak	9
Karnal	10
Jind	11
Sonepat	12
Yamunanagar	13
Panchkula	14
Faridabad	15
Bhiwani	16
Kaithal	17
Gurgaon	18
Panipat	19

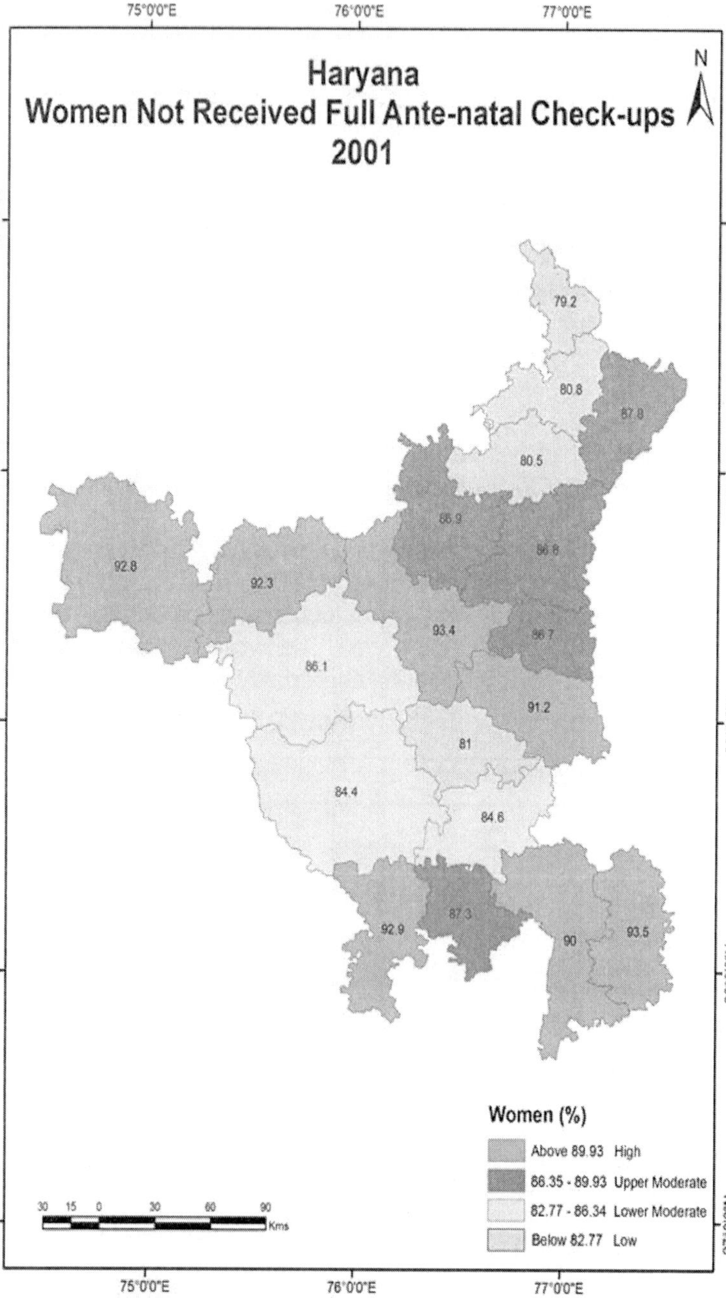
75°0'0"E
76°0'0"E
77°0'0"E
Haryana
Women Not Received Full Ante-natal Check-ups
2001
N
31°0'0"N
30°0'0"N
29°0'0"N
28°0'0"N
27°0'0"N
79.2
80.8
87.8
80.5
88.9
88.8
92.8
92.3
93.4
88.7
86.1
91.2
81
84.4
84.6
87.3
92.9
90
93.5
Women (%)
Above 89.93 High
86.35 - 89.93 Upper Moderate
82.77 - 86.34 Lower Moderate
Below 82.77 Low
30 15 0 30 60 90
Kms

Map 5.5

level here is observed as low as 2.60 per cent thereby awarded the last rank. The maximum number (8) of districts, covering all parts of the state, has also restricted the deprivation level between 22.45 per cent and 42.29 per cent thereby grouped in the lower moderate category. The deprivation level in Hisar (59.10 per cent) and Fatehabad (53.50 per cent) districts is high enough to place them in the category of upper moderate deprivation level. Both of these districts are located in the western part of the state.

Ambala, Rewari and Kurukshetra districts have shown high deprivation in terms of both the variables pertaining to health infrastructure. The districts like Yamunanagar, Panchkula, Gurgaon and Jind which demonstrate high deprivation in terms of government health facility have shown reasonably better performance in terms of facility of doctors thereby awarded lower rank of derivation whereas the opposite trend is shown by the districts of Hisar, Rohtak, Fatehabad and Jhajjar. The deprivation level is consistently low in the districts of Panipat, Kaithal, Karnal and Faridabad in terms of both the variables of health infrastructure (compare Table 5.3 and Table 5.4).

The three variables focussing on the deprivation in health awareness of the people have been examined. Map 5.5 reflects district-wise deprivation level in terms of women not receiving ante-natal check-ups during pregnancy and their rankings are presented in Table 5.5. The

Table 5.5: Women Not Received Full Ante-natal Check-ups (2001)

District	*Rankings*
Faridabad	1
Jind	2
Mahendergarh	3
Sirsa	4
Fatehabad	5
Sonepat	6
Gurgaon	7
Yamunanagar	8
Rewari	9
Kaithal	10
Karnal	11
Panipat	12
Hisar	13
Jhajjar	14
Bhiwani	15
Rohtak	16
Ambala	17
Kurukshetra	18
Panchkula	19

given data reveals that this significant component of safe motherhood is highly neglected in the state as 88.20 per cent of the population in this segment did not get full ante-natal check-ups. Since the deprivation level is too high across all the districts, inter-district variations are not as high as observed in the other dimensions. An east to west strip can be seen in the central part of the state indicating the districts that have deprivation level above 90 per cent. The situation of southern districts is also no better. However, some of the northern districts have come up with relatively low deprivation but it is, too, hovering near 80 per cent mark.

A comparative analysis of Table 5.4 and Table 5.5 brings out that Kurukshetra and Ambala districts, which have captured the front seat with high deprivation level in terms of government doctor, are standing behind as regards to non-receipt of full ante-natal check-ups.

Undoubtedly non-institutional deliveries increase the health risk not only for the mother but also for the newborn baby. This is why; it has been an important thrust area of the government to encourage institutional deliveries in proper hygienic conditions under the supervision of trained health professionals. Taking little note of government's efforts 64.90 per cent of the women in the state have undergone non-institutional deliveries. Map 5.6 depicts district-wise deprivation level in terms of non-institutional deliveries and Table 5.6 shows their rankings.

Table 5.6: Non-institutional Deliveries (2001)

District	*Rankings*
Gurgaon	1
Jind	2
Kaithal	3
Faridabad	4
Yamunanagar	5
Hisar	6
Sirsa	7
Karnal	8
Panipat	9
Bhiwani	10
Mahendergarh	11
Fatehabad	12
Sonepat	13
Rohtak	14
Panchkula	15
Rewari	16
Jhajjar	17
Kurukshetra	18
Ambala	19

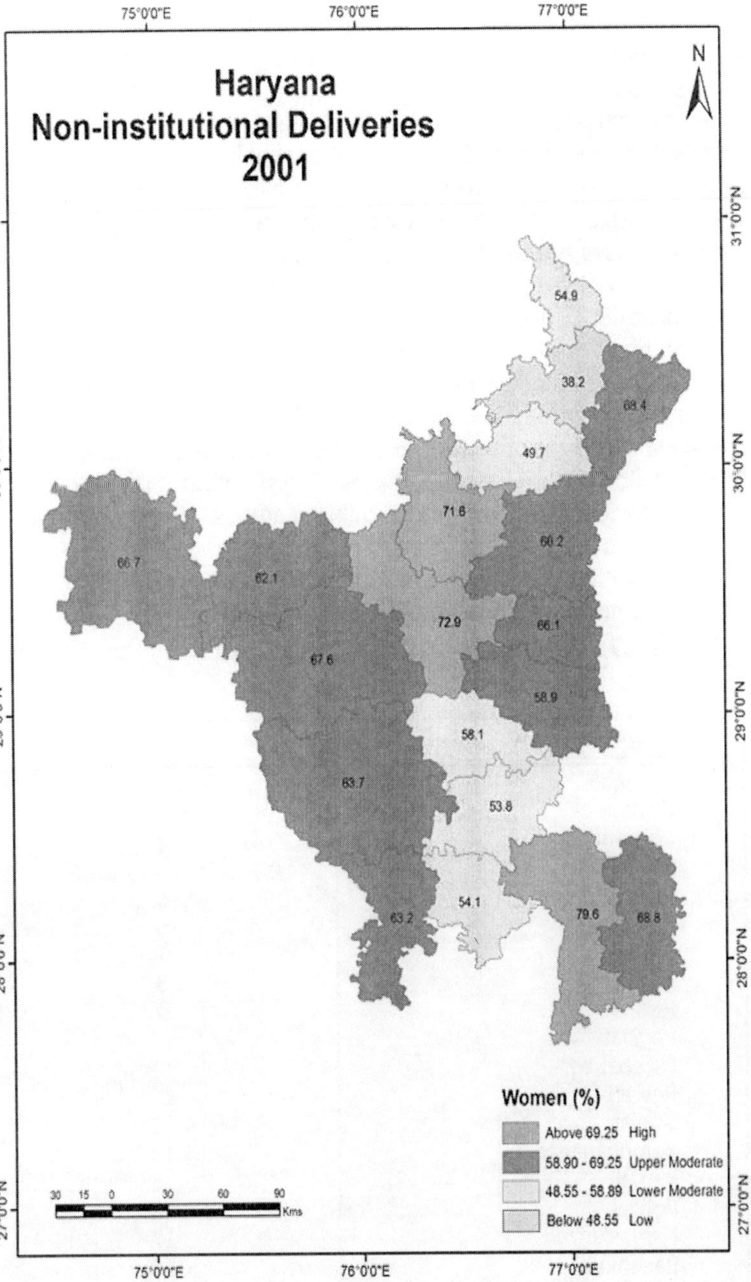
Haryana
Non-institutional Deliveries
2001
N
75°0'0"E
76°0'0"E
77°0'0"E
31°0'0"N
30°0'0"N
29°0'0"N
28°0'0"N
27°0'0"N
54.9
38.2
68.4
49.7
71.6
60.2
66.7
62.1
72.9
66.1
67.6
58.9
58.1
63.7
53.8
54.1
63.2
79.6
68.8
Women (%)
Above 69.25 High
58.90 - 69.25 Upper Moderate
48.55 - 58.89 Lower Moderate
Below 48.55 Low
30 15 0 30 60 90
Kms

Map 5.6

Three districts have appeared in the category of high deprivation level where more than 69.20 per cent of the women have had non-institutional deliveries. Gurgaon tops the list with a figure of 79.60 per cent which is followed by Jind (72.90 per cent) and Kaithal (71.60 per cent) districts with second and third ranks respectively. Lowest level of deprivation is found in Ambala district where only 38.20 per cent of the women have experienced non-institutional deliveries and it is the only district that has been placed in the category of low deprivation. It is in contrast with the very high deprivation level recorded by Ambala in both the indicators of health infrastructure. The highest number (10) of districts has come up with upper moderate deprivation level ranging from 58.90 per cent to 69.25 per cent.

The immunization of children against six serious but preventable diseases is the main component of the child survival programme. The Government of India has initiated the programme in every district of the country with the objective of reducing morbidity, mortality and disabilities among children from the six diseases. The situation is rather critical in Haryana as 37.10 per cent of the children age 12-35 months have not been covered in the full vaccination programme as a whole. The district wise deprivation level in terms vaccination has been shown in Map 5.7 and their rankings are presented in Table 5.7.

Table 5.7: Children Age 12-35 Months Not Fully Vaccinated (2001)

District	*Rankings*
Gurgaon	1
Kaithal	2
Bhiwani	3
Sirsa	4
Mahendergarh	5
Faridabad	6
Sonepat	7
Jind	8
Hisar	9
Panipat	10
Fatehabad	11
Rewari	12
Jhajjar	13
Yamunanagar	14
Karnal	15
Rohtak	16
Kurukshetra	17
Panchkula	18
Ambala	19

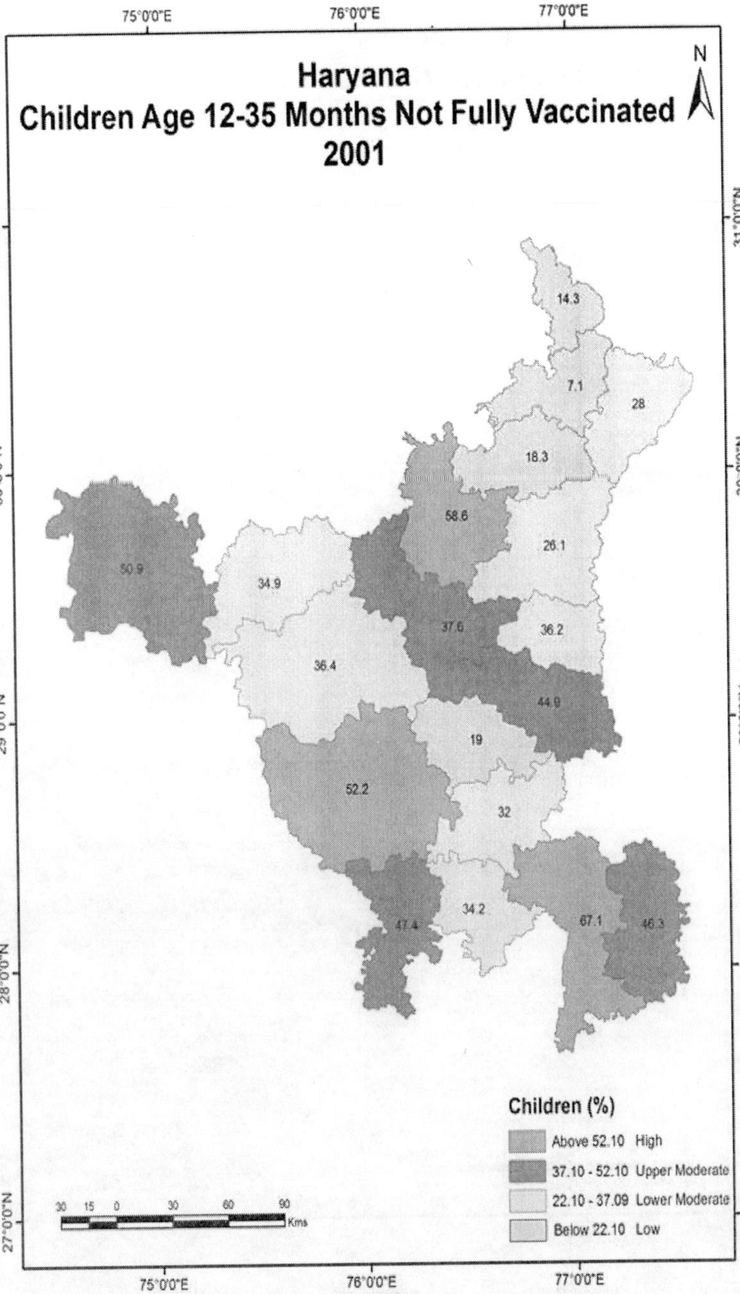
Haryana
Children Age 12-35 Months Not Fully Vaccinated
2001
N
75°0'0"E
76°0'0"E
77°0'0"E
31°0'0"N
30°0'0"N
29°0'0"N
28°0'0"N
27°0'0"N
14.3
7.1
28
18.3
58.6
26.1
50.9
34.9
37.6
36.2
36.4
44.9
19
52.2
32
34.2
47.4
67.1
46.3
Children (%)
Above 52.10 High
37.10 - 52.10 Upper Moderate
22.10 - 37.09 Lower Moderate
Below 22.10 Low
30 15 0 30 60 90
Kms

Map 5.7

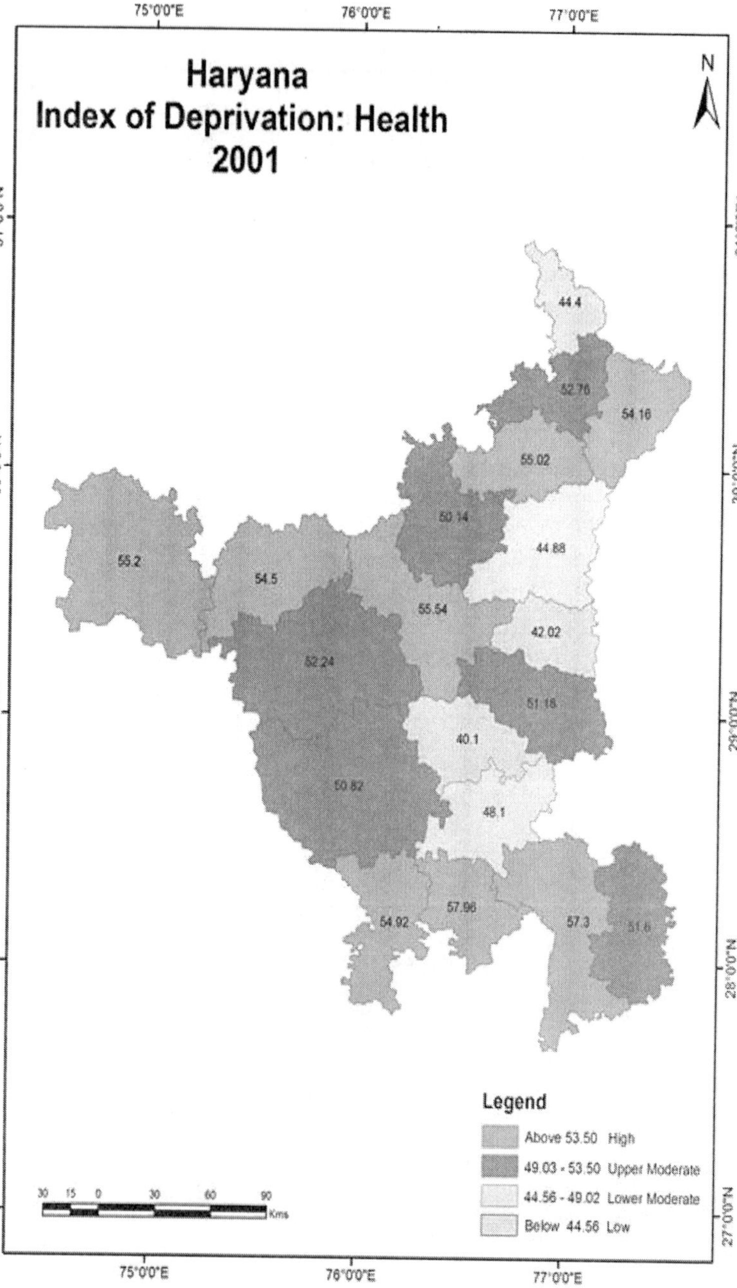
Haryana
Index of Deprivation: Health
2001
N
44.4
52.76
54.16
55.02
50.14
44.88
55.2
54.5
55.54
42.02
52.24
51.18
40.1
50.82
48.1
57.96
54.92
57.3
51.6
Legend
Above 53.50 High
49.03 - 53.50 Upper Moderate
44.56 - 49.02 Lower Moderate
Below 44.56 Low
Kms
75°0'0"E
76°0'0"E
77°0'0"E
31°0'0"N
30°0'0"N
29°0'0"N
28°0'0"N
27°0'0"N

Map 5.8

Gurgaon leads the category of high deprivation with a value as high as 67.10 per cent and thus it has been awarded top rank. The second ranked district Kaithal (58.60 per cent) and the third ranked district Bhiwani (52.20 per cent) have also joined the category of high deprivation level. The category of low deprivation is appropriately represented by Ambala district with the lowest value of 7.10 per cent thereby awarded bottom rank. Three other districts i.e. Panchkula (14.30 per cent), Kurukshetra (18.30 per cent) and Rohtak (19.00 per cent) have also found place in this category. A huge difference of 60.00 per centage points between the deprivation levels of districts with two extremes strongly advocates the existence of great deal of inter-district variations in this perspective.

Having discussed all the five variables focusing on the health issues, IOD-health is now computed by combining all of them. As a whole the deprivation level as regards to health is 51.96 per cent at the state level, which is fairly high on the scale. Notwithstanding the sound income base (IOD-income is as low as 10.21 per cent) and satisfactory education base (IOD-education confines to 30.32 per cent) the deprivation level on health is reasonably high. Though, it has resulted in the modest inter-district variation on IOD-health.

District-wise trend as depicted in Map 5.8 reflects that high deprivation level persists in eight districts where IOD-health is found above 53.50 per cent. Most of the districts situated in the southern and western parts of

Table 5.8: Index of Deprivation in Health (2001)

District	*Rankings*
Rewari	1
Gurgaon	2
Jind	3
Sirsa	4
Kurukshetra	5
Mahendergarh	6
Fatehabad	7
Yamunanagar	8
Ambala	9
Hisar	10
Faridabad	11
Sonepat	12
Bhiwani	13
Kaithal	14
Jhajjar	15
Karnal	16
Panchkula	17
Panipat	18
Rohtak	19

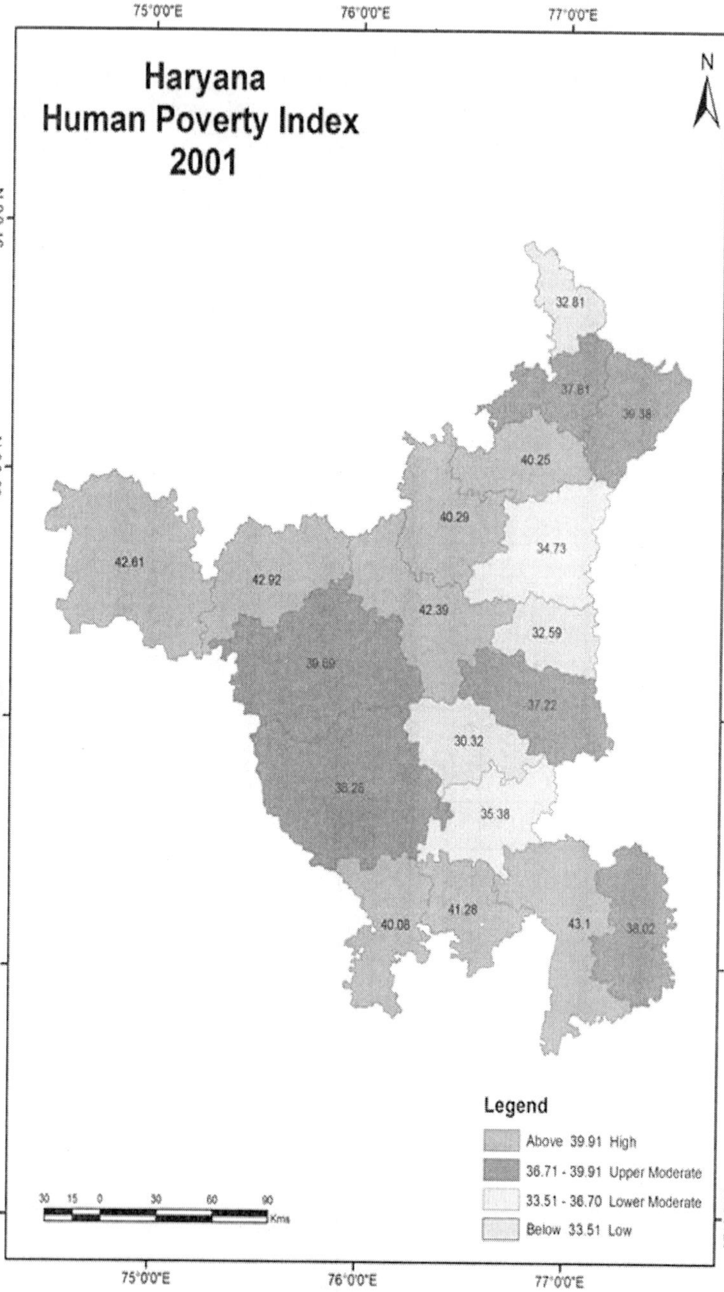
75°0'0"E
76°0'0"E
77°0'0"E
Haryana
Human Poverty Index
2001
N
31°0'0"N
30°0'0"N
29°0'0"N
28°0'0"N
27°0'0"N
32.81
37.81
39.38
40.25
40.29
34.73
42.61
42.92
42.39
32.59
39.69
37.22
30.32
38.26
35.38
41.28
40.08
43.1
38.02
Legend
Above 39.91 High
36.71 - 39.91 Upper Moderate
33.51 - 36.70 Lower Moderate
Below 33.51 Low
30 15 0 30 60 90
Kms

Map 5.9

Table 5.9: Human Poverty Index (2001)

District	*Rankings*
Gurgaon	1
Fatehabad	2
Sirsa	3
Jind	4
Rewari	5
Kaithal	6
Kurukshetra	7
Mahendergarh	8
Hisar	9
Yamunanagar	10
Bhiwani	11
Faridabad	12
Ambala	13
Sonepat	14
Jhajjar	15
Karnal	16
Panchkula	17
Panipat	18
Rohtak	19

the state have demonstrated high deprivation level on health as Rewari being the leader with the highest value of 57.96 per cent. Maximum numbers of districts have found place in two middle categories by keeping their deprivation level moderate between 44.56 per cent and 53.50 per cent. Rohtak district has been placed at the bottom as it has recorded the lowest (40.10 per cent) deprivation level. Panipat and Panchkula districts have joined Rohtak in the category of low deprivation. District-wise rankings are given in Table 5.8.

A perusal of tables depicting the rankings of districts as regards to five health variables brings out that the top rank awarded to Rewari district on IOD-health is largely because of the prevalence of high deprivation on health infrastructure. While the high deprivation level on health awareness has a great bearing on the second ranked district of Gurgaon. The case of third ranked district of Jind is somewhat different as it has obtained high deprivation in three variables associated with both the sub-sectors i.e. health infrastructure as well as health awareness.

Besides, the high degree of deprivation level in health infrastructure has up scaled Ambala district into middle ranked districts albeit its lowest rankings on health awareness. The situation of Kurukshetra is no different. Almost opposite is the case of Fatehabad district.

Human Poverty Index

Map 5.9 portrays Human Poverty Index. At the state level it is 38.74. Poverty is highly pervasive in as many as eight districts across the state where the HPI is found above 39.91 per cent. The highest HPI value of 43.10 is visible in Gurgaon thereby it has been awarded top rank (Table 5.9). Districts like Fatehabad (42.92), Sirsa (42.61) and Jind (42.39) are closely behind it with second, third and fourth ranks respectively. However, Rohtak district represents the lower end of the scale with HPI value as low as 30.32 thereby awarded bottom rank. Panipat (32.59) and Panchkula (32.81) have also found place in the category of low HPI. All the remaining districts have been placed in the two moderate categories as they have contained their HPI value between 33.51 and 39.91. The difference of 13.10 index points between the top ranked and bottom ranked districts, once again gives support to higher inter-district disparities in the state.

As explained earlier that the HPI is an outcome of extent of deprivation suffered by a district in terms of three dimensions of development, it becomes pertinent to examine whether an individual dimension or a combination of dimensions have significantly affected the product. In this regard, Table 5.10 provides some revealing conclusions as described below:

- Surprisingly, Gurgaon district in the vicinity of the National Capital has appeared as the highest deprived district in terms of human development by obtaining HPI value of 43.10 per cent. The reasons are quite obvious. The district excels in one of the three dimensions i.e. income by virtue of renowned industrial development restricted to its urban areas, but on the contrary the degree of deprivation in terms of all the three dimensions is as high over the large rural tracts as it has been bounced up at the top end of HPI scale.
- On account of highest deprivation on health dimension, Rewari district has been included in the top five districts with the highest deprivation even though it has shown lower deprivation on the other two dimensions of income and education.
- Jhajjar district has achieved a lower 15th rank in two of the three dimensions and 14th rank in the third dimension. By virtue of its consistency it has been awarded 15th rank on the HPI. None of the other districts in the state has shown such consistency. However, the districts like Sirsa, Jind (with higher deprivation) and Rohtak, Panchkula, Sonepat (with lower deprivation) are somewhat consistent.

Table 5.10: Construction of Human Poverty Index: District-wise Rankings (2001)

Districts	*IOD-income*	*IOD-education*	*IOD-health*	*HPI*
Gurgaon	11	5	2	1
Fatehabad	9	1	7	2
Sirsa	3	3	4	3
Jind	1	4	3	4
Rewari	10	18	1	5
Kaithal	8	2	14	6
Kurukshetra	4	10	5	7
Mahendergarh	18	11	6	8
Hisar	6	6	10	9
Yamunanagar	7	13	8	10
Bhiwani	2	7	13	11
Faridabad	14	12	11	12
Ambala	19	19	9	13
Sonepat	16	15	12	14
Jhajjar	15	14	15	15
Karnal	5	8	16	16
Panchkula	13	17	17	17
Panipat	17	9	18	18
Rohtak	12	16	19	19
Correlation between the ranks of individual dimensions with the HPI	**0.42**	**0.61**	**0.87**	

- Highly diverse ranks on the three dimensions in the cases of three southern districts i.e. Gurgaon, Rewari and Mahendergarh reflect that deprivation is not pervasive in all dimensions and these districts can considerably bring down the deprivation level by improving their status in one or two dimensions.
- A high positive correlation of 0.87 between the ranks of IOD-health and of the HPI suggests that the deprivation level on health has a greater bearing on the HPI as compared to the other two dimensions. However, the bearing of income dimension has been the lowest (lowest correlation of 0.42) on the HPI.

Sum up

Considering the three dimensions, health is highly neglected dimension in the state. This is why; it has put decisive impact on Human Poverty Index (HPI) whereas income dimension has properly taken care of thereby associated insignificantly with the HPI. Not only the inter-district disparities but intra-district disparities are considerably high. Gurgaon district in the vicinity of the National Capital has appeared as the highest deprived district in terms of human development. It excels in income dimension by virtue of renowned industrial development restricted to its urban areas, but on the contrary the degree of deprivation in terms of all the three dimensions is reasonably high over the large rural tracts. Jhajjar is the only district that has consistently shown lower deprivation in all the three dimensions. While highly diverse ranks on the three dimensions in the cases of three southern districts i.e. Gurgaon, Rewari and Mahendergarh reflect that deprivation is not pervasive in all dimensions and these districts can considerably bring down the deprivation level by improving their status in one or two dimensions.

6

Human Development Index, 2011

Human Development Index (2011) has been carried out using the same set of variables and the methodology so as to focus on the decadal changes therein. The description is given in the succeeding section.

Income Dimension

The state income index during 2011 has been 0.59. The district-wise rankings have been presented in Table 6.1 and the distribution of districts in different income categories is presented in Map 6.1.

The statistics reveals that Gurgaon district has outpaced all other districts by attaining income index as high as 0.74. Panipat (0.67), Faridabad (0.64) and Panchkula (0.64) have been placed at second, third and fourth place respectively. However, Gurgaon is the only district that occupies a place in the category of high development whereas the other three have been grouped in the category of upper moderate attainment level. Mahendergarh district (0.49), on the other hand, has been placed at last rank which is immediately preceded by Kaithal (0.51) and Bhiwani (0.51) districts. Four districts namely Hisar, Sonepat, Karnal and Yamunanagar, with an equal strength of income index (0.56) have shown bright prospects for development; however, Ambala district in the north and Rewari district in the south lead these districts in the category of lower moderate attainment level. A reasonable difference of 0.25 index points between top and bottom ranked districts underlines great income disparities among the districts. Less than one-third of the districts have attained index value greater than the state average which reflects that higher ranking districts have great bearing on the state index value. The districts located in the National Capital Region (NCR) have shown fairly high income index.

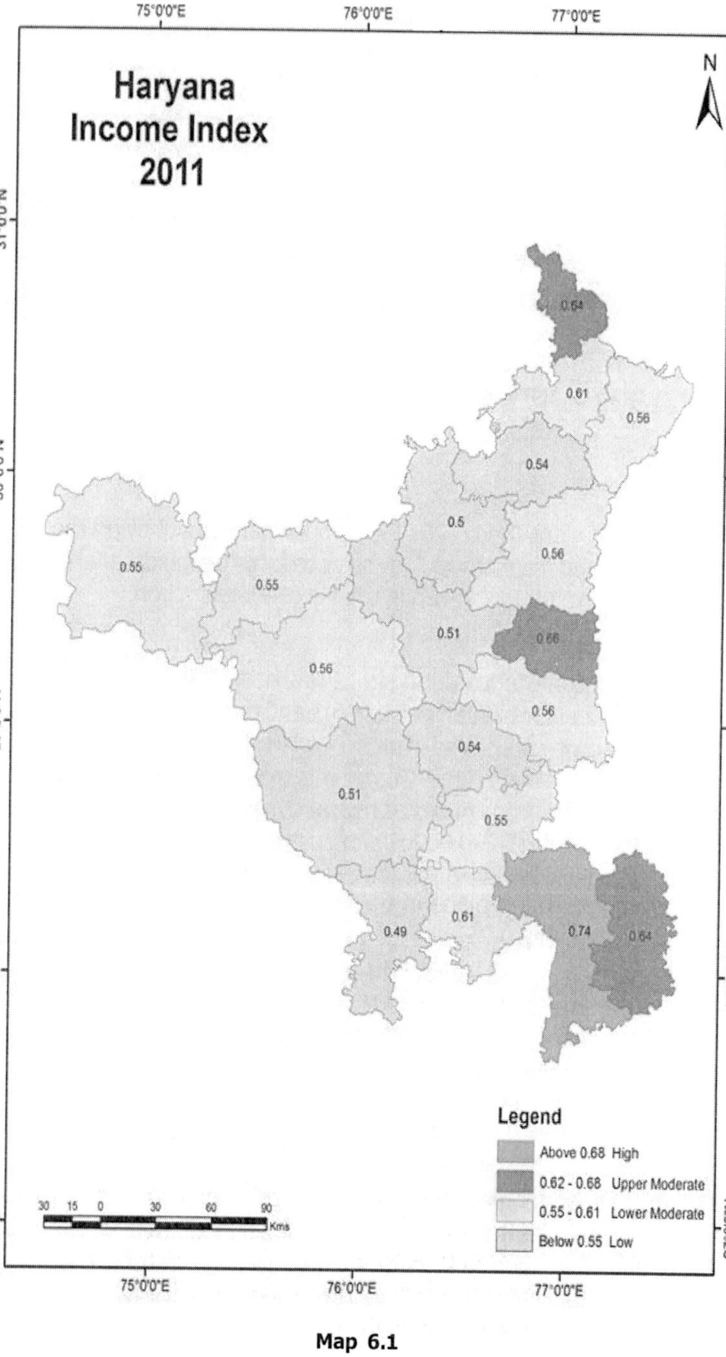
75°0'0"E
76°0'0"E
77°0'0"E
Haryana
Income Index
2011
N
31°0'0"N
30°0'0"N
29°0'0"N
28°0'0"N
27°0'0"N
0.64
0.61
0.56
0.54
0.5
0.56
0.55
0.55
0.51
0.66
0.56
0.56
0.54
0.51
0.55
0.61
0.49
0.74
0.64
Legend
Above 0.68 High
0.62 - 0.68 Upper Moderate
0.55 - 0.61 Lower Moderate
Below 0.55 Low
30 15 0 30 60 90
Kms

Map 6.1

Table 6.1: Income Index (2001)

Districts	*Rankings*
Gurgaon	1
Panipat	2
Faridabad	3
Panchkula	4
Ambala	5
Rewari	6
Hisar	7
Sonepat	8
Karnal	9
Yamunanagar	10
Sirsa	11
Fatehabad	12
Jhajjar	13
Kurukshetra	14
Rohtak	15
Jind	16
Bhiwani	17
Kaithal	18
Mahendergarh	19

Education Dimension

Considering the literacy levels of population, education index has been carried out. As a whole the education index of the state for 2011 amounts to 0.77. Out of the total (19), as many as ten districts have recorded education index above the state average. Map 6.2 illustrates the geographical distribution of districts into four categories of attainment level whereas the rankings of districts are depicted in Table 6.2. Most of the districts have found place in the first two categories by recording education index above 0.75.

Two districts in the extreme north i.e. Panchkula (0.83) and Ambala (0.83) on the one hand, and the two districts in the south i.e. Rewari (0.82) and Jhajjar (0.81), on the other hand, have attained the top four ranks respectively thereby placed in the category of high development. Sonepat district has also joined these districts in this category. Fatehabad (0.69), Sirsa (0.70) and Kaithal (0.71) districts represent the darker side of development as these districts have been placed in the last category i.e. category of low development by recording education index below 0.72. These districts are concentrated in the western part of the state. Keeping in mind the size and geographical conditions of the state, the difference of 0.14 index points between the education indexes of districts with two extremes indicates that inter-district disparities are fairly high in this context.

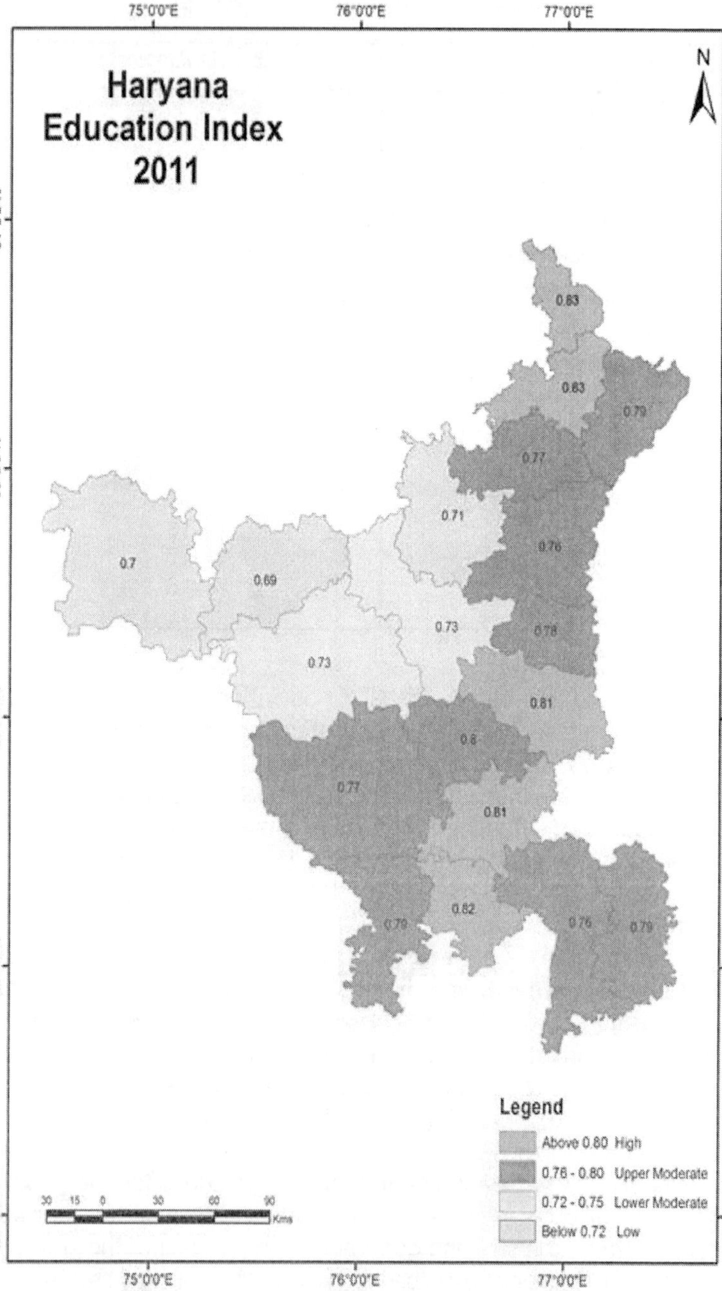
Haryana
Education Index
2011
N
75°0'0"E
76°0'0"E
77°0'0"E
31°0'0"N
30°0'0"N
29°0'0"N
28°0'0"N
27°0'0"N
0.83
0.83
0.79
0.77
0.71
0.76
0.7
0.69
0.73
0.78
0.73
0.81
0.8
0.77
0.81
0.82
0.79
0.76
0.79
Legend
Above 0.80 High
0.76 - 0.80 Upper Moderate
0.72 - 0.75 Lower Moderate
Below 0.72 Low
30 15 0 30 60 90
Kms

Map 6.2

Table 6.2: Education Index (2011)

Districts	*Rankings*
Panchkula	1
Ambala	2
Rewari	3
Jhajjar	4
Sonepat	5
Rohtak	6
Mahendergarh	7
Yamunanagar	8
Faridabad	9
Panipat	10
Bhiwani	11
Kurukshetra	12
Gurgaon	13
Karnal	14
Hisar	15
Jind	16
Kaithal	17
Sirsa	18
Fatehabad	19

Health Dimension

To evaluate health dimension, five indicators covering both the aspects of health i.e. health infrastructure and health awareness have been analysed. Health index is then worked out by averaging the attainment

Table 6.3: Villages with Government Health Facility (2011)

Districts	*Rankings*
Hisar	1
Rohtak	2
Jhajjar	3
Fatehabad	4
Sonepat	5
Jind	6
Kaithal	7
Sirsa	8
Bhiwani	9
Panipat	10
Rewari	11
Kurukshetra	12
Karnal	13
Ambala	14
Mahendergarh	15
Panchkula	16
Gurgaon	17
Faridabad	18
Yamunanagar	19

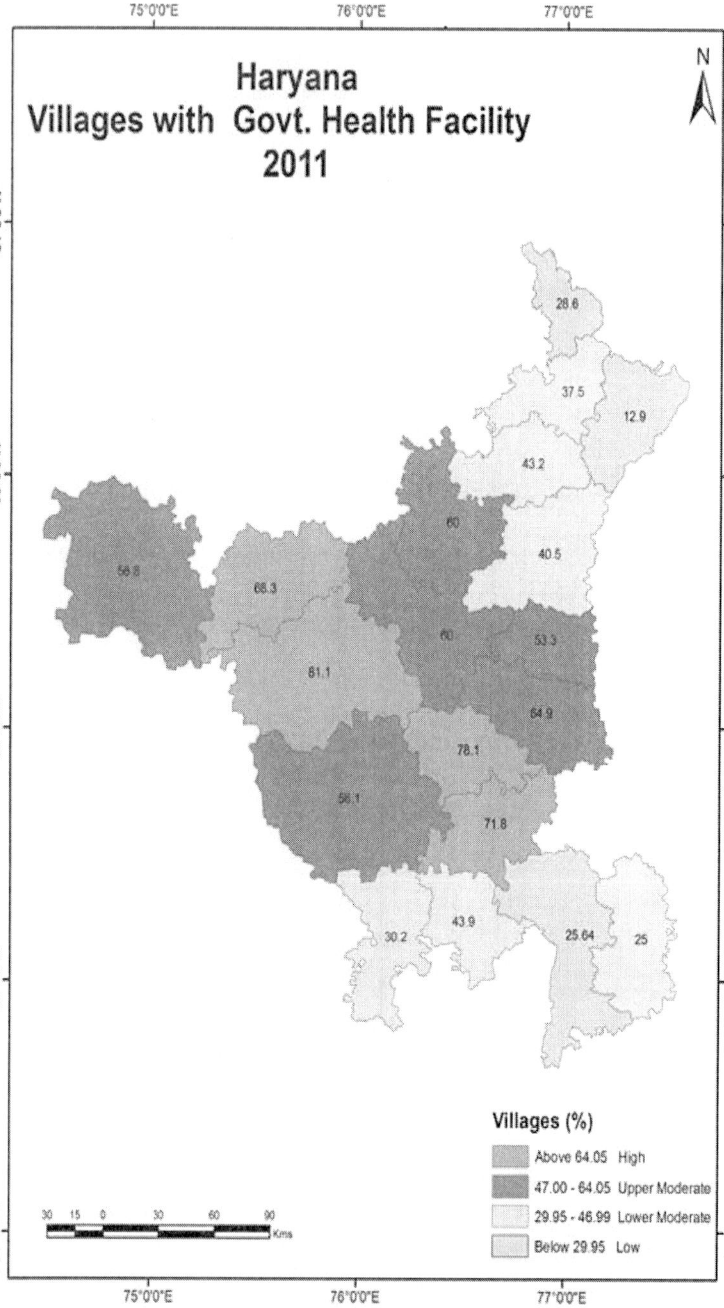
Haryana
Villages with Govt. Health Facility
2011
N
75°0'0"E
76°0'0"E
77°0'0"E
31°0'0"N
30°0'0"N
29°0'0"N
28°0'0"N
27°0'0"N
28.6
37.5
12.9
43.2
60
40.5
56.8
68.3
60
53.3
81.1
64.9
78.1
56.1
71.8
43.9
30.2
25.64
25
Villages (%)
Above 64.05 High
47.00 - 64.05 Upper Moderate
29.95 - 46.99 Lower Moderate
Below 29.95 Low
30 15 0 30 60 90
Kms

Map 6.3

Table 6.4: Villages with Doctor (2011)

Districts	*Rankings*
Karnal	1
Kurukshetra	2
Panipat	3
Sonepat	4
Panchkula	5
Kaithal	6
Ambala	7
Yamunanagar	8
Jind	9
Sirsa	10
Rewari	11
Rohtak	12
Gurgaon	13
Hisar	14
Bhiwani	15
Fatehabad	16
Mahendergarh	17
Jhajjar	18
Faridabad	19

levels of all these five indicators. The attainment levels with respect to all these five indicators as well the health index is discussed separately in the succeeding section.

There are 49.10 per cent of the villages in the state that are equipped with government health facility. Hisar and Yamunanagar districts portray the two extremes of the attainment level where the former is at the top end with an index value of 81.10 per cent and the latter is at the bottom with the index value as low as 12.90 per cent (Map 6.3 and Table 6.3). Rohtak (78.10 per cent), Jhajjar (71.80 per cent), Fatehabad (68.30 per cent) and Sonepat (64.90 per cent) are amongst the districts that have shown high attainment level. The two highly industrialised districts of the state located in the southern part i.e. Gurgaon (25.64 per cent) and Faridabad (25.00 per cent) are lagging behind in government health infrastructure thereby placed in the category of low attainment level. One can clearly detect that the districts located in the west-central part have performed better whereas the attainment level is fairly low in the two pockets of the state- one pocket is in the north and the other is in the south.

So far as the availability of doctor in the villages is concerned, the situation in the state is not encouraging. As a whole there are only

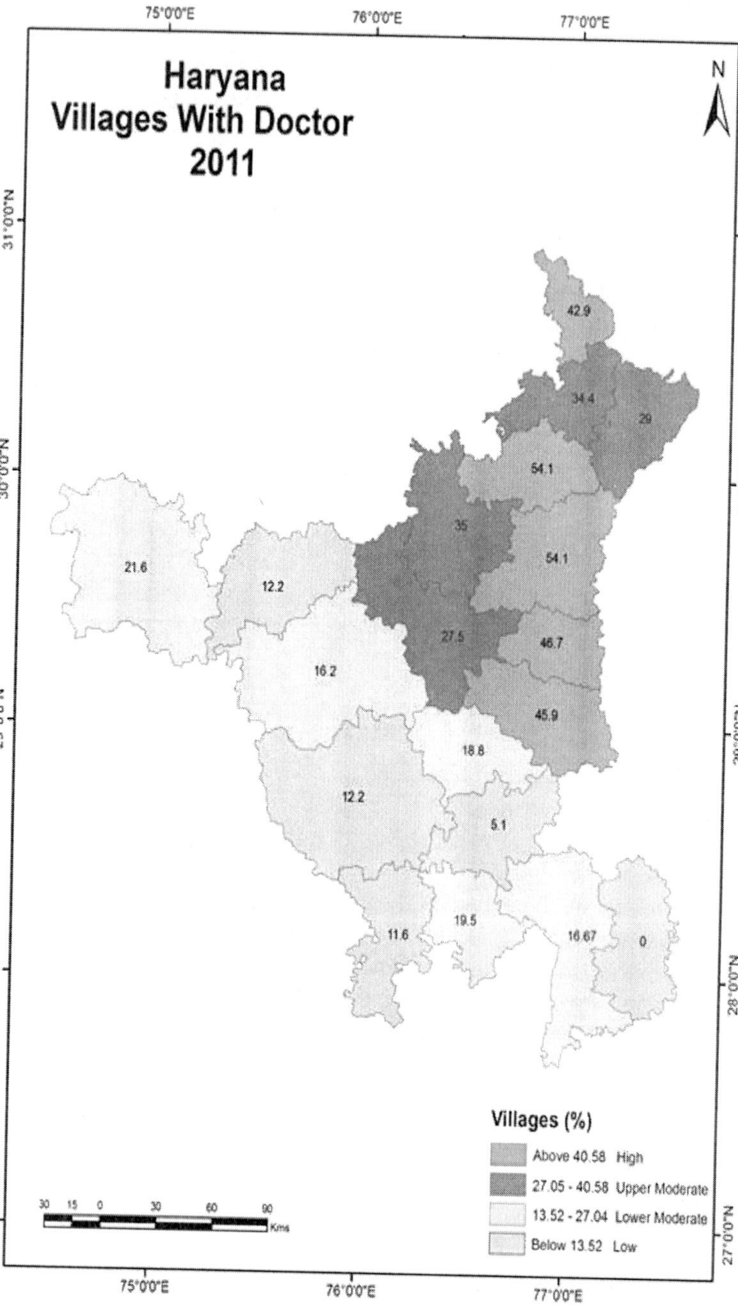
Haryana
Villages With Doctor
2011
75°0'0"E
76°0'0"E
77°0'0"E
31°0'0"N
30°0'0"N
29°0'0"N
28°0'0"N
27°0'0"N
N
42.9
34.4
29
54.1
35
54.1
21.6
12.2
27.5
46.7
16.2
45.9
18.8
12.2
5.1
11.6
19.5
16.67
0
Villages (%)
Above 40.58 High
27.05 - 40.58 Upper Moderate
13.52 - 27.04 Lower Moderate
Below 13.52 Low
30 15 0 30 60 90
Kms

Map 6.4

25.80 per cent of the villages in the state where facility of doctor is available. Surprisingly, the situation is quite alarming in Faridabad district where the facility of doctor has been reported nil in the surveyed villages. The situation of Jhajjar (5.10 per cent) is no better. Some other districts with the attainment level below 13.52 per cent like Mahendergarh (11.60 per cent), Fatehabad (12.20 per cent) and Bhiwani (12.20 per cent) have also been placed in the last category representing low attainment level along with Jhajjar and Faridabad districts (Map 6.4 and Table 6.4). On the other hand, Karnal and Kurukshetra districts have topped the tally where 54.10 per cent of the villages are found with the facility of doctors. Similarly, Panipat (46.70 per cent), Sonepat (45.90 per cent) and Panchkula (42.90 per cent) are other high ranked districts in this respect. However, it is disheartening to realise that there are only seven districts in the state where doctor facility has been found in more than one-third of the villages. These districts are concentrated in the northern part of the state. The attainment level in rest of the twelve districts is far below satisfactory level. Moreover, a high degree of inter-district variation can also be noticed in the state.

Some revealing conclusions can be drawn from the district-wise rankings with regard to the attainment levels of both the dimensions of health infrastructure. A comparative analysis of Table 6.3 and Table 6.4 reflects that only Rewari district has attained the same rank (11th rank) in both the dimensions. On one side there are districts with higher ranks in

Table 6.5: Women Received Full Ante-natal Check-ups (2011)

Districts	*Rankings*
Rohtak	1
Kaithal	2
Yamunanagar	3
Rewari	4
Panchkula	5
Sirsa	6
Ambala	7
Karnal	8
Jhajjar	9
Sonepat	10
Kurukshetra	11
Gurgaon	12
Hisar	13
Jind	14
Fatehabad	15
Faridabad	16
Mahendergarh	17
Bhiwani	18
Panipat	19

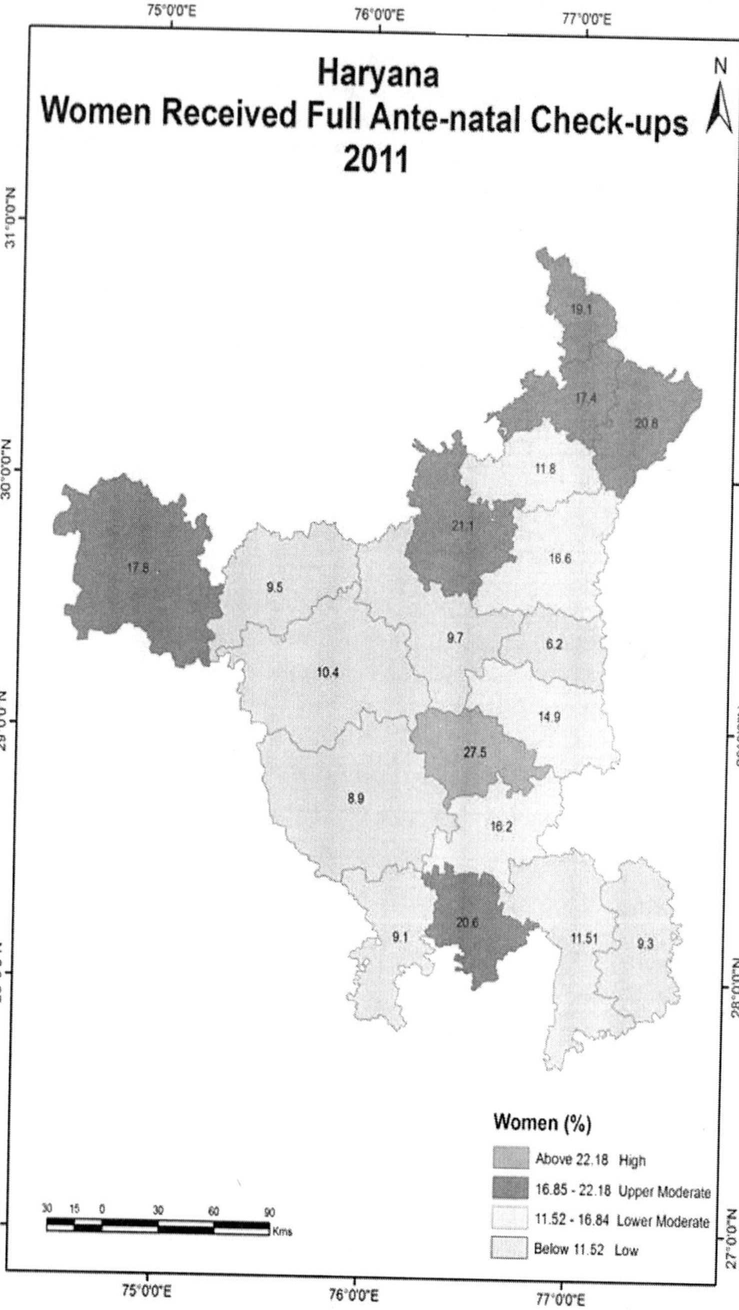
Haryana
Women Received Full Ante-natal Check-ups
2011
N
75°0'0"E
76°0'0"E
77°0'0"E
31°0'0"N
30°0'0"N
29°0'0"N
28°0'0"N
27°0'0"N
19.1
17.4
20.8
11.8
21.1
16.6
17.8
9.5
9.7
6.2
10.4
14.9
27.5
8.9
16.2
20.6
9.1
11.51
9.3
Women (%)
Above 22.18 High
16.85 - 22.18 Upper Moderate
11.52 - 16.84 Lower Moderate
Below 11.52 Low
30 15 0 30 60 90
Kms

Map 6.5

'Govt. Health Facility' but lagging far behind with respect to the 'Villages with Doctors'. These include Hisar, Rohtak, Jhajjar and Fatehabad districts. On the other side there are districts like Karnal, Kurukshetra, Panipat and Panchkula that have attained higher rankings with respect to the 'Villages with Doctors' but they are far behind in respect of 'Govt. Health Facility'. In this way none of the districts has registered higher rankings in both the health infrastructure dimensions. Though there are districts like Faridabad, Gurgaon and Mahendergarh which have shown poor health infrastructure regarding both the dimensions.

Ante-natal check-up is one of the most vital variables as it ensures the safe delivery of the baby. Despite its importance, it is not practiced to a great extent by the women in the state. The data reveals that only 13.20 per cent of the women have had full ante-natal check-ups in the state in 2011.

Consider the case of Rohtak district that has outpaced all the districts and obtained the top rank but here also only 27.50 per cent of the women have received full ante-natal check-ups. Kaithal district which occupies the second rank is fairly behind with a figure of 21.10 per cent. Kaithal is closely followed by Yamunanagar (20.80 per cent) and Rewari (20.60 per cent) districts. On the darker side, there are as many as eight districts where the attainment level is below 11.52 per cent thus these districts have been placed in the category of low development. These districts

Table 6.6: Institutional Deliveries (2011)

Districts	*Rankings*
Rewari	1
Panchkula	2
Kurukshetra	3
Mahendergarh	4
Ambala	5
Sonepat	6
Sirsa	7
Rohtak	8
Yamunanagar	9
Karnal	10
Fatehabad	11
Hisar	12
Jhajjar	13
Kaithal	14
Jind	15
Faridabad	16
Panipat	17
Bhiwani	18
Gurgaon	19

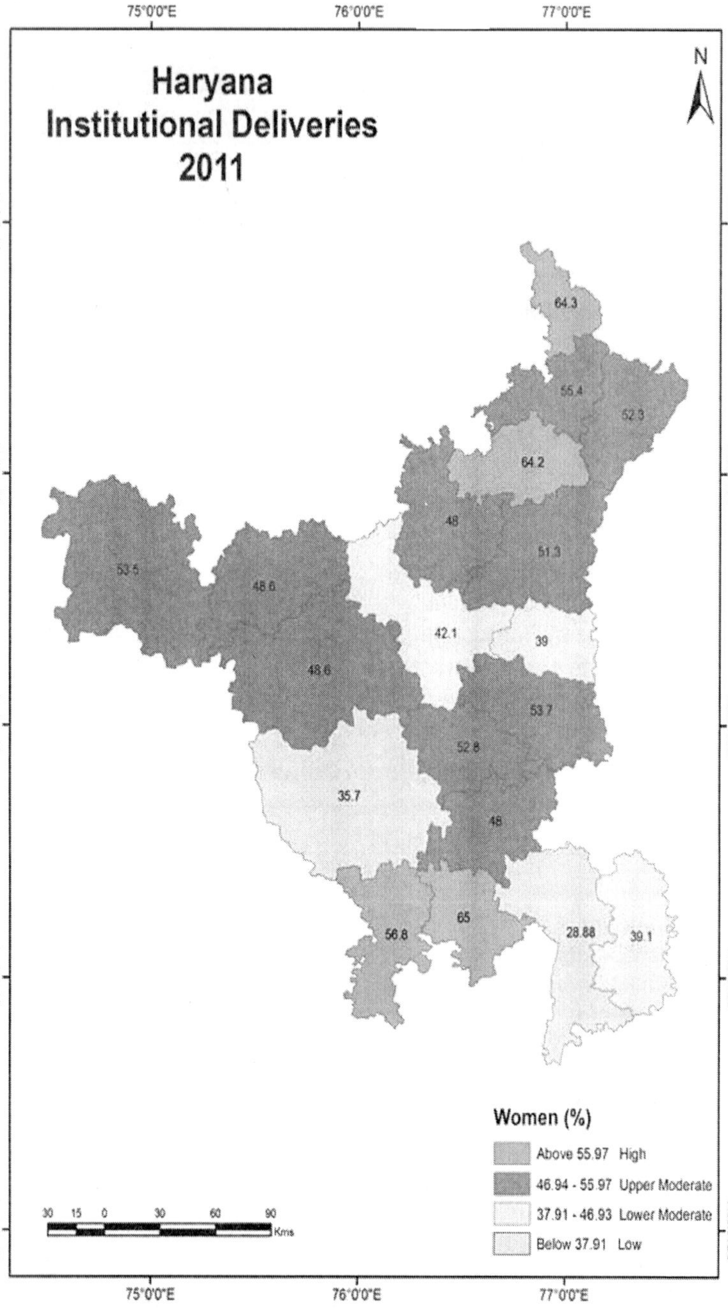
Haryana
Institutional Deliveries
2011
N
75°0'0"E
76°0'0"E
77°0'0"E
31°0'0"N
30°0'0"N
29°0'0"N
28°0'0"N
27°0'0"N
64.3
55.4
52.3
64.2
48
51.3
53.5
48.6
42.1
39
48.6
53.7
52.8
35.7
48
65
56.8
28.88
39.1
Women (%)
Above 55.97 High
46.94 - 55.97 Upper Moderate
37.91 - 46.93 Lower Moderate
Below 37.91 Low
30 15 0 30 60 90
Kms

Map 6.6

include Panipat (6.20 per cent), Bhiwani (8.90 per cent), Mahendergarh (9.10 per cent), Faridabad (9.30 per cent), Fatehabad (9.50 per cent) and Jind (9.70 per cent) where less than 10 per cent of the women have received full ante-natal check-ups (Map 6.5 and Table 6.5).

Table 6.7: Children Age 12-35 Months Fully Vaccinated (2011)

Districts	*Rankings*
Ambala	1
Panchkula	2
Rohtak	3
Karnal	4
Sonepat	5
Kaithal	6
Yamunanagar	7
Kurukshetra	8
Mahendergarh	9
Rewari	10
Jhajjar	11
Fatehabad	12
Sirsa	13
Bhiwani	14
Panipat	15
Hisar	16
Jind	17
Faridabad	18
Gurgaon	19

It seems that the unresponsiveness of the women towards the full ante-natal check-ups has not put adverse effect on the incidence of institutional deliveries. This is why, as against a meek 13.20 per cent women who had received full ante-natal check-ups, 46.80 per cent of the women in the state have undergone institutional deliveries during the given point of time. In this regard Rewari (65.00 per cent) district has achieved the top rank which is narrowly followed by Panchkula (64.30 per cent) and Kurukshetra (64.20 per cent). Mahendergarh (56.80 per cent) district has also found place in the category of high attainment level. It is quite encouraging to note that there are as many as 10 districts in the state where more than 50 per cent of the women have undergone institutional deliveries. On the other hand, Gurgaon district has demonstrated the gloomier side of health awareness where only 28.88 per cent of the women have had institutional deliveries which is preceded by Bhiwani (35.70 per cent) and Panipat (39.00 per cent) districts. The corresponding figures of Fatehabad, Hisar, Jhajjar and Kaithal are hovering between 48 per cent and 49 per cent (Map 6.6 and Table 6.6).

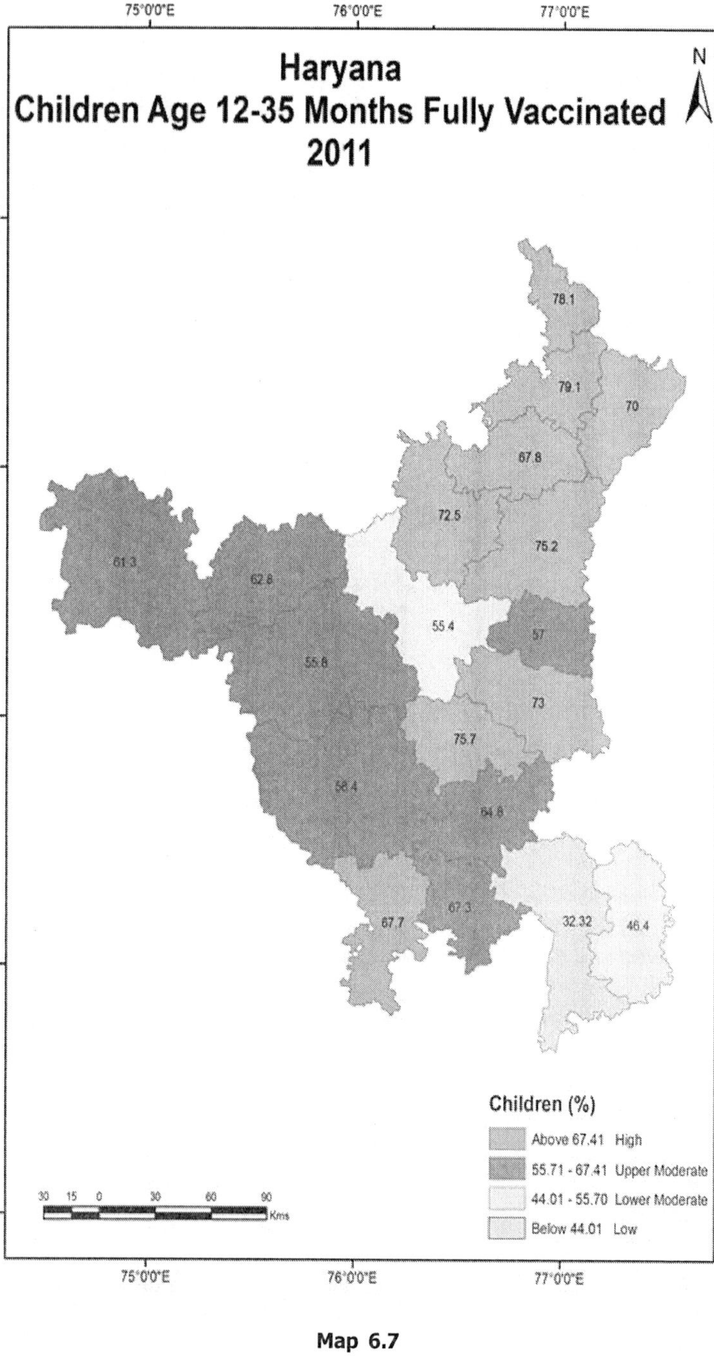
Haryana
Children Age 12-35 Months Fully Vaccinated
2011
N
75°0'0"E
76°0'0"E
77°0'0"E
31°0'0"N
30°0'0"N
29°0'0"N
28°0'0"N
27°0'0"N
78.1
79.1
70
67.8
72.5
75.2
61.3
62.8
55.4
57
55.8
73
75.7
58.4
64.8
67.3
67.7
32.32
46.4
Children (%)
Above 67.41 High
55.71 - 67.41 Upper Moderate
44.01 - 55.70 Lower Moderate
Below 44.01 Low
30 15 0 30 60 90
Kms

Map 6.7

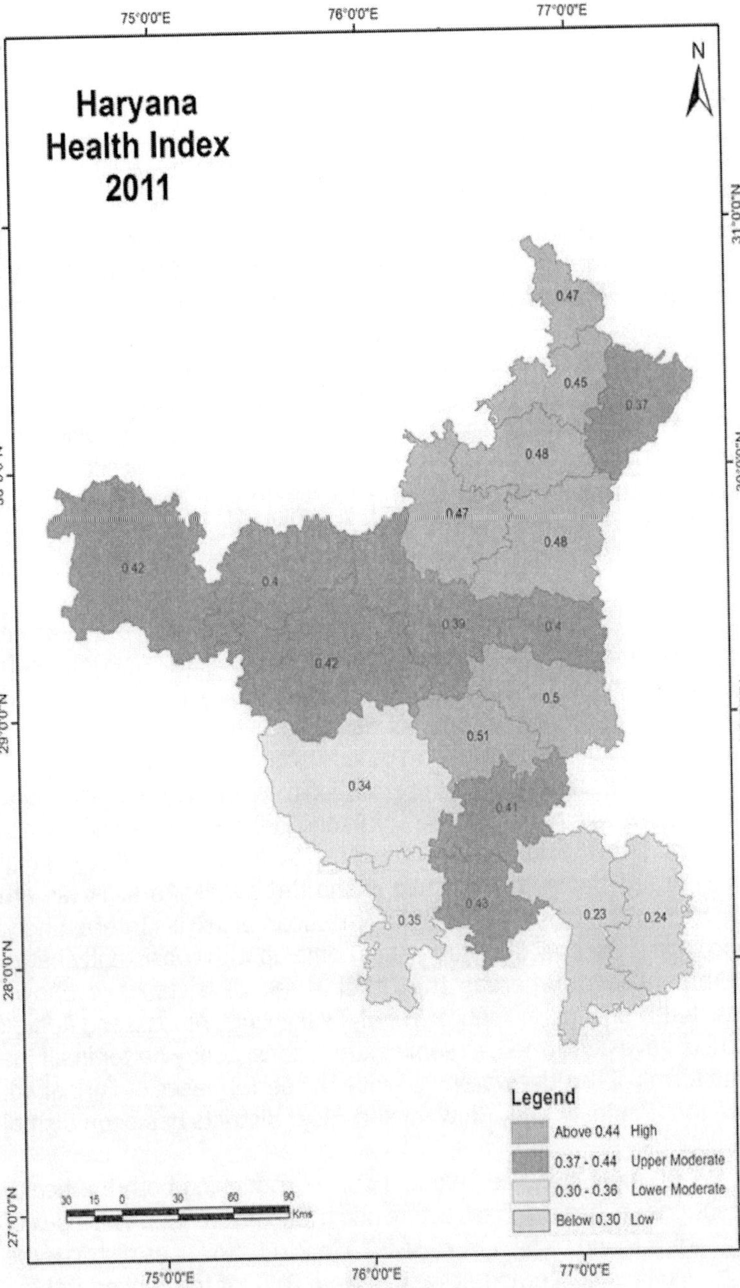
Haryana
Health Index
2011
75°0'0"E
76°0'0"E
77°0'0"E
31°0'0"N
30°0'0"N
29°0'0"N
28°0'0"N
27°0'0"N
N
0.47
0.45
0.37
0.48
0.47
0.48
0.42
0.4
0.39
0.4
0.42
0.5
0.51
0.34
0.41
0.43
0.35
0.23
0.24
Legend
Above 0.44 High
0.37 - 0.44 Upper Moderate
0.30 - 0.36 Lower Moderate
Below 0.30 Low
30 15 0 30 60 90
Kms

Map 6.8

There are nearly 60 per cent of the children that are fully vaccinated in the state in 2011. The district-wise attainment levels have been depicted in Map 6.7 and the rankings are presented in Table 6.7. It is heartening to realise that as many as nine districts have found place in the category of high attainment level. The two northern most districts i.e. Ambala (79.10 per cent) and Panchkula (78.10 per cent) of the state have captured the first two positions. Rohtak (75.70 per cent) has successfully taken marginal lead over Karnal (75.20 per cent) and acquired the third place. Sonepat, Kaithal and Yamunanagar districts have succeeded in attaining the vaccination level of 70 per cent and above. Once again, the two southernmost districts of Haryana are crawling underneath. Gurgaon with a poor attainment level of 32.30 per cent is preceded by its neighbouring district Faridabad (46.40 per cent). However, there is a visible difference of more than 14 per centage points between the attainment levels of the two bottom districts and this is why Faridabad district has successfully found a place in the category of lower moderate level. Interestingly there are only three districts that have appeared in the last two categories while as many as sixteen districts have been placed in the first two categories.

Some interesting inferences may be drawn on the basis of attainment levels of the districts as regards to the three indicators pertaining to health awareness (Consider Tables 6.5, 6.6 and 6.7). Firstly, attainment level is so fluctuating that none of the districts has obtained the same rank in all the three indicators. In other words, the attainment levels of the districts differ considerably from one indicator to another which shows that a district with higher/lower rank in one indicator has not performed better/worse in the other two. Secondly, there are only four districts that have obtained same rank in two of the three indicators. These are Panchkula, Bhiwani, Gurgaon and Faridabad districts. Interestingly, Panchkula is the only district that has come up with consistently better attainment level whereas the other three districts have shown consistently poor performance. Thirdly; Panchkula, Ambala and Rohtak districts have performed, to some extent, consistently better in all the three forms of health awareness while the performance of Faridabad, Gurgaon, Panipat, Jind, Bhiwani and Hisar districts has been dismal throughout.

Health index has been worked out by combining both the health dimensions i.e. health infrastructure and health awareness. The index of the state is found to be a modest 0.39 in 2011. So far as district-wise health index is concerned, it ranges from 0.51 of top ranked Rohtak district to 0.23 of bottom ranked Gurgaon district. Except Rohtak, Sonepat (0.50), Kurukshetra (0.48) and Karnal (0.48) are amongst the districts

Table 6.8: Health Index (2011)

Districts	*Rankings*
Rohtak	1
Sonepat	2
Kurukshetra	3
Karnal	4
Kaithal	5
Panchkula	6
Ambala	7
Rewari	8
Hisar	9
Sirsa	10
Jhajjar	11
Panipat	12
Fatehabad	13
Jind	14
Yamunanagar	15
Mahendergarh	16
Bhiwani	17
Faridabad	18
Gurgaon	19

that have appeared in the category of high attainment level. Faridabad (0.24), Bhiwani (0.34) and Mahendergarh (0.35) districts represent the last category characterised with poor health index (Map 6.8 and Table 6.8).

The districts with higher health index are concentrated in the central and northern parts whereas the index is quite poor in the southern parts of the state. The difference of 0.28 index points between the districts with two extreme attainment levels signifies that there exist high inter-district disparities in health attainment level in the state.

A careful study of Tables 6.3 to 6.8 brings out the makeup of health index. Rohtak, the top ranked district has performed convincingly well in three of the five health parameters and its performance was moderate in the remaining two. The performance of Sonepat, the second ranked district has been consistently fair in four parameters, though it does not get second rank in any of the parameters. The third rank obtained by Kurukshetra district is mainly because it has secured second rank in one of the health infrastructure indicators and third rank in one of the health awareness indicators. The districts like Rewari, Hisar, Jhajjar and Yamunanagar have to pay the penalty of inconsistent performance thereby obtained moderate or poor health index. Consider the example of Panchkula which has performed reasonably well in four of the five health

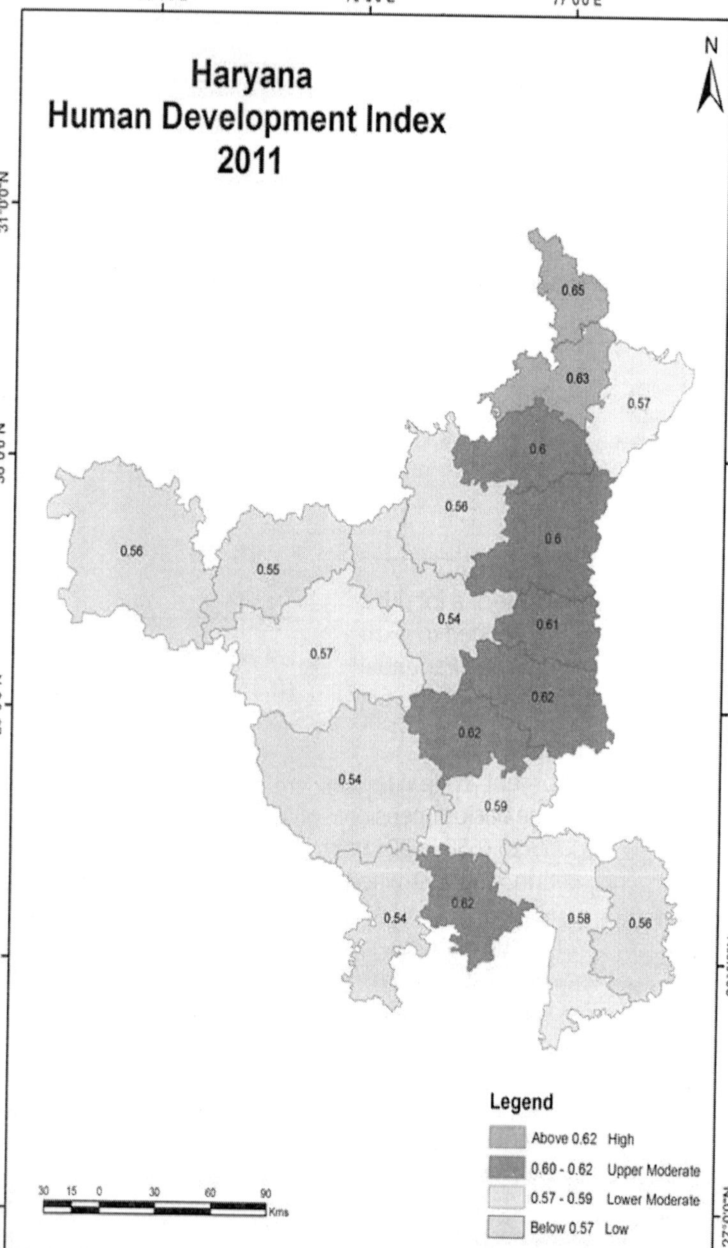
Haryana
Human Development Index
2011
N
75°0'0"E
76°0'0"E
77°0'0"E
31°0'0"N
30°0'0"N
29°0'0"N
28°0'0"N
27°0'0"N
0.65
0.63
0.57
0.6
0.56
0.6
0.56
0.55
0.54
0.61
0.57
0.62
0.62
0.54
0.59
0.62
0.54
0.58
0.56
Legend
Above 0.62 High
0.60 - 0.62 Upper Moderate
0.57 - 0.59 Lower Moderate
Below 0.57 Low
30 15 0 30 60 90
Kms

Map 6.9

Table 6.9: Human Development Index (2011)

Districts	*Rankings*
Panchkula	1
Ambala	2
Sonepat	3
Rewari	4
Rohtak	5
Panipat	6
Karnal	7
Kurukshetra	8
Jhajjar	9
Gurgaon	10
Yamunanagar	11
Hisar	12
Kaithal	13
Sirsa	14
Faridabad	15
Fatehabad	16
Jind	17
Mahendergarh	18
Bhiwani	19

parameters but has to suffer a lot due to its poor 'Govt. Health Facility' in the rural areas thereby slipped to sixth position. The consistent but poor performance of Gurgaon and Faridabad districts as regards to all the five parameters has driven them at the bottom of health index tally.

Human Development Index

Human Development Index is now extracted considering the performance in the three basic dimensions- income, education and health. The state HDI amounts to 0.58 in 2011. The geographical distribution of districts can be seen in Map 6.9 whereas their rankings are given in Table 6.9.

The HDI earned by the districts, in some cases, is such that it is not possible to delineate one district from the other if the figure is presented up to two decimals. This is why; the index value has been calculated up to three decimals to facilitate the interpretation more precise in these cases. Panchkula district is at the top with an index value of 0.65 followed by Ambala (0.63). These are the two districts that have registered their presence in the first category representing high human development. Six districts from third to eighth ranks namely Sonepat (0.624), Rewari (0.620), Rohtak (0.616), Panipat (0.613), Karnal (0.600) and Kurukshetra (0.597) have found place in the second category of upper moderate level. In this way one can easily deduce from Map 6.9 that the districts with high HDI are mainly concentrated in the north-eastern part of the state. As many

Table 6.10: Construction of Human Development Index: District-wise Rankings (2011)

Districts	*Income Index*	*Education Index*	*Health Index*	*Human Development Index*
Panchkula	4	1	6	1
Ambala	5	2	7	2
Sonepat	8	5	2	3
Rewari	6	3	8	4
Rohtak	15	6	1	5
Panipat	2	10	12	6
Karnal	9	14	4	7
Kurukshetra	14	12	3	8
Jhajjar	13	4	11	9
Gurgaon	1	13	19	10
Yamunanagar	10	8	15	11
Hisar	7	15	9	12
Kaithal	18	17	5	13
Sirsa	11	18	10	14
Faridabad	3	9	18	15
Fatehabad	12	19	13	16
Jind	16	16	14	17
Mahendergarh	19	7	16	18
Bhiwani	17	11	17	19
Correlation of individual dimension with HDI	**0.54**	**0.65**	**0.67**	

as seven districts have shown poor performance by recording HDI below 0.57 thereby placed in the last category representing low level of human development. These districts are concentrated either in the south or in the western part of the state. Bhiwani (0.539) district is at the bottom, however, the situation of Mahendergarh (0.542) and Jind (0.542) is no better. Interestingly nine districts (from first to ninth rank) have recorded HDI above the state average and equal number of districts (from 11th to 19th) below the state average. However, Gurgaon district has achieved HDI equal to the state average.

It is pertinent to figure out the relative role of the three basic dimensions in the construction of HDI. District wise rankings of the three dimensions as well the rankings of HDI have been presented in Table 6.10. Some meaningful conclusions drawn from the table are listed below:

- None of the districts is too consistent in its performance to obtain the same rank in all the three basic dimensions. However, relatively high consistency can be seen in Panchkula, Ambala, Sonepat, Rewari (higher ranked districts); and Bhiwani, Jind, Fatehabad and Sirsa (lower ranked districts). The performance of Bhiwani district is equally poor (17th rank) in both the income and health dimensions. Similar is the performance of Jind district (16th rank) as regards to income and education dimensions.
- Higher correlation of education and health dimensions with the HDI reflects that these two dimensions have greater bearing over the construction of the HDI as compared to the income dimension.
- The unparallel performance of Gurgaon district fails to enhance its position in the sphere of human development due to fairly poor performance in the other two basic dimensions of education and health. Similar is the case of Faridabad district. Both of these can improve the level of human development on the lines of Panipat district.
- The development trend of Rohtak district is rather interesting. It has successfully overcome its weakness of the income dimension by achieving top rank on health and a fairly higher rank on education dimension thereby achieved fifth rank on HDI.
- The two northern districts i.e. Karnal and Kurukshetra have shown better prospects for human development what they need is a light thrust in the spheres of income and education dimensions.

Sum up

As a whole there is a lot of scope to enhance the human development level in the state which amounts to a fairly moderate level in 2011. As far as district level performance is concerned, the districts located in the northern part of the state like Panchkula and Ambala have achieved higher development level whereas vigorous efforts are required in the districts located in the south-western part of the state like Bhiwani, Mahendergarh, Jind, Fatehabad and Sirsa to reach the satisfactory level of human development. Higher correlation of education and health dimensions with the HDI reflects that these two dimensions have greater bearing over the construction of the HDI as compared to the income dimension. Even after exemplary performance in income dimension, Faridabad and Gurgaon districts have failed to enhance their HDI rank due to fairly poor performance in the other two basic dimensions of education and health. On the other hand Rohtak district has achieved respectable position on HDI albeit its poor performance in income dimension. Karnal and Kurukshetra have shown better prospects for human development.

7

Gender Development Index, 2011

Gender Development Index (GDI) has been carried out for 2011 following the same methodology as adopted for 2001. At first the three basic dimensions have been discussed separately for both the genders and GDI has been taken into analysis in the end.

Income Dimension

The district-wise distribution of Economically Active Population (EAP) with respect to males is illustrated in Map 7.1 and their rankings are in given in Table 7.1.

Table 7.1: Economically Active Population – Males (2001)

Districts	*Rankings*
Yamunanagar	1
Ambala	2
Faridabad	3
Karnal	4
Kurukshetra	5
Panipat	6
Rohtak	7
Gurgaon	8
Kaithal	9
Panchkula	10
Jhajjar	11
Sonepat	12
Sirsa	13
Fatehabad	14
Hisar	15
Jind	16
Rewari	17
Bhiwani	18
Mahendergarh	19

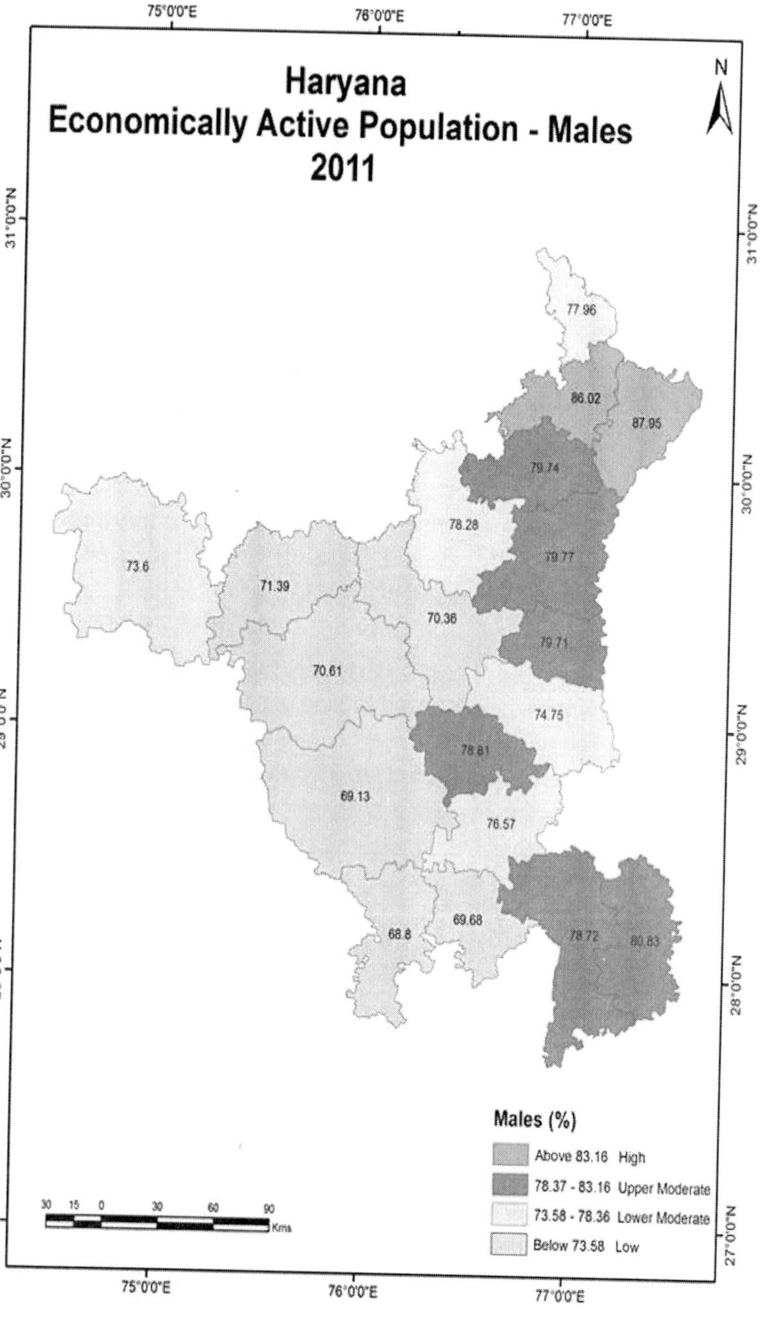
Haryana
Economically Active Population - Males
2011
N
75°0'0"E
76°0'0"E
77°0'0"E
31°0'0"N
30°0'0"N
29°0'0"N
28°0'0"N
27°0'0"N
77.96
86.02
87.95
79.74
78.28
73.6
71.39
79.77
70.36
79.71
70.61
74.75
78.81
69.13
76.57
69.68
68.8
78.72
80.83
Males (%)
Above 83.16 High
78.37 - 83.16 Upper Moderate
73.58 - 78.36 Lower Moderate
Below 73.58 Low
30 15 0 30 60 90
Kms

Map 7.1

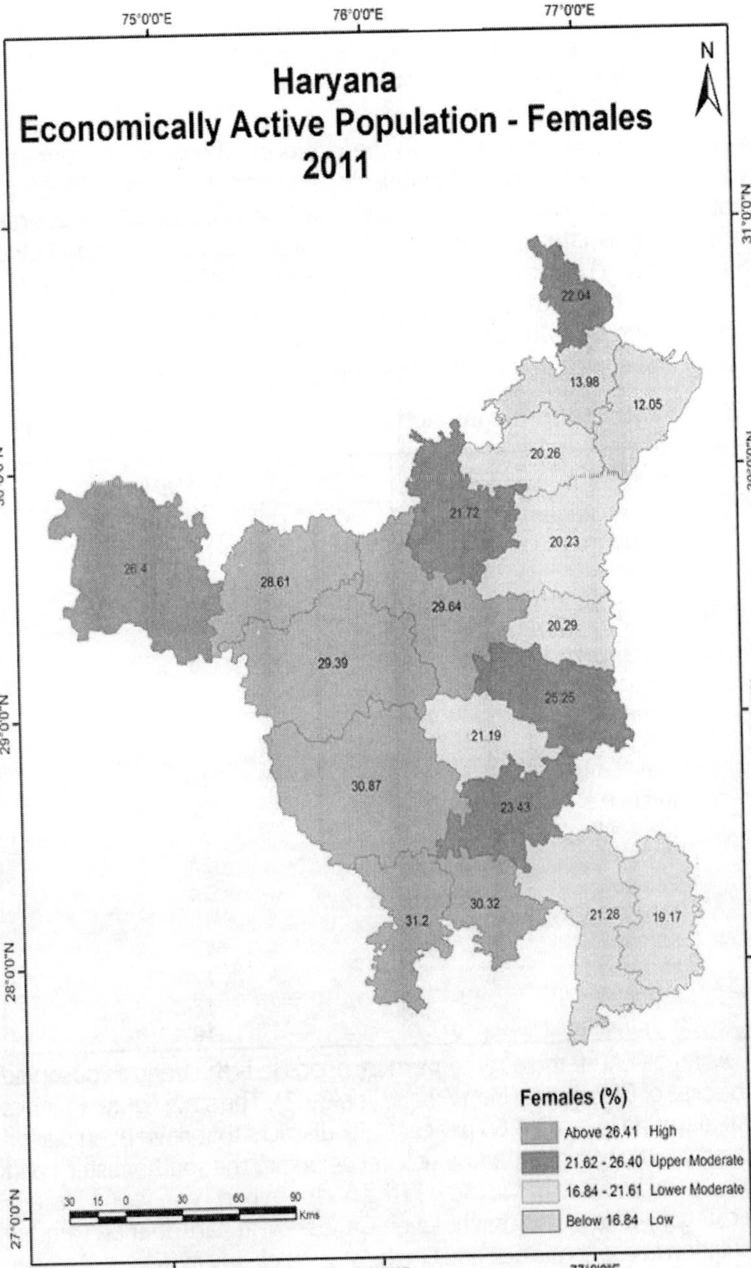
Haryana
Economically Active Population - Females
2011
N
22.04
13.98
12.05
20.26
21.72
20.23
26.4
28.61
29.64
20.29
29.39
25.25
21.19
30.87
23.43
30.32
31.2
21.28
19.17
Females (%)
Above 26.41 High
21.62 - 26.40 Upper Moderate
16.84 - 21.61 Lower Moderate
Below 16.84 Low
Kms

Map 7.2

Altogether 76.34 per cent of the EAP in the state belongs to masculine gender. There are three districts in the state where more than 80 per cent of the EAP is composed of males. Out of these two districts located in the northern part, namely Yamunanagar (87.95 per cent) the top ranked district and Ambala (86.02 per cent) with the second position have been placed in the category of high attainment level. On the contrary, six districts have found place in the category of low attainment level where the proportion of EAP-males has been found below 73.58 per cent. Mahendergarh (68.80 per cent) district has obtained the last rank which is immediately preceded by Bhiwani (69.13 per cent) and Rewari (69.68 per cent) districts. Distribution pattern of districts over space clearly reflects that the districts with higher EAP-males are concentrated in the north-eastern part whereas the concentration of districts with lower EAP-males can be seen in the south-western part.

Table 7.2: Economically Active Population – Females (2011)

Districts	*Rankings*
Mahendergarh	1
Bhiwani	2
Rewari	3
Jind	4
Hisar	5
Fatehabad	6
Sirsa	7
Sonepat	8
Jhajjar	9
Panchkula	10
Kaithal	11
Gurgaon	12
Rohtak	13
Panipat	14
Kurukshetra	15
Karnal	16
Faridabad	17
Ambala	18
Yamunanagar	19

As far as EAP-females is concerned, opposite is the trend as observed in the case of EAP-males (Map 7.2 and Table 7.2). The state figure amounts to an alarming low of 24.66 per cent. Six districts that have been placed in the category of high attainment level belong to the south-western part whereas the two districts located in the northern part have found place in the category of low attainment level. Gender-wise participation trend of population in economic activities in the state is clearly in favour of males. Even the top ranked Mahendergarh district occupies less than one-third

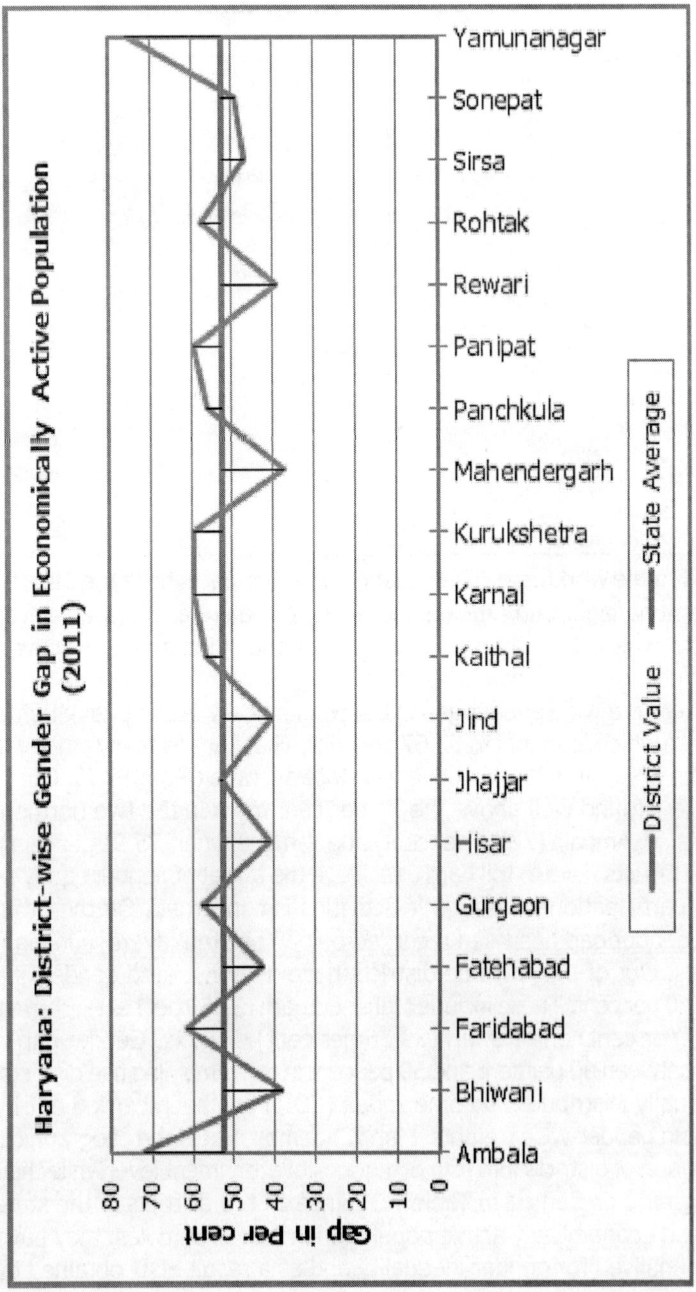
Haryana: District-wise Gender Gap in Economically Active Population (2011)
Gap in Per cent
80
70
60
50
40
30
20
10
0
Ambala
Bhiwani
Faridabad
Fatehabad
Gurgaon
Hisar
Jhajjar
Jind
Kaithal
Karnal
Kurukshetra
Mahendergarh
Panchkula
Panipat
Rewari
Rohtak
Sirsa
Sonepat
Yamunanagar
District Value
State Average

Fig. 7.1

Table 7.3: Equally Distributed Income Index (2011)

Districts	*Rankings*
Gurgaon	1
Panipat	2
Rewari	3
Panchkula	4
Faridabad	5
Hisar	6
Sonepat	7
Fatehabad	8
Sirsa	9
Jhajjar	10
Karnal	11
Ambala	12
Jind	13
Bhiwani	14
Rohtak	15
Kurukshetra	16
Mahendergarh	17
Kaithal	18
Yamunanagar	19

of the female workforce. The situation is rather pathetic in the districts like Yamunanagar and Ambala. Moreover, there are as many as eleven districts where less than 25 per cent of the females have actively contributed in the economic activities.

There is a wide gender gap in the economically active population in the state which amounts to 52.67 per cent. There are as many as eleven districts where it is found above the state average (Figure 7.1). Out of these it is found well above the 70 per cent mark in the two northern districts i.e. Ambala (72.04 per cent) and Yamunanagar (75.91 per cent). These districts have to toil hard to achieve the target of gender equity as far as participation in economic activities is concerned. On the other hand, gender gap has been recorded below the state average in eight districts. Out of these, three districts have demonstrated gender gap below 40 per cent. These include Mahendergarh (37.59 per cent), Bhiwani (38.26 per cent) and Rewari (39.36 per cent) districts. Gender gap is found between 40 per cent and 50 per cent in the remaining five districts.

Equally Distributed Income Index (EDII) has been carried out by awarding gender-wise weights. Map 7.3 demonstrates the geographical distribution of districts into four categories of attainment level while their rankings are presented in Table 7.3. Since all the districts in the state have had economically active population in favour of males, they have been penalised for gender inequality and as a result EDII obtained by

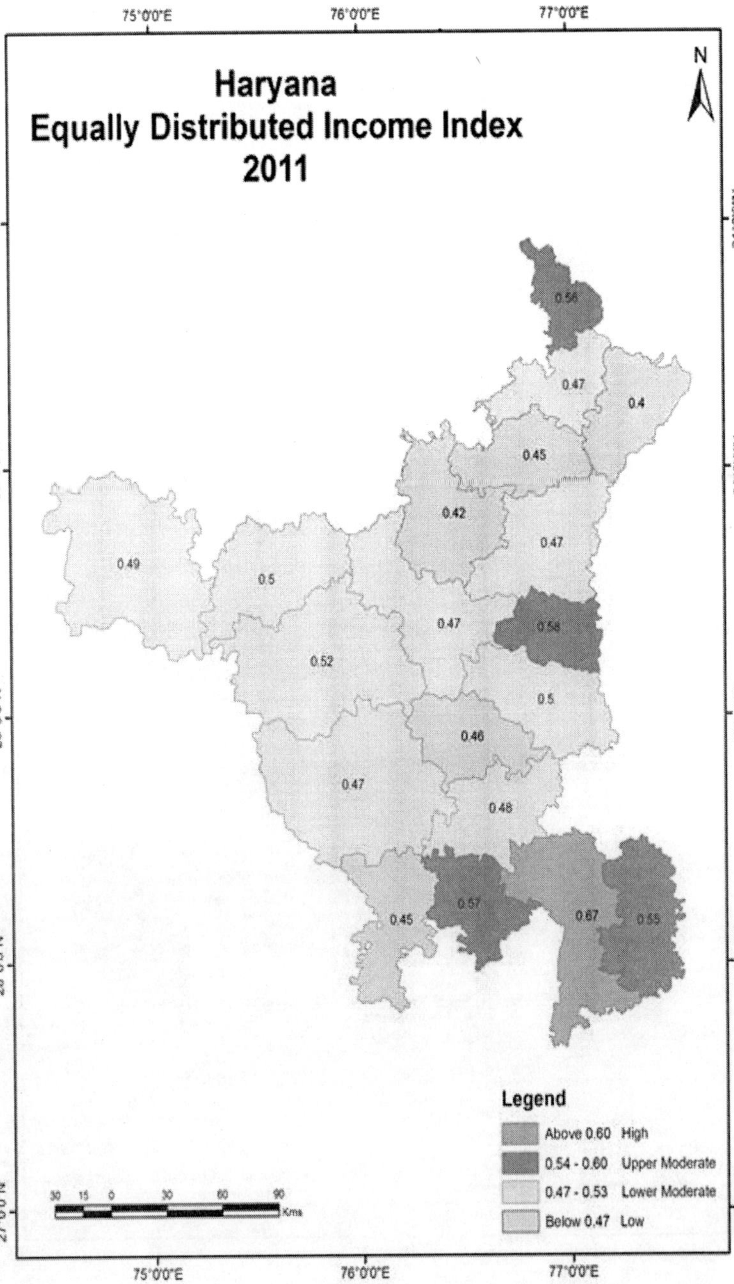
Haryana
Equally Distributed Income Index
2011
N
75°0'0"E
76°0'0"E
77°0'0"E
31°0'0"N
29°0'0"N
28°0'0"N
27°0'0"N
Legend
Above 0.60 High
0.54 - 0.60 Upper Moderate
0.47 - 0.53 Lower Moderate
Below 0.47 Low
Kms

Map 7.3

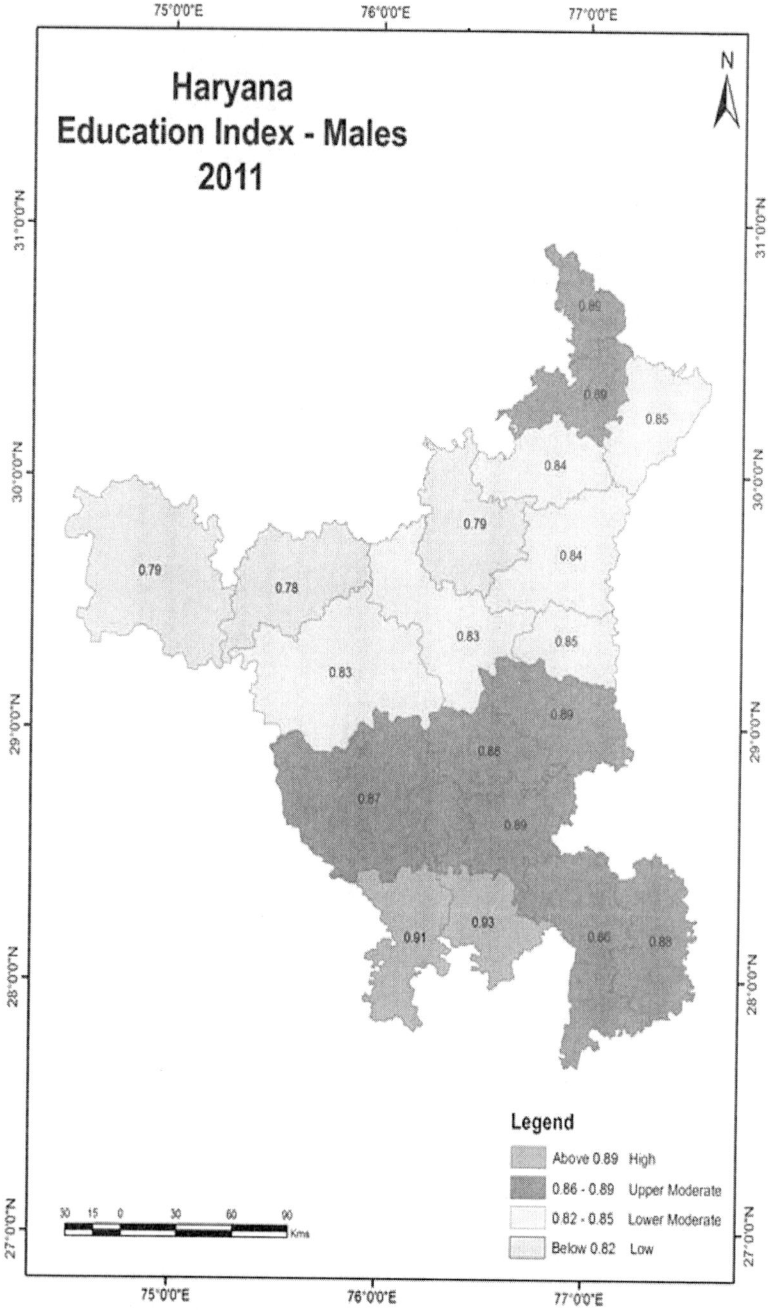
Haryana
Education Index - Males
2011
N
75°0'0"E
76°0'0"E
77°0'0"E
31°0'0"N
30°0'0"N
29°0'0"N
28°0'0"N
27°0'0"N
0.89
0.89
0.85
0.84
0.79
0.84
0.79
0.78
0.83
0.85
0.83
0.89
0.88
0.87
0.89
0.93
0.91
0.88
0.88
Legend
Above 0.89 High
0.86 - 0.89 Upper Moderate
0.82 - 0.85 Lower Moderate
Below 0.82 Low
30 15 0 30 60 90
Kms

Map 7.4

Table 7.4: Education Index- Males (2011)

Districts	*Rankings*
Rewari	1
Mahendergarh	2
Jhajjar	3
Sonepat	4
Panchkula	5
Ambala	6
Rohtak	7
Faridabad	8
Bhiwani	9
Gurgaon	10
Panipat	11
Yamunanagar	12
Karnal	13
Kurukshetra	14
Hisar	15
Jind	16
Kaithal	17
Sirsa	18
Fatehabad	19

them is lesser than that of EAP-males. However, difference in the real per capita GDP earned by the districts is also an affecting factor. Gurgaon (0.67) district has obtained the top rank by leaving Panipat (0.58) district far behind which has granted second rank. This is why; Gurgaon is the only district that has found place in the category of high attainment level. Higher real per capita GDP of Gurgaon is accountable for this difference. Five districts have recorded their presence in the second category representing upper moderate attainment level. In addition to Panipat, Rewari (0.57), Panchkula (0.56) and Faridabad (0.55) are the other districts that found place in this category. Consider the cases of three southern districts, namely Mahendergarh, Bhiwani and Rewari which have shown the lowest gender gap in EAP. Out of these, only Rewari district has come up with an appreciable EDII (0.57) and placed in the category of upper moderate attainment level whereas the corresponding values for Mahendergarh and Bhiwani are 0.45 and 0.47 and as a result Mahendergarh district has been placed in the category of low attainment level while Bhiwani district in the category of lower moderate level. In fact, difference in the real per capita GDP has made all the difference which has taken into consideration in calculating EDII. Take another example of Yamunanagar district which has appeared with the highest gender gap in EAP in favour of males. Moreover, real per capita GDP of the district is not impressive too. As a result it is placed at the bottom of

EDII. The case of Kaithal district is also attention-grabbing as it has been placed in the category of moderate attainment level as regards to EAP-males and EAP-females. But due to poor real per capita GDP it has been thrown back in the category of low attainment level as regards to EDII.

Education Dimension

At first gender-wise education indexes have been worked out and then Equally Distributed Education Index (EDEI) has been calculated by combining both the aspects. The state EI-males has been 0.85 in 2011. Geographical distribution of districts falling in different categories of EI-males is mapped in Map 7.4.

The ranks obtained by each district are presented in Table 7.4. Only two districts have appeared in the category of high attainment level by recording an index value above 0.89. Rewari district being at the first place has acquired EI-males as high as 0.93. Its neighbouring district Mahendergarh has also obtained an impressive index value of 0.91. The highest number of districts (8) has found place in the category of upper moderate level by achieving index value between 0.86 and 0.89. These districts are scattered over a larger part of the state without showing specific concentration pattern. However, two districts, namely Fatehabad and Sirsa located in the western part of the state have been awarded 19th and 18th ranks respectively thereby placed in the category of low attainment level. Kaithal has also joined the last category by recording EI-males below 0.82. There is a reasonable difference of 0.15 index

Table 7.5: Education Index- Females (2011)

Districts	*Rankings*
Panchkula	1
Ambala	2
Yamunanagar	3
Rohtak	4
Jhajjar	5
Sonepat	6
Rewari	7
Kurukshetra	8
Faridabad	9
Karnal	10
Panipat	11
Mahendergarh	12
Bhiwani	13
Gurgaon	14
Hisar	15
Jind	16
Sirsa	17
Kaithal	18
Fatehabad	19

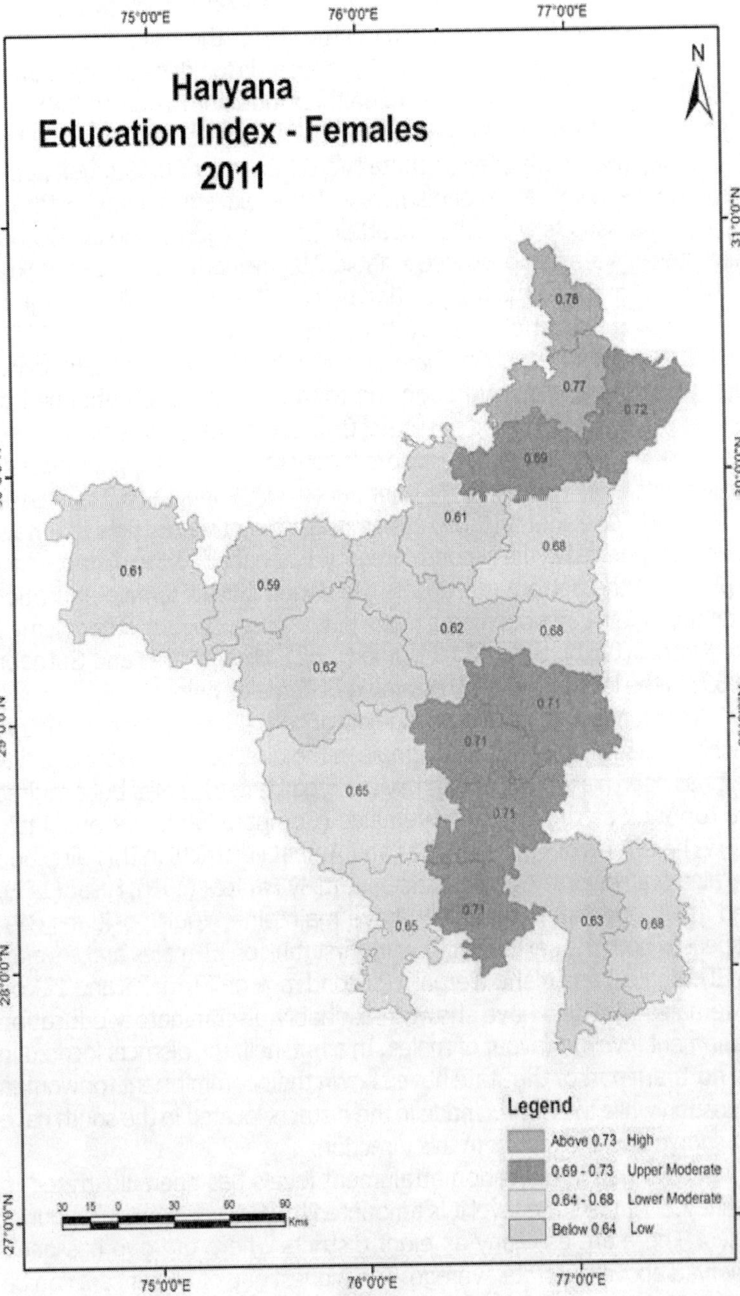
Haryana
Education Index - Females
2011
N
75°0'0"E
76°0'0"E
77°0'0"E
31°0'0"N
30°0'0"N
29°0'0"N
28°0'0"N
27°0'0"N
0.78
0.77
0.72
0.69
0.61
0.68
0.61
0.59
0.62
0.68
0.62
0.71
0.71
0.65
0.71
0.71
0.65
0.63
0.68
Legend
Above 0.73 High
0.69 - 0.73 Upper Moderate
0.64 - 0.68 Lower Moderate
Below 0.64 Low
30 15 0 30 60 90
Kms

Map 7.5

points between the top ranked and bottom ranked districts which needs to be taken seriously keeping in mind the size of the state.

Gender biasness is clearly visible as regards to education attainment levels in the state. As against a healthier index of EI-males 0.85, the figure of 0.67 seems fairly poor for the feminine sex. Inter-district disparities are also higher as there is a difference of 0.19 index points between the index values of districts with two extremes. Map 7.5 throws light on the districts with different attainment categories and the district-wise rankings are demonstrated in Table 7.5. The northernmost Panchkula district has grabbed the top position by acquiring EI-females as high as 0.78 which is closely followed by its neighbouring district Ambala (0.77). In this way both the districts have secured their place in the category of high attainment level. Although the third rank has been obtained by Yamunanagar (0.72), another district from the northern part of the state, yet it has been pushed in the second category representing upper moderate attainment level. Rohtak (0.71), Jhajjar (0.71), Sonepat (0.71), Rewari (0.71) and Kurukshetra (0.69) are amongst the other districts that have been incorporated in the second category. Fatehabad (0.59) district which is placed at the bottom represents the darker side of female education attainment level by obtaining a meek index value. It leads other districts like Kaithal (0.61), Sirsa (0.61), Jind (0.62), Hisar (0.62) and Gurgaon (0.63) in the last category by attaining EI-females below 0.64.

A comparison of education indexes of both the sexes brings out that Panchkula district has set an example in the direction of gender equality as it has been placed at the fifth rank as regards to EI-males but acquired the top rank as regards to EI-females (Compare Table 7.4 and Table 7.5). The efforts of Yamunanagar and Ambala districts in this direction are also praiseworthy. Four districts, namely Panipat (11th), Hisar (14th), Jind (16th) and Fatehabad (19th) have maintained their positions with respect to both the sexes. But Rewari (first rank on EI-males and seventh on EI-females) and Mahendergarh (second rank on EI-males and 12th on EI-females) districts have shown reasonably discriminatory education attainment levels in favour of males. In a nutshell, the districts located in the northern part of the state have shown their commitment for women education while the efforts made in the districts located in the south have not shown positive results in this direction.

Gender gap in education attainment levels has been illustrated in Figure 7.2. At the state level it is amounted to 18.60 per cent in favour of males. There are as many as eight districts where the gap has been observed above the state average. The highest gap of 26 per cent can be seen in Mahendergarh district. It is the only district that has shown the gap above 25 per cent. Most of the other districts that have shown the

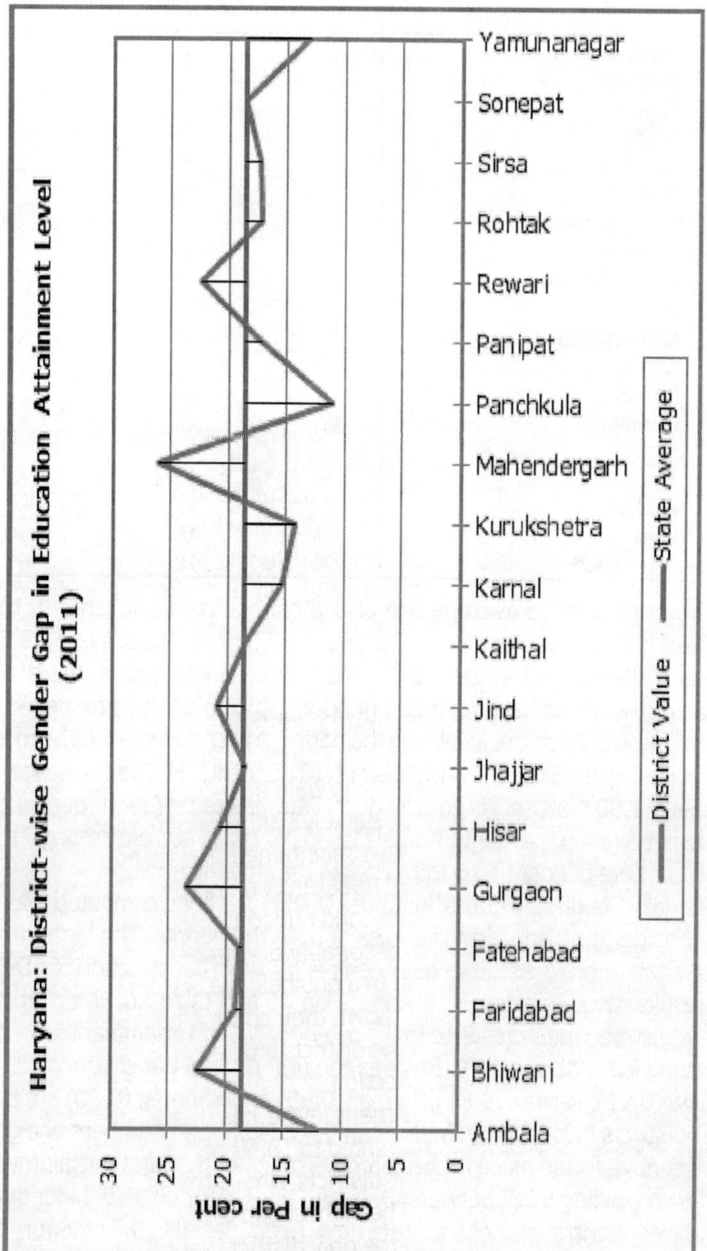
Haryana: District-wise Gender Gap in Education Attainment Level (2011)
Gap in Per cent
30
25
20
15
10
5
0
Ambala
Bhiwani
Faridabad
Fatehabad
Gurgaon
Hisar
Jhajjar
Jind
Kaithal
Karnal
Kurukshetra
Mahendergarh
Panchkula
Panipat
Rewari
Rohtak
Sirsa
Sonepat
Yamunanagar
District Value
State Average

Fig. 7.2

Table 7.6: Equally Distributed Education Index (2011)

Districts	*Rankings*
Panchkula	1
Ambala	2
Rewari	3
Jhajjar	4
Sonepat	5
Rohtak	6
Yamunanagar	7
Faridabad	8
Mahendergarh	9
Panipat	10
Kurukshetra	11
Karnal	12
Bhiwani	13
Gurgaon	14
Hisar	15
Jind	16
Kaithal	17
Sirsa	18
Fatehabad	19

gap above the state average are also those which are located in the southern part of the state such as Gurgaon (23.50 per cent), Bhiwani (22.60 per cent), Rewari (22.40 per cent), etc. On the brighter side, there are eleven districts that have recorded gender gap below the state average. Most of these districts are located in the northern part of Haryana. The most minuscule gap is visible in Panchkula (11.10 per cent). The performance of Ambala (11.90 per cent) is equally good. Yamunanagar (13.10 per cent), Kurukshetra (14.30 per cent), Karnal (15.40 per cent), etc. are amongst the districts where gender gap is found below the state average.

Equally Distributed Education Index (EDEI) has been computed taking into consideration education indexes of both the gender. The higher the gender gap, more the district has been penalised in construction of EDEI. The results have been demonstrated in Map 7.6 and Table 7.6. Five districts have registered their presence in the category of high attainment level by achieving EDEI above 0.79. Besides the first ranked Panchkula (0.83); Ambala (0.82), Rewari (0.81), Jhajjar (0.80) and Sonepat (0.80) are the other districts incorporated in this category. Maximum numbers of eight districts have found place in the category of upper moderate attainment level by recording EDEI between 0.76 and 0.79. Four districts belonging to the west-central part of the state have been placed in the category of low development out of which Fatehabad district is at the bottom with the lowest EDEI (0.68).

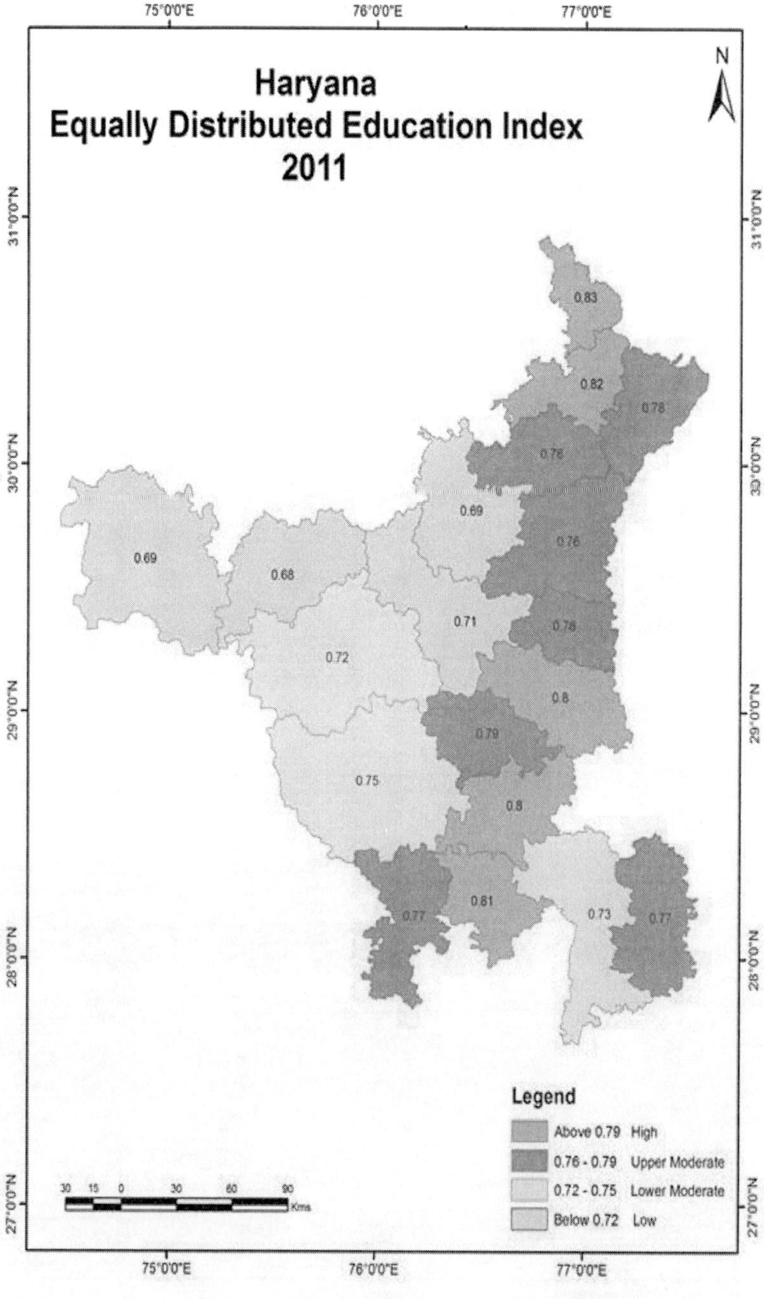
Haryana
Equally Distributed Education Index
2011
N
75°0'0"E
76°0'0"E
77°0'0"E
31°0'0"N
30°0'0"N
29°0'0"N
28°0'0"N
27°0'0"N
0.83
0.82
0.78
0.76
0.69
0.69
0.68
0.76
0.71
0.78
0.72
0.8
0.79
0.75
0.8
0.81
0.77
0.73
0.77
Legend
Above 0.79 High
0.76 - 0.79 Upper Moderate
0.72 - 0.75 Lower Moderate
Below 0.72 Low
30 15 0 30 60 90
Kms

Map 7.6

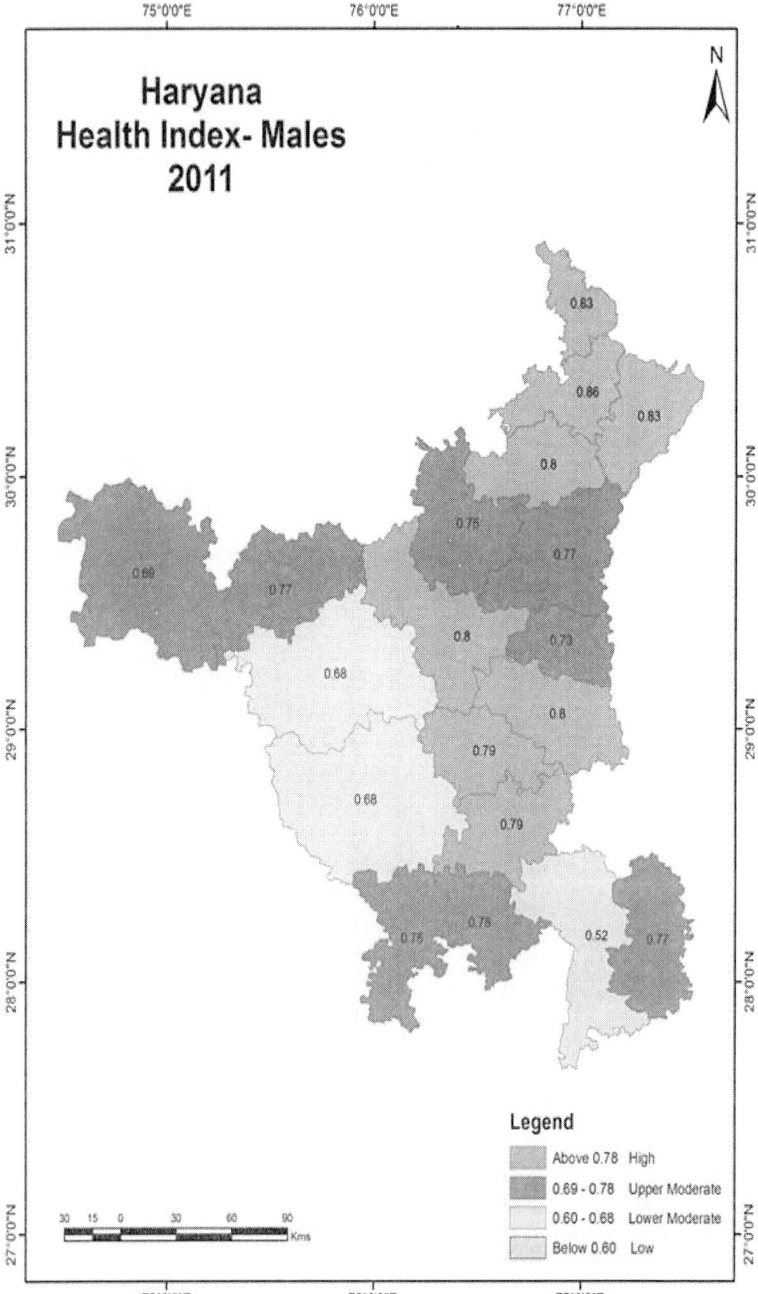
Haryana
Health Index- Males
2011
N
75°0'0"E
76°0'0"E
77°0'0"E
31°0'0"N
30°0'0"N
29°0'0"N
28°0'0"N
27°0'0"N
0.83
0.86
0.83
0.8
0.75
0.77
0.69
0.77
0.8
0.73
0.68
0.8
0.79
0.68
0.79
0.78
0.75
0.52
0.77
Legend
Above 0.78 High
0.69 - 0.78 Upper Moderate
0.60 - 0.68 Lower Moderate
Below 0.60 Low
30 15 0 30 60 90
Kms

Map 7.7

The methodology involves in the computation of EDEI is such that the districts with lesser gender biasness are granted weightage and as a result the districts that performed better as regards to EI-females have obtained higher ranks on EDEI albeit a moderate rank on EI-males (Compare Tables 7.4, 7.5 and 7.6). The cases of Panchkula, Ambala and Yamunanagar are worth mentioning here. Districts like Sonepat, Jhajjar and Rohtak have performed consistently better with respect to education indexes of both the sexes thereby obtained better rank on EDEI. On the other hand, there are districts that have performed very well as regards to EI-males but failed to maintain the performance as regards to EI-females thereby thrown away back on EDEI. Consider the case of Mahendergarh district that has been granted second rank on EI-males but a poor 12th rank on EI-females has pushed it to a meek ninth rank on EDEI. Rewari district, to some extent, has also paid the penalty of inequitable development.

Health Index – Males

Health status of the population has been determined using the variable 'marriages above the legal age of marriage' as it not only ensures the health of the married couple but also the good health of the newborn. District-wise figures as well as different categories of health index pertaining to masculine sex are depicted in Map 7.7 whereas district-wise rankings are tabulated in Table 7.7.

Table 7.7: Health Index- Males (2011)

Districts	*Rankings*
Ambala	1
Yamunanagar	2
Panchkula	3
Sonepat	4
Jind	5
Kurukshetra	6
Jhajjar	7
Rohtak	8
Rewari	9
Faridabad	10
Fatehabad	11
Karnal	12
Mahendergarh	13
Kaithal	14
Panipat	15
Sirsa	16
Bhiwani	17
Hisar	18
Gurgaon	19

Eight districts have successfully found place in the category of high attainment level. Ambala district appears as the top ranked district with an index value as high as 0.86 while its neighbouring two districts i.e. Yamunanagar (0.83) and Panchkula (0.83) standing closely behind it by capturing second and third positions respectively. Sonepat, Jind and Kurukshetra are the other districts with high attainment level. Equal number (8) of districts is incorporated in the second category representing upper moderate attainment level by acquiring index value between 0.69 and 0.78. In this way only three districts have been placed in the last two categories. Gurgaon district in the southern part of the state presents the gloomiest picture of health status of males and stands isolated in the last category with a meek index value of 0.52. The districts of Hisar (0.68) and Bhiwani (0.68) immediately preceding to Gurgaon have had reasonably higher index value than the bottom district thereby put together in the category of lower moderate attainment level.

The district-wise ranks of health index of feminine sex for 2011 have been given in the Table 7.8 whereas the distribution pattern of districts in different attainment categories has been portrayed in Map 7.8. Once again Ambala district has captured the top rank with an index value of 0.97. It is closely followed by Panchkula (0.97), Yamunanagar (0.96) and Sonepat (0.96) districts. In this way the top three ranks are claimed by the same northern most districts as noted in the case of health index of

Table 7.8: Health Index- Females (2011)

Districts	*Rankings*
Ambala	1
Panchkula	2
Yamunanagar	3
Kurukshetra	4
Sonepat	5
Panipat	6
Rohtak	7
Sirsa	8
Karnal	9
Kaithal	10
Rewari	11
Jhajjar	12
Faridabad	13
Fatehabad	14
Jind	15
Bhiwani	16
Hisar	17
Gurgaon	18
Mahendergarh	19

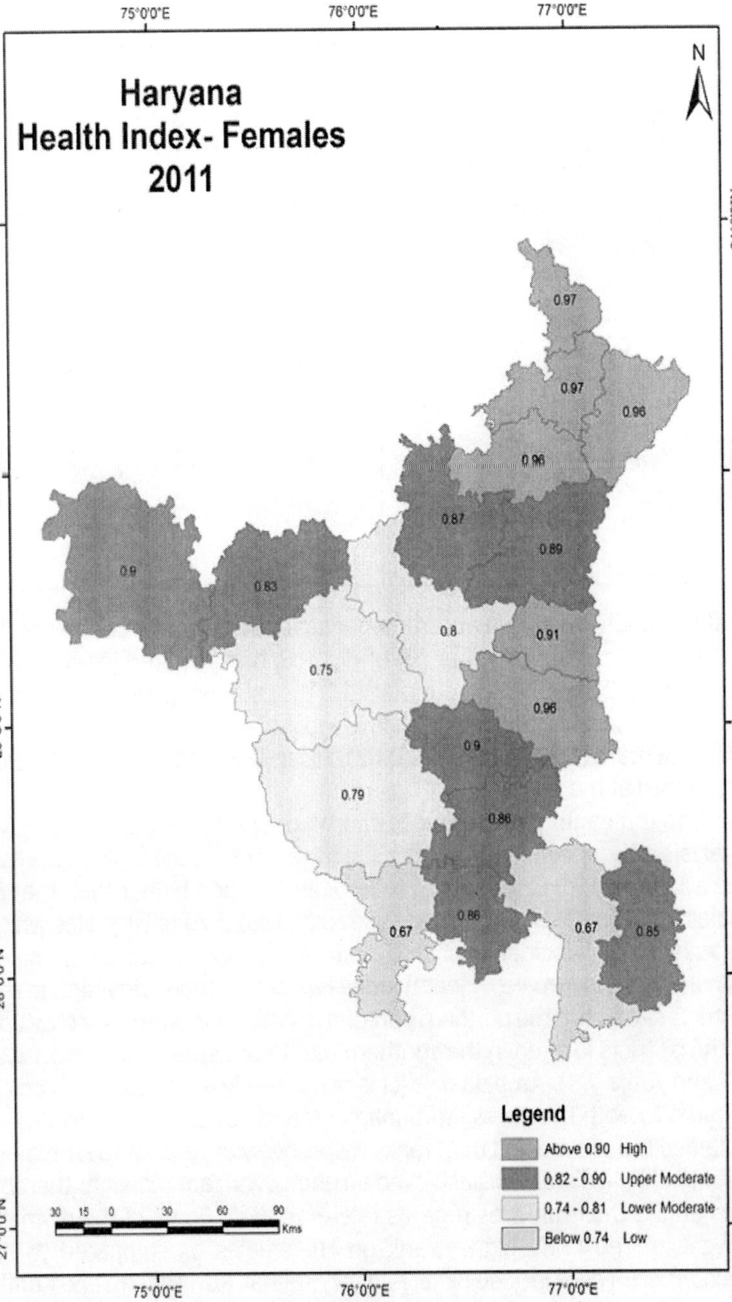
75°0'0"E
76°0'0"E
77°0'0"E
Haryana
Health Index- Females
2011
N
31°0'0"N
30°0'0"N
29°0'0"N
28°0'0"N
27°0'0"N
0.97
0.97
0.96
0.96
0.87
0.89
0.9
0.83
0.8
0.91
0.75
0.96
0.9
0.79
0.86
0.86
0.67
0.67
0.85
Legend
Above 0.90 High
0.82 - 0.90 Upper Moderate
0.74 - 0.81 Lower Moderate
Below 0.74 Low
30 15 0 30 60 90
Kms

Map 7.8

Table 7.9: Equally Distributed Health Index (2011)

Districts	*Rankings*
Ambala	1
Yamunanagar	2
Panchkula	3
Sonepat	4
Kurukshetra	5
Rohtak	6
Karnal	7
Jhajjar	8
Rewari	9
Faridabad	10
Panipat	11
Jind	12
Kaithal	13
Fatehabad	14
Sirsa	15
Bhiwani	16
Mahendergarh	17
Hisar	18
Gurgaon	19

males though Panchkula and Yamunanagar have exchanged their ranks this time. Maximum number (8) of districts has acquired index values between 0.82 and 0.90 thereby placed in the category of upper moderate attainment level. The districts mainly located in the southern parts like Mahendergarh (0.67), Gurgaon (0.67), Hisar (0.75), Bhiwani (0.79), etc., are placed at the bottom.

Some meaningful inferences can be drawn from the comparative analysis of health indexes of both the sexes. It is at the first time when the attainment level pertaining to females is found higher than that of males as HI-females amounts to 0.84 as against 0.73 of HI-males which reflects that the incidence of child marriage is more prevalent in males as compared to females. Health index has been found fairly high in the districts situated in the northern part of the state. Opposite is the situation in the districts located in the southern part of the state (Compare Table 7.7 and Table 7.8). Ambala district is consistently at the top position as regards to both the sexes. Yamunanagar and Panchkula districts have obtained the second and third ranks respectively as regards to HI-males. But Panchkula district has achieved an edge over Yamunanagar thereby exchanged their ranks as regards to HI-females. Some of the districts have acquired fairly higher rank on HI-females as compared to its counterpart. These include Sirsa, Panipat, Kaithal, Kurukshetra and Karnal

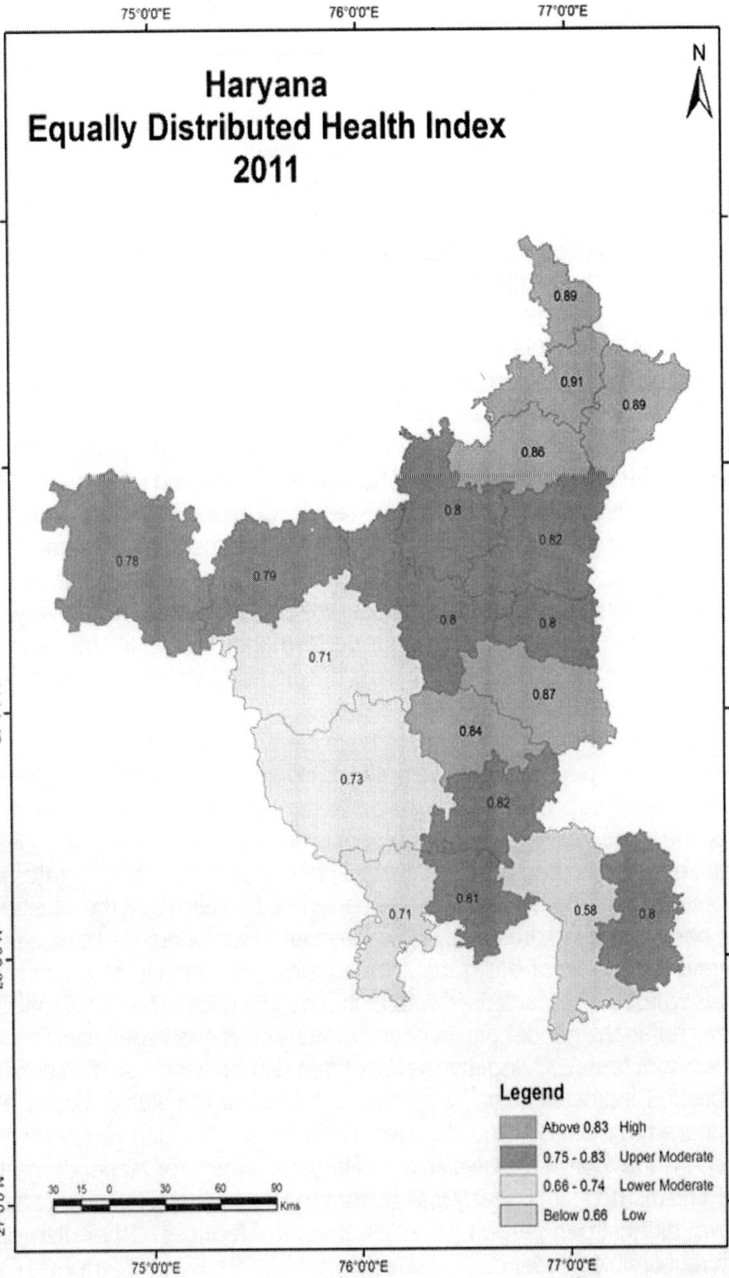
Haryana
Equally Distributed Health Index
2011
N
75°0'0"E
76°0'0"E
77°0'0"E
31°0'0"N
30°0'0"N
29°0'0"N
28°0'0"N
27°0'0"N
0.89
0.91
0.89
0.86
0.8
0.82
0.78
0.79
0.8
0.8
0.71
0.87
0.84
0.73
0.82
0.81
0.71
0.58
0.8
Legend
Above 0.83 High
0.75 - 0.83 Upper Moderate
0.66 - 0.74 Lower Moderate
Below 0.66 Low
30 15 0 30 60 90
Kms

Map 7.9

districts. On the contrary certain districts have shown poorer ranks as regards to HI-females. To name a few- Jind, Mahendergarh, and Jhajjar and Faridabad districts.

Equally Distributed Health Index (EDHI) has been worked out by considering the attainment levels of both the sexes. The district-wise ranks have been given in Table 7.9 and the spatial distribution of districts in four attainment categories has been presented in Map 7.13. It is worthwhile to mention that as many as fifteen districts have been grouped into the top two categories of attainment level leaving only four districts in the last two categories. The performance of Ambala district has been very sound in the health dimension and has been placed at the top rank with EDHI as high as 0.91. Its neighbouring districts i.e. Yamunanagar (0.89) and Panchkula (0.89) have performed fairly well in the health aspect and thereby placed at second and third ranks respectively. Sonepat, Kurukshetra and Rohtak are the other better performing districts in this dimension. Gurgaon district, on the contrary, has been placed at the bottom with the EDHI as low as 0.58 which is far behind its immediately preceding district Hisar (0.71). As a result, Gurgaon is the only district that has been placed in the category of low attainment level. In addition to Hisar, Mahendergarh (0.71) and Bhiwani (0.73) are the other districts that have come up with lower moderate performance. In this way, a concentration of districts with poor performance can easily be seen in the southern parts of the state whereas the districts located in the northern part have excelled in health dimension.

Gender parity in development is an ideal situation which is seldom achieved for a period lasting very short. However, it is one of the prime objectives of social and economic planners to work restlessly in this direction as gender gap in development is not desirable. In a country like India, gender gap had been a universal phenomenon across the states in favour of masculine gender. But it is heartening to realise that the situation has been changing drastically nowadays and fruitful results have been achieved by some of the states. Nonetheless, Haryana is amongst the states which are characterised with higher gender gaps in favour of males. But as far as the gender gap in health dimension is concerned, it is found in favour of females. Negative value of gender gap which can be seen in Figure 7.3 indicates that the attainment level of females is better as compared to males. At the state level gender gap is found -0.12. It can be seen in favour of females all over Haryana except for Mahendergarh and Jind districts. It is clearly visible from the figure that Sirsa district has shown highest gender gap (-0.21) in favour of females. Other districts with reasonable gender gap include Panipat (-0.18), Kurukshetra (-0.16), Sonepat (-0.15) and Gurgaon (-0.15). Gender gap is found above the

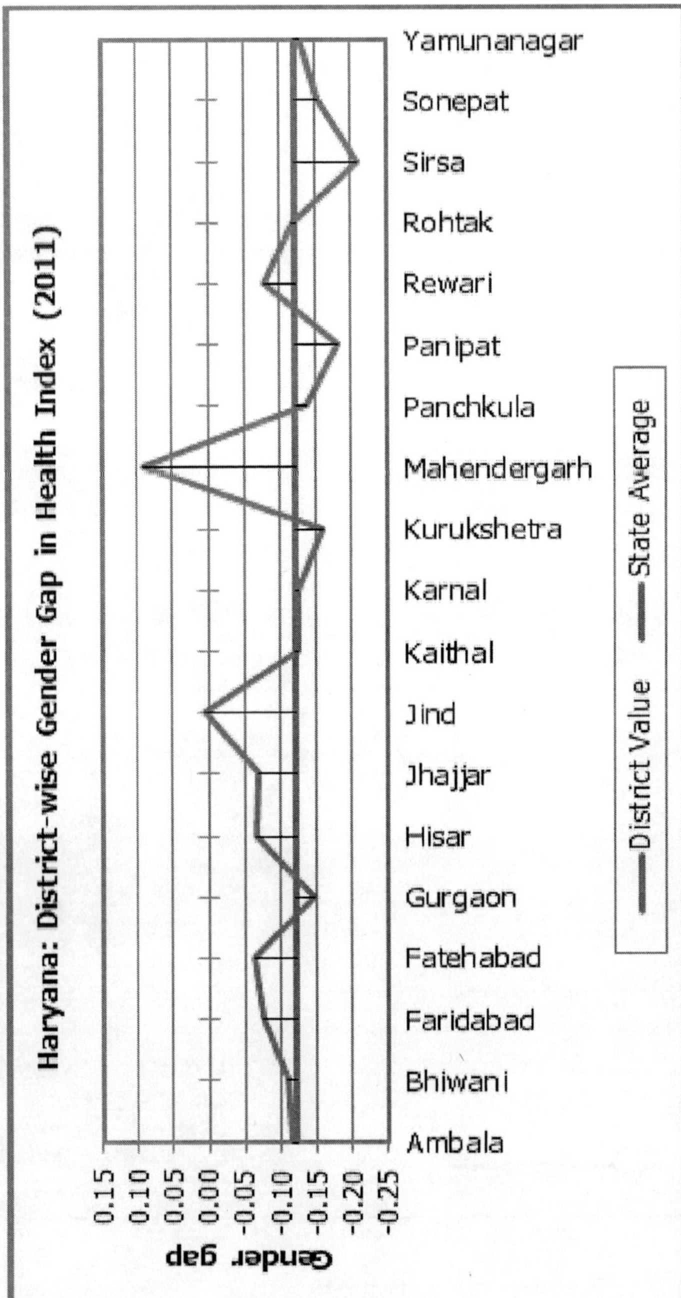
Haryana: District-wise Gender Gap in Health Index (2011)
Gender gap
0.15
0.10
0.05
0.00
-0.05
-0.10
-0.15
-0.20
-0.25
Yamunanagar
Sonepat
Sirsa
Rohtak
Rewari
Panipat
Panchkula
Mahendergarh
Kurukshetra
Karnal
Kaithal
Jind
Jhajjar
Hisar
Gurgaon
Fatehabad
Faridabad
Bhiwani
Ambala
District Value
State Average

Fig. 7.3

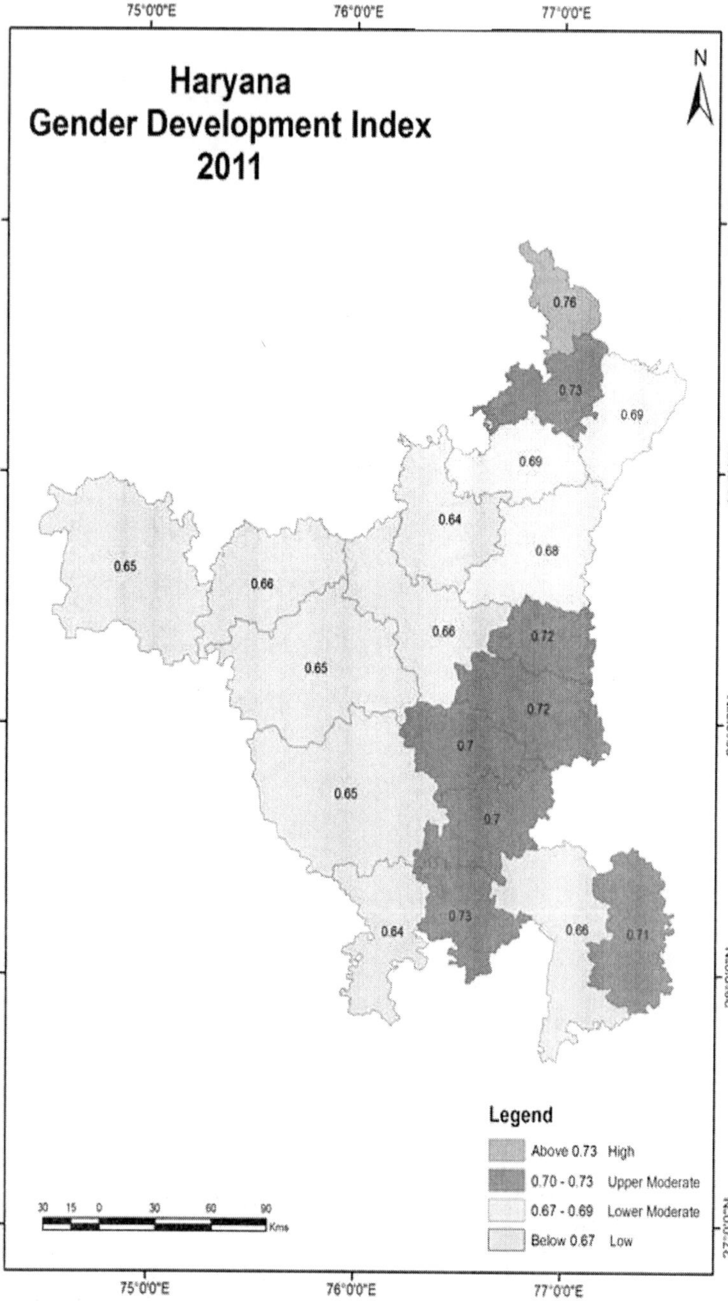
Haryana
Gender Development Index
2011
N
75°0'0"E
76°0'0"E
77°0'0"E
31°0'0"N
30°0'0"N
29°0'0"N
28°0'0"N
27°0'0"N
0.76
0.73
0.69
0.69
0.64
0.68
0.65
0.66
0.66
0.72
0.65
0.72
0.7
0.65
0.7
0.73
0.64
0.66
0.71
Legend
Above 0.73 High
0.70 - 0.73 Upper Moderate
0.67 - 0.69 Lower Moderate
Below 0.67 Low
30 15 0 30 60 90
Kms

Map 7.10

state average in districts like Rewari (-0.08), Faridabad (-0.08), Jhajjar (-0.07), Hisar (-0.07), Fatehabad (-0.06), Bhiwani (-0.01), etc. yet it is in favour of females. On the contrary, Mahendergarh district has shown exceptional trend by registering gender gap (0.09) in favour of males. One can observe that Jind district has almost achieved the ideal situation of gender equality. Here, gender gap is found as low as 0.005.

Gender Development Index

After obtaining the Equally Distributed Indexes (EDI) of all the three basic dimensions, Gender Development Index (GDI) has been carried out. The findings have been illustrated in Map 7.10 and Table 7.10.

Only the top ranked Panchkula district has found place in the category of high attainment level by capturing GDI as high as 0.76. The second ranked district Ambala (0.73) and the third ranked district Rewari (0.73) have failed to find place in this category by narrow margin thereby placed in the second category representing upper moderate attainment level. Besides, five other districts that have achieved GDI between 0.70 and 0.73 also been grouped in this category. The highest number (8) of districts has appeared in the last category pertaining to low attainment level by registering GDI below 0.67. GDI is found lowest in Kaithal district which amounts to a humble 0.64 mark. The situation of Mahendergarh (0.64) district is no better. One can easily infer from Map 7.10 that majority of districts located in the south-western tracts of the state are lagging behind in this context.

Some interesting conclusions can be drawn from Table 7.10 regarding the construction of GDI.

- Ambala district has given tough competition to Panchkula district in both the education and health dimensions but its performance in the third dimension (income) has pushed it back at second rank on GDI. While Panchkula district has been benefitted on account of its consistent and admirable performance in all the three dimensions thereby honoured with the top rank.
- None of the district has been found too consistent to obtain the same rank in all the three dimensions. However there are three districts that have obtained the same rank in two of the three dimensions. Rewari district has acquired appreciable third rank in both the income and education dimensions whereas Rohtak district has achieved respectable sixth rank in both education and health dimensions. The lower ranked district Mahendergarh has obtained poor 17th rank in both income and health dimensions. Such consistent performance has affected the GDI rankings of these districts to a large extent and

Table 7.10: Gender Development Index: District-wise Rankings (2011)

DISTRICT	*Equally Distributed Income Index*	*Equally Distributed Education Index*	*Equally Distributed Health Index*	*Gender Development Index*
Panchkula	4	1	3	1
Ambala	12	2	1	2
Rewari	3	3	9	3
Sonepat	7	5	4	4
Panipat	2	10	11	5
Faridabad	5	8	10	6
Jhajjar	10	4	8	7
Rohtak	15	6	6	8
Kurukshetra	16	11	5	9
Yamunanagar	19	7	2	10
Karnal	11	12	7	11
Gurgaon	1	14	19	12
Jind	13	16	12	13
Fatehabad	8	19	14	14
Sirsa	9	18	15	15
Hisar	6	15	18	16
Bhiwani	14	13	16	17
Mahendergarh	17	9	17	18
Kaithal	18	17	13	19
Correlation between the ranks of individual dimensions with the GDI	0.46	0.82	0.75	

resultantly Rewari has obtained an appreciable third rank, Rohtak district has succeeded to obtain a respectable eighth rank whereas Mahendergarh district has been awarded a poor 18th rank on GDI.

- Gurgaon district demonstrates the most inconsistent development trend as it has outpaced all the districts as regards to income dimension but found itself at the bottom as regards to health dimension. Furthermore, it has recorded a poor 14th rank in terms of education dimension. Exemplary performance in the income sector could not stand against the poor performance with respect to the other two dimensions and as a result it has slipped to a moderate 12th rank as regards to GDI.
- Although all the three dimensions have shown positive correlation with the GDI yet education dimension is highly (0.82) associated with it. Health dimension has also shown significant (0.75) association whereas low positive correlation of income dimension with the GDI suggests that the districts with high attainment level as regards to income dimension are not necessarily be successful in achieving a respectable position on GDI and vice versa. Consider the cases of Gurgaon, Hisar, Fatehabad and Sirsa districts (high rank on EDII but low rank on GDI), on one hand, and Ambala, Rohtak, Kurukshetra, Yamunanagar districts (low rank on EDII but high rank on GDI) on the other.

Sum up

The gist of the above discussion is that the state has to travel long way to reach the desired destination of gender parity. As of now the intensity of gender discrimination in the state is such that only the top ranked district i.e. Panchkula has found place in the category of high attainment level by performing consistently well in all the three dimensions. Although Ambala district has given tough competition to Panchkula district in both the education and health dimensions but its performance in the third dimension (income) has pushed it back at second rank on GDI. Generally the districts located in the northern part of the state have moved forwards to achieve gender parity whereas the districts situated in the southern part of the state have not shown such spirit. Although all the three dimensions have shown positive correlation with the GDI yet education dimension is highly associated with the GDI.

Health dimension has also shown significant association whereas less significant positive correlation of income dimension with the GDI suggests that the districts with high attainment level as regards to income dimension are not necessarily be successful in achieving a respectable position on GDI and vice versa.

8

Human Poverty Index, 2011

Human Development Index (HDI) and Gender Development Index (GDI) measure the level of development of population. On the contrary, Human Poverty Index (HPI), as the name suggests, focuses on the level of deprivation in terms of three basic dimensions i.e. income, education and health. Similar to that of HDI and GDI the three dimensions have been discussed in the beginning and then HPI has been constructed and analysed in the end. Here the index value ranges from 0 to 100. The value of 100 indicates that the whole population is deprived of descent standard of living whereas the index value of 0 reflects that the entire population has been provided with the minimum basic amenities required to live a descent life.

Income Deprivation

The proportion of population Below Poverty Line (BPL) has been used to measure the Index of Deprivation- Income (IOD- Income). The index values are presented in per centage term. The higher the proportion of BPL population or rank, higher is the deprivation level. At the state level 22.96 per cent of the population has been found below poverty line. The spatial distribution of districts belonging to different income deprivation categories is shown in Map 8.1. Nearly 30 per cent of the population is found below poverty line in each of the four districts (Kaithal, Jind, Fatehabad and Bhiwani) that have been grouped in the category of high deprivation level. There are as many as 14 districts where the deprivation level is above 20 per cent. Even the remaining five districts (Panchkula, Faridabad, Panipat, Jhajjar and Gurgaon) have not presented very bright picture as none of the districts has had deprivation level below 15 per cent. One district in the extreme north i.e. Panchkula (15.52) and one

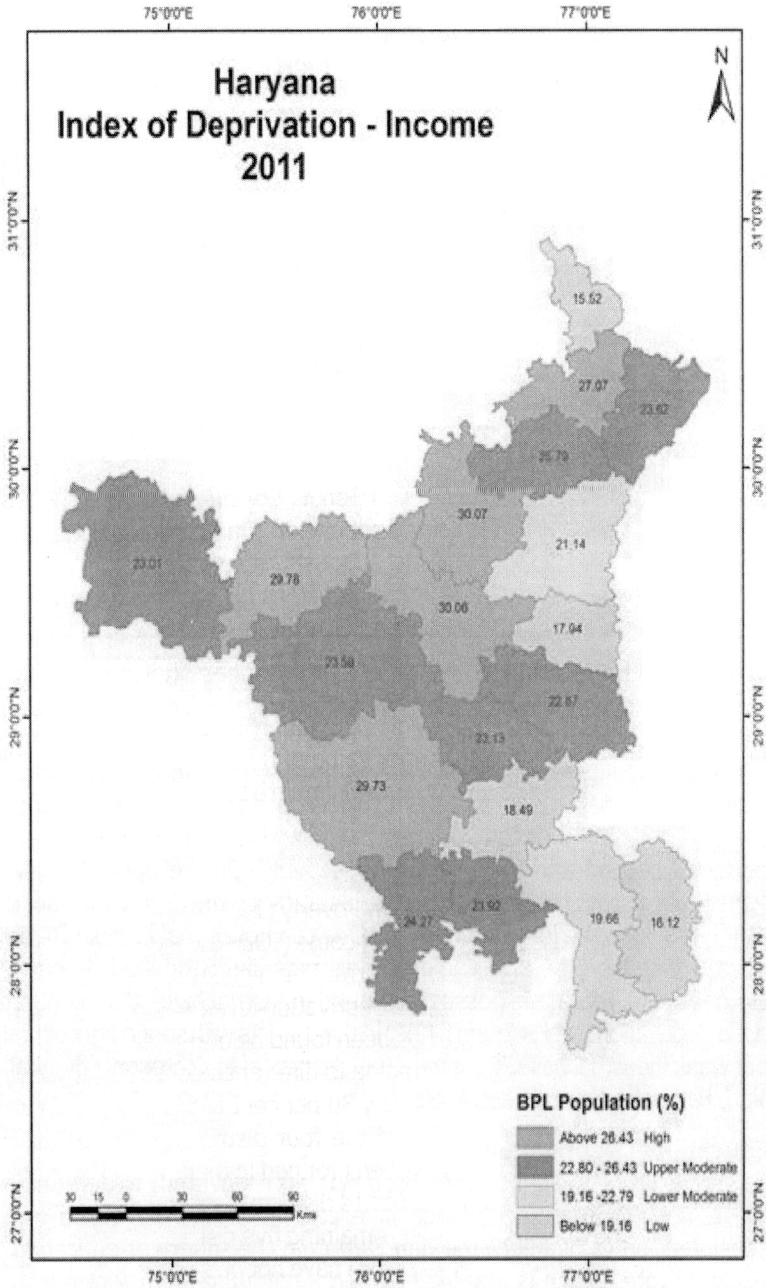
Haryana
Index of Deprivation - Income
2011
N
75°0'0"E
76°0'0"E
77°0'0"E
31°0'0"N
30°0'0"N
29°0'0"N
28°0'0"N
27°0'0"N
15.52
27.07
30.07
21.14
29.78
30.06
17.94
23.58
22.67
23.13
29.73
18.49
23.92
24.27
19.66
16.12
BPL Population (%)
Above 26.43 High
22.80 - 26.43 Upper Moderate
19.16 -22.79 Lower Moderate
Below 19.16 Low
30 15 0 30 60 90
Kms

Map 8.1

Table 8.1: Index of Deprivation in Income (2011)

Districts	*Rankings*
Kaithal	1
Jind	2
Fatehabad	3
Bhiwani	4
Ambala	5
Kurukshetra	6
Mahendergarh	7
Rewari	8
Yamunanagar	9
Hisar	10
Rohtak	11
Sirsa	12
Sonepat	13
Karnal	14
Gurgaon	15
Jhajjar	16
Panipat	17
Faridabad	18
Panchkula	19

in the extreme south i.e. Faridabad (16.12) has shown minimum deprivation level. A concentration of districts with high deprivation level can be seen in the north-western and south-western parts of the state.

Table 8.1 illustrates the district-wise rankings during 2011. Being a district with highest proportion of BPL population Kaithal has been awarded the top rank as regards to IOD-income. Jind and Fatehabad districts have obtained second and third ranks respectively. On the opposite side, Panchkula district has been given the last rank on the deprivation scale as it has shown the least deprivation. One can notice that comparatively lower ranks have been obtained by districts like Faridabad, Panipat, Gurgaon, etc. that have possessed sound industrial base. On the other hand deprivation level is found higher in the districts with sound agricultural but weak industrial base. To name a few districts in this category – Kaithal, Jind, Fatehabad, Kurukshetra, etc.

Educational Deprivation

While literacy rate has been used in the present study to determine the education attainment level, illiteracy rate has been taken into consideration to highlight the deprivation in the sphere of education. Illiteracy rate, which is obtained by subtracting the literacy rate from 100, is here termed as Index of Deprivation- Education (IOD-education). Hence the index values are given in per centage term. District-wise

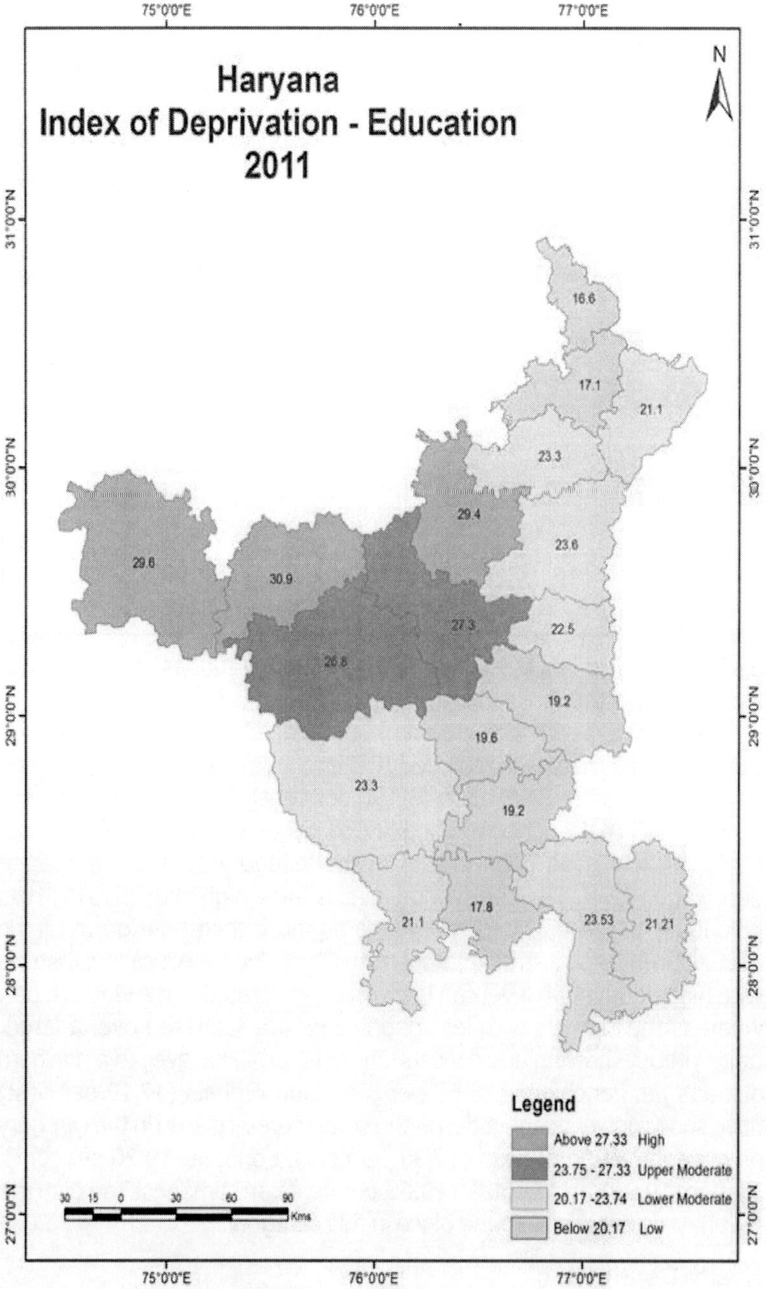
Haryana
Index of Deprivation - Education
2011
N
75°0'0"E
76°0'0"E
77°0'0"E
31°0'0"N
30°0'0"N
29°0'0"N
28°0'0"N
27°0'0"N
16.6
17.1
21.1
23.3
29.4
23.6
29.6
30.9
27.3
22.5
26.8
19.2
19.6
23.3
19.2
17.8
21.1
23.53
21.21
Legend
Above 27.33 High
23.75 - 27.33 Upper Moderate
20.17 -23.74 Lower Moderate
Below 20.17 Low
30 15 0 30 60 90
Kms

Map 8.2

Table 8.2: Index of Deprivation in Education (2011)

Districts	*Rankings*
Fatehabad	1
Sirsa	2
Kaithal	3
Jind	4
Hisar	5
Karnal	6
Gurgaon	7
Bhiwani	8
Kurukshetra	9
Panipat	10
Faridabad	11
Mahendergarh	12
Yamunanagar	13
Rohtak	14
Jhajjar	15
Sonepat	16
Rewari	17
Ambala	18
Panchkula	19

deprivation level has been classified into four categories and mapped in Map 8.2 while the ranks are presented in Table 8.2.

The districts with top three ranks are placed in the category of high deprivation as they have recorded IOD-education above 27.33 per cent. These districts are Fatehabad (30.90 per cent), Sirsa (29.60 per cent) and Kaithal (29.40 per cent). Jind (27.30 per cent) and Hisar (26.80 per cent) districts have been placed in the category of upper moderate deprivation level. The deprivation level is fairly high in the five districts belonging to the first two categories as more than one-fourth of the population in these districts has been found deprived of education. Districts with high deprivation level can be seen concentrated in the western part whereas the districts with less deprivation are scattered over a larger tract without showing any concentration pattern. However, two northern districts i.e. Panchkula (16.60 per cent) and Ambala (17.10 per cent) have shown lowest deprivation in the state thereby placed in the category of low deprivation. Rewari (17.80 per cent), Sonepat (19.20 per cent), Jhajjar (19.20) and Rohtak (19.60 per cent) are amongst the districts that have successfully found place in this category.

Health Deprivation

This is the third and last dimension to be considered to work out the HPI. The same five variables pertaining to the health aspect that had

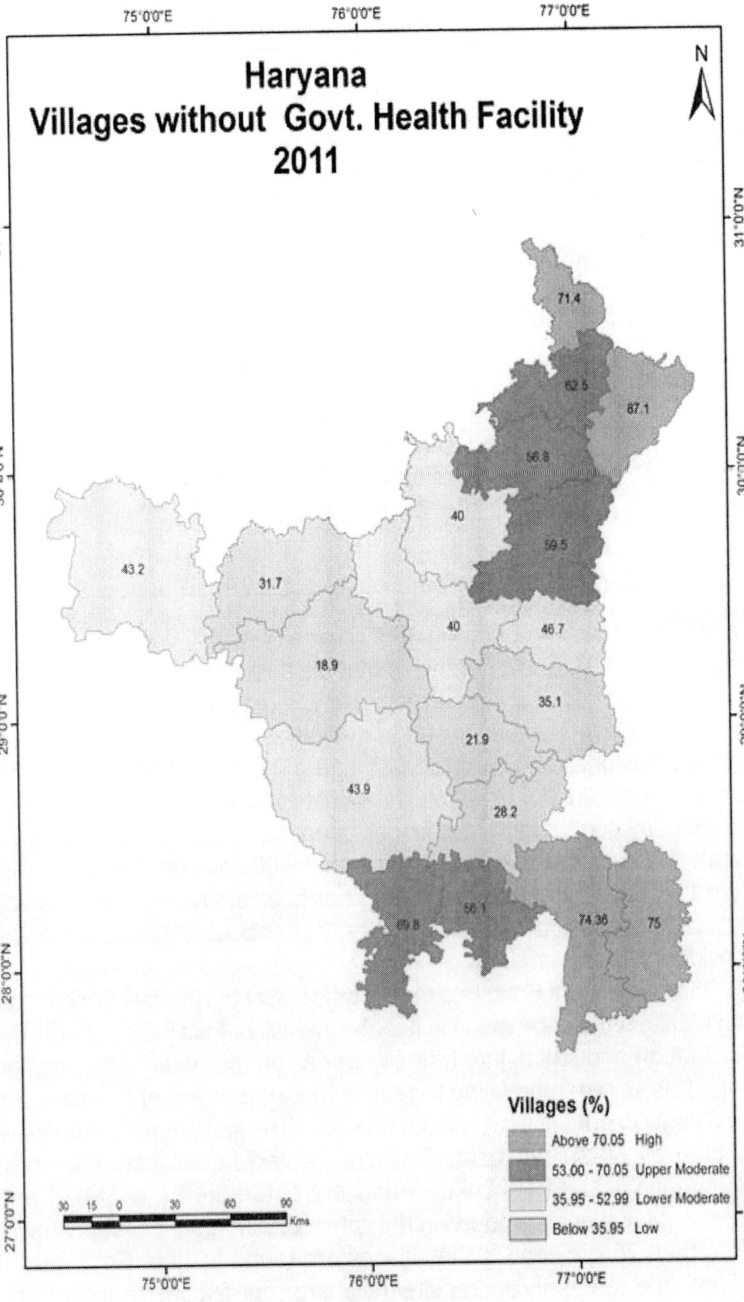
Haryana
Villages without Govt. Health Facility
2011
N
75°0'0"E
76°0'0"E
77°0'0"E
31°0'0"N
30°0'0"N
29°0'0"N
28°0'0"N
27°0'0"N
71.4
62.5
87.1
56.8
40
59.5
43.2
31.7
40
46.7
18.9
35.1
21.9
43.9
28.2
69.8
56.1
74.36
75
Villages (%)
Above 70.05 High
53.00 - 70.05 Upper Moderate
35.95 - 52.99 Lower Moderate
Below 35.95 Low
30 15 0 30 60 90
Kms

Map 8.3

Table 8.3: Villages without Govt. Health Facility (2011)

Districts	*Rankings*
Yamunanagar	1
Faridabad	2
Gurgaon	3
Panchkula	4
Mahendergarh	5
Ambala	6
Karnal	7
Kurukshetra	8
Rewari	9
Panipat	10
Bhiwani	11
Sirsa	12
Jind	13
Kaithal	14
Sonepat	15
Fatehabad	16
Jhajjar	17
Rohtak	18
Hisar	19

been used in the computation of HDI have been taken into analyses to carry out the HPI. The difference is that the data pertaining to attainment level had been used in the former case whereas the data pertaining to deprivation level has been used in the latter. Deprivation level of each variable has been acquired by subtracting the attainment level of that variable from 100. For example, the statistics for the variable 'population without any govt. health facility' has been extracted by subtracting the data pertaining to the variable 'population with any govt. health facility' from 100. Each of these five variables has been analysed separately and Index of Deprivation- Health (IOD-health) has been obtained in the end considering these variables.

'Villages without Govt. Health Facility' is one of the five health indicators that highlight the deprivation in health dimension. Map 8.3 illustrates the distribution of districts into four categories on the basis of deprivation level. It is very demoralising to realise that rural areas of the state are appallingly devoid of Govt. health facilities. The state figure amounts to as high as 50.90 per cent. Districts located in the extreme north (Yamunanagar and Panchkula) and extreme south (Faridabad and Gurgaon) have been grouped in the category of high deprivation where more than 70 per cent of the villages are found without Govt. health facility. One can easily appreciate the sharp contrast between rural and urban areas of these districts as regards to Govt. health facility. Deprivation level is fairly low in the districts like Hisar (18.90), Rohtak (21.90), Jhajjar (28.20) and Fatehabad (31.70).

Table 8.3 illustrates the district-wise rankings on the basis of index of deprivation in this aspect. Yamunanagar has come into sight as the highest deprived district in the state followed by the two industrialised districts i.e. Faridabad and Gurgaon. Surprisingly, Panchkula is also found among the districts with high deprivation. On the opposite side Hisar district which has occupied the last rank in terms of non-availability of Govt. health facility in the villages.

Not only the health facilities (in terms of health centres) but the availability of doctors at the health centres is equally important as the health centres without doctors serve no purpose. In Haryana, 74.20 per cent of the villages have been found without doctors. The districts have been classified into four categories of deprivation (Map 8.4). One can easily figures out that the highest deprivation is pervasive in Faridabad district where none of the villages has been found with doctor (DLHS III survey, 2007-08).

Moreover, 75 per cent of the villages of this district are found without Govt. health facility (Map 8.3). In this way rural areas of Faridabad district are awfully devoid of health infrastructure (Govt. health facility and Doctors)

Table 8.4: Villages without Doctor (2011)

Districts	*Rankings*
Faridabad	1
Jhajjar	2
Mahendergarh	3
Fatehabad	4
Bhiwani	5
Hisar	6
Gurgaon	7
Rohtak	8
Rewari	9
Sirsa	10
Jind	11
Yamunanagar	12
Ambala	13
Kaithal	14
Panchkula	15
Sonepat	16
Panipat	17
Kurukshetra	18
Karnal	19

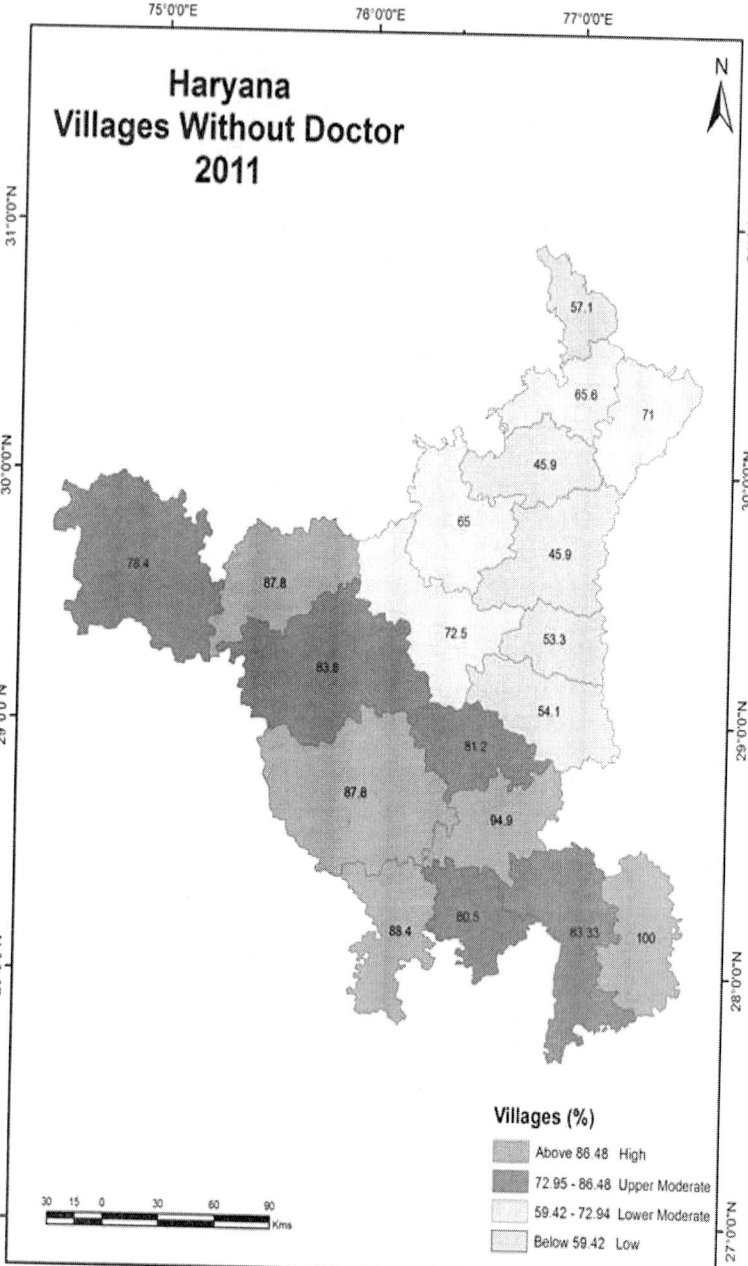
Haryana
Villages Without Doctor
2011
N
75°0'0"E
76°0'0"E
77°0'0"E
31°0'0"N
30°0'0"N
29°0'0"N
28°0'0"N
27°0'0"N
57.1
65.6
71
45.9
65
45.9
78.4
87.8
72.5
53.3
83.8
54.1
81.2
87.8
94.9
80.5
88.4
83.33
100
Villages (%)
Above 86.48 High
72.95 - 86.48 Upper Moderate
59.42 - 72.94 Lower Moderate
Below 59.42 Low
30 15 0 30 60 90
Kms

Map 8.4

which is a matter of grave concern. The situation of Jhajjar (94.90 per cent), Mahendergarh 88.40 per cent), Bhiwani (87.80 per cent), Fatehabad (87.80 per cent), Hisar (83.80 per cent), Gurgaon (83.33 per cent) and Rohtak (81.20 per cent) districts is equally critical as far as availability of doctors in the villages is concerned. Even the districts with the lowest figure i.e. Karnal (45.90 per cent) and Kurukshetra (45.90 per cent) have had fairly high deprivation level which suggests that the health infrastructure in the rural hinterland of the state is in a pitiable condition and demands urgent attention.

Rankings have been given to each district in view of intensity of deprivation i.e. villages without doctor (Table 8.4). Faridabad district stands at the top with highest deprivation level which is followed by Jhajjar, Mahendergarh and Fatehabad districts. On the other hand, the lowest rank has been awarded to Karnal district. Other districts like Kurukshetra, Panipat, Sonepat, etc. also have obtained lower ranks.

A comparative study of Table 8.3 and Table 8.4 brings out that majority of the districts have shown contrast in deprivation level with respect to the two health infrastructure variables. In other words a district appears with high deprivation in one variable shows low deprivation in the other. Consider the case of Yamunanagar district which appears with the highest deprivation level as regards to 'villages without Govt. health facility' but it has performed satisfactorily as regards to 'villages without doctor'. In

Table 8.5: Women not Received Full Ante-natal Check-ups (2011)

Districts	*Rankings*
Panipat	1
Bhiwani	2
Mahendergarh	3
Faridabad	4
Fatehabad	5
Jind	6
Hisar	7
Gurgaon	8
Kurukshetra	9
Sonepat	10
Jhajjar	11
Karnal	12
Ambala	13
Sirsa	14
Panchkula	15
Rewari	16
Yamunanagar	17
Kaithal	18
Rohtak	19

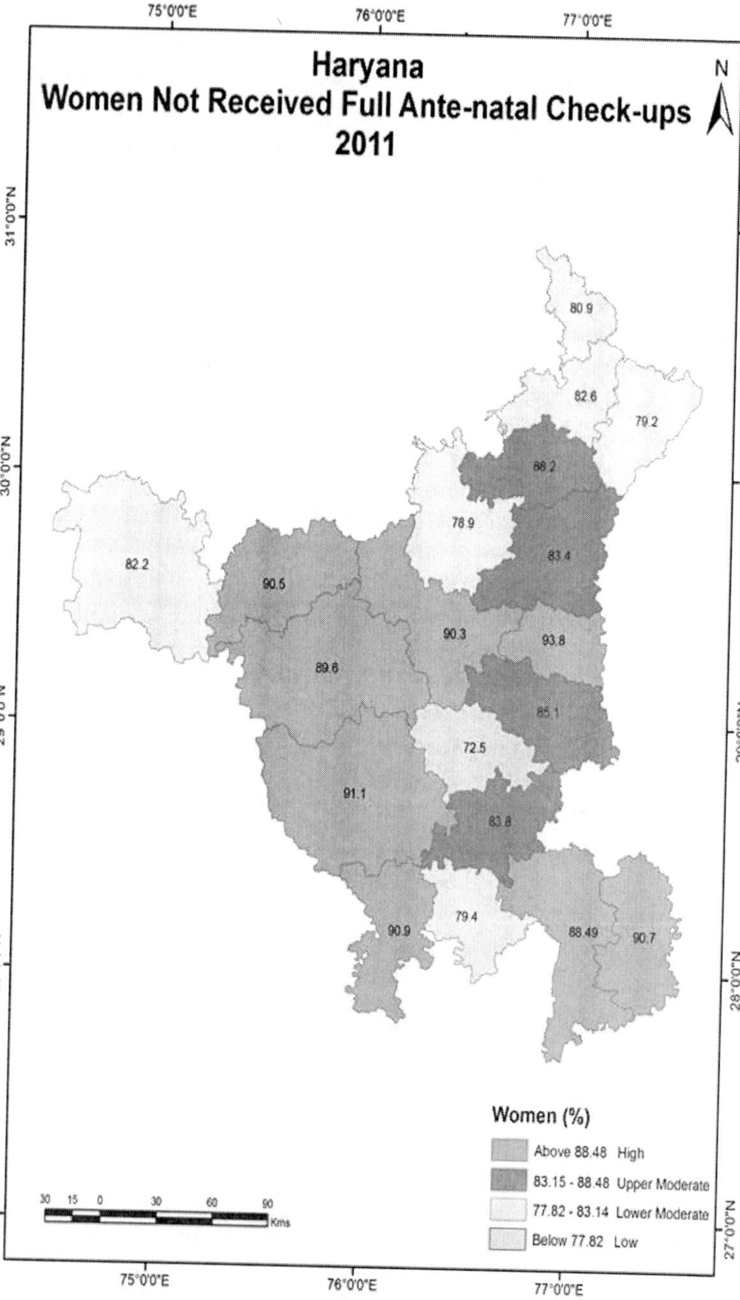
Haryana
Women Not Received Full Ante-natal Check-ups
2011
N
75°0'0"E
76°0'0"E
77°0'0"E
31°0'0"N
30°0'0"N
29°0'0"N
28°0'0"N
27°0'0"N
80.9
82.6
79.2
86.2
78.9
83.4
82.2
90.5
90.3
93.8
89.6
85.1
72.5
91.1
83.8
79.4
90.9
88.49
90.7
Women (%)
Above 88.48 High
83.15 - 88.48 Upper Moderate
77.82 - 83.14 Lower Moderate
Below 77.82 Low
30 15 0 30 60 90
Kms

Map 8.5

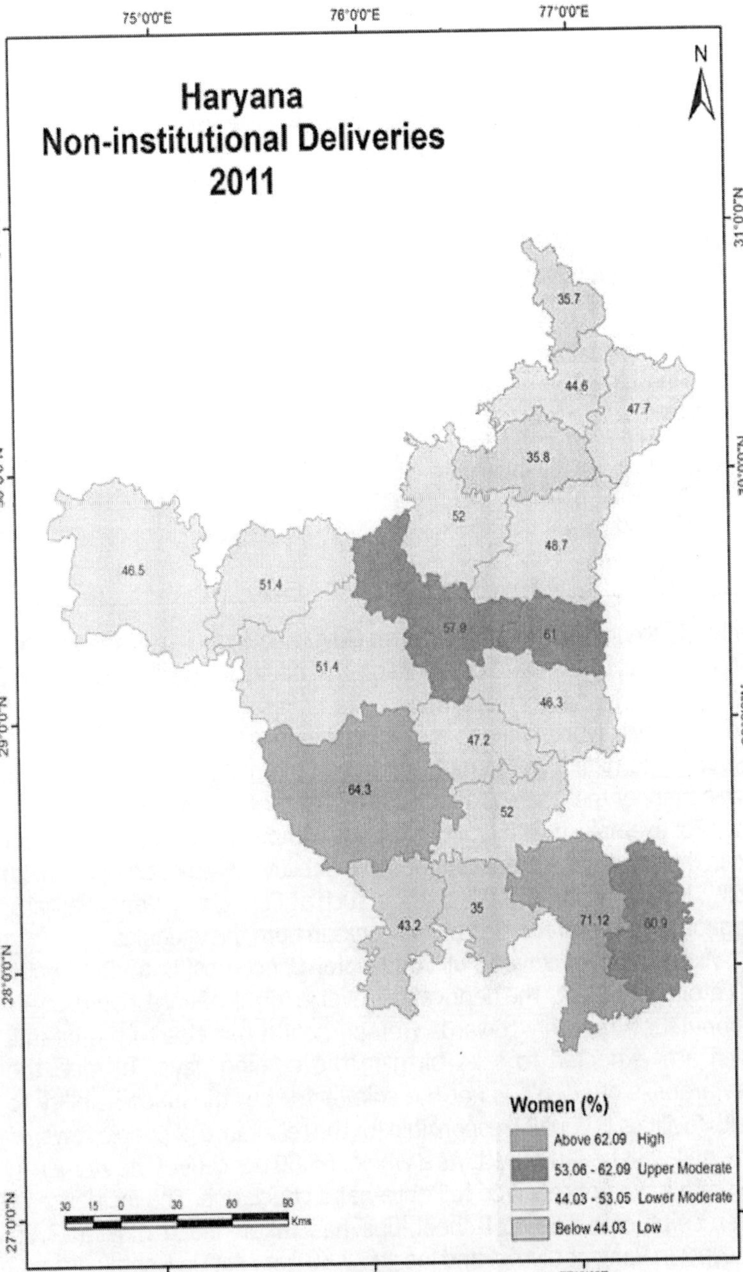
Haryana
Non-institutional Deliveries
2011
N
75°0'0"E
76°0'0"E
77°0'0"E
31°0'0"N
30°0'0"N
29°0'0"N
28°0'0"N
27°0'0"N
35.7
44.6
47.7
35.8
52
48.7
46.5
51.4
57.9
61
51.4
46.3
47.2
64.3
52
35
43.2
71.12
60.9
Women (%)
Above 62.09 High
53.06 - 62.09 Upper Moderate
44.03 - 53.05 Lower Moderate
Below 44.03 Low
30 15 0 30 60 90
Kms

Map 8.6

Table 8.6: Non-institutional Deliveries (2011)

Districts	*Rankings*
Gurgaon	1
Bhiwani	2
Panipat	3
Faridabad	4
Jind	5
Kaithal	6
Jhajjar	7
Hisar	8
Fatehabad	9
Karnal	10
Yamunanagar	11
Rohtak	12
Sirsa	13
Sonepat	14
Ambala	15
Mahendergarh	16
Kurukshetra	17
Panchkula	18
Rewari	19

contrast, Jhajjar district offers better Govt. health facility (17th rank) but deprivation level as regards to availability of doctors is pretty high (second rank). Similarly, the corresponding ranks of Hisar district have been 19th and sixth. It is worthwhile to mention here that the above two aspects pertaining to health infrastructure are complementary to each other in such a manner that there is a little use of one facility in the absence of the other. For example, health facility is useless without the availability of doctor and in the same way doctor cannot serve effectively without proper health facility. However, some of the districts such as Faridabad, Mahendergarh, Gurgaon, etc. have recorded higher ranks in both the variables.

'Women not received Full Ante-natal Check-ups' is a vital health indicator that reflects the deprivation level in terms of unresponsiveness of population not only towards women health but also to the infants which are expected to take birth in the coming days. In fact, the unawareness of people is not the sole factor but the inaccessibility to health facilities is equally responsible for the reluctance of people towards this significant health aspect. As a whole, 86.80 per cent of the women in the state have not received full ante-natal check-ups. The incidence of non-receipt of ante-natal check-ups has taken place most (93.80 per cent) in Panipat district and least (72.50 per cent) in Rohtak district. This is why; the former has been placed at the top and the latter at the bottom (Table 8.5). The magnitude of deprivation level is illustrated in Map 8.5 where the districts have been classified into four categories. The deprivation level is appallingly high not only in the category of high deprivation but also in the fourth category of lowest deprivation (below 77.80 per cent). However, a close look of Map 8.5 brings out that low to moderate deprivation level persists by and large in the northern part (Kaithal, Yamunanagar, Panchkula, Ambala) while moderate to high deprivation level is pervasive in the southern part (Gurgaon, Hisar, Fatehabad, Faridabad, Mahendergarh, Bhiwani) of the state.

There is a constant risk of health not only of the women but also of the infants who take birth when deliveries occur outside the health institutions. These institutions not only provide the hygienic conditions for safe deliveries but also the facilities of qualified doctors and/or nursing staff. The occurrence of non-institutional deliveries is one of the significant indicators showing deprivation in health dimension.

It is disheartening to realise that 53.20 per cent of the women in the state have opted for non-institutional deliveries. A perusal of Table 8.6 and Map 8.6 brings out that Gurgaon district is at the top as regard to deprivation level where 71.12 per cent of the women have undergone non-institutional deliveries. Bhiwani (64.30 per cent), Panipat (61 per cent) and Faridabad (60.90 per cent) districts have been placed at

Table 8.7: Children Age 12-35 Months not fully Vaccinated (2011)

Districts	*Rankings*
Gurgaon	1
Faridabad	2
Jind	3
Hisar	4
Panipat	5
Bhiwani	6
Sirsa	7
Fatehabad	8
Jhajjar	9
Rewari	10
Mahendergarh	11
Kurukshetra	12
Yamunanagar	13
Kaithal	14
Sonepat	15
Karnal	16
Rohtak	17
Panchkula	18
Ambala	19

second, third and fourth ranks respectively. On the other side, deprivation level is found lowest in Rewari district where only 35 per cent of the non-institutional deliveries have taken place thereby it has been placed at the bottom of deprivation tally. Similarly, the deprivation level is fairly low in the districts like Panchkula (35.70 per cent) and Kurukshetra (35.80 per cent). Interestingly, the districts with lower ranks (lower deprivation) are mainly located in northern pockets (Panchkula, Kurukshetra, Ambala) whereas districts with higher ranks (higher deprivation) are concentrated in southern part (Gurgaon, Bhiwani, Faridabad) of the state. However Rewari and Mahendergarh districts in the southern part have had exceptionally lower ranks/deprivation level.

'Children age 12-35 months not fully vaccinated' is also an important indicator of deprivation in health dimension which reflects the level of health unconsciousness of the people. As much as 40.40 per cent of the children in the above age group have not been fully vaccinated in the state. Table 8.7 throws light on the district-wise rankings; the four categories of districts based on the intensity of deprivation are presented in Map 8.7. Again Gurgaon district is at the top with the deprivation level as high as 67.70 per cent. The second rank has been occupied by Faridabad district where 53.60 per cent of the children have not been fully vaccinated. In this way the two most developed districts (in terms of industrial development) of the state are most deprived with respect to this health dimension. Ambala (20.90 per cent) district has found place at the other end of the scale with the lowest deprivation accompanied by Panchkula (21.90 per cent), Rohtak (24.30 per cent) and Karnal (24.80 per cent) districts. The concentration of districts with 'high to moderate' deprivation (Gurgaon, Faridabad, Hisar, Bhiwani, Sirsa and Fatehabad) can be seen in the south-western part whereas the districts with 'low to moderate' deprivation (Ambala, Panchkula, Karnal, Yamunanagar, and Kaithal) are concentrating in the north-eastern part of the state.

Index of deprivation in health (IOD- Health) has been calculated by taking into account all the five indicators pertaining to health deprivation. At the state level it arrives at an alarming height of 61.10 per cent. The spatial distribution of districts into four categories of deprivation has been illustrated in Map 8.8. District-wise rankings can be seen in Table 8.8. Gurgaon (77.00 per cent) district has emerged at the top rank as regard to IOD-health characterised with highest deprivation in two of the five health indicators and fairly higher ranks in the remaining three. Its neighbouring district Faridabad (76.04 per cent) has obtained second rank. Ironically, only these two industrially advanced districts have been incorporated in the category of high deprivation as regards to health

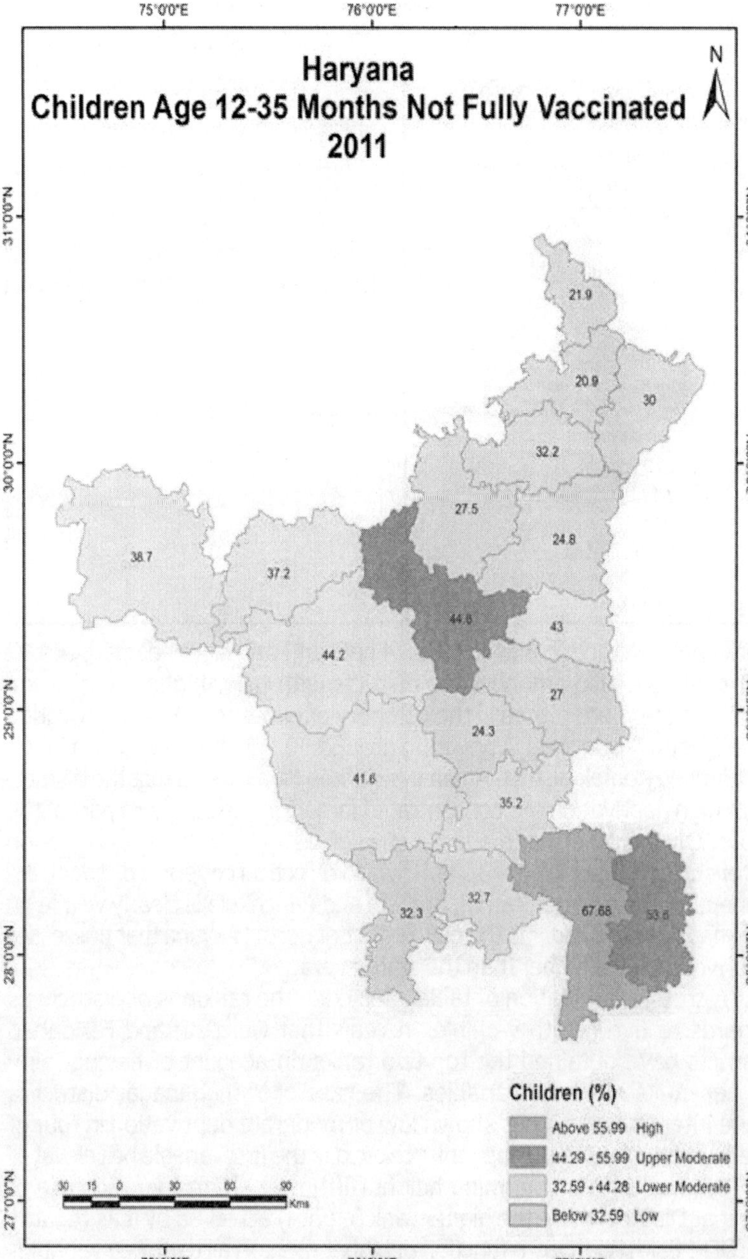
Haryana
Children Age 12-35 Months Not Fully Vaccinated
2011
N
75°0'0"E
76°0'0"E
77°0'0"E
31°0'0"N
30°0'0"N
29°0'0"N
28°0'0"N
27°0'0"N
21.9
20.9
30
32.2
27.5
24.8
38.7
37.2
44.8
43
44.2
27
24.3
41.6
35.2
32.3
32.7
67.68
53.6
Children (%)
Above 55.99 High
44.29 - 55.99 Upper Moderate
32.59 - 44.28 Lower Moderate
Below 32.59 Low
30 15 0 30 60 90
Kms

Map 8.7

Table 8.8: Index of Deprivation- Health (2011)

Districts	*Rankings*
Gurgaon	1
Faridabad	2
Bhiwani	3
Mahendergarh	4
Yamunanagar	5
Jind	6
Fatehabad	7
Panipat	8
Jhajjar	9
Sirsa	10
Hisar	11
Rewari	12
Ambala	13
Panchkula	14
Kaithal	15
Karnal	16
Kurukshetra	17
Sonepat	18
Rohtak	19

parameters. Although Bhiwani (65.74 per cent) and Mahendergarh (64.92 per cent) are also amongst the districts with fairly higher deprivation level but these are placed in the category of upper moderate deprivation level. Deprivation level is hovering around 50 per cent mark even in the last ranked Rohtak district. An analysis of the Map reveals that the districts with high deprivation are concentrated largely in the southern part of the state. On the other hand a large strip of districts with low deprivation level starting from Rohtak to northward direction covering districts like Sonepat, Kurukshetra, Karnal, Ambala and Panchkula is clearly visible on the map. Yamunanagar is the only district of north Haryana that possesses deprivation level higher than the state average.

A cross-examination of tables depicting the rankings of districts as regards to five health variables reveals that Gurgaon and Faridabad districts have obtained the top two ranks on account of having fairly higher ranks in all the variables. The case of Yamunanagar district is quite interesting as it has shown low or moderate deprivation in four of the five variables but the top rank achieved in the first variable has elevated its IOD-health to an alarming height (fifth rank). Consider the case of Panipat District where the higher rank (eighth) achieved by it as regards to IOD-health is largely a function of higher ranks in all the three variables pertaining to health unawareness. Ambala and Panchkula districts could have bring their deprivation level down considerably just by bringing down the deprivation level in the first variable only.

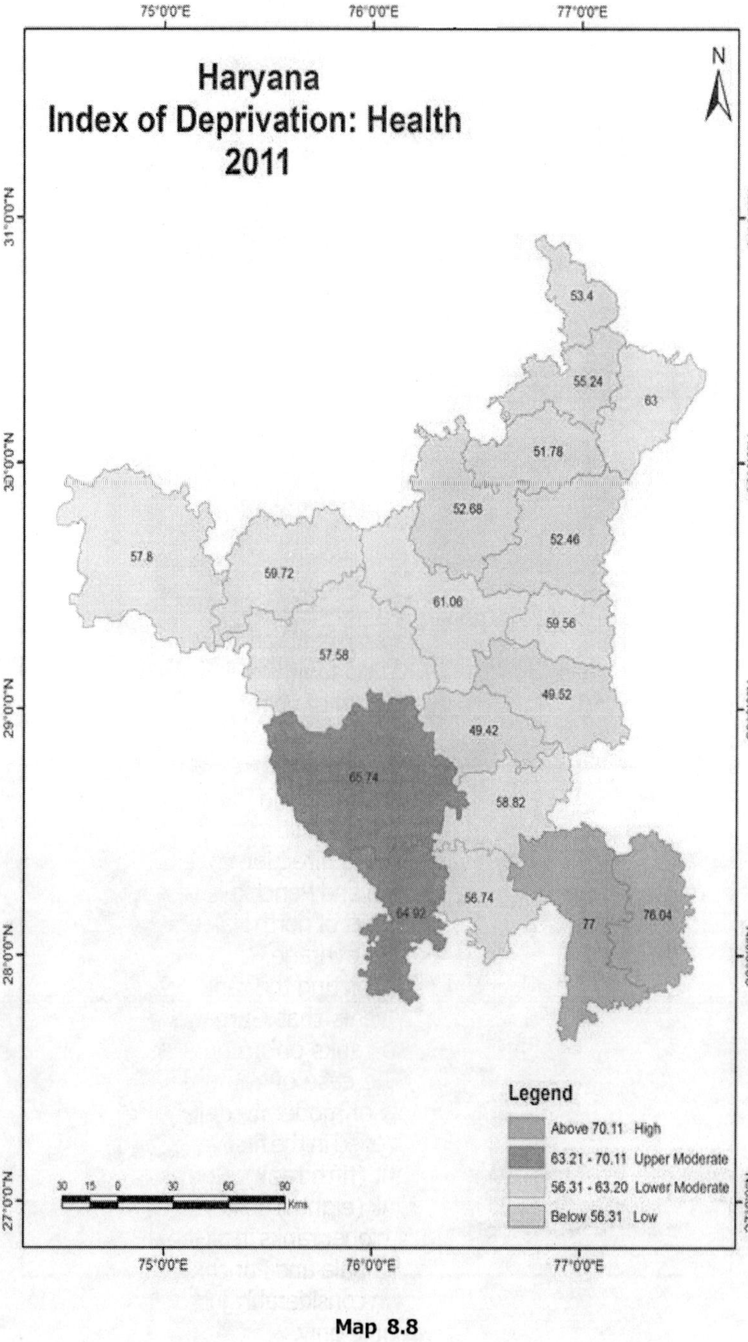

Haryana
Index of Deprivation: Health
2011
N
75°0'0"E
76°0'0"E
77°0'0"E
31°0'0"N
30°0'0"N
29°0'0"N
28°0'0"N
27°0'0"N
53.4
55.24
63
51.78
52.68
52.46
57.8
59.72
61.06
59.56
57.58
49.52
49.42
65.74
58.82
56.74
64.92
77
76.04
Legend
Above 70.11 High
63.21 - 70.11 Upper Moderate
56.31 - 63.20 Lower Moderate
Below 56.31 Low
30 15 0 30 60 90 Kms

Map 8.8

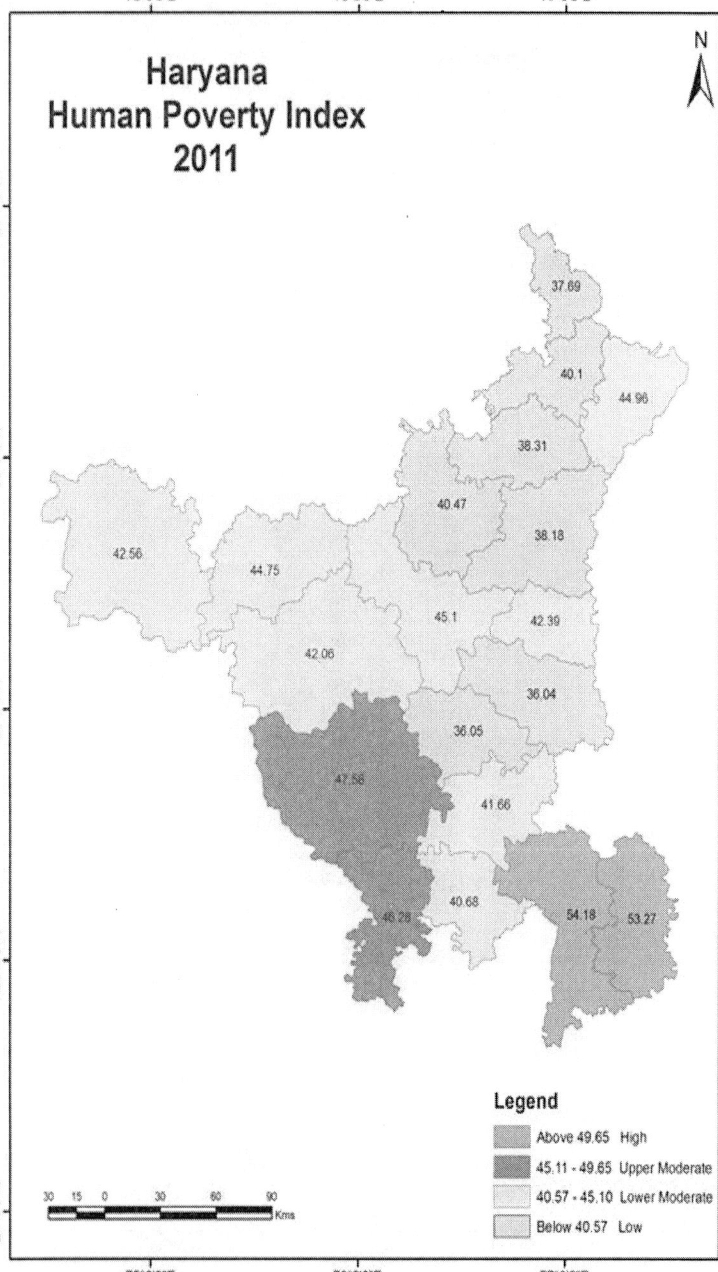
Haryana
Human Poverty Index
2011
N
75°0'0"E
76°0'0"E
77°0'0"E
31°0'0"N
30°0'0"N
29°0'0"N
28°0'0"N
27°0'0"N
37.69
40.1
44.96
38.31
40.47
38.18
42.56
44.75
45.1
42.39
42.06
36.04
36.05
47.58
41.66
40.68
40.28
54.18
53.27
Legend
Above 49.65 High
45.11 - 49.65 Upper Moderate
40.57 - 45.10 Lower Moderate
Below 40.57 Low
30 15 0 30 60 90
Kms

Map 8.9

Human Poverty Index

Considering the three broad dimensions of deprivation, Human Poverty Index (HPI) has finally been worked out. At the state level it is found 43.85. Surprisingly Gurgaon and Faridabad, the highly industrialised districts located in the National Capital Region, have appeared in the category of high HPI recording index values of 54.18 and 53.27 thereby placed at the first and second rank respectively (Map 8.9 and Table 8.9).

Table 8.9: Human Poverty Index (2011)

Districts	*Rankings*
Gurgaon	1
Faridabad	2
Bhiwani	3
Mahendergarh	4
Jind	5
Yamunanagar	6
Fatehabad	7
Sirsa	8
Panipat	9
Hisar	10
Jhajjar	11
Rewari	12
Kaithal	13
Ambala	14
Kurukshetra	15
Karnal	16
Panchkula	17
Rohtak	18
Sonepat	19

The third ranked Bhiwani (47.58) district is fairly behind its preceding district. Bhiwani and Mahendergarh districts have found place in the category of upper moderate level by registering HPI between 45.11 and 49.65. Highest number (8) of districts has been placed in the category of lower moderate HPI level whereas seven districts have found place in the fourth category pertaining to low HPI level. The intensity of deprivation level is such that it is fairly high (36.04) even in the bottom ranked Sonepat district. Nonetheless the difference of 18.14 index points between the HPI values of top and bottom ranked districts is still appallingly high indicating higher inter-district disparities.

It is now pertinent to identify the nature of relationship of the three broad dimensions with the Human Poverty Index. The relevant statistics has been tabulated in Table 8.10. Some meaningful conclusions have been drawn from the table as detailed below:

Table 8.10: Construction of Human Poverty Index: District-wise Rankings (2011)

Districts	*IOD-income*	*IOD-education*	*IOD-health*	*HPI*
Gurgaon	15	7	1	1
Faridabad	18	11	2	2
Bhiwani	4	8	3	3
Mahendergarh	7	12	4	4
Jind	2	4	6	5
Yamunanagar	9	13	5	6
Fatehabad	3	1	7	7
Sirsa	12	2	10	8
Panipat	17	10	8	9
Hisar	10	5	11	10
Jhajjar	16	15	9	11
Rewari	8	17	12	12
Kaithal	1	3	15	13
Ambala	5	18	13	14
Kurukshetra	6	9	17	15
Karnal	14	6	16	16
Panchkula	19	19	14	17
Rohtak	11	14	19	18
Sonepat	13	16	18	19
Correlation between the ranks of individual dimensions with the HPI	0.11	0.41	0.97	

- Although Gurgaon, the highly industrialised district has earned a reputation not only in India but also in the world thereby IOD-income is quite low, but the deprivation level as regards to the other two dimensions pertaining to education and health is too high to neutralise the effect of low deprivation as regards to the income dimension. As a result, it has been awarded top rank on the HPI scale. Similar is the situation of second ranked Faridabad district though it has shown lower deprivation with regard to income and education dimensions as compared to Gurgaon district.
- None of the districts has come up with the same rank in all the three dimensions which suggests that the deprivation level has not been consistently higher/lower in a district in these dimensions. However, Panchkula has recorded the same 19th rank both in income and education dimensions thereby shown somewhat consistent performance.
- Faridabad (by bringing down health deprivation) and Kaithal (by bringing down income deprivation) districts can improve their positions considerably just by bringing down deprivation level in one dimension.
- IOD-health is significantly and positively (0.97) associated with the HPI which indicates that the performance of a district in health dimension has a great bearing on the magnitude of the HPI. In other words, a district showing lower deprivation as regards to health aspect has been successful in attaining lower rank in the HPI scale.
- Contrary to health, income dimension has demonstrated insignificant but positive correlation with the HPI thereby put inconsequential impact on the construction of the latter. Consider the case of Kaithal district that has attained top rank as regards to income deprivation but acquired moderate (13th) rank on the HPI. Take other examples of Faridabad, Gurgaon and Panipat districts that have acquired fairly higher rank on the HPI irrespective of lower ranks on income deprivation. However, the correlation between education dimension and the HPI is somewhat significant.

Sum up

The deprivation level is highly pervasive in the state. The intensity of deprivation level is such that it is rather high even in the bottom ranked Sonepat district. The two industrially advanced districts of Gurgaon and Faridabad have failed to provide normative facilities of education and health to a major chunk of their residents. However, Panchkula has successfully contained its deprivation level especially in income and education dimensions. Faridabad and Kaithal districts have shown better prospects as they can bring down their poverty levels significantly just by bringing down deprivation level in one dimension. Health dimension is significantly and positively associated with the HPI while income dimension has been ineffective in the making of human poverty index.

9

Spatio-temporal Analysis of Human Development Index, 2001-2011

This chapter focuses on the temporal changes that have taken place in the HDI during 2001-2011. Two facets viz. 'absolute change' and 'proportional change' of temporal or decadal changes have been carried out. Absolute change refers to the actual change occurred in the index values of an aspect in the given time whereas proportional change reflects the per centage change. Proportional change has had an added advantage as absolute change underestimates the change occurred in the districts with low index values and overestimates in the districts with high index values. Hence, proportional change gives more realistic picture especially when inter-district disparities persist in attainment level. In addition to this, temporal movement of districts in their rankings has also been carried out to identify the direction (upward/downward) of change over the period. At first various components on the basis of which HDI has been constructed are discussed separately while temporal changes in the HDI have been discussed in the end.

Income Dimension

It is disheartening to realise that the state income index has come down from 0.642 in 2001 to 0.595 in 2011 thereby registered absolute and proportional decline of 0.047 and 7.31 per cent respectively. The decline has been witnessed all across the districts (Table 9.1).

The highest decadal decline both in terms of 'absolute change' as well as 'proportional change' has been observed in Jind district which amounts to 0.095 and 15.66 per cent respectively. Kaithal, Fatehabad, Sirsa, Bhiwani, Hisar are amongst the districts that have registered considerable decline in

Table 9.1: Spatio-temporal Analysis of Income Index (2001-2011)

Districts	*Index 2001*	*Index 2011*	*Absolute Change*	*Proportional Change (%)*
Gurgaon	0.744	0.738	-0.007	-0.89
Panchkula	0.649	0.636	-0.014	-2.11
Panipat	0.687	0.662	-0.024	-3.56
Faridabad	0.676	0.639	-0.037	-5.48
Rewari	0.644	0.606	-0.038	-5.86
Sonepat	0.608	0.561	-0.046	-7.61
Jhajjar	0.594	0.546	-0.049	-8.18
Ambala	0.662	0.608	-0.054	-8.21
Kurukshetra	0.608	0.545	-0.063	-10.38
Rohtak	0.604	0.540	-0.064	-10.60
Yamunanagar	0.628	0.561	-0.067	-10.66
Karnal	0.629	0.561	-0.068	-10.79
Mahendergarh	0.545	0.486	-0.059	-10.85
Hisar	0.641	0.564	-0.077	-12.00
Bhiwani	0.578	0.508	-0.070	-12.16
Sirsa	0.632	0.550	-0.082	-12.99
Fatehabad	0.638	0.548	-0.090	-14.15
Kaithal	0.589	0.503	-0.086	-14.66
Jind	0.606	0.511	-0.095	-15.66
Haryana	**0.642**	**0.595**	**-0.047**	**-7.31**

Table 9.2: Income Index: Temporal Movement in the Ranking of Districts (2001-2011)

Districts	*Rank in 2001*	*Rank in 2011*	*Temporal Movement*
Gurgaon	1	1	◆
Panipat	2	2	◆
Faridabad	3	3	◆
Ambala	4	5	↓
Panchkula	5	4	↑
Rewari	6	6	◆
Hisar	7	7	◆
Fatehabad	8	12	↓
Sirsa	9	11	↓
Karnal	10	9	↑
Yamunanagar	11	10	↑
Sonepat	12	8	↑
Kurukshetra	13	14	↓
Jind	14	16	↓
Rohtak	15	15	◆
Jhajjar	16	13	↑
Kaithal	17	18	↓
Bhiwani	18	17	↑
Mahendergarh	19	19	◆
Rank Correlation Coefficient (r)			**+0.95**

terms of both the facets of change. On the other hand Gurgaon district has, by and large, maintained its income level. Panchkula, Panipat, Faridabad and Rewari are amongst the districts that have registered modest decline. One can easily deduce from the given statistics that the districts with higher index values have registered a modest decline whereas the districts with lower index values have suffered a sharp decadal decline. The decline in the income index is a function of decline in real per capita GDP (PPP$) even though per capita GDP (Rs) of the state has increased over time.

Temporal movement of the districts has been worked out on the basis of ranks obtained by these districts in both the time periods (Table 9.2). Seven districts have maintained their ranks during the period under study which include three top ranked districts viz. Gurgaon, Panipat and Faridabad. Mahendergarh district remains at the bottom. Rewari and Hisar districts have maintained their sixth and seventh ranks respectively. Six districts have improved their positions by registering upward movement (though slight) during the decade. These districts include higher ranked district of Panchkula, middle ranked districts of Karnal, Yamunanagar and Sonepat; and lower raked districts of Jhajjar and Bhiwani. The highest jump of four ranks is achieved by Sonepat district. Contrarily, six districts have registered downward movements which include higher ranked Ambala district, middle ranked Fatehabad and Sirsa districts; and lower ranked Kurukshetra, Jind and Kaithal districts. Fatehabad district has suffered sharpest plunge of four ranks.

To make the interpretation more precise, rank correlation coefficient has also been calculated between the ranks obtained by the districts over the two time periods i.e. 2001 and 2011. The higher (positive) the coefficient lesser is the inter-district deviation during the given time period and vice-versa. A significantly high positive correlation (0.95) of income index reflects that the decadal movement is far from significant during the period. Generally speaking, the districts have maintained their status with regard to income index during 2001-2011 and no significant shifting in the relative positions of the districts has been noticed.

Education Dimension

The state education index which was 0.679 in 2001 has increased to 0.766 in 2011 thereby recorded an absolute increase of 0.087 index points and proportional increase of 12.86 per cent. The increase can be seen across all the districts. Gurgaon district has appeared with the highest temporal change with reference to both the aspects of change which is followed by Kaithal and Fatehabad districts (Table 9.3).

Jind, Sirsa, Bhiwani and Hisar are amongst the districts that have registered decadal change above the state average in proportional terms.

Table 9.3: Spatio-temporal Analysis of Education Index (2001-2011)

Districts	*Index 2001*	*Index 2011*	*Absolute Change*	*Proportional Change (%)*
Gurgaon	0.629	0.765	0.136	21.55
Kaithal	0.590	0.706	0.116	19.62
Fatehabad	0.580	0.691	0.111	19.18
Jind	0.621	0.727	0.106	17.03
Sirsa	0.606	0.704	0.099	16.27
Bhiwani	0.675	0.767	0.093	13.71
Hisar	0.648	0.732	0.084	12.91
Mahendergarh	0.699	0.789	0.090	12.89
Karnal	0.677	0.764	0.087	12.78
Panchkula	0.740	0.834	0.094	12.70
Faridabad	0.700	0.788	0.088	12.51
Panipat	0.692	0.775	0.083	12.04
Jhajjar	0.724	0.808	0.084	11.63
Sonepat	0.728	0.808	0.080	11.00
Yamunanagar	0.716	0.789	0.073	10.15
Ambala	0.753	0.829	0.076	10.08
Kurukshetra	0.699	0.767	0.068	9.76
Rewari	0.753	0.822	0.070	9.24
Rohtak	0.737	0.804	0.067	9.06
Haryana	**0.679**	**0.766**	**0.087**	**12.86**

Panchkula and Faridabad districts have also recorded change marginally above the state average but only in absolute terms and not in proportional terms. Rohtak district has recorded lowest change which is immediately preceded by Rewari and Kurukshetra districts where decadal change is found below 10 per cent. Generally the intensity of change is found higher in the districts with lesser index values whereas it is found lesser in the districts where it has already reached at a higher level.

District-wise ranks as well as temporal movement have been depicted in Table 9.4. A very high positive correlation (0.96) strongly suggests that the decadal movement of districts has been very insignificant notwithstanding the fact that only three districts have kept themselves stable on the same status during both the periods. The data reveals that out of the nine districts that have observed downward movement as many as six districts have descended only one step. The other three districts have relegated two steps only. Similar tendency can be seen in the districts with upward movement. It can be inferred from the given statistics that educational development has taken place all over the state without any significant decadal variation.

Health Dimension

Unfortunately, the decadal change in the attainment level of 'Govt. Health Facility' reflects a negative trend in the state (Table 9.5). At the state level absolute change of -0.149 index points reaches at -23.28 per cent in terms of proportional change. Majority of districts in the state have registered negative change. As far as the intensity of absolute change is concerned, the sharpest decline can be noticed in Faridabad (0.402) district. Karnal (0.386), Mahendergarh (0.333) and Gurgaon (0.318) districts have also shown steep decline in absolute terms. But as regards to proportional terms, Yamunanagar (64.36 per cent) district has shown sharpest decline whereas in absolute terms the figure is 0.233 which is well below the corresponding figures of Faridabad, Karnal, Mahendergarh, Gurgaon and Panipat. As stated earlier the absolute change underrates the change in the case of district like Yamunanagar which possesses low index value. On the contrary, three districts have come up with positive change. Surprisingly, Jind district has registered highest change both in absolute and proportional terms albeit its poor performance in income dimension and modest performance in education dimension as observed in the preceding section. Jhajjar district has joined it with a handsome positive change. However, Sonepat has shown modest increase during the period. It can be inferred from the statistics that the rural areas of even the industrially advanced districts are in a critically poor condition as regards to health facility.

Table 9.4: Education Index: Temporal Movement

Districts	*Rank in 2001*	*Rank in 2011*	*Temporal Movement*
Ambala	1	2	↓
Rewari	2	3	↓
Panchkula	3	1	↑
Rohtak	4	6	↓
Sonepat	5	5	◆
Jhajjar	6	4	↑
Yamunanagar	7	8	↓
Faridabad	8	9	↓
Mahendergarh	9	7	↑
Kurukshetra	10	12	↓
Panipat	11	10	↑
Karnal	12	14	↓
Bhiwani	13	11	↑
Hisar	14	15	↓
Gurgaon	15	13	↑
Jind	16	16	◆
Sirsa	17	18	↓
Kaithal	18	17	↑
Fatehabad	19	19	◆
Rank Correlation Coefficient (r)			**+0.96**

Table 9.5: Spatio-temporal Analysis of Govt. Health Facility (2001-2011)

Districts	*Index 2001*	*Index 2011*	*Absolute Change*	*Proportional Change (%)*
Jind	0.502	0.600	0.098	19.52
Jhajjar	0.646	0.718	0.072	11.15
Sonepat	0.63	0.649	0.019	3.02
Fatehabad	0.703	0.683	-0.020	-2.84
Bhiwani	0.579	0.561	-0.018	-3.11
Hisar	0.88	0.811	-0.069	-7.84
Rohtak	0.864	0.781	-0.083	-9.61
Sirsa	0.64	0.568	-0.072	-11.25
Ambala	0.443	0.375	-0.068	-15.35
Kurukshetra	0.536	0.432	-0.104	-19.40
Kaithal	0.763	0.600	-0.163	-21.36
Rewari	0.565	0.439	-0.126	-22.30
Panipat	0.815	0.533	-0.282	-34.60
Panchkula	0.465	0.286	-0.179	-38.49
Karnal	0.791	0.405	-0.386	-48.80
Mahendergarh	0.635	0.302	-0.333	-52.44
Gurgaon	0.574	0.256	-0.318	-55.33
Faridabad	0.652	0.250	-0.402	-61.66
Yamunanagar	0.362	0.129	-0.233	-64.36
Haryana	**0.640**	**0.491**	**-0.149**	**-23.28**

Table 9.6: Govt. Health Facility: Temporal Movement in the Ranking of Districts (2001-2011)

Districts	*Rank in 2001*	*Rank in 2011*	*Temporal Movement*
Hisar	1	1	◆
Rohtak	2	2	◆
Panipat	3	10	↓
Karnal	4	13	↓
Kaithal	5	6	↓
Fatehabad	6	4	↑
Faridabad	7	18	↓
Jhajjar	8	3	↑
Sirsa	9	8	↑
Mahendergarh	10	15	↓
Sonepat	11	5	↑
Bhiwani	12	9	↑
Gurgaon	13	17	↓
Rewari	14	11	↑
Kurukshetra	15	12	↑
Jind	16	7	↑
Panchkula	17	16	↑
Ambala	18	14	↑
Yamunanagar	19	19	◆
Rank Correlation Coefficient (r)			**+0.58**

Table 9.7: Spatio-temporal Analysis of Villages with Doctor (2001-2011)

Districts	*Index 2001*	*Index 2011*	*Absolute Change*	*Proportional Change (%)*
Kurukshetra	0.198	0.541	0.343	173.23
Ambala	0.180	0.344	0.164	91.11
Karnal	0.756	0.541	-0.215	-28.44
Rewari	0.293	0.195	-0.098	-33.45
Sonepat	0.761	0.459	-0.302	-39.68
Panchkula	0.799	0.429	-0.370	-46.31
Panipat	0.974	0.467	-0.507	-52.05
Hisar	0.409	0.162	-0.247	-60.39
Kaithal	0.901	0.350	-0.551	-61.15
Yamunanagar	0.772	0.290	-0.482	-62.44
Jind	0.760	0.275	-0.485	-63.82
Sirsa	0.704	0.216	-0.488	-69.32
Rohtak	0.712	0.188	-0.524	-73.60
Fatehabad	0.465	0.122	-0.343	-73.76
Gurgaon	0.928	0.167	-0.761	-82.04
Mahendergarh	0.654	0.116	-0.538	-82.26
Bhiwani	0.883	0.122	-0.761	-86.18
Jhajjar	0.653	0.051	-0.602	-92.19
Faridabad	0.854	0.000	-0.854	-100.00
Haryana	**0.664**	**0.258**	**-0.406**	**-61.14**

The temporal movement of the districts has been depicted in Table 9.6. A moderate positive correlation coefficient (0.58) shows that the decadal movement of the districts has affected their status in a fairly impressive way. Only three districts have maintained their positions during the decade. Out of these, Hisar and Rohtak have maintained their first and second positions respectively whereas Yamunanagar remains at the bottom. As many as ten districts have improved their ranks. Jind district which was at a humble 16th rank in 2001 has shown exemplary improvement of nine ranks thereby reached at seventh rank in 2011. The other districts with appreciable upward movement are Sonepat and Jhajjar. On the contrary, six districts have downgraded their positions. Most of the districts are those which possessed higher ranks in 2001. Consider the situations of Panipat and Karnal districts that had obtained third and fourth ranks respectively in the earlier point of time. In 2011, they have slipped to meek tenth and 13th ranks thereby registered a sharp plunge of seven and nine ranks respectively. However, the sharpest downfall of 11 ranks has been noticed in Faridabad district.

As far as the availability of doctors is concerned, the present statistics brings out that the health aspect of rural masses has been neglected in the state. A fair state index amounting to 0.664 in 2001 has dipped to a meek 0.258 in 2011 thereby registered a sharp plunge of 0.406 index points in terms of absolute change whereas in proportional terms it amounts to 61.14 per cent (Table 9.7). The incidence of negative temporal change has been conspicuous across most of the districts, though with the diverse magnitude. In terms of proportional change, Faridabad district has suffered the sharpest decline of 100 per cent as none of the villages surveyed has been found with facility of doctor in 2011. The other districts with noticeable negative change are Jhajjar (92.19 per cent), Bhiwani (86.18 per cent), Mahendergarh (82.26 per cent) and Gurgaon (82.04 per cent). Contrary to this, a ray of hope can be seen in Kurukshetra and Ambala districts as they have recorded positive decadal change as regards to the availability of doctor in the rural hinterland. It is quite interesting to compare the trend of two neighbouring districts i.e. Kurukshetra and Karnal, located in the northern part of the state. Both of these have been placed at the top rank in 2011 with an index value of 0.541. Kurukshetra district has achieved the top rank by recording an appreciable growth of 173.23 per cent whereas Karnal district shares the top rank by losing its earlier strength by 28.44 per cent.

Temporal movement of the districts with respect to the availability of doctor in the rural areas has been illustrated in Table 9.8. A negligible positive correlation (0.1) strongly indicates that the districts have experienced large scale reshuffling in their ranks with respect to the

Table 9.8: Villages with Doctor: Temporal Movement in the Ranking of Districts (2001-2011)

Districts	*Rank in 2001*	*Rank in 2011*	*Temporal Movement*
Panipat	1	3	↓
Gurgaon	2	13	↓
Kaithal	3	6	↓
Bhiwani	4	15	↓
Faridabad	5	19	↓
Panchkula	6	5	↑
Yamunanagar	7	8	↓
Sonepat	8	4	↑
Jind	9	9	◆
Karnal	10	1	↑
Rohtak	11	12	↓
Sirsa	12	10	↑
Mahendergarh	13	17	↓
Jhajjar	14	18	↓
Fatehabad	15	16	↓
Hisar	16	14	↑
Rewari	17	11	↑
Kurukshetra	18	2	↑
Ambala	19	7	↑
Rank Correlation Coefficient (r)			**+0.10**

Table 9.9: Spatio-temporal Analysis of Women Received Full Ante-natal Check-ups (2001-2011)

Districts	*Index 2001*	*Index 2011*	*Absolute Change*	*Proportional Change (%)*
Sirsa	0.072	0.178	0.106	147.22
Yamunanagar	0.122	0.208	0.086	70.49
Sonepat	0.088	0.149	0.061	69.32
Rewari	0.127	0.206	0.079	62.20
Kaithal	0.131	0.211	0.08	61.07
Jind	0.066	0.097	0.031	46.97
Rohtak	0.19	0.275	0.085	44.74
Faridabad	0.065	0.093	0.028	43.08
Mahendergarh	0.071	0.091	0.02	28.17
Karnal	0.132	0.166	0.034	25.76
Fatehabad	0.077	0.095	0.018	23.38
Gurgaon	0.100	0.115	0.015	15.11
Jhajjar	0.154	0.162	0.008	5.19
Panchkula	0.208	0.191	-0.017	-8.17
Ambala	0.192	0.174	-0.018	-9.38
Hisar	0.139	0.104	-0.035	-25.18
Kurukshetra	0.195	0.118	-0.077	-39.49
Bhiwani	0.156	0.089	-0.067	-42.95
Panipat	0.133	0.062	-0.071	-53.38
Haryana	**0.118**	**0.132**	**0.014**	**11.86**

Table 9.10: Women Received Full Ante-natal Check-ups: Temporal Movement in the Ranking of Districts (2001-2011)

Districts	*Rank in 2001*	*Rank in 2011*	*Temporal Movement*
Panchkula	1	5	↓
Kurukshetra	2	11	↓
Ambala	3	7	↓
Rohtak	4	1	↑
Bhiwani	5	18	↓
Jhajjar	6	9	↓
Hisar	7	13	↓
Panipat	8	19	↓
Karnal	9	8	↑
Kaithal	10	2	↑
Rewari	11	4	↑
Yamunanagar	12	3	↑
Gurgaon	13	12	↑
Sonepat	14	10	↑
Fatehabad	15	15	◆
Sirsa	16	6	↑
Mahendergarh	17	17	◆
Jind	18	14	↑
Faridabad	19	16	↑
Rank Correlation Coefficient (r)			**+0.30**

attainment level of villages with doctor. The data reveals that all the districts have witnessed shifting in their ranks during the decade apart from Jind district which is consistently stable at ninth rank over the given period. Interestingly, five top ranked districts of 2001 have moved downward whereas the upward movement is visible in the four bottom ranked districts. The most alarming movement can be seen in Faridabad district that has slipped to the last position in 2011 from a respectable fifth position in 2001. The situation of Gurgaon and Bhiwani districts is also critical as each district has downgraded its earlier position by 11 ranks. Kurukshetra district, on the other hand, has set an example in the state by moving at the top from the bottom over the period. Karnal district has captured top rank (shared with Kurukshetra) even after recording negative decadal change. It occurred on account of sharper decline experienced by the other higher ranked districts like Faridabad, Gurgaon, Bhiwani, Jhajjar and Kaithal as compared to Karnal district.

As regards to the incidence of full ante-natal check-ups, district-wise attainment levels and the temporal changes therein are presented in Table 9.9. Although the attainment level of the state is not at all pleasing yet it has registered an increasing trend by recording proportional change up to 11.86 per cent. Nearly two-third of the districts have recorded positive change above the state level. Sirsa district has recorded the highest boost by gaining 0.106 index points in its earlier strength thereby its proportional change reaches at 147.22 per cent. The other districts with conspicuous positive proportional change include Yamunanagar (70.49 per cent), Sonepat (69.32 per cent), Rewari (62.20 per cent) and Kaithal (61.07 per cent).

It is mesmerising fact that districts like Faridabad and Gurgaon that have experienced a sharp negative change in both the health infrastructure indicators (observed in the preceding section) have come up with positive decadal change, though their attainment levels are still low. The districts with negative decadal change are lead by Panipat which has suffered a decline of 53.38 per cent in terms of proportional change though the sharpest decline in terms of absolute change can be seen in Kurukshetra district. Bhiwani and Hisar are amongst the districts that have registered noteworthy descending trend.

Most of the districts have experienced temporal shifting in their corresponding ranks (Table 9.10). Furthermore, the intensity of shifting is also quite significant as the correlation coefficient is fairly low (0.3). Only two districts i.e. Fatehabad and Mahendergarh with the lower ranks have remained firm over the period. All the higher ranked districts in 2001 have shifted downwards except Rohtak district. Kurukshetra district which was at second rank in 2001 has slipped to eleventh rank in 2011.

Table 9.11: Spatio-temporal Analysis of Women who had Institutional Deliveries (2001-2011)

Districts	*Index 2001*	*Index 2011*	*Absolute Change*	*Proportional Change (%)*
Kaithal	0.284	0.48	0.196	69.01
Yamunanagar	0.316	0.523	0.207	65.51
Sirsa	0.333	0.535	0.202	60.66
Jind	0.271	0.421	0.15	55.35
Mahendergarh	0.368	0.568	0.200	54.35
Karnal	0.338	0.513	0.175	51.78
Hisar	0.324	0.486	0.162	50.00
Panchkula	0.451	0.643	0.192	42.57
Rewari	0.459	0.65	0.191	41.61
Gurgaon	0.204	0.289	0.085	41.56
Fatehabad	0.379	0.486	0.107	28.23
Kurukshetra	0.503	0.642	0.139	27.63
Rohtak	0.419	0.528	0.109	26.01
Faridabad	0.312	0.391	0.079	25.32
Panipat	0.339	0.39	0.051	15.04
Jhajjar	0.462	0.48	0.018	3.90
Bhiwani	0.363	0.357	-0.006	-1.65
Ambala	0.618	0.554	-0.064	-10.36
Haryana	**0.351**	**0.468**	**0.117**	**33.33**

Similarly Bhiwani has slipped from fifth to eighteenth rank, Hisar from seventh to thirteenth rank and Panipat has plunged from eighth rank to the bottom in the corresponding period. On the brighter side, Rohtak district has moved three steps upward thereby succeed to capture top rank in 2011. None of the lower ranked districts have faced downward movement. Appreciable upward shift has been observed by Sirsa (ten steps), Yamunanagar (nine steps), Kaithal (eight steps) and Rewari (seven steps).

The district-wise temporal change as regards to prevalence of institutional deliveries has been tabulated in Table 9.11. As a whole the state has gained strength over time in this health aspect. As many as eleven districts have performed better than the state as a whole. The best performing three districts are Kaithal, Yamunanagar and Sirsa that have registered proportional change above 60 per cent. In terms of absolute change the best performing three districts are Yamunanagar, Sirsa and Mahendergarh. Kaithal district has been underestimated (due to lower index values) while Mahendergarh has been overestimated (due to higher index values) in terms of absolute change. The performance of districts like Jind, Karnal, Hisar, Panchkula and Rewari is also praiseworthy both in terms of absolute change as well as proportional change. But the situation is not heartening in Ambala and Bhiwani districts where negative growth has been recorded. Ambala district has failed to sustain its high attainment level and registered the highest decadal decline of 10.36 per cent against the general trend of positive change in the state during the period. However, Bhiwani district has experienced insignificant decline.

It is evident from the moderate value of correlation coefficient (0.67) that the degree of decadal movement has not been very significant throughout the state (Table 9.12). The two lower ranked districts i.e. Faridabad and Gurgaon have shown no enhancement in their positions and remained steady at 16th and 19th ranks respectively. The other lower ranked districts like Jind, Kaithal, Yamunanagar, Hisar, Sirsa and Karnal have improved their positions up to six steps. Some of the districts with middle and upper middle ranks have also enhanced their positions. As a whole ten districts have moved upward. Again, the districts with the top three ranks in 2001 could not sustain their positions. Out of them Jhajjar (third rank in 2001) district has faced a sharp dip of 10 steps thereby thrown at the 13th rank. Bhiwani and Panipat districts, with moderate ranks in 2001 have faced reasonable slide of eight and six steps respectively thereby awarded fairly lower ranks in 2011.

It is quite disappointing to note that decadal change in one of the most vital health indicators pertaining to the vaccination of children has been negative during 2001-2011. The overall state figure comes down by 5.25 per cent (Table 9.13). As many as twelve districts have suffered

Table 9.12: Women who had Institutional Deliveries: Temporal Movement in the Ranking of Districts (2001-2011)

Districts	*Rank in 2001*	*Rank in 2011*	*Temporal Movement*
Ambala	1	5	↓
Kurukshetra	2	3	↓
Jhajjar	3	13	↓
Rewari	4	1	↑
Panchkula	5	2	↑
Rohtak	6	8	↓
Sonepat	7	6	↑
Fatehabad	8	11	↓
Mahendergarh	9	4	↑
Bhiwani	10	18	↓
Panipat	11	17	↓
Karnal	12	10	↑
Sirsa	13	7	↑
Hisar	14	12	↑
Yamunanagar	15	9	↑
Faridabad	16	16	◆
Kaithal	17	14	↑
Jind	18	15	↑
Gurgaon	19	19	◆
Rank Correlation Coefficient (r)			**+0.67**

Table 9.13: Spatio-temporal Analysis of Children Age 12-35 Months Fully Vaccinated (2001-2011)

Districts	*Index 2001*	*Index 2011*	*Absolute Change*	*Proportional Change (%)*
Kaithal	0.414	0.725	0.311	75.12
Sonepat	0.551	0.73	0.179	32.49
Mahendergarh	0.526	0.677	0.151	28.71
Sirsa	0.491	0.613	0.122	24.85
Bhiwani	0.478	0.584	0.106	22.18
Rewari	0.658	0.673	0.015	2.28
Karnal	0.739	0.752	0.013	1.76
Gurgaon	0.329	0.323	-0.004	-1.77
Yamunanagar	0.72	0.7	-0.02	-2.78
Fatehabad	0.651	0.628	-0.023	-3.53
Jhajjar	0.68	0.648	-0.032	-4.71
Rohtak	0.81	0.757	-0.053	-6.54
Panchkula	0.857	0.781	-0.076	-8.87
Panipat	0.638	0.57	-0.068	-10.66
Jind	0.624	0.554	-0.07	-11.22
Hisar	0.636	0.558	-0.078	-12.26
Faridabad	0.537	0.464	-0.073	-13.59
Ambala	0.929	0.791	-0.138	-14.85
Kurukshetra	0.817	0.678	-0.139	-17.01
Haryana	**0.629**	**0.596**	**-0.033**	**-5.25**

negative growth. The negative change ranges from 1.77 per cent (lowest in Gurgaon) to 17.01 per cent (highest in Kurukshetra). Against the overall negative trend of the state there are seven districts that have appeared with the positive change. Kaithal district has outpaced other districts by recording an impressive figure of 75.12 per cent in terms of proportional change. Moreover, it is well ahead of other districts in terms of absolute change also. Sonepat, Mahendergarh, Sirsa and Bhiwani districts have also recorded appreciable growth. One can take a note from the table that the districts with lower index values have registered positive change whereas the districts with higher index values have suffered decline. Gurgaon, being an exception has registered negative change.

A glance of Table 9.14 brings out that seven districts have augmented their earlier positions while the highest numbers of nine districts have recorded downward movement. The value of correlation coefficient (0.64) reflects that the degree of decadal movement has been moderate except for Kaithal district which has recorded phenomenal improvement of 12 steps. Kurukshetra, Panipat, Hisar and Jind districts have downgraded their positions moderately by five steps as compared to the earlier point of time. The moderate but upward movement of the lower ranked districts can be seen in the present case also, though the districts with higher ranks have shown some resistance against downward movement as the two top ranked districts (Ambala and Panchkula) have remained unmoved albeit negative decadal growth observed by these districts (Compare Table 9.13 and Table 9.14). On the other end of the scale, Gurgaon has shown no improvement and remained at the bottom. However, Sonepat and Mahendergarh districts have recorded impressive upward movement of eight and six steps respectively.

As regard to health index, the district-wise attainment levels for both the periods under study and the decadal change therein have been presented in Table 9.15. Unfortunately the state has experienced unenthusiastic development over time. A negative absolute change of 0.091 index points, which is equal to 19.03 per cent in terms of proportional change, underlines that the status of health parameters has been deteriorating considerably over time in the state. The deterioration in health status has been observed in as many as sixteen districts out of the nineteen, though the magnitude of deterioration varies to a great extent. The most alarming situation is faced by the two southernmost districts i.e. Faridabad and Gurgaon which have not only suffered a steep decline of 50.50 per cent and 46.13 per cent respectively but they have weakened their already frail health parameters over the period. The situation of other two southern districts i.e. Bhiwani and Mahendergarh is no better as the health index in these districts has been found below the state

Table 9.14: Children Age 12-35 Months Fully Vaccinated: Temporal Movement in the Ranking of Districts (2001-2011)

Districts	*Rank in 2001*	*Rank in 2011*	*Temporal Movement*
Ambala	1	1	◆
Panchkula	2	2	◆
Kurukshetra	3	8	↓
Rohtak	4	3	↑
Karnal	5	4	↑
Yamunanagar	6	7	↓
Jhajjar	7	11	↓
Rewari	8	10	↓
Fatehabad	9	12	↓
Panipat	10	15	↓
Hisar	11	16	↓
Jind	12	17	↓
Sonepat	13	5	↑
Faridabad	14	18	↓
Mahendergarh	15	9	↑
Sirsa	16	13	↑
Bhiwani	17	14	↑
Kaithal	18	6	↑
Gurgaon	19	19	◆
Rank Correlation Coefficient (r)			**+0.64**

Table 9.15: Spatio-temporal Analysis of Health Index (2001-2011)

Districts	*Index 2001*	*Index 2011*	*Absolute Change*	*Proportional Change (%)*
Kurukshetra	0.450	0.482	0.032	7.20
Sonepat	0.488	0.505	0.017	3.40
Rewari	0.420	0.433	0.012	2.90
Kaithal	0.499	0.473	-0.025	-5.09
Ambala	0.472	0.448	-0.025	-5.25
Sirsa	0.448	0.422	-0.026	-5.80
Hisar	0.478	0.424	-0.053	-11.18
Fatehabad	0.455	0.403	-0.052	-11.47
Jind	0.445	0.389	-0.055	-12.42
Karnal	0.551	0.475	-0.076	-13.75
Rohtak	0.599	0.506	-0.093	-15.56
Panchkula	0.556	0.466	-0.090	-16.19
Yamunanagar	0.458	0.370	-0.088	-19.28
Jhajjar	0.519	0.412	-0.107	-20.66
Mahendergarh	0.451	0.351	-0.100	-22.18
Panipat	0.580	0.404	-0.175	-30.25
Bhiwani	0.492	0.343	-0.149	-30.34
Gurgaon	0.427	0.230	-0.197	-46.13
Faridabad	0.484	0.240	-0.244	-50.50
Haryana	**0.480**	**0.389**	**-0.091**	**-19.03**

Table 9.16: Health Index: Temporal Movement

Districts	*Rank in 2001*	*Rank in 2011*	*Temporal Movement*
Rohtak	1	1	◆
Panipat	2	12	↓
Panchkula	3	6	↓
Karnal	4	4	◆
Jhajjar	5	11	↓
Kaithal	6	5	↑
Bhiwani	7	17	↓
Sonepat	8	2	↑
Faridabad	9	18	↓
Hisar	10	9	↑
Ambala	11	7	↑
Yamunanagar	12	15	↓
Fatehabad	13	13	◆
Mahendergarh	14	16	↓
Kurukshetra	15	3	↑
Sirsa	16	10	↑
Jind	17	14	↑
Gurgaon	18	19	↓
Rewari	19	8	↑
Rank Correlation Coefficient (r)			**+0.38**

average in 2011 and they have suffered a decline higher than that of the state. However, three districts spread over different parts of the state have registered modest but positive decadal change. Generally districts located in the south-eastern part of the state have experienced sharper decline than that of the state average whereas the performance is better in the north-western part of the state. However, Rewari district is an exception.

Again, a humble correlation coefficient (0.38) underlines that the temporal movement in the rankings of districts with regard to the attainment level of health index has undergone a significant shifting (Table 9.16). Out of the sixteen districts that have shifted their positions, eight districts have moved upward. Amongst these the performance of Kurukshetra district has been spectacular as it has recorded a boost of 12 steps thereby reached at a respectable third place in 2011 as against a poor 15th rank in 2001. Rewari district has also improved its position by achieving a remarkable boost of 11 steps thereby reached at a moderate level from the bottom during the corresponding period. On the other hand, Panipat district has appeared as the greatest sufferer of 10 steps which slipped from a respectable second rank in 2001 to a docile 12th rank in 2011. Bhiwani and Faridabad districts are amongst the main sufferers that have downgraded their positions by ten steps and nine steps respectively. However, three districts i.e. Rohtak, Karnal and Fatehabad have maintained their first, fourth and thirteenth ranks respectively during the decade albeit the negative decadal change as observed in the preceding table (Table 9.15). It is because the decline they suffered was not sharper than that of the state average.

Human Development Index

At the state level the HDI is found 0.58 in 2011 as against 0.60 in 2001 thereby registered a decline of 2.83 per cent (Table 9.17). As far as district level decadal change is concerned, fifteen districts out of the nineteen have suffered negative change. Out of these fifteen, nine districts have suffered sharper decline than that of the state as a whole. In the present case, the trend of absolute change corresponds to the trend of proportional change. The sharpest decline of 10.42 per cent is faced by Faridabad district which is preceded by Bhiwani (7.28 per cent) and Panipat (5.95 per cent) districts. One can take a pleasing note that four districts have recorded positive change, nonetheless, modest in magnitude. These districts are- Sonepat, Rewari, Kurukshetra and Kaithal. Besides, Ambala, Panchkula and Sirsa districts have appeared with negligible decline. Rewari district has emerged as an oasis in a desert by recording positive trend in the southern part of the state.

Table 9.17: Spatio-temporal Analysis of Human Development Index (2001-2011)

Districts	*Index 2001*	*Index 2011*	*Absolute Change*	*Proportional Change (%)*
Sonepat	0.608	0.625	0.017	2.77
Rewari	0.606	0.620	0.015	2.42
Kurukshetra	0.585	0.598	0.012	2.13
Kaithal	0.559	0.561	0.001	0.24
Ambala	0.629	0.628	-0.001	-0.17
Panchkula	0.648	0.645	-0.003	-0.50
Sirsa	0.562	0.559	-0.003	-0.57
Fatehabad	0.558	0.547	-0.010	-1.87
Hisar	0.589	0.573	-0.016	-2.64
Jind	0.557	0.542	-0.015	-2.65
Karnal	0.619	0.600	-0.019	-3.07
Gurgaon	0.600	0.577	-0.023	-3.78
Jhajjar	0.612	0.589	-0.024	-3.90
Mahendergarh	0.565	0.542	-0.023	-4.07
Yamunanagar	0.601	0.573	-0.028	-4.59
Rohtak	0.647	0.617	-0.030	-4.66
Panipat	0.653	0.614	-0.039	-5.95
Bhiwani	0.581	0.539	-0.042	-7.28
Faridabad	0.620	0.555	-0.065	-10.42
Haryana	**0.600**	**0.583**	**-0.017**	**-2.83**

Table 9.18: Human Development Index: Temporal Movement in the Ranking of Districts (2001-2011)

Districts	*Rank in 2001*	*Rank in 2011*	*Temporal Movement*
Panipat	1	6	↓
Panchkula	2	1	↑
Rohtak	3	5	↓
Ambala	4	2	↑
Faridabad	5	15	↓
Karnal	6	7	↓
Jhajjar	7	9	↓
Sonepat	8	3	↑
Rewari	9	4	↑
Yamunanagar	10	11	↓
Gurgaon	11	10	↑
Hisar	12	12	◆
Kurukshetra	13	8	↑
Bhiwani	14	19	↓
Mahendergarh	15	18	↓
Sirsa	16	14	↑
Kaithal	17	13	↑
Fatehabad	18	16	↑
Jind	19	17	↑
Rank Correlation Coefficient (r)			**+0.76**

Table 9.18 illustrates the direction as well as intensity of temporal movement in the rankings obtained by the districts on the basis of their attainment levels as regard to the HDI. High positive correlation (0.76) between the districts-wise rankings of two periods strongly advocates that the intensity of shifting is fairly low in majority of the districts, nonetheless eighteen districts out of the nineteen have experienced shift in their respective ranks. As many as ten districts have been incorporated in the category of upward movement whereas eight districts have shown downward movement. As regards to upward movement, three districts viz. Sonepat, Rewari and Panchkula have recorded a leap of five ranks each. On account of this spectacular jump, these districts have successfully achieved positive change in the HDI (See Table 9.17). Kaithal district has also enhanced effectively its position by four steps thereby appeared with positive change in the HDI. No significant upward movement has been seen in the left over districts in this category. Out of the eight districts that have registered downward movement, the sharpest slide of ten steps has been faced by Faridabad district which has pushed it to a humiliating 15th rank in 2011 from a reputable fifth rank in 2001. Panipat and Bhiwani districts have experienced a slide of five steps each. The left over districts have registered insignificant downward movement. Hisar is the only district that has remained unmoved at 12th position.

Sum up

The gist of the above discussion is that the state, as a whole, could not improve its earlier attainment levels in two (income and health) of the three broad dimensions. Although, the state has recorded visible improvement in the third dimension i.e. education sector yet it is not of a great extent to neutralise the negative impact of the former two dimensions. As a result, Human Development Index, which is an outcome of these three dimensions, has become poorer in the given point of time. Furthermore, the temporal change in the attainment levels of some of the districts vary to a great extent in such a manner that they have witnessed considerable shifting in the ranks obtained by them. Generally the districts with higher ranks in the base year have suffered downward movement whereas the districts with lower ranks have moved upward over time.

10

Spatio-temporal Analysis of Gender Development Index, 2001-2011

Since Spatio-temporal analysis is the central point of investigation of the present study, this chapter focuses on the gender-wise changes that take place in the attainment levels during 2001-2011. At first decadal changes occurred in the three broad dimensions have been taken for analysis, GDI has been discussed in the end. It is worthwhile to mention here that the index values pertaining to some of the dimensions have been shown up to three decimal places so as to facilitate the interpretation.

Income Dimension

Masculine gender not only forms the major part of the Economically Active Population (EAP) but also it is gaining strength with time. Males consist of more than three-fourth (76.34 per cent) of the economically active population in the state in 2011 as compared to 68.22 per cent in 2001 (Table 10.1). The positive change is persistent all over the state except a humble decline (0.61 per cent) experienced by Panchkula district. Jhajjar district has recorded highest increase in terms of absolute change (13.59 per cent) and proportional change (21.58 per cent) as well. Gurgaon and Mahendergarh districts have also shown impressive decadal change in favour of males. By and large the districts located in the southern part of the state have recorded sharper increase as compared to the districts located in the northern part. It is because the districts belonging to northern part have already possessed greater proportion of EAP-males leaving a little scope for further increase.

Table 10.1: Spatio-temporal Analysis of Economically Active Population- Males (2001-2011)

Districts	*Index 2001*	*Index 2011*	*Absolute Change*	*Proportional Change (%)*
Jhajjar	62.98	76.57	13.59	21.58
Gurgaon	65.94	78.72	12.79	19.39
Mahendergarh	57.78	68.80	11.02	19.07
Rohtak	67.67	78.81	11.14	16.46
Rewari	60.07	69.68	9.61	16.00
Sonepat	66.05	74.75	8.70	13.18
Panipat	70.50	79.71	9.22	13.07
Bhiwani	61.28	69.13	7.85	12.81
Kaithal	69.80	78.28	8.48	12.15
Fatehabad	64.15	71.39	7.24	11.29
Sirsa	66.17	73.60	7.42	11.22
Jind	63.44	70.36	6.92	10.90
Faridabad	73.37	80.83	7.46	10.17
Hisar	64.73	70.61	5.88	9.08
Kurukshetra	73.42	79.74	6.33	8.62
Karnal	75.29	79.77	4.48	5.95
Yamunanagar	83.29	87.95	4.67	5.60
Ambala	85.24	86.02	0.78	0.91
Panchkula	78.44	77.96	-0.48	-0.61
Haryana	**68.22**	**76.34**	**8.11**	**11.89**

Table 10.2: Economically Active Population- Males (2001-2011)

Districts	*Rank in 2001*	*Rank in 2011*	*Temporal Movement*
Ambala	1	2	↓
Yamunanagar	2	1	↑
Panchkula	3	10	↓
Karnal	4	4	◆
Kurukshetra	5	5	◆
Faridabad	6	3	↑
Panipat	7	6	↑
Kaithal	8	9	↓
Rohtak	9	7	↑
Sirsa	10	13	↓
Sonepat	11	12	↓
Gurgaon	12	8	↑
Hisar	13	15	↓
Fatehabad	14	14	◆
Jind	15	16	↓
Jhajjar	16	11	↑
Bhiwani	17	18	↓
Rewari	18	17	↑
Mahendergarh	19	19	◆
Rank Correlation Coefficient (r)			**+0.89**

Table 10.3: Spatio-temporal Analysis of Economically Active Population- Females (2001-2011)

Districts	*Index 2001*	*Index 2011*	*Absolute Change*	*Proportional Change (%)*
Panchkula	21.56	22.04	0.48	2.22
Ambala	14.76	13.98	-0.78	-5.28
Hisar	35.27	29.39	-5.88	-16.66
Karnal	24.71	20.23	-4.48	-18.12
Jind	36.56	29.64	-6.92	-18.92
Fatehabad	35.85	28.61	-7.24	-20.20
Bhiwani	38.72	30.87	-7.85	-20.27
Sirsa	33.83	26.40	-7.42	-21.95
Kurukshetra	26.58	20.26	-6.33	-23.80
Rewari	39.93	30.32	-9.61	-24.07
Sonepat	33.95	25.25	-8.70	-25.64
Mahendergarh	42.22	31.20	-11.02	-26.10
Yamunanagar	16.71	12.05	-4.67	-27.92
Faridabad	26.63	19.17	-7.46	-28.02
Kaithal	30.20	21.72	-8.48	-28.08
Panipat	29.50	20.29	-9.22	-31.24
Rohtak	32.33	21.19	-11.14	-34.45
Jhajjar	37.02	23.43	-13.59	-36.71
Gurgaon	34.06	21.28	-12.79	-37.54
Haryana	**31.78**	**23.66**	**-8.11**	**-25.53**

Table 10.4: Economically Active Population- Females: Temporal Movement in the Ranking of Districts (2001-2011)

Districts	*Rank in 2001*	*Rank in 2011*	*Temporal Movement*
Mahendergarh	1	1	◆
Rewari	2	3	↓
Bhiwani	3	2	↑
Jhajjar	4	9	↓
Jind	5	4	↑
Fatehabad	6	6	◆
Hisar	7	5	↑
Gurgaon	8	12	↓
Sonepat	9	8	↑
Sirsa	10	7	↑
Rohtak	11	13	↓
Kaithal	12	11	↑
Panipat	13	14	↓
Faridabad	14	17	↓
Kurukshetra	15	15	◆
Karnal	16	16	◆
Panchkula	17	10	↑
Yamunanagar	18	19	↓
Ambala	19	18	↑
Rank Correlation Coefficient (r)			**+0.89**

Temporal movement of districts as regard to EAP-males is depicted in Table 10.2. High correlation coefficient (0.89) between the district-wise rankings of two points of time indicates that the intensity of movement has little significance. Out of the eight districts that have registered downward movement, only Panchkula district has shown significant movement of seven steps (third rank in 2001 to tenth rank in 2011). As regards to upward movement, none of the seven districts has shown significant shifting except for a modest increase of five steps registered by Jhajjar district (16th rank in 2001 to 11th rank in 2011). Two districts with higher ranks (Karnal and Kurukshetra) and two districts with lower ranks (Mahendergarh and Fatehabad) have remained unmoved.

Even though efforts have been and are being made for gender equality; feminine gender is facing hard time as far as participation in economic activities is concerned. Table 10.3 brings out that the proportion of females, which was already far from unity, is becoming lesser with time. At the state level EAP-females has reduced by 8.11 index points in terms of absolute change and 25.53 per cent in terms of proportional change. In this way the proportion EAP-females has come down to less than 25 per cent in 2011. The reducing trend is persistent across the districts except a humble increase of 2.22 per cent observed in Panchkula district. The negative change ranges from 5.28 per cent in Ambala to as high as 37.54 per cent in Gurgaon district. As many as eight districts in the state have recorded negative change above the state average. In general, districts located in the south and eastern parts of the state have shown higher decline as compared to the districts located in the north and western parts.

Again the high correlation coefficient (0.89) rules out notable shifting in the rankings of districts during the decade (Table 10.4). Four districts, including top ranked Mahendergarh district and the lower ranked Karnal district have maintained their earlier ranks. Out of the eight districts which appeared with upward movement Panchkula is the solitary district that has experienced visible boost of seven steps (from 17th rank in 2001 to 10th rank in 2011). This phenomenal increase is owed to positive decadal change as depicted in Table 10.3. On the opposite direction, Jhajjar district has downgraded its earlier position by five steps (fourth rank in 2001 to ninth rank in 2011) on account of high negative change.

EAP-females have a great bearing over Equally Distributed Income Index (EDII) which turns its temporal change to negative. At the state level EDII has gone down by 0.081 index points in terms of absolute change and 13.27 per cent in terms of proportional change. Both the aspects of change correspond to each other (Table 10.5). None of the districts in the state has shown positive change over time and their

Table 10.5: Spatio-temporal Analysis of Equally Distributed Income Index (2001-2011)

Districts	*Index 2001*	*Index 2011*	*Absclute Change*	*Proportional Change (%)*
Panchkula	0.582	0.564	-0.018	-3.04
Gurgaon	0.719	0.666	-0.053	-7.35
Rewari	0.628	0.566	-0.062	-9.94
Panipat	0.651	0.583	-0.068	-10.45
Faridabad	0.630	0.550	-0.080	-12.64
Ambala	0.542	0.472	-0.070	-12.93
Sonepat	0.583	0.504	-0.079	-13.51
Hisar	0.618	0.521	-0.097	-15.69
Mahendergarh	0.532	0.445	-0.087	-16.30
Bhiwani	0.561	0.467	-0.093	-16.64
Jhajjar	0.575	0.478	-0.098	-16.97
Karnal	0.571	0.473	-0.099	-17.25
Kurukshetra	0.557	0.455	-0.102	-18.32
Sirsa	0.604	0.493	-0.111	-18.41
Fatehabad	0.615	0.499	-0.116	-18.82
Rohtak	0.574	0.458	-0.115	-20.13
Jind	0.586	0.468	-0.118	-20.18
Kaithal	0.552	0.420	-0.132	-23.96
Yamunanagar	0.523	0.397	-0.126	-24.16
Haryana	**0.610**	**0.529**	**-0.081**	**-13.27**

Table 10.6: Equally Distributed Income Index: Temporal Movement in the Ranking of Districts (2001-2011)

Districts	*Rank in 2001*	*Rank in 2011*	*Temporal Movement*
Gurgaon	1	1	◆
Panipat	2	2	◆
Faridabad	3	5	↓
Rewari	4	3	↑
Hisar	5	6	↓
Fatehabad	6	8	↓
Sirsa	7	9	↓
Jind	8	13	↓
Sonepat	9	7	↑
Panchkula	10	4	↑
Jhajjar	11	10	↑
Rohtak	12	15	↓
Karnal	13	11	↑
Bhiwani	14	14	◆
Kurukshetra	15	16	↓
Kaithal	16	18	↓
Ambala	17	12	↑
Mahendergarh	18	17	↑
Yamunanagar	19	19	◆
Rank Correlation Coefficient (r)			**+0.89**

earlier strength has been reduced in diverse magnitude. In proportional terms, it ranges from 3.04 per cent in Panchkula to 24.16 per cent in Yamunanagar.

Interestingly, one northern district (Panchkula) has shown lowest change whereas the other (Yamunanagar) has come up with highest change in the state. Majority of the districts have recorded higher decline as compared to the state average. However, districts located in the southern part such as Gurgaon, Rewari, Faridabad, etc. have shown lower decline.

Similar to EAP-males and EAP-females, the significant coefficient of correlation (0.89) forbids large scale reshuffling in the district-wise rankings over time (Table 10.6). Four districts including top ranked Gurgaon and bottom ranked Yamunanagar districts have sustained their earlier positions. Out of the eight districts that belong to the category of downward movement, only Jind has distinctively moved five steps flipside (eighth rank in 2001 to thirteenth rank in 2011). On the other hand, seven districts have improved their rankings. With the lowest decadal decline as observed in the foregoing section Panchkula district has succeeded in recording the remarkable thrust of six steps (tenth rank in 2001 to fourth rank in 2011). Another northern district i.e. Ambala has also registered a notable upward movement of five steps thereby placed along with moderate ranked districts. None of the left over districts has recorded noteworthy shifting in either of direction.

Education Dimension

Like income dimension, masculine gender has registered positive growth in education dimension also. The state education index which was 0.785 in 2001 has increased up to 0.854 in 2011 by recording an increase of 0.069 index points in terms of absolute change and 8.80 per cent in terms of proportional change (Table 10.7).

The increase is experienced by all the districts in the state though with diverse magnitude. It ranges from 5.03 per cent (lowest in Rewari district) to 14.68 per cent (highest in Kaithal district). In addition to Kaithal, Fatehabad, Gurgaon, Sirsa and Jind districts have registered impressive growth above ten per cent in proportional terms. As many as eleven districts have observed decadal change below the state average. In addition to Rewari, Rohtak and Kurukshetra are the other districts that have observed growth even below seven per cent.

Since the temporal change in EI-males has been observed in the same direction, the reshuffling in the rankings of districts has been negligible. A very high positive correlation coefficient (0.94) gives strength to the above statement (Table 10.8).

Table 10.7: Spatio-temporal Analysis of Education Index- Males (2001-2011)

Districts	*Index 2001*	*Index 2011*	*Absolute Change*	*Proportional Change (%)*
Kaithal	0.692	0.793	0.102	14.68
Fatehabad	0.682	0.781	0.099	14.48
Gurgaon	0.762	0.863	0.101	13.31
Sirsa	0.701	0.786	0.085	12.21
Jind	0.738	0.825	0.087	11.76
Karnal	0.763	0.837	0.074	9.71
Panchkula	0.809	0.886	0.077	9.56
Bhiwani	0.803	0.874	0.071	8.90
Panipat	0.785	0.854	0.069	8.79
Hisar	0.766	0.828	0.062	8.14
Yamunanagar	0.788	0.851	0.063	7.97
Mahendergarh	0.847	0.913	0.066	7.77
Sonepat	0.831	0.894	0.063	7.63
Ambala	0.823	0.885	0.062	7.52
Faridabad	0.815	0.876	0.061	7.49
Jhajjar	0.833	0.894	0.061	7.36
Kurukshetra	0.781	0.835	0.054	6.97
Rohtak	0.832	0.884	0.052	6.21
Rewari	0.885	0.929	0.045	5.03
Haryana	**0.785**	**0.854**	**0.069**	**8.80**

Table 10.8: Education Index - Males: Temporal Movement in the Ranking of Districts (2001-2011)

Districts	*Rank in 2001*	*Rank in 2011*	*Temporal Movement*
Rewari	1	1	◆
Mahendergarh	2	2	◆
Jhajjar	3	4	↓
Rohtak	4	7	↓
Sonepat	5	3	↑
Ambala	6	6	◆
Faridabad	7	8	↓
Panchkula	8	5	↑
Bhiwani	9	9	◆
Yamunanagar	10	12	↓
Panipat	11	11	◆
Kurukshetra	12	14	↓
Hisar	13	15	↓
Karnal	14	13	↑
Gurgaon	15	10	↑
Jind	16	16	◆
Sirsa	17	18	↓
Kaithal	18	17	↑
Fatehabad	19	19	◆
Rank Correlation Coefficient (r)			**+0.94**

Table 10.9: Spatio-temporal Analysis of Education Index - Females (2001-2011)

Districts	*Index 2001*	*Index 2011*	*Absolute Change*	*Proportional Change (%)*
Gurgaon	0.478	0.628	0.151	31.51
Kaithal	0.473	0.607	0.134	28.30
Fatehabad	0.465	0.593	0.128	27.44
Jind	0.485	0.616	0.131	26.98
Sirsa	0.499	0.612	0.113	22.57
Bhiwani	0.530	0.648	0.118	22.26
Hisar	0.511	0.623	0.112	21.97
Faridabad	0.563	0.684	0.121	21.46
Mahendergarh	0.541	0.653	0.112	20.75
Jhajjar	0.597	0.710	0.114	19.03
Panchkula	0.657	0.775	0.119	18.05
Karnal	0.580	0.683	0.103	17.82
Panipat	0.580	0.682	0.102	17.65
Sonepat	0.607	0.709	0.102	16.84
Rewari	0.608	0.705	0.097	15.90
Kurukshetra	0.606	0.692	0.086	14.17
Rohtak	0.626	0.712	0.086	13.76
Ambala	0.674	0.766	0.092	13.67
Yamunanagar	0.634	0.720	0.086	13.58
Haryana	**0.557**	**0.668**	**0.111**	**19.86**

Table 10.10: Education Index - Females: Temporal Movement in the Ranking of Districts (2001-2011)

Districts	*Rank in 2001*	*Rank in 2011*	*Temporal Movement*
Ambala	1	2	↓
Panchkula	2	1	↑
Yamunanagar	3	3	◆
Rohtak	4	4	◆
Rewari	5	7	↓
Sonepat	6	6	◆
Kurukshetra	7	8	↓
Jhajjar	8	5	↑
Karnal	9	10	↓
Panipat	10	11	↓
Faridabad	11	9	↑
Mahendergarh	12	12	◆
Bhiwani	13	13	◆
Hisar	14	15	↓
Sirsa	15	17	↓
Jind	16	16	◆
Gurgaon	17	14	↑
Kaithal	18	18	◆
Fatehabad	19	19	◆
Rank Correlation Coefficient (r)			**+0.97**

As many as seven districts with diverse ranks remained firm at their earlier positions. Only Gurgaon district has observed noteworthy boost of five steps (15th rank in 2001 to 10th rank in 2011). Credit goes to the high positive growth of 13.31 per cent registered by the district as depicted in Table 10.7. Except Gurgaon, none of the districts has recorded notable movement in either of direction.

As far as decadal change in EI-females is concerned, it is encouraging to note that the feminine gender has recorded higher positive growth as compared to its counterpart (Compare Table 10.7 and Table 10.9). At the state level, it has almost touched the 20 per cent mark in terms of proportional change. All the districts have enjoyed positive change. Gurgaon district has recorded highest increase of 31.51 per cent thereby appeared as the solitary district with a change above 30 per cent. Kaithal (28.30 per cent), Fatehabad (27.44 per cent) and Jind (26.98 per cent) districts have also registered impressive growth. The lowest growth in terms of absolute change can be seen in Yamunanagar, Rohtak and Kurukshetra districts as all these districts have gained 0.086 index points over time. However, Yamunanagar district is at the bottom by acquiring lowest growth of 13.58 per cent in terms of proportional change. Consider the case of Ambala district, which has gained 0.092 index points (higher than Rohtak and Kurukshetra districts) but has recorded lower (13.67 per cent) proportional growth (as compared to Rohtak and Kurukshetra districts). This is on account of absolute change that has overestimated the change in Ambala district where attainment level is higher. It can be concluded from the trend of change in EI-females that the steps taken to achieve gender equality in terms of education dimension have been fruitful during the given point of time.

Since the positive change has been persistent all over the state, there is a little scope for inter-district shifting during the given point of time. The robust value of correlation coefficient (0.97) which is hovering around unity strongly signifies the steadiness of districts. A perusal of Table 10.10 brings out that as many as eight districts have remained firm at the same ranks in 2011 as assigned to them in 2001. Although seven districts have shifted their ranks, yet none of them has shown significant movement. As far as upward movement is concerned, only four districts have appeared in this category. Out of these, two districts (Jhajjar and Gurgaon) have moderately enhanced their positions by three steps.

Both the genders have shown steady growth in the education dimension. As a result, positive trend is visible in respect of Equally Distributed Education Index (EDEI). The state EDEI which was 0.660 in 2001 has increased to 0.756 thereby added 14.45 per cent in its earlier strength (Table 10.11). Eight districts have registered proportional change above the state average.

Table 10.11: Spatio-temporal Analysis of Equally Distributed Education Index (2001-2011)

Districts	*Index 2001*	*Index 2011*	*Absolute Change*	*Proportional Change (%)*
Gurgaon	0.597	0.735	0.138	23.20
Kaithal	0.570	0.693	0.123	21.60
Fatehabad	0.560	0.679	0.119	21.29
Jind	0.595	0.712	0.117	19.69
Sirsa	0.589	0.693	0.104	17.59
Bhiwani	0.647	0.751	0.104	16.08
Mahendergarh	0.666	0.769	0.102	15.31
Hisar	0.623	0.718	0.095	15.27
Faridabad	0.677	0.775	0.098	14.43
Karnal	0.665	0.757	0.091	13.73
Panchkula	0.732	0.831	0.098	13.45
Jhajjar	0.705	0.798	0.093	13.27
Panipat	0.676	0.765	0.088	13.05
Sonepat	0.711	0.798	0.087	12.23
Rewari	0.728	0.808	0.080	10.93
Yamunanagar	0.708	0.784	0.076	10.72
Ambala	0.746	0.825	0.079	10.52
Kurukshetra	0.689	0.761	0.072	10.52
Rohtak	0.723	0.795	0.072	9.94
Haryana	**0.660**	**0.756**	**0.095**	**14.45**

The highest change of 23.20 per cent has been observed in Gurgaon district. In addition to this, Kaithal (21.60 per cent) and Fatehabad (21.29 per cent) are among the districts that have registered handsome growth above 20 per cent. On the other hand, Rohtak is the solitary district that has attained decadal growth below 10 per cent. The degree of decadal change is such that the districts with higher attainment levels have shown lesser growth (Rohtak, Kurukshetra, Ambala, Yamunanagar and Rewari districts) as there was little scope left for these districts whereas the districts with lesser attainment levels have shown higher decadal growth (Gurgaon, Kaithal, Fatehabad, Jind and Sirsa).

The steady positive growth observed throughout the state rules out large scale reshuffling in the district-wise ranks. One can easily substantiate the assertion in view of very high positive coefficient of correlation (0.97). Table 10.12 brings out that highest numbers (7) of districts have remained unmoved. Six districts have found place in each category of downward movement and upward movement. Kurukshetra district in the category of downward movement and Jhajjar district in the category of upward movement have shown moderate shifting of three steps in their respective categories. Insignificant movement is evident in the left over ten districts from both the categories. Consider the case of Ambala and Panchkula districts that have been awarded first and second ranks respectively in 2001. They have exchanged their positions in 2011. Even though Ambala district has recorded positive decadal growth (10.52 per cent) but Panchkula superseded the former by recording higher growth (13.45 per cent) (See Table 10.11).

Health Index- Males

Table 10.13 throws light on the decadal changes observed in the districts with regard to health index pertaining to males. Since majority of the districts have recorded positive change the overall change observed in the state has been positive. The state HI-males has improved slightly by 2.25 per cent. Faridabad district improves its health status appreciably by 0.183 index points thereby obtained an index value of 0.77 in the latter decade. In terms of proportional change it has recorded a spectacular increase of 31.18 per cent. Similarly, Jind and Mahendergarh districts have also shown impressive temporal change. A large number of districts dispersed in the state have remained free from significant decadal change in either direction. A little change (-0.55 per cent) can be seen in Panipat district. In addition to Panipat there are as many as five districts that have registered negative change. These are Hisar, Rohtak, Ambala, Jhajjar and Panchkula districts. Highest decline of 8.70 per cent is visible in Hisar district. No regional pattern of change can be seen in the state as the

Table 10.12: Equally Distributed Education Index: Temporal Movement in the Ranking of Districts (2001-2011)

Districts	*Rank in 2001*	*Rank in 2011*	*Temporal Movement*
Ambala	1	2	↓
Panchkula	2	1	↑
Rewari	3	3	◆
Rohtak	4	6	↓
Sonepat	5	5	◆
Yamunanagar	6	7	↓
Jhajjar	7	4	↑
Kurukshetra	8	11	↓
Faridabad	9	8	↑
Panipat	10	10	◆
Mahendergarh	11	9	↑
Karnal	12	12	◆
Bhiwani	13	13	◆
Hisar	14	15	↓
Gurgaon	15	14	↑
Jind	16	16	◆
Sirsa	17	18	↓
Kaithal	18	17	↑
Fatehabad	19	19	◆
Rank Correlation Coefficient (r)			**+0.97**

Table 10.13: Spatio-temporal Analysis of Health Index- Males (2001-2011)

Districts	*Index 2001*	*Index 2011*	*Absolute Change*	*Proportional Change (%)*
Faridabad	0.587	0.770	0.183	31.18
Jind	0.657	0.803	0.146	22.22
Mahendergarh	0.635	0.759	0.124	19.53
Kaithal	0.664	0.745	0.081	12.20
Fatehabad	0.720	0.766	0.046	6.39
Yamunanagar	0.793	0.834	0.041	5.17
Sirsa	0.662	0.690	0.028	4.23
Karnal	0.743	0.766	0.023	3.10
Sonepat	0.782	0.804	0.022	2.81
Gurgaon	0.514	0.524	0.010	1.85
Bhiwani	0.674	0.683	0.009	1.34
Rewari	0.768	0.778	0.010	1.30
Kurukshetra	0.790	0.796	0.006	0.76
Panipat	0.732	0.728	-0.004	-0.55
Panchkula	0.842	0.827	-0.015	-1.78
Jhajjar	0.802	0.786	-0.016	-2.00
Ambala	0.878	0.856	-0.022	-2.51
Rohtak	0.823	0.786	-0.037	-4.50
Hisar	0.747	0.682	-0.065	-8.70
Haryana	**0.710**	**0.726**	**0.016**	**2.25**

Table 10.14: Health Index- Males: Temporal Movement in the Ranking of Districts (2001-2011)

Districts	*Rank in 2001*	*Rank in 2011*	*Temporal Movement*
Ambala	1	1	◆
Panchkula	2	3	↓
Rohtak	3	8	↓
Jhajjar	4	7	↓
Yamunanagar	5	2	↑
Kurukshetra	6	6	◆
Sonepat	7	4	↑
Rewari	8	9	↓
Hisar	9	18	↓
Karnal	10	12	↓
Panipat	11	15	↓
Fatehabad	12	11	↑
Bhiwani	13	17	↓
Kaithal	14	14	◆
Sirsa	15	16	↓
Jind	16	5	↑
Mahendergarh	17	13	↑
Faridabad	18	10	↑
Gurgaon	19	19	◆
Rank Correlation Coefficient (r)			**+0.67**

districts with diverse magnitude of change are scattered all over the state.

The districts have been ranked on the basis of the index value obtained by them in the two decades (Table 10.14). The coefficient of correlation amounting to 0.67 indicates that there has been a controlled decadal movement of districts in their respective ranks with regard to health index pertaining to males. The decadal change in the rankings of the districts reveals that five districts have maintained the same ranks in 2011 as obtained by them in 2001. These include the top (Ambala) and bottom (Gurgaon) ranked districts of the state. Downward trend in the rankings has been observed in as many as nine districts consisting of higher ranked Panchkula, Rohtak and Jhajjar districts. On the other hand, five districts namely, Jind, Faridabad, Mahendergarh, Sonepat and Yamunanagar have improved their rankings. Most of these belong to the category of lower ranked districts in 2001. Out of these, Jind district has shown a spectacular increase with a bounce of 11 steps and capture fifth rank in 2011 as against the 16th rank in 2001. In addition to this, Faridabad district has improved its position by joining the districts with moderate ranks as it has propelled eight steps upward from a poor 18th rank in 2001.

Health Index- Females

As a whole the health index of females has experienced a positive temporal change in the state. It was 0.722 in 2001 and increased up to 0.841 in 2011 thereby registered an increase of 0.119 index points as regards to absolute change (Table 10.15). The increasing trend has been observed all across the districts, though with different magnitude, except for the top ranked Ambala district which experienced a humble decline of 0.013 index points reaches at 1.32 per cent in proportional terms. There are as many as nine districts where the decadal change has been observed above the state average. Interestingly, higher positive decadal change has been registered by the districts that possessed lower index in the former decade. These include Bhiwani, Faridabad, Kaithal, Panipat, Sonepat, etc. This is why, Ambala has successfully maintained its top position even after a humble decline and Bhiwani district is far behind it even after recording highest increase of 44.44 per cent.

A reasonably high positive correlation (0.76) between the ranks obtained by the districts during the two decades indicates that the decadal deviation of the districts from their earlier ranks has been trifling though most of the districts have reshuffled their positions (Table 10.16). However, Ambala district is consistently enjoying the top rank. The ten districts that have improved their positions include the bottom districts of Gurgaon and Bhiwani as well as the higher ranked districts like Panchkula and

Table 10.15: Spatio-temporal Analysis of Health Index- Females (2001-2011)

Districts	*Index 2001*	*Index 2011*	*Absolute Change*	*Proportional Change (%)*
Bhiwani	0.549	0.793	0.244	44.44
Gurgaon	0.509	0.672	0.163	32.02
Panipat	0.706	0.911	0.205	29.04
Sonepat	0.742	0.956	0.214	28.84
Kaithal	0.687	0.872	0.185	26.93
Faridabad	0.670	0.847	0.177	26.42
Rohtak	0.732	0.904	0.172	23.50
Sirsa	0.763	0.899	0.136	17.82
Mahendergarh	0.575	0.668	0.093	16.17
Hisar	0.655	0.748	0.093	14.20
Yamunanagar	0.855	0.962	0.107	12.51
Panchkula	0.881	0.966	0.085	9.65
Jhajjar	0.781	0.855	0.074	9.48
Jind	0.734	0.798	0.064	8.72
Fatehabad	0.764	0.828	0.064	8.38
Karnal	0.844	0.893	0.049	5.81
Rewari	0.835	0.858	0.023	2.75
Kurukshetra	0.940	0.956	0.016	1.70
Ambala	0.984	0.971	-0.013	-1.32
Haryana	**0.722**	**0.841**	**0.119**	**16.67**

Table 10.16: Health Index- Females: Temporal Movement in the Ranking of Districts (2001-2011)

Districts	*Rank in 2001*	*Rank in 2011*	*Temporal Movement*
Ambala	1	1	◆
Kurukshetra	2	5	↓
Panchkula	3	2	↑
Yamunanagar	4	3	↑
Karnal	5	9	↓
Rewari	6	11	↓
Jhajjar	7	12	↓
Fatehabad	8	14	↓
Sirsa	9	8	↑
Sonepat	10	4	↑
Jind	11	15	↓
Rohtak	12	7	↑
Panipat	13	6	↑
Kaithal	14	10	↑
Faridabad	15	13	↑
Hisar	16	17	↓
Mahendergarh	17	19	↓
Bhiwani	18	16	↑
Gurgaon	19	18	↑
Rank Correlation Coefficient (r)			**+0.76**

Yamunanagar. Besides, most of the districts with moderate ranks (between 9 and 15) have registered upward movement. The most spectacular upward movement of seven ranks can be seen in Panipat district which was at a humble 13th rank in 2001 has acquired a respectable sixth rank. As many as eight districts have downgraded their earlier positions. In addition to the second ranked Kurukshetra district; Karnal, Rewari and Jhajjar are the other better ranked districts that have suffered downward movement. The sharpest plunge of six ranks has been observed in Fatehabad district whereas Rewari and Jhajjar districts have descended by five ranks each.

The EDHI has improved convincingly from 0.716 in 2001 to 0.776 in 2011 thereby registered an increase of 0.060 index points (Table 10.17). Inter-district variations in the decadal change are also not as high as observed in respect of feminine health index. Except Ambala, all the districts have recorded positive decadal change. Faridabad district has experienced the highest increase of 0.18 index points and as a result its EDHI has crossed the mark of 0.80 in 2011. The other districts that have registered appreciable increase include Kaithal, Bhiwani, Jind and Mahendergarh. Compare the patterns of Kurukshetra and Hisar districts as both of these have recorded lowest positive growth. Whereas the former has already achieved a respectable index (0.864), the latter is still lagging far behind with a meek index value of 0.711. Even though the districts like Faridabad, Bhiwani, Kaithal, Mahendergarh, etc. are lagging far behind as compared to Ambala district but they have shown enthusiastic spirit to achieve the targeted index value (target is to achieve index value equal to unity). On the other hand, Ambala district has moved flipside before achieving it.

Table 10.18 throws light on the decadal movement in the ranks obtained by the individual districts over the period under study. A high degree of correlation

Coefficient (0.86) suggests that no significant decadal movement in the ranks of districts has occurred in the state. Four districts have consistently maintained their earlier positions. These include the top ranked Ambala district on one hand and the bottom ranked Gurgaon district on the other. Karnal and Panipat have maintained seventh and eleventh ranks respectively. Out of the fifteen districts that have changed their earlier positions, eight districts have recorded improvement in their earlier ranks. Most of these districts are characterised with lower ranks. The highest upward movement of six ranks has been enjoyed by Faridabad. Credit goes to the highest positive growth recorded by Faridabad in the state (see Table 10.17). Sonepat district, too, has registered an impressive bounce of five ranks. Out of the seven districts that have descended their positions incorporates high ranked districts like Panchkula (second rank)

Table 10.17: Spatio-temporal Analysis of Equally Distributed Health Index (2001-2011)

Districts	*Index 2001*	*Index 2011*	*Absolute Change*	*Proportional Change (%)*
Faridabad	0.622	0.804	0.182	29.24
Bhiwani	0.609	0.731	0.121	19.94
Kaithal	0.674	0.800	0.125	18.55
Mahendergarh	0.605	0.713	0.108	17.91
Jind	0.690	0.801	0.110	15.98
Gurgaon	0.512	0.584	0.072	14.08
Sonepat	0.763	0.867	0.104	13.66
Panipat	0.720	0.803	0.083	11.47
Sirsa	0.706	0.775	0.069	9.83
Yamunanagar	0.821	0.889	0.069	8.38
Rohtak	0.779	0.837	0.058	7.47
Fatehabad	0.740	0.794	0.054	7.33
Karnal	0.787	0.821	0.034	4.34
Panchkula	0.859	0.886	0.027	3.16
Jhajjar	0.792	0.816	0.024	3.06
Rewari	0.798	0.814	0.016	1.95
Hisar	0.702	0.711	0.010	1.36
Kurukshetra	0.853	0.864	0.011	1.27
Ambala	0.924	0.906	-0.018	-1.94
Haryana	**0.716**	**0.776**	**0.060**	**8.33**

Table 10.18: Equally Distributed Health Index: Temporal Movement in the Ranking of Districts (2001-2011)

Districts	*Rank in 2001*	*Rank in 2011*	*Temporal Movement*
Ambala	1	1	◆
Panchkula	2	3	↓
Kurukshetra	3	5	↓
Yamunanagar	4	2	↑
Rewari	5	9	↓
Jhajjar	6	8	↓
Karnal	7	7	◆
Rohtak	8	6	↑
Sonepat	9	4	↑
Fatehabad	10	14	↓
Panipat	11	11	◆
Sirsa	12	15	↓
Hisar	13	18	↓
Jind	14	12	↑
Kaithal	15	13	↑
Faridabad	16	10	↑
Bhiwani	17	16	↑
Mahendergarh	18	17	↑
Gurgaon	19	19	◆
Rank Correlation Coefficient (r)			**+0.86**

Table 10.19: Spatio-temporal Analysis of Gender Development Index (2001-2011)

Districts	*Index 2001*	*Index 2011*	*Absolute Change*	*Proportional Change (%)*
Faridabad	0.643	0.710	0.067	10.37
Gurgaon	0.609	0.662	0.053	8.62
Bhiwani	0.606	0.650	0.044	7.28
Mahendergarh	0.601	0.642	0.041	6.86
Kaithal	0.599	0.637	0.039	6.46
Jind	0.624	0.660	0.036	5.84
Sonepat	0.686	0.723	0.038	5.47
Panipat	0.683	0.717	0.034	5.02
Panchkula	0.724	0.760	0.036	4.97
Sirsa	0.633	0.654	0.021	3.25
Fatehabad	0.638	0.658	0.019	3.01
Rewari	0.718	0.729	0.011	1.52
Karnal	0.674	0.683	0.009	1.34
Jhajjar	0.691	0.697	0.007	0.97
Yamunanagar	0.684	0.690	0.006	0.89
Rohtak	0.692	0.697	0.005	0.70
Hisar	0.648	0.650	0.003	0.39
Ambala	0.738	0.734	-0.003	-0.43
Kurukshetra	0.699	0.693	-0.006	-0.89
Haryana	**0.662**	**0.677**	**0.015**	**2.22**

and Kurukshetra (third rank); and districts with moderate ranks namely Hisar (13th rank) and Sirsa (12th rank). It is worthwhile to take a note of Hisar district which has suffered the sharpest downfall of five ranks in its already modest position and thrown away reasonably back at 18th rank in 2011. All the three districts located in the western part of the state viz. Hisar, Fatehabad and Sirsa have undergone descending movement which indicate that the region has not been able to make pace with the other parts of the state as regards to health dimension.

After discussing the trend of change as regards to three broad dimensions namely, income, education and health separately for both the genders, the temporal change in the Gender Development Index (GDI) has been taken into analysis. As a whole, the GDI has increased slightly by 2.22 per cent in the state (Table 10.19). The positive change is visible in as many as seventeen districts. Out of these, eleven districts have achieved positive change above the state average. Faridabad district has appeared with the highest positive change both in terms of absolute change (0.067 index points) as well as in terms of proportional change (10.37 per cent). It is attention-grabbing fact that four districts (Faridabad, Gurgaon, Bhiwani and Mahendergarh) with highest positive change belong to the southern part of the state. On the contrary, two districts (Kurukshetra and Ambala) that have suffered negative change are located in the northern part of the state. Furthermore, the districts located in the northern part of the state have already achieved higher GDI whereas the southern districts are still behind in the race of gender development. In this way the district-wise trend of change reflects that inter-district disparities have been decreasing over time.

There is always a possibility of shifting in the rankings of the districts as they show diverse development trend. However, in the present case high positive correlation coefficient (0.87) between the district-wise rankings of two points of time rules out a large scale shifting (Table 10.20). In addition to the third ranked Rewari district, three bottom ranked districts (Kaithal, Mahendergarh and Bhiwani) have remained unmoved at their respective ranks. Nine districts have downgraded their ranks. Out of these a notable decline of five steps (fourth in 2001 to ninth in 2011) is evident in Kurukshetra district which has driven it out from the category of districts with higher ranks. Similarly Hisar is also expelled from a moderate 11th rank and placed at a poor 16th rank in 2011. Out of the six districts that have shown upward movement, Faridabad district has registered a noteworthy thrust of six steps (twelveth in 2001 to sixth in 2011). The reason behind it is the highest positive growth registered in the district during the decade (See Table 10.19). Gurgaon (lower ranked)

Table 10.20: Gender Development Index: Temporal Movement in the Ranking of Districts (2001-2011)

Districts	*Rank in 2001*	*Rank in 2011*	*Temporal Movement*
Ambala	1	2	↓
Panchkula	2	1	↑
Rewari	3	3	◆
Kurukshetra	4	9	↓
Rohtak	5	8	↓
Jhajjar	6	7	↓
Sonepat	7	4	↑
Yamunanagar	8	10	↓
Panipat	9	5	↑
Karnal	10	11	↓
Hisar	11	16	↓
Faridabad	12	6	↑
Fatehabad	13	14	↓
Sirsa	14	15	↓
Jind	15	13	↑
Gurgaon	16	12	↑
Bhiwani	17	17	◆
Mahendergarh	18	18	◆
Kaithal	19	19	◆
Rank Correlation Coefficient (r)			**+0.87**

and Panipat (moderate ranked) districts have advanced four steps each. Insignificant movement is noticed in the other districts of the state.

Sum up

The state has advanced slowly but steadily towards gender development. The females of the state have marched substantially ahead of males in the education and health dimensions. However, the feminine sex of the state is facing hard time as far as participation in economic activities is concerned. As regards to spatio-temporal analysis of the state, the districts with lower index values have recorded higher positive change whereas the districts with higher index values have either recorded lesser positive growth or negative growth. However, the decadal shifting in the rankings has been well under control.

11

Spatio-temporal Analysis of Human Poverty Index, 2001-2011

Similar to that of Human Development Index (HDI) and Gender Development Index (GDI), the Spatio-temporal changes that occurred in the Human Poverty Index (HPI) have been examined. The three basic dimensions as well as the trend of change in the HPI have been discussed in the succeeding section.

Income Dimension

Some revealing conclusions can be drawn on the basis of the trends of temporal change in the deprivation level (income) as depicted in Table 11.1.

Firstly, the deprivation level is on the rise at alarming rate in the state. It was 10.21 per cent in 2001 which has risen to a considerable height (more than double) at 22.96 per cent in 2011. Secondly, none of the districts has shown descending trend in the deprivation level. (It is pertinent to mention here that the trend is largely an outcome of biased BPL list on which questions are raised from time to time as a large number of ineligible persons succeed in including their names in the BPL list by hook or by crook so that they can take the benefit of Government Schemes meant for the people below poverty line). Thirdly, Ambala district has surprisingly registered a huge bounce of 364.33 per cent in terms of proportional change to reach at a deprivation level as high as 27.07 per cent in 2011 as compared to a docile deprivation level of 5.83 per cent in 2001. The districts like Mahendergarh (272.78 per cent), Sonepat (189.85 per cent), Fatehabad (181.76 per cent), Kaithal (172.35 per cent) and many more have observed a steep hike in the deprivation level over

Table 11.1: Spatio-temporal Analysis of Index of Deprivation- Income (2001-2011)

Districts	*Index 2001*	*Index 2011*	*Absolute Change*	*Proportional Change (%)*
Ambala	5.83	27.07	21.24	364.33
Mahendergarh	6.51	24.27	17.76	272.78
Sonepat	7.89	22.87	14.98	189.85
Fatehabad	10.57	29.78	19.21	181.76
Kaithal	11.04	30.07	19.03	172.35
Panipat	6.95	17.94	10.99	158.09
Rohtak	9.98	23.13	13.15	131.77
Jhajjar	7.98	18.49	10.51	131.69
Rewari	10.54	23.92	13.38	126.92
Bhiwani	13.61	29.73	16.12	118.47
Kurukshetra	12.01	25.79	13.78	114.77
Jind	14.26	30.06	15.80	110.81
Yamunanagar	11.32	23.62	12.30	108.69
Hisar	11.47	23.58	12.11	105.57
Faridabad	8.06	16.12	8.06	100.04
Gurgaon	10.13	19.66	9.53	94.06
Karnal	11.94	21.14	9.20	77.07
Sirsa	13.47	23.01	9.54	70.85
Panchkula	9.36	15.52	6.16	65.81
Haryana	**10.21**	**22.96**	**12.75**	**124.91**

Table 11.2: Index of Deprivation- Income: Temporal Movement in the Ranking of Districts (2001-2011)

Districts	*Rank in 2001*	*Rank in 2011*	*Temporal Movement*
Jind	1	2	↓
Bhiwani	2	4	↓
Sirsa	3	12	↓
Kurukshetra	4	6	↓
Karnal	5	14	↓
Hisar	6	10	↓
Yamunanagar	7	9	↓
Kaithal	8	1	↑
Fatehabad	9	3	↑
Rewari	10	8	↑
Gurgaon	11	15	↓
Rohtak	12	11	↑
Panchkula	13	19	↓
Faridabad	14	18	↓
Jhajjar	15	16	↓
Sonepat	16	13	↑
Panipat	17	17	◆
Mahendergarh	18	7	↑
Ambala	19	5	↑
Rank Correlation Coefficient (r)			**+0.41**

the period. Fourthly, in contradiction to Ambala district, Panchkula district which was among the bottom districts with deprivation level as low as 9.36 per cent in 2001 has maintained its status in 2011 by registering lowest decadal change (though it has also registered decadal increase of 65.81 per cent). Fifth, absolute change does not show parity with the proportional change in many of the districts which indicates that a number of districts with lower deprivation levels have been underrated while the districts with higher deprivation levels have been overrated. Compare the trend of Sonepat (low deprivation level) and Jind (high deprivation level) districts. The absolute change occurred in the former district is lesser than that of the latter but in terms of proportional change the figures are 189.85 per cent and 11.81 per cent respectively. In this way absolute change occurred in Jind district is overestimated. Similar examples may be quoted of Mahendergarh and Fatehabad; Sonepat and Kaithal; Panipat and Yamunanagar districts, etc.

A significant decadal movement in the ranks of districts regarding the deprivation level (income) is visible in Table 11.2. The modest value of correlation coefficient (0.41) suggests that there is insignificant association between the ranks obtained by the districts during the two decades. Except for low ranked Panipat district, all the districts have changed their positions. Eleven districts have descended their positions whereas seven have recorded upward movement. The highest upward movement of fourteen ranks can be seen in Ambala which was at the last rank in 2001 now reached at a fairly higher fifth rank. In other words, Ambala district has appeared as a highly deprived district in 2011 while it was least deprived in 2001. The other districts with notable upward movement are Mahendergarh (eleven steps), Kaithal (seven steps) and Fatehabad (six steps). Out of the eleven districts with the downward movement, Sirsa and Karnal districts have recorded sharpest decline of nine ranks each and as a result the former district has slipped from third rank in 2001 to 12th rank in 2011 whereas the latter has descended from fifth rank to 14th rank in the corresponding time. The descending ranks indicate here that the deprivation level has been increasing in these districts but the degree of change is comparatively less.

Education Dimension

IOD-education throws light on the deprivation of people with respect to literacy rate. Luckily, the deprivation level is decreasing sharply in the state. The state figure which was 32.09 in 2001 has reduced considerably to 23.36 in 2011 thereby recorded a decennial decline of 27.20 per cent in proportional terms (Table 11.3).

Table 11.3: Spatio-temporal Analysis of Index of Deprivation- Education (2001-2011)

Districts	*Index 2001*	*Index 2011*	*Absolute Change*	*Proportional Change (%)*
Kurukshetra	30.12	23.30	-6.82	-22.64
Hisar	35.17	26.80	-8.37	-23.80
Sirsa	39.45	29.60	-9.85	-24.97
Rohtak	26.28	19.60	-6.68	-25.42
Yamunanagar	28.37	21.10	-7.27	-25.63
Fatehabad	42.02	30.90	-11.12	-26.46
Karnal	32.26	23.60	-8.66	-26.84
Panipat	30.83	22.50	-8.33	-27.02
Jind	37.88	27.30	-10.58	-27.93
Rewari	24.75	17.80	-6.95	-28.08
Kaithal	40.98	29.40	-11.58	-28.26
Bhiwani	32.55	23.30	-9.25	-28.42
Faridabad	29.97	21.21	-8.76	-29.23
Sonepat	27.21	19.20	-8.01	-29.44
Mahendergarh	30.11	21.10	-9.01	-29.92
Jhajjar	27.62	19.20	-8.42	-30.49
Ambala	24.69	17.10	-7.59	-30.74
Panchkula	26.00	16.60	-9.40	-36.15
Gurgaon	37.09	23.53	-13.56	-36.56
Haryana	**32.09**	**23.36**	**-8.73**	**-27.20**

Table 11.4: Index of Deprivation- Education: Temporal Movement in the Ranking of Districts (2001-2011)

Districts	*Rank in 2001*	*Rank in 2011*	*Temporal Movement*
Fatehabad	1	1	◆
Kaithal	2	3	↓
Sirsa	3	2	↓
Jind	4	4	◆
Gurgaon	5	7	↓
Hisar	6	5	↓
Bhiwani	7	8	↓
Karnal	8	6	↑
Panipat	9	10	↓
Kurukshetra	10	9	↑
Mahendergarh	11	12	↓
Faridabad	12	11	↑
Yamunanagar	13	13	◆
Jhajjar	14	15	↓
Sonepat	15	16	↓
Rohtak	16	14	↑
Panchkula	17	19	◆
Rewari	18	17	↑
Ambala	19	18	↑
Rank Correlation Coefficient (r)			**+0.98**

The declining trend is pervasive all across the districts ranging from 22.64 per cent in Kurukshetra to 36.56 per cent in Gurgaon. Most of the districts which possessed higher deprivation level in the base year (2001) have shown inflated sharper decline in terms of absolute change. These include Fatehabad, Kaithal and Jind districts. On the other hand there are districts like Panchkula, Ambala, Jhajjar, etc. with fairly low deprivation level in the base year have demonstrated appreciable decline (in terms of proportional change). The intensity of decline in these districts is rather underrated in terms of absolute change.

As all the districts have shown descending trend with minimum inter-district variation in the intensity of temporal change, there is hardly any scope for significant shifting among the districts. A very high degree of positive correlation (0.98) which is near to unity provides strong support to it. Although fifteen districts have changed their earlier positions yet the intensity of change is far from significant to affect their status to a substantial manner (Table 11.4).

Against the general perception that the health facilities are spreading over space with time, it can be noticed from Table 11.5 that more than 50 per cent of the villages in the state are found devoid of Govt. health facility in 2011 whereas the corresponding figure was 36 per cent in 2001. The deprivation level has increased all across the state apart from Jind, Jhajjar and Sonepat districts. An awful increase of 40.20 index points in terms of absolute change has been recorded by Faridabad district which signifies that three-fourth of villages in the district are found underprivileged of any Govt. health facility in 2011. In terms of proportional change, Karnal demonstrates the most depressing figure of 184.69 per cent. The decadal change observed in Mahendergarh, Gurgaon and Panipat districts is not at all encouraging. Surprisingly all these districts had deprivation level well under control in the earlier decade. On the other end of the scale, Jind district has reduced its deprivation level by 9.80 index points (in terms of absolute change) to reach at a modest figure of 40 per cent in 2011. Jhajjar district has brought the corresponding figure below 30 per cent by recording sharpest decline of 20.34 per cent in terms of proportional change. Rather insignificant decadal change can be seen in Sonepat and Bhiwani districts but in the opposite directions.

Moderate value (0.58) of correlation coefficient suggests that the decadal movement in the district-wise rankings as regards to 'villages without Govt. health facility' has been illustrious (Table 11.6). The positions of only three districts, one at the top (Yamunanagar) and two at the bottom (Hisar and Rohtak), have remain unchanged. A downward movement is recorded by ten districts. Out of these Jind, Jhajjar and Sonepat districts have shown noteworthy slide of nine ranks, six ranks

Table 11.5: Spatio-temporal Analysis of Villages without Govt. Health Facility (2001-2011)

Districts	*Index 2001*	*Index 2011*	*Absolute Change*	*Proportional Change (%)*
Karnal	20.90	59.50	38.60	184.69
Panipat	18.50	46.70	28.20	152.43
Faridabad	34.80	75.00	40.20	115.52
Mahendergarh	36.50	69.80	33.30	91.23
Gurgaon	42.60	74.40	31.76	74.55
Kaithal	23.70	40.00	16.30	68.78
Rohtak	13.60	21.90	8.30	61.03
Hisar	12.00	18.90	6.90	57.50
Yamunanagar	63.80	87.10	23.30	36.52
Panchkula	53.50	71.40	17.90	33.46
Rewari	43.50	56.10	12.60	28.97
Kurukshetra	46.40	56.80	10.40	22.41
Sirsa	36.00	43.20	7.20	20.00
Ambala	55.70	62.50	6.80	12.21
Fatehabad	29.70	31.70	2.00	6.73
Bhiwani	42.10	43.90	1.80	4.28
Sonepat	37.00	35.10	-1.90	-5.14
Jind	49.80	40.00	-9.80	-19.68
Jhajjar	35.40	28.20	-7.20	-20.34
Haryana	**36.00**	**50.90**	**14.90**	**41.39**

Table 11.6: Villages without Govt. Health Facility:
Temporal Movement in the Ranking of Districts (2001-2011)

Districts	*Rank in 2001*	*Rank in 2011*	*Temporal Movement*
Yamunanagar	1	1	◆
Ambala	2	6	↓
Panchkula	3	4	↓
Jind	4	13	↓
Kurukshetra	5	8	↓
Rewari	6	9	↓
Gurgaon	7	3	↑
Bhiwani	8	11	↓
Sonepat	9	15	↓
Mahendergarh	10	5	↑
Sirsa	11	12	↓
Jhajjar	12	17	↓
Faridabad	13	2	↑
Fatehabad	14	16	↓
Kaithal	15	14	↑
Karnal	16	7	↑
Panipat	17	10	↑
Rohtak	18	18	◆
Hisar	19	19	◆
Rank Correlation Coefficient (r)			**+0.58**

Table 11.7: Spatio-temporal Analysis of Villages without Doctor (2001-2011)

Districts	*Index 2001*	*Index 2011*	*Absolute Change*	*Proportional Change (%)*
Panipat	2.60	53.30	50.70	1950.00
Gurgaon	7.20	83.30	76.10	1057.41
Bhiwani	11.70	87.80	76.10	650.43
Faridabad	14.60	100.00	85.40	584.93
Kaithal	9.90	65.00	55.10	556.57
Yamunanagar	22.80	71.00	48.20	211.40
Jind	24.00	72.50	48.50	202.08
Panchkula	20.10	57.10	37.00	184.08
Rohtak	28.80	81.20	52.40	181.94
Jhajjar	34.70	94.90	60.20	173.49
Sirsa	29.60	78.40	48.80	164.86
Mahendergarh	34.60	88.40	53.80	155.49
Sonepat	23.90	54.10	30.20	126.36
Karnal	24.40	45.90	21.50	88.11
Fatehabad	53.50	87.80	34.30	64.11
Hisar	59.10	83.80	24.70	41.79
Rewari	70.70	80.50	9.80	13.86
Ambala	82.00	65.60	-16.40	-20.00
Kurukshetra	80.20	45.90	-34.30	-42.77
Haryana	**33.60**	**74.20**	**40.60**	**120.83**

and five ranks respectively. The other six districts have come up with upward movement. Although the number of districts in the category of upward movement is lesser as compared to the districts with downward movement, yet the intensity of movement is fairly higher. The notable upward movement has been experienced by Faridabad (11 ranks), Karnal (nine ranks) and Panipat (seven ranks) districts.

The data pertaining to deprivation level regarding 'villages without doctor' for two time periods and decadal change therein is quite striking (Table 11.7). As a whole the state has experienced a sharp increase in the deprivation level as the figure was as moderate as 33.60 in 2001 which has risen appallingly at a point as high as 74.20 thereby recording an increase of 40.60 index points in terms of absolute change. Proportionally the state deprivation level has increased by 120.83 per cent. The other eye catching fact is that the decadal change is quite high in most of the districts. As many as thirteen districts have enhanced their deprivation level sharper than the state average. Consider some of the districts that have experienced increase in the deprivation level. Faridabad, Gurgaon and Panipat are the three most advanced districts with respect to industrial development and they have achieved appreciable attainment level in income dimension but surprisingly they are awfully devoid of doctor's facility in their rural hinterland. In this way these districts have demonstrated a wide rural-urban gap in development. However, two districts i.e. Kurukshetra and Ambala have come up with a decline in deprivation level. While Kurukshetra district has brought its deprivation level at a moderate level of 45.90 index points by recording absolute decline of 34.30 index points, it is still high (65.60 index points) in Ambala district albeit a decline of 16.40 index points.

Table 11.8 focuses on the temporal movement experienced by the districts over the period. The ranks achieved by the districts in the base year have shown negligible correlation (0.06) with the ranks of 2011 which strongly indicate that a large scale inter-district reshuffling has taken place during 2001-2011. Ten districts have experienced upward movement whereas downward movement is visible in eight districts. The most noteworthy change can be seen in Kurukshetra district which has brought its rank significantly down (from second to eighteenth) during 2001-2011. It implies that it has reduced its deprivation level more than that of 17 districts.

The other districts with notable downward movement include Ambala and Karnal districts with a decline of 12 ranks and nine ranks respectively. Out of the ten districts that have experienced upward movement in their ranks over time, the most significant change occurs in Faridabad (upward movement of 14 ranks), Bhiwani (upward movement of 11 ranks) and

Table 11.8: Villages without Doctor: Temporal Movement in the Ranking of Districts (2001-2011)

Districts	*Rank in 2001*	*Rank in 2011*	*Temporal Movement*
Ambala	1	13	↓
Kurukshetra	2	18	↓
Rewari	3	9	↓
Hisar	4	6	↓
Fatehabad	5	4	↑
Jhajjar	6	2	↑
Mahendergarh	7	3	↑
Sirsa	8	10	↓
Rohtak	9	8	↑
Karnal	10	19	↓
Jind	11	11	◆
Sonepat	12	16	↓
Yamunanagar	13	12	↑
Panchkula	14	15	↓
Faridabad	15	1	↑
Bhiwani	16	5	↑
Kaithal	17	14	↑
Gurgaon	18	7	↑
Panipat	19	17	↑
Rank Correlation Coefficient (r)			**+0.06**

Gurgaon (upward movement of 11 ranks) which reflects that the deprivation level in these districts has increased sharply with time. Jind district, moderately placed at 11th rank in 2001, however, has remained unmoved over the given point of time. It can be concluded from the table that northern districts (Ambala and Kurukshetra) have reduced their deprivation level whereas it has increased considerably in southern districts (Gurgaon and Faridabad).

Even after a slight decrease of 1.4 index points in 2011; the intensity of deprivation level in terms of 'women received full ante-natal check-ups' is still reasonably high in the state (Table 11.9). As far as district-wise deprivation level is concerned, a fairly diverse trend of change can be seen. Nearly one-third of the districts have augmented their deprivation level. In the present case the two facets of temporal change are concurrent to each other which reflect that none of the districts has shown overestimation/underestimation in terms of absolute change. Panipat district has emerged as the highest deprived district (with an increase of 7.10 index points) in the state in 2011 as 93.80 per cent of the eligible women here have not received full ante-natal check-ups. However, the highest decadal increase of 7.70 index points (in terms of absolute change) has been noticed in Kurukshetra district which propels its deprivation level above the state average. Similarly, Bhiwani district has experienced handsome increase to become the second most deprived district with the deprivation level as high as 91.10 index points.

On the opposite side, Sirsa district has brought its deprivation level down considerably from 92.80 per cent in 2001 to 82.20 per cent in 2011 with the highest plunge of 10.60 index points. The decline is also conspicuous in Yamunanagar, Rohtak, Kaithal and Rewari districts.

Table 11.10 focuses on the temporal movement of districts in their respective position as regards to women not received ante-natal check-ups. It is evident from the poor association (r = 0.30) between the ranks obtained by each district during the two points of time that decadal movement has been quite significant. As a whole, seventeen districts have changed their ranks in 2011. Out of these, ten districts have moved downward and the remaining seven have moved upward. Most of the high ranked districts have experienced downward movement while the upward movement is conspicuous in lower ranked districts. A notable upward movement can be seen in Bhiwani (15th rank to 2nd rank), Panipat (12th rank to 1st rank), Kurukshetra (18th rank to ninth rank) and Hisar (13th rank to 7th rank). The districts with the distinguished downward movement include Sirsa (4th rank to 14th rank), Yamunanagar (8th rank to 17th rank), Kaithal (10th rank to 18th rank) and Rewari (9th rank to 16th rank). Only two districts that have maintained their earlier positions are

Table 11.9: Spatio-temporal Analysis of Women not Received Full Ante-natal Check-ups (2001-2011)

Districts	*Index 2001*	*Index 2011*	*Absolute Change*	*Proportional Change (%)*
Kurukshetra	80.50	88.20	7.70	9.57
Panipat	86.70	93.80	7.10	8.19
Bhiwani	84.40	91.10	6.70	7.94
Hisar	86.10	89.60	3.50	4.07
Ambala	80.80	82.60	1.80	2.23
Panchkula	79.20	80.90	1.70	2.15
Jhajjar	84.60	83.80	-0.80	-0.95
Gurgaon	90.00	88.50	-1.50	-1.68
Fatehabad	92.30	90.50	-1.80	-1.95
Mahendergarh	92.90	90.90	-2.00	-2.15
Faridabad	93.50	90.70	-2.80	-2.99
Jind	93.40	90.30	-3.10	-3.32
Karnal	86.80	83.40	-3.40	-3.92
Sonepat	91.20	85.10	-6.10	-6.69
Rewari	87.30	79.40	-7.90	-9.05
Kaithal	86.90	78.90	-8.00	-9.21
Yamunanagar	87.80	79.20	-8.60	-9.79
Rohtak	81.00	72.50	-8.50	-10.49
Sirsa	92.80	82.20	-10.60	-11.42
Haryana	**88.20**	**86.80**	**-1.40**	**-1.59**

Table 11.10: Women not Received Full Ante-natal Check-ups: Temporal Movement in the Ranking of Districts (2001-2011)

Districts	*Rank in 2001*	*Rank in 2011*	*Temporal Movement*
Faridabad	1	4	↓
Jind	2	6	↓
Mahendergarh	3	3	◆
Sirsa	4	14	↓
Fatehabad	5	5	◆
Sonepat	6	10	↓
Gurgaon	7	8	↓
Yamunanagar	8	17	↓
Rewari	9	16	↓
Kaithal	10	18	↓
Karnal	11	12	↓
Panipat	12	1	↑
Hisar	13	7	↑
Jhajjar	14	11	↑
Bhiwani	15	2	↑
Rohtak	16	19	↓
Ambala	17	13	↑
Kurukshetra	18	9	↑
Panchkula	19	15	↑
Rank Correlation Coefficient (r)			**+0.30**

Table 11.11: Spatio-temporal Analysis of Non-institutional Deliveries (2001-2011)

Districts	*Index 2001*	*Index 2011*	*Absolute Change*	*Proportional Change (%)*
Ambala	38.20	44.60	6.40	16.75
Bhiwani	63.70	64.30	0.60	0.94
Jhajjar	53.80	52.00	-1.80	-3.35
Panipat	66.10	61.00	-5.10	-7.72
Gurgaon	79.60	71.10	-8.50	-10.65
Faridabad	68.80	60.90	-7.90	-11.48
Fatehabad	62.10	51.40	-10.70	-17.23
Rohtak	58.10	47.20	-10.90	-18.76
Jind	72.90	57.90	-15.00	-20.58
Sonepat	58.90	46.30	-12.60	-21.39
Hisar	67.60	51.40	-16.20	-23.96
Karnal	66.20	48.70	-17.50	-26.44
Kaithal	71.60	52.00	-19.60	-27.37
Kurukshetra	49.70	35.80	-13.90	-27.97
Yamunanagar	68.40	47.70	-20.70	-30.26
Sirsa	66.70	46.50	-20.20	-30.28
Mahendergarh	63.20	43.20	-20.00	-31.65
Panchkula	54.90	35.70	-19.20	-34.97
Rewari	54.10	35.00	-19.10	-35.30
Haryana	**64.90**	**53.20**	**-11.70**	**-18.03**

Table 11.12: Non-institutional Deliveries: Temporal Movement in the Ranking of Districts (2001-2011)

Districts	*Rank in 2001*	*Rank in 2011*	*Temporal Movement*
Gurgaon	1	1	◆
Jind	2	5	↓
Kaithal	3	7	↓
Faridabad	4	4	◆
Yamunanagar	5	11	↓
Hisar	6	9	↓
Sirsa	7	13	↓
Karnal	8	10	↓
Panipat	9	3	↑
Bhiwani	10	2	↑
Mahendergarh	11	16	↓
Fatehabad	12	8	↑
Sonepat	13	14	↓
Rohtak	14	12	↑
Panchkula	15	18	↓
Rewari	16	19	↓
Jhajjar	17	6	↑
Kurukshetra	18	17	↑
Ambala	19	15	↑
Rank Correlation Coefficient (r)			**+0.64**

Fatehabad (fifth rank) and Mahendergarh (third rank). In this way both of these maintained their higher ranks.

The incidence of non-institutional deliveries was quite high in the state in 2001 when 64.90 per cent of the deliveries took place outside the health institutions. The figure has come down to 53.20 per cent in 2011 still it is fairly high. The district wise decadal change presented in Table 11.11 reflects that the deprivation level has decreased all across the districts except Ambala and Bhiwani districts. It is worthwhile to note that the deprivation level was lowest in Ambala district in 2001.

This is why it has successfully maintained it in the lower ranked districts in 2011 even after a reasonable increase of 16.75 per cent in terms of proportional change during 2001-2011. On the other hand Bhiwani district has recorded a little (0.94 per cent) increase but it has become the second most deprived district after Gurgaon in 2011 owing to its already high deprivation level in 2001. Out of the seventeen districts that have reduced their deprivation level, the highest decline (20.70 index points in terms of absolute change) has been registered by Yamunanagar district and as a result it has succeeded to bring its deprivation well below 50 per cent in 2011. Similarly, Sirsa, Mahendergarh, Panchkula, Rewari and Karnal districts have also brought their deprivation level below the 50 per cent mark by registering notable decline. As far as proportional change is concerned, Rewari district has appeared with sharpest decline of 35.30 per cent. Here, the decline registered by Yamunanagar district has been overestimated in terms of absolute change due to its greater size of deprivation as compared to Rewari district. Similar overestimation is evident in Sirsa, Mahendergarh and Kaithal districts. It is heartening to realise that most of the districts with high deprivation level in 2001 have shown decreasing trend in 2011.

Moderate coefficient of correlation (0.64) puts forward that there has not been a large scale shifting in the relative positions of the districts over time as regards to their deprivation level. Gurgaon and Faridabad, the two higher ranked districts have maintained their first and fourth positions respectively (Table 11.12). Majority of the districts have descended their positions. Some of the districts with notable downward movement are Yamunanagar and Sirsa (descended six ranks each) and Mahendergarh (descended five ranks). Nonetheless the number of districts with upward movement is fewer (7) than that of districts with downward movement (10), yet the intensity of movement is higher. Jhajjar, Bhiwani and Panipat districts have shown a significant upward movement of ten ranks, eight ranks and six ranks respectively. Again the districts with 'low to moderate' deprivation level have moved upward whereas the districts

Table 11.13: Spatio-temporal Analysis of Children Age 12-35 Months not Fully Vaccinated (2001-2011)

Districts	*Index 2001*	*Index 2011*	*Absolute Change*	*Proportional Change (%)*
Ambala	7.10	20.90	13.80	194.37
Kurukshetra	18.30	32.20	13.90	75.96
Panchkula	14.30	21.90	7.60	53.15
Rohtak	19.00	24.30	5.30	27.89
Hisar	36.40	44.20	7.80	21.43
Panipat	36.20	43.00	6.80	18.78
Jind	37.60	44.60	7.00	18.62
Faridabad	46.30	53.60	7.30	15.77
Jhajjar	32.00	35.20	3.20	10.00
Yamunanagar	28.00	30.00	2.00	7.14
Fatehabad	34.90	37.20	2.30	6.59
Gurgaon	67.10	67.70	0.60	0.87
Rewari	34.20	32.70	-1.50	-4.39
Karnal	26.10	24.80	-1.30	-4.98
Bhiwani	52.20	41.60	-10.60	-20.31
Sirsa	50.90	38.70	-12.20	-23.97
Mahendergarh	47.40	32.30	-15.10	-31.86
Sonepat	44.90	27.00	-17.90	-39.87
Kaithal	58.60	27.50	-31.10	-53.07
Haryana	**37.10**	**40.40**	**3.30**	**8.89**

with 'high to moderate' deprivation level have either retained their positions or moved downward.

As far as the tendency of non-receipt of full vaccination is concerned, the deprivation level in the state accounts for 37.10 per cent in 2001 which has increased by 3.30 per cent thereby reached at 40.40 per cent in 2011 (Table 11.13). The deprivation level has been increased in twelve districts. Ambala district has registered highest increase of 194.37 per cent in proportional terms. However, the inflated value in terms of absolute change has put forward Kurukshetra district with the highest increase. Out of the seven districts that have experienced negative decadal change, the remarkable change of 53.07 per cent has been observed in Kaithal district. As a result it has reduced its deprivation level to 27.50 per cent in 2011. Other districts which reduced their deprivation level effectively include Sonepat (39.87 per cent), Mahendergarh (31.86 per cent), Sirsa (23.97 per cent) and Bhiwani (20.31 per cent).

Compare the intensity and trend of change of non-institutional deliveries with non-vaccination. As a whole the deprivation level in terms of non-vaccination is lesser in the state than that of non-institutional deliveries but it has been increasing with time contrary to the decreasing trend of the latter (Compare Table 11.11 and Table 11.13). Besides, the inter-district range of decadal change is quite broad as regards to deprivation in vaccination (194.37 per cent to -53.07 per cent) as compared to non-institutional deliveries (16.75 per cent to -35.30 per cent).

Table 11.14 illustrates district-wise rankings and temporal movement thereof as regards to non-vaccination. The value of correlation coefficient (0.64) indicates that there has been controlled decadal movement of districts in their respective ranks. No movement has been experienced in three districts (Gurgaon at the top and Ambala and Panchkula at the bottom). Sixteen districts have registered movement in their respective ranks; however the intensity of movement has been fairly controlled except for a few districts that have experienced remarkably high movement. These include Kaithal (movement of 12 ranks), Sonepat (movement of eight ranks), and Mahendergarh (movement of six ranks). Interestingly all these districts have registered downward movement. Even though the number of districts is higher in the category of upward movement, yet the intensity of shifting is rather insignificant. The highest bounce of five ranks is visible in Jind, Hisar, Panipat and Kurukshetra districts.

Unfortunately, IOD-health has been increasing with time as far as the temporal change is concerned. At the state level, it was 52.00 in 2001 which has reached at 61.10 in 2011 thereby registered a remarkable increase of 9.10 index points. In other words the deprivation level of

Table 11.14: Children Age 12-35 Months not fully Vaccinated: Temporal Movement in the Ranking of Districts (2001-2011)

Districts	*Rank in 2001*	*Rank in 2011*	*Temporal Movement*
Gurgaon	1	1	◆
Kaithal	2	14	↓
Bhiwani	3	6	↓
Sirsa	4	7	↓
Mahendergarh	5	11	↓
Faridabad	6	2	↑
Sonepat	7	15	↓
Jind	8	3	↑
Hisar	9	4	↑
Panipat	10	5	↑
Fatehabad	11	8	↑
Rewari	12	10	↑
Jhajjar	13	9	↑
Yamunanagar	14	13	↑
Karnal	15	16	↓
Rohtak	16	17	↓
Kurukshetra	17	12	↑
Panchkula	18	18	◆
Ambala	19	19	◆
Rank Correlation Coefficient (r)			**+0.64**

Table 11.15: Spatio-temporal Analysis of Index of Deprivation- Health (2001-2011)

Districts	*Index 2001*	*Index 2011*	*Absolute Change*	*Proportional Change (%)*
Faridabad	51.60	76.00	24.44	47.36
Panipat	42.00	59.60	17.54	41.74
Gurgaon	57.30	77.00	19.70	34.37
Bhiwani	50.80	65.70	14.92	29.36
Rohtak	40.10	49.40	9.32	23.24
Jhajjar	48.10	58.80	10.72	22.29
Panchkula	44.40	53.40	9.00	20.27
Mahendergarh	54.90	64.90	10.00	18.21
Karnal	44.90	52.50	7.58	16.89
Yamunanagar	54.20	63.00	8.84	16.32
Hisar	52.20	57.60	5.34	10.22
Jind	55.50	61.10	5.52	9.94
Fatehabad	54.50	59.70	5.22	9.58
Kaithal	50.10	52.70	2.54	5.07
Sirsa	55.20	57.80	2.60	4.71
Ambala	52.80	55.20	2.48	4.70
Rewari	58.00	56.70	-1.22	-2.10
Sonepat	51.20	49.50	-1.66	-3.24
Kurukshetra	55.00	51.80	-3.24	-5.89
Haryana	**52.00**	**61.10**	**9.14**	**17.59**

Table 11.16: Index of Deprivation- Health: Temporal Movement in the Ranking of Districts (2001-2011)

Districts	*Rank in 2001*	*Rank in 2011*	*Temporal Movement*
Rewari	1	12	↓
Gurgaon	2	1	↑
Jind	3	6	↓
Sirsa	4	10	↓
Kurukshetra	5	17	↓
Mahendergarh	6	4	↑
Fatehabad	7	7	◆
Yamunanagar	8	5	↑
Ambala	9	13	↓
Hisar	10	11	↓
Faridabad	11	2	↑
Sonepat	12	18	↓
Bhiwani	13	3	↑
Kaithal	14	15	↓
Jhajjar	15	9	↑
Karnal	16	16	◆
Panchkula	17	14	↑
Panipat	18	8	↑
Rohtak	19	19	◆
Rank Correlation Coefficient (r)			**+0.38**

health has increased by 17.59 per cent in terms of proportional change during 2001-2011 (Table 11.15).

Talking in terms of proportional change, the highest increase of 47.36 per cent has been recorded in Faridabad district. In this way the IOD-health in this district has reached up to an appalling height of 76.00 in 2011. The situation of Gurgaon district is even grimmer. Panipat, Bhiwani, Jhajjar and Mahendergarh districts have also added considerably in their already high deprivation level. As a whole sixteen districts have experienced increasing trend in IOD-health. The left over three districts (Kurukshetra, Sonepat and Rewari) scattering in the different parts of the state have registered a humble decline of 5.89 per cent, 3.24 per cent and 2.10 per cent respectively.

The diversified magnitude of decadal change in the IOD-health (as seen in Table 11.15) has resulted in restructuring of district-wise ranks over time. The districts that have registered relatively higher change (positive or negative) have experienced higher change in their positions (upward or downward) as shown in Table 11.16. Poor coefficient of correlation (0.38) indicates that the reshuffling has taken place at large scale. Eight districts have registered upward movement during 2001-2011. The movement is reasonably high in majority of the districts. The highest bounce of 10 ranks each can be seen in Bhiwani and Panipat districts. In this manner these districts have reached at third and eighth places respectively in 2011. Besides, conspicuous change can also be seen in Faridabad (upward movement of nine ranks) and Jhajjar (upward movement of six ranks) districts. Equal numbers (8) of districts have descended their positions; however, the movement is even sharper. Kurukshetra district has slipped sharply to 17th place in 2011 from fifth rank in 2001 thereby recorded downward movement of 12 steps. In the same manner, Rewari has descended by 11 ranks as it was at the top in 2001 but slipped to 12th rank in 2011. Downward movement of six ranks each is visible in Sirsa and Sonepat districts. However, the positions of three districts in the state have remained unchanged during the decade. These are Fatehabad (seventh rank), Karnal (16th rank) and Rohtak (19th rank).

Human Poverty Index

Human Poverty Index (HPI) reflects the combined deprivation levels in respect of the three basic dimensions discussed above. It is very depressing to realise that the overall deprivation level of the people has increased in the state despite various efforts of the government to improve their living conditions. The HPI value which was 38.74 in the base year has increased to 43.85 in 2011 thereby recorded an increase of 13.20 per cent in proportional terms (Table 11.17). Fifteen districts have

Table 11.17: Spatio-temporal Analysis of Human Poverty Index (2001-2011)

Districts	*Index 2001*	*Index 2011*	*Absolute Change*	*Proportional Change (%)*
Faridabad	38.02	53.27	15.25	40.11
Panipat	32.59	42.39	9.80	30.06
Gurgaon	43.10	54.18	11.08	25.70
Bhiwani	38.28	47.58	9.30	24.29
Rohtak	30.32	36.05	5.73	18.91
Jhajjar	35.38	41.66	6.28	17.75
Mahendergarh	40.08	46.28	6.19	15.45
Panchkula	32.81	37.69	4.88	14.88
Yamunanagar	39.38	44.96	5.58	14.18
Karnal	34.73	38.18	3.45	9.93
Jind	42.39	45.10	2.70	6.38
Ambala	37.81	40.10	2.29	6.06
Hisar	39.69	42.06	2.37	5.98
Fatehabad	42.92	44.75	1.83	4.26
Kaithal	40.29	40.47	0.18	0.44
Sirsa	42.61	42.56	-0.05	-0.12
Rewari	41.28	40.68	-0.60	-1.45
Sonepat	37.22	36.04	-1.18	-3.16
Kurukshetra	40.25	38.31	-1.94	-4.83
Haryana	**38.74**	**43.85**	**5.11**	**13.20**

Table 11.18: Human Poverty Index: Temporal Movement in the Ranking of Districts (2001-2011)

Districts	*Rank in 2001*	*Rank in 2011*	*Temporal Movement*
Gurgaon	1	1	◆
Fatehabad	2	7	↓
Sirsa	3	8	↓
Jind	4	5	↓
Rewari	5	12	↓
Kaithal	6	13	↓
Kurukshetra	7	15	↓
Mahendergarh	8	4	↑
Hisar	9	10	↓
Yamunanagar	10	6	↑
Bhiwani	11	3	↑
Faridabad	12	2	↑
Ambala	13	14	↓
Sonepat	14	19	↓
Jhajjar	15	11	↑
Karnal	16	16	◆
Panchkula	17	17	◆
Panipat	18	9	↑
Rohtak	19	18	↑
Rank Correlation Coefficient (r)			**0.53**

registered increase in the HPI. Out of these, nine districts have registered sharper increase than that of the state average.

The highest boost is visible in Faridabad district followed by Panipat and Gurgaon districts. Surprisingly these three districts have earned a good name in the state as regards to industrial development. It implies that the other aspects of human development have not been on the priority of the stake holders. However, the HPI figure has declined, though slightly, in four districts. Out of these Kurukshetra, Rewari and Sirsa districts have brought down their deprivation levels below the state average in 2011 by recording negative proportional change of 4.83 per cent, 1.45 per cent and 0.12 per cent respectively. Sonepat district has diminished its HPI figure which was already below the state average and emerged as a district with the lowest HPI.

A moderate coefficient of correlation (0.53) signifies that majority of the districts have undergone notable shifting in their respective ranks as regards to magnitude of HPI. Table 11.18 demonstrates that nine districts have lowered their ranks. Out of the seven top ranked districts, six districts have moved downward. On account of highest negative change as evident in Table 11.17, Kurukshetra district has experienced sharpest plunge of eight ranks (seventh in 2001 to 15th in 2011). The other districts with conspicuous downward movement include Kaithal and Rewari districts that have enjoyed a plunge of seven steps each. Besides, Sirsa and Fatehabad districts have also brought down their deprivation level by five steps each. On the other hand, seven districts have registered sharp decadal hike in their HPI value on account of which their ranks have been enhanced considerably in 2011 as compared to 2001. The most noteworthy thrust of ten steps is experienced by Faridabad. Credit goes to highest increase observed by it in its HPI value. Reasonable upward movement has also been observed in Panipat (18th rank in 2001 to ninth rank in 2011) and Bhiwani (11th rank in 2001 to third rank in 2011) districts. However, Gurgaon district has remained firm at the top position as regards to human poverty in the state during the given point of time.

One can infer from the trend depicted in Table 11.18 that the districts with higher deprivation level are gaining concentration in the southern parts of the state as the top ranked four districts in 2011 viz. Gurgaon, Faridabad, Bhiwani and Mahendergarh belong to southern region. On the contrary, the districts of north Haryana, except Yamunanagar, have either maintained their lower ranks or recorded downward movement thereby reduced human poverty level relatively.

Sum up

As against the spirit of development goals, the deprivation level in the state is increasing with time. Although it has decreased all across the state in education dimension yet the situation with respect to income and health dimensions has generally been critical. This is why; most of the districts have suffered an undesirable increase in the HPI value. Moreover, a large scale fluctuation in the deprivation level of districts as regards to income and health dimensions intensifies the decadal movement in the district-wise rankings which is undesirable in bringing down the deprivation level in the state. Regional pattern of the HPI suggests that the districts located in the southern part are more deprived as compared to the northern part of the state.

12

Conclusions and Policy Implications

The chapters in this study have discussed various aspects of human development in Haryana, giving a contemporary picture of two points of time as well as spatio-temporal changes that took place in the state. The present chapter recapitulates the main findings and discusses policy implications for improving human development all over the state.

Conclusions

As mentioned in the introductory chapter, Haryana has had unique identity in several respects such as it was one of the cradles of Indian culture and civilisation; it was one of the few pioneer states which adopted green revolution; its distinctive demographic experience; and its remarkable progress in the industrial development especially during the last two decades. These unique features have raised numerous far-reaching issues on the strategies which have been adopted and to be followed in improving human development.

The introductory chapter has pointed out that Haryana comprises of 2.09 per cent population of India and stands at 16th place on the state wise population tally as per latest census. Not only the density of population but the decennial growth of population is higher in the state than that of India. The state has an undesirable distinction of ranking at the bottom of the scale amongst the Indian states as regards to sex ratio. However, the latest trend of change is encouraging.

The state has performed better in a number of health parameters as compared to the country. Life expectancy at birth of females is considerably higher; birth rates as well as death rates are lower than the national average. The participation rates of the population in various health awareness programmes pertaining to women and children are higher than the national average. The prevalence of child marriage in respect of females is lower in the state; however it is found higher in respect of males. Life expectancy at birth of males (LEB- males) and Infant Mortality Rates (IMR) are largely at par with the country except for urban areas. The health infrastructure of the state is better than that of the nation.

As far as the literacy rate is concerned, it is slightly higher in the state as compared to the national average. The state has been placed at the 15th rank on the state-wise tally of total literacy rate in census 2011. The state has an edge over the national average as regards to gender-wise literacy rates also. Besides, the state has developed impressive educational infrastructure not only to provide elementary education but also for higher and technical education especially during the last decade.

The economic development in the state is rather remarkable. The Quick Estimates of the Gross State Domestic Product (GSDP) at factor cost at constant prices (2004-05) reveal that the state has recorded an impressive growth of 9.9 per cent during the year 2009-10. At current prices, the GSDP has shown an appreciable growth of 18.2 per cent during 2009-10. As regards to inter-sector growth of economy, it was 0.7 per cent, 10.3 per cent and 12.9 per cent for Primary Sector, Secondary Sector and Tertiary Sector respectively in 2009-10. Stumpy growth of Primary sector is mainly due to the discouraging growth of 0.6 per cent in Agriculture Sector. On the other hand, the encouraging growth of GSDP recorded in Secondary Sector is exclusively because of the excellent growth of 10.5 per cent each recorded in the Manufacturing and Construction Sectors. Similarly, a heartening growth of Tertiary Sector was chiefly due to the spectacular growth of 20.1 per cent registered in Trade Sector. The per capita income (Per Capita Net State Domestic Product) in real terms at constant prices (2004-05) has been estimated at Rs 55214 during 2009-10 as against Rs 51016 during 2008-09 showing an annual boost of 8.2 per cent. At current prices the per capita income has been estimated as Rs 78781 in 2009-10 with an annual increase of 16.3 per cent. The economy of Haryana reflects a structural shift from Primary Sector to Tertiary Sector, which is a sign of healthy economy. Agriculture Sector still continues to occupy a significant position in state's economy, although the share of this sector in the GSDP is declining consistently. The preponderance of Agriculture Sector is, to a great extent, responsible for instability in the growth rate of economy due to fluctuations in agricultural production. Moreover, rapidly increasing share of Services Sector in the state GDP adds to the decline in the share of Agriculture Sector. The share of Agriculture and Allied Sectors has declined from 22 per cent during 2004-05 to 16.1 per cent during 2009-10 as against 30.5 per cent and 53.4 per cent in Secondary and Tertiary Sectors respectively.

As far as Plan-wise outlay and expenditure of the state since inception is concerned, a consistent increase in the approved outlay till the Fourth Plan and a sharp increase in the subsequent Plans has been the characteristic feature of the state's outlay history. While allocating plan outlays for the departments, highest priority has been accorded to the social service sector in the 11th Plan period which is 47.71 per cent of the total outlay. Among the social services, due importance has been given to the three basic services of Water Supply, General Education and Technical Education and Health Care. The second highest priority has been given to the development/improvement of infrastructure of Irrigation, Energy, Roads and Road Transport Sectors by earmarking 37.76 per cent of the total outlay.

Haryana, the state known for its agricultural production is located strategically close to Delhi and one-third of its area falls within the National Capital Region. This region represents one of the biggest trade and consumption centres in the country. Between 1994 and 2003, the economy of Haryana grew at an average rate of 6.5 per cent per annum. Haryana has the fourth highest per capita income in India. Haryana offers significant potential for agro-based industries, property development and retailing. With investment currently underway, it is expected to emerge as the principal hub for downstream chemicals in north India. Keeping apart the above facts, it is disheartening to note that the industrial development is restricted to a few districts located in the radius of 60 kilometres from Delhi and the far off districts are lagging behind in the race. As a result, the rank achieved by the state with respect to Human Development Index is quite disappointing. It has been awarded depressing 15th rank in 1981 and 16th rank in 1991 amongst the Indian states.

HDI, 2001

The state HDI worked out in the present study for 2001 has been moderately at 0.60. Panipat district appears at the top with an index value of 0.65 whereas Jind district occupies the last seat with a humble HDI value of 0.56. In this way, the difference of 0.0954 index points of HDI value between the top and bottom ranked districts signifies inter-district disparities. Geographical distribution of the districts suggests that majority of top ranked districts are concentrated in north-eastern part while the bottom ranked five districts show their concentration in north-western part (Ghaggar Basin) of the state. Furthermore, none of the districts located in the vicinity of New Delhi (and Chandigarh also) has showed HDI value below the state average. This statistics provides a reasonable ground in favour of the statement that the Capital Cities have put positive impact on the overall human development parameters. The five districts that have been grouped in the lowest performing class in respect of HDI demonstrate insignificant intra-class difference in their attainment levels.

A good number of studies have highlighted the complimentary relationship between economic development and human development. The importance of economic development to enhance the people's income level is beyond any debate for achieving higher standards of living as it gives ability to buy goods and services and widens the range of consumption options. But in order to achieve high income level the negligence of education and health dimensions put fairly adverse impact on the HDI as observed in Gurgaon and Faridabad districts in the present case. Nonetheless, high literacy and better health can be achieved even with low per capita income. Rohtak and Jhajjar districts have successfully attained high HDI on account of better performance in education and health dimensions even though these are lagging behind in income dimension. Moreover, the districts like Karnal, Sonepat, Mahendergarh, Yamunanagar, Bhiwani and Mahendergarh have performed better either in education or in health dimension without having higher income level. One more striking feature which can be noticed from HDI statistics, 2001 is that none of the districts is perfectly consistent in the attainment level of all the three dimensions, whether it is on the upper end or on the lower end of the scale. On one hand, the most advanced districts have shown weakness in one or another dimension while on the other hand; the most backward districts have shown a ray of hope in one or another dimension of human development. The correlation coefficients explain that education dimension has put most significant impact on construction of the HDI, though the role of health dimension cannot be underrated. On the other hand, the income dimension is far less influential as it has a moderate (0.46) correlation with the HDI.

GDI, 2001

It is rightly said that high economic development is meaningless in a society which is characterised with gender discrimination and inequality. To highlight this aspect, GDI has been obtained by computing the simple average of the equally distributed indexes pertaining to three dimensions-income, education and health. The three districts i.e. Ambala, Panchkula and Rewari that find place in the first category of high development have been awarded top three ranks respectively. The seven districts which are characterised with the upper moderate development forms a unique pattern in the eastern part of the state. In north-south order, these districts are Yamunanagar, Kurukshetra, Karnal, Panipat, Sonepat, Rohtak and Jhajjar. However, the attainment level is found lowest in as many as five districts dispersed all over the state. Kaithal district is at the bottom which is preceded by Mahendergarh, Bhiwani, Gurgaon and Jind districts.

Only three districts all over the state have shown consistent performance in all the three dimensions. By virtue of it, Rewari district has been placed higher on GDI tally whereas Kaithal and Bhiwani districts have been placed at bottom as these districts have performed consistently poor in all the three dimensions. Ambala and Panchkula districts that have attained top two positions have shown admirable performance as regards to education and health dimensions but none of them perform up to the mark in income dimension. But their poor performance in the income dimension is well compensated by the other two. On the other hand, Gurgaon district has failed to recover from its pitiable position in respect of education and health, even though it has outraced all the districts in income dimension. A high positive correlation can be seen between the rankings of two dimensions i.e. education and health with the GDI. A district performing well in one dimension is also performing well in the other dimension or vice versa. Again, income dimension has insignificant negative correlation (-0.09) with the GDI. Hence, a district performing well as regards to income dimension shows poor performance in remaining two dimensions i.e. education and health. This is why; the better performing districts in income dimension could not succeed in attaining better GDI rank. Gurgaon, Panipat, Faridabad, etc. are amongst such districts. However, Rewari district is an exception.

HPI, 2001

Human Poverty Index (HPI) has been estimated to reflect the depressing perspective on development on the basis of multiple variables. Like HDI, these variables of deprivation have been put in three broad groups- Income Deprivation, Educational Deprivation and Health Deprivation. The state HPI amounts to 38.74. Surprisingly, Gurgaon district in the vicinity of the National Capital has appeared as the highest deprived district in terms of human development. The statistics reveals that Gurgaon excels in one of the three dimensions i.e. income by virtue of renowned industrial development restricted to its urban areas; on the contrary the degree of deprivation in terms of other two dimensions is quite high particularly over the large rural tracts resultantly it has been placed at the top end of HPI scale. Jhajjar is the only district that has consistently shown lower deprivation in all the three dimensions. While highly diverse ranks on the three dimensions in the cases of three southern districts i.e. Gurgaon, Rewari and Mahendergarh reflect that deprivation is not pervasive in all dimensions and these districts can considerably bring down the deprivation level by improving their status in one or two dimensions. On account of highest deprivation on health dimension, Rewari district has been included in the top five districts with the highest deprivation even though it has shown lower deprivation on the other two dimensions of income and education. It suggests that the deprivation level on health has a greater bearing on the HPI as compared to the other two dimensions. However, the bearing of income dimension has been the lowest on the HPI.

HDI, 2011

The state HDI amounts to 0.58 in 2011. The HDI earned by the districts, in some cases, is such that it is not possible to delineate one district from the other if the figure is presented up to two decimals. In these cases the index value is given up to three decimals. Panchkula district is at the top with an index value of 0.65 followed by Ambala (0.63). These are the two districts that have registered their presence in the first category of high human development. Six districts namely, Sonepat, Rewari, Rohtak, Panipat, Karnal and Kurukshetra have found place in the second category of upper moderate level. In this way one can easily deduce from the present statistics that the districts with high HDI are mainly concentrated in the north-eastern part of the state. As many as seven districts have shown poor performance by recording HDI below 0.57 thereby placed in the last category of human development. These districts are concentrated either in the south or in the western part of the state. Bhiwani (0.54) district is at the bottom, however, the situation of Mahendergarh and Jind is no better. None of the districts is too consistent in its performance to obtain the same rank in all the three basic dimensions. However, relatively high consistency can be seen in Panchkula, Ambala, Sonepat, Rewari (high ranked districts); and Bhiwani, Jind, Fatehabad and Sirsa (lower ranked districts). The performance of Bhiwani district is equally poor in both the income and health dimensions. Similar is the performance of Jind district as regards to income and education dimensions. Higher correlation of education and health dimensions with the HDI reflects that these two dimensions have greater bearing over the construction of the HDI as compared to the income dimension. The unparallel performance of Gurgaon districts fails to enhance the district in the sphere of high human development due to fairly poor performance in the other two basic dimensions of education and health. Similar is the case of Faridabad district. Both of these can improve the level of human development on the lines of Panipat district. The development trend of Rohtak district is rather interesting. It has successfully overcome its weakness of the income dimension by achieving top rank on health and a fairly higher rank on education dimension thereby respectable position on HDI. The two northern districts i.e. Karnal and Kurukshetra have shown better prospects for human development what they need is a light thrust in the spheres of income and education.

GDI, 2011

The intensity of gender discrimination in the state is such that only the top ranked district i.e. Panchkula has found place in the category of high attainment level with an index value of 0.76. Ambala and Rewari districts have failed to find place in this category by narrow margin thereby placed in the second category belonging to upper moderate attainment level. Besides, five other districts that have achieved GDI between 0.70 and 0.73 also been grouped in this category. The highest number (8) of districts has appeared in the last category pertaining to low attainment level by registering GDI below 0.67. GDI is found lowest in Kaithal district which amounts to a humble 0.64 mark. The situation of Mahendergarh district is no better. One can easily infer from the data that majority of districts located in the south-western tracts of the state are lagging behind in this context. Ambala district has given tough competition to Panchkula district in both the education and health dimensions but its performance in the third dimension (income) has pushed it to second rank on GDI. While Panchkula district has get the benefit of its relatively consistent and admirable performance in all the three dimensions thereby honoured with the top rank. None of the districts has been found too consistent to obtain the same rank in all the three dimensions. However, there are three districts that have obtained the same rank in two of the three dimensions. Rewari district has acquired appreciable third rank in both the income and education dimensions whereas Rohtak district has achieved respectable sixth rank in both the education and health dimensions. The lower ranked district Mahendergarh has obtained poor 17th rank in both the income and health dimensions. Such consistent performance has affected the GDI rankings of these districts to a large extent and as result Rewari has obtained an appreciable third rank on GDI, Rohtak district has succeeded to obtain a respectable eighth rank whereas Mahendergarh district has been awarded a poor 18th rank on GDI. On the contrary, Gurgaon district demonstrates the most inconsistent development trend as it has outpaced all the districts as regards to income dimension but thrown at the bottom as regards to health dimension. Furthermore, it has recorded a low 14th rank on the third dimension. Exemplary performance in the income sector could not stand against the poor performance with respect to the two dimensions and as a result it has slipped to a moderate 12th rank as regards to GDI. Although all the three dimensions have shown positive correlation with the GDI yet education dimension is highly (0.82) associated with the GDI. Health dimension has also shown significant (0.75) association whereas low positive correlation of income dimension with the GDI suggests that the districts with high attainment level as regards to income dimension are not necessarily be successful in achieving a respectable position on GDI and vice versa. Consider the cases of Gurgaon, Hisar, Fatehabad and Sirsa districts (high rank on income dimension but low rank on GDI), on the one hand; and Ambala, Rohtak, Kurukshetra, Yamunanagar districts (low rank on income dimension but high rank on GDI) on the other.

HPI, 2011

At the state level it is recorded 43.85 in 2011. Again Gurgaon, the highly industrialised district located in the National Capital Region, has come up with the highest deprivation level in the state. Its neighbouring Faridabad district has joined it in this category. Bhiwani and Mahendergarh districts have found place in the category of upper moderate level. Highest numbers (8) of districts have been placed in the category of lower moderate HPI level whereas as seven districts found place in the fourth category pertaining to low HPI level. The intensity of deprivation level is such that it is rather high (36.04) even in the bottom ranked Sonepat district. Nonetheless the difference of 18.14 index points between the HPI values of top and bottom ranked districts is still appallingly high indicating higher inter-district disparities. Although, Gurgaon, the highly industrialised district has earned a reputation not only in India but also in the world thereby income deprivation is quite low, but the deprivation level as regards to the other two dimensions pertaining to education and health is too high to neutralise the effect of low deprivation as regards to the income dimension. As a result, it has been awarded top rank on the HPI scale. Similar is the situation of second ranked Faridabad district though it has shown lower deprivation with regard to income and education dimensions as compared to Gurgaon district. None of the districts has come up with the same rank in all the three dimensions which suggest that the deprivation level has not been consistently higher/lower in a district in these dimensions. However, Panchkula has recorded the same 19th rank both in income and education dimensions thereby shown somewhat consistent performance. Faridabad (by bringing down health deprivation) and Kaithal (by bringing down income deprivation) districts can improve their positions considerably just by bringing down deprivation level in one dimension. Health dimension is significantly and positively associated with the HPI which indicates that the performance of a district in health dimension has a great bearing on the magnitude of the HPI. Contrarily, income dimension has demonstrated insignificant but positive correlation with the HPI thereby put inconsequential impact on the construction of the latter. However, the correlation between education dimension and the HPI is somewhat significant.

Spatio-temporal Change in HDI (2001-2011)

The state, as a whole, could not maintain its attainment levels in two (income and health) of the three broad dimensions. Although, the state has recorded visible improvement in the third dimension i.e. education sector yet it is not to a great extent to neutralise the negative impact of the former two dimensions. As a result, Human Development Index, which is an outcome of these three dimensions, has turned out to be poor in the given point of time. At the state level it is found 0.58 in 2011 as against 0.60 in 2001. The SWOT analysis of districts is depicted in Figure 12.1.

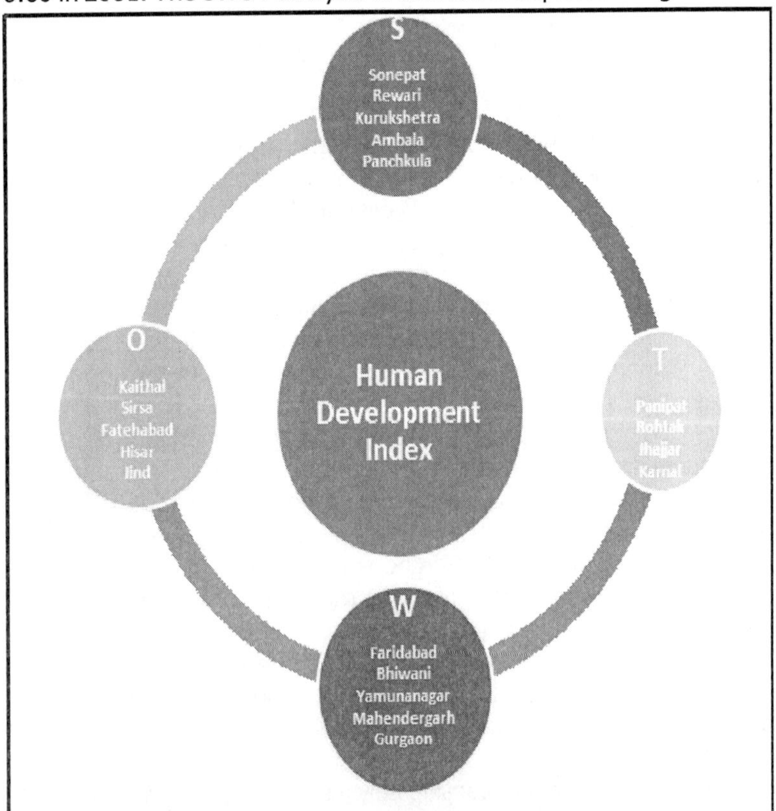

Figure 12.1. Human Development Index (2001-2011): SWOT Analysis of Districts.

S (Strength) and W (Weakness) are the two extreme categories which represent high and low attainment levels respectively. O (Opportunity) category represents the districts that have had low attainment levels but recorded higher decadal change as compared to the state average while T (Threat) category represents the districts that have had higher attainment levels but recorded lower decadal change. The higher the concentration of districts in the two extreme categories, higher shall be the intensity of inter-district disparities and vice versa. As regards to HDI five districts have shown strength by recording higher index values as well as decadal change above the state average. Majority of these districts belong to the northern part of the state. Equal number (five) of districts has shown weakness in their attainment levels thereby placed in 'W' category. Majority of districts in this category belong to southern part of the state. Four districts located in the east-central part of the state have posed threat as they have had HDI higher than the state average but losing their strength sharply by registering decadal change below the state average. On the other hand, five districts representing 'O' category, mainly located in the west-central part of the state have shown bright prospects as regards to human development by recording decadal change above the state average yet they possess index values lesser than that of the state as a whole.

High positive correlation between the districts-wise rankings of two periods strongly suggests that the intensity of shifting is fairly low, nonetheless eighteen districts out of the nineteen have experienced shift in their respective ranks. As many as ten districts have been incorporated in the category of upward movement whereas eight districts have shown downward movement. As regards to upward movement, three districts viz. Sonepat, Rewari and Panchkula have recorded spectacular increase in the HDI thereby observed a leap of five ranks each. Similarly, Kaithal district has also enhanced effectively its position by four steps. No significant upward movement has been seen in the left over districts in this category. Out of the eight districts that have registered downward movement, the sharpest slide of ten steps has been faced by Faridabad district which has thrown it at a humiliating 15th rank in 2011 from a reputable fifth rank in 2001. Panipat and Bhiwani districts have experienced a slide of five steps each. Downward movement has been insignificant in the other districts of this category. Hisar is the only district that has remained unmoved at 12th position.

Spatio-temporal Change in GDI (2001-2011)

Unlike HDI, GDI has recorded a slight decadal increase in the state. Seventeen districts have recorded positive change. SWOT analysis of districts reveals that four districts namely, Faridabad, Sonepat, Panipat and Panchkula located along the eastern border of the state have shown appreciable strength by recording higher GDI as well as higher decadal change as compared to the state average and grouped in 'S' category while Hisar is the solitary district that represents 'W' category characterised with lesser index value as well as decadal change below state average. Although Kurukshetra, Ambala, Rohtak, Yamunanagar, Jhajjar, Karnal and Rewari districts have also obtained higher index values yet they have created a threat by recording decadal change below the state average thereby placed in 'T' category. Out of these, Kurukshetra and Ambala have registered negative decadal change. On the contrary, equal number (seven) of districts has come up with opportunities i.e. 'O' category with respect to gender development as they have shown higher decadal change albeit lesser index values. Interestingly, as many as fourteen districts have found place in the

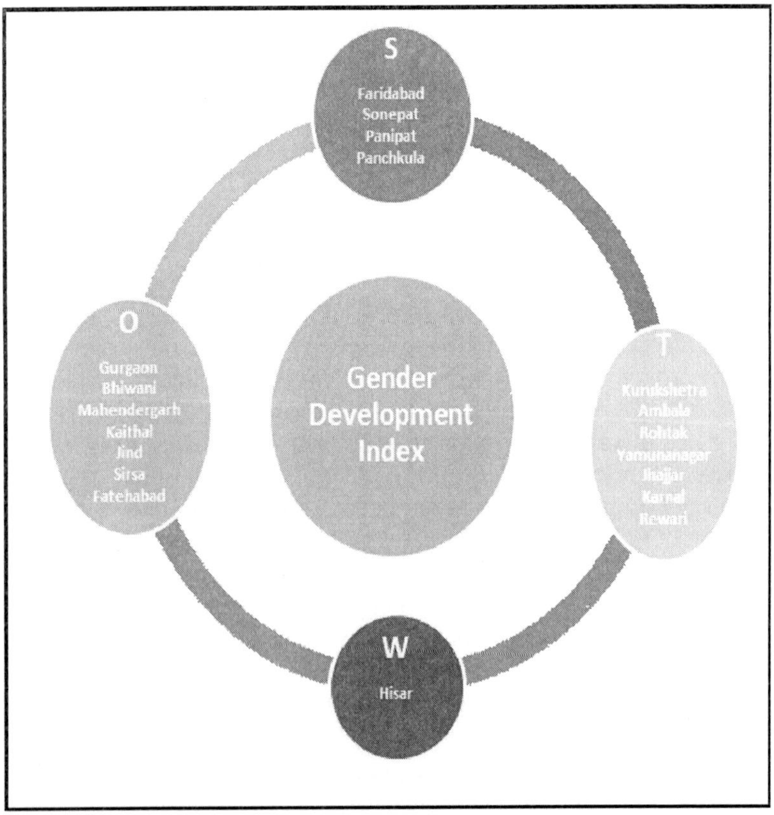

Figure 12.2. Gender Development Index (2001-2011): SWOT Analysis of Districts.

two central categories i.e. 'T' and 'O' categories left only five districts in extreme categories which implies that inter-district disparities have come down considerably in the state over the given point of time.

The state has experienced controlled inter-district shifting over the period. In addition to the third ranked Rewari district, three bottom ranked districts (Kaithal, Mahendergarh and Bhiwani) have remained unmoved at their respective ranks. Nine districts have downgraded their ranks. Out of these a notable decline of five is observed in Kurukshetra district which has driven it out from the category of districts with higher ranks. Similarly, Hisar is also expelled from a moderate 11th rank and placed at a poor 16th rank in 2011. Out of the six districts that have shown upward movement, Faridabad district with highest positive growth during the decade has registered a noteworthy thrust of six steps (12th in 2001 to sixth in 2011). Gurgaon (lower ranked) and Panipat (moderate ranked) districts have advanced four steps each. Insignificant movement is noticed in the remaining districts of the state.

Spatio-temporal Change in HPI (2001-2011)

It is very depressing to realise that the overall deprivation level of the people has increased in the state despite various efforts of the government

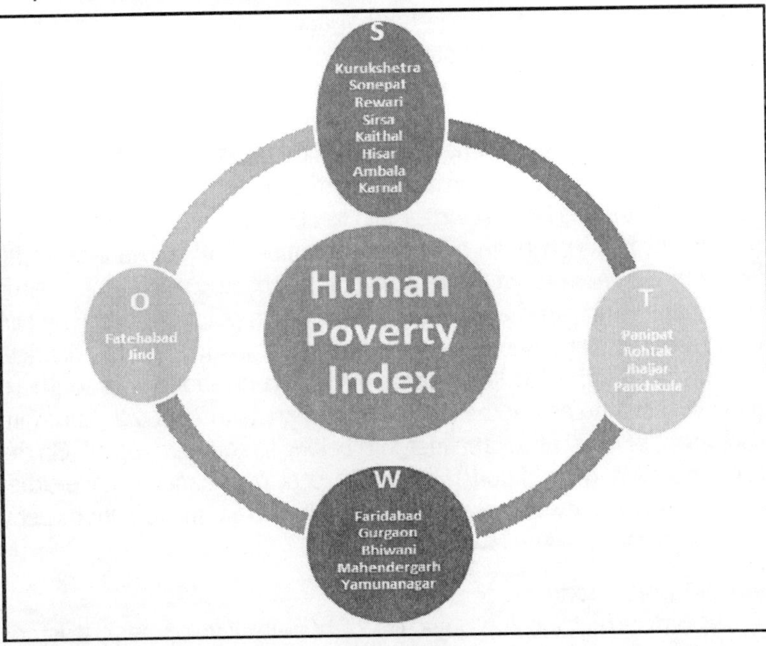

Figure 12.3. Human Poverty Index (2001-2011): SWOT Analysis of Districts.

to improve their living conditions. The HPI value which was 38.74 in the base year has increased to 43.85 in 2011 thereby recorded an increase of 13.20 per cent in proportional terms.

As many as eight districts spread over different parts of the state have appeared in 'S' category by recording lesser index values and decadal change below the state average. While four of the five districts that have been placed in 'W' category characterised with the higher deprivation level and decadal change above state average, belong to the southern part of the state. In this way, thirteen districts have been grouped in the two extreme categories which indicate that there exist significant inter-district disparities with respect to poverty levels in the state. However, only Fatehabad and Jind districts have shown prospects by bringing down their deprivation level below the state average. Panipat, Rohtak, Jhajjar and Panchkula districts have to toil hard to bring down the rate of decadal change so as to reach in 'S' category otherwise there shall be a persistent fear of inclusion of these districts in 'W' category. Majority of the districts have undergone notable shifting in their respective ranks over the period as regards to HPI. Nine districts have lowered their ranks. Out of the top ranked seven districts, six districts have moved downward. On account of highest negative decadal change, Kurukshetra district has registered the sharpest plunge of eight ranks. The other districts with handsome downward movement include Kaithal and Rewari districts that have enjoyed a plunge of seven steps each. Besides, Sirsa and Fatehabad districts are two other districts that have descended their ranks by five steps. On the other hand, seven districts have registered sharp decadal hike in their HPI value thereby enhanced their ranks in 2011 as compared to 2001. The most noteworthy thrust of ten steps is experienced by Faridabad resulting highest increase in its HPI value. Reasonable upward movement has also been observed in Panipat and Bhiwani districts. However, Gurgaon district has remained firm at the top position as regards to human poverty in the state during the given point of time. One can infer from the trend depicted in the present statistics that the districts with higher deprivation level are gaining concentration in the southern parts of the state as the top ranked four districts in 2011 viz. Gurgaon, Faridabad, Bhiwani and Mahendergarh belong to southern region. On the contrary, the districts of north Haryana, except Yamunanagar, have either maintained their lower ranks or recorded downward movement thereby reduced human poverty level relatively.

Policy Implications

In order to attain the objective of human development, it is not adequate merely to identify the flaws in education system, healthcare and economic growth. It is equally important to create a framework which ensures sustainability of suggested development strategies. The outcomes of human development in a state depend on historical and geographical factors, policies of central government and the state government. The state government is a major agency which not only formulates the development strategies but ensures budget allocations and effective implementation; hence it bears the prime responsibility for human development. Inclusive growth is the need of the hour. The benefits should reach all the sections of society. Although there has been a considerable progress in the state still there exists a substantial degree of poverty, inadequate human development, problems in employment sector and above all there are significant regional, social and gender disparities. The state government has to concentrate on the broad based development so as to achieve inclusive and equitable growth.

Based on the analysis of the present research work, major issues and policy implications for enhancing human development have been discussed in the succeeding section.

Regional Disparities

One of the most significant issues identified in the present study is that there exist appalling regional disparities in economic and social spheres of development in the state. Some districts have benefitted from the ongoing development process while some are neglected thereby lagging behind in economic and social fronts. In fact favourable geographical and political factors play the role of catalyst in the development of a region. However, in some spheres of development there are signs of improvement while in others the disparities are on the rise.

As far as regional disparities in demographic attributes is concerned, the population of Haryana is growing at a rate slightly higher than the national average, however, a great regional variation can be observed within the state. The population of Gurgaon is growing rapidly at galloping pace of more than 70 per cent whereas there are districts like Jhajjar, Jind, Ambala, etc. where it is restricted near about 10 per cent during the period under study. The most interesting example of inter-district disparities which can be quoted here is that of literacy rate of Gurgaon. Mewat district has been carved out of Gurgaon during the last inter-census period. Taking the literacy rate of the two districts separately, Gurgaon is at the top by attaining literacy rate well above 80 per cent while Mewat is at the bottom with a meek corresponding figure below 60 per cent in 2011.

Inter-district disparities as regards to income dimensions have been highlighted in the third, sixth and ninth chapters. The gist of these observations is that the districts such as Gurgaon, Faridabad, Panipat,

Rewari, etc. that have experienced appreciable advancement in industrial sector have outpaced all other districts. These districts are concentrated in the close vicinity of National Capital. On the other hand, the far off districts are lagging appallingly behind in this context. Furthermore, the districts with sound income base have succeeded in maintaining their status whereas the districts with weak income base such as Mahendergarh, Kaithal, Bhiwani, Jind, etc. could not sustain it successfully thereby the gap has widened over time.

Undoubtedly the gap has been bridged over time as far as regional disparities in education dimension are concerned. The attainment level of education has increased consistently in the state. Districts like Rohtak, Rewari, Ambala, Kurukshetra, Jhajjar, Sonepat, etc. which possessed higher attainment levels in the base year have recorded lesser decadal increase whereas districts like Gurgaon, Fatehabad, Kaithal, Jind, Sirsa, etc. have registered remarkable increase thereby bridged the inter-district gap to a great extent.

Not only the regional disparities as regards to five health indicators have increased but the attainment level in majority of cases has come down over time. The most alarming situation is faced by the two southernmost districts i.e. Faridabad and Gurgaon which have not only suffered a steep decline in their attainment levels but also weakened their already frail health parameters over the period under study. The situation of other two southern districts i.e. Bhiwani and Mahendergarh is no better as the health index in these districts has been found below the state average in 2011 and they have suffered a decline higher than that of the state. Generally districts located in the south-eastern part of the state have experienced sharper decline than that of the state average whereas the performance is better in the north-western part of the state. In this way the gap has widened between the districts located in these two different geographical locations.

Regional disparities are critically high with respect to the provision of basic amenities. As against the state figure of 45.83 per cent, the provision of safe drinking water has been observed remarkably high in districts like Sirsa (69.31 per cent), Panchkula (68.03 per cent), and Ambala (65.81 per cent) whereas it is available to only 10.90 per cent of the population of Mewat district. Similar magnitude of disparities can be observed with respect to other household amenities such as provision of latrine within premises, provision of electricity, provision of LPG/CNG for cooking, etc. Three districts namely, Mewat, Palwal and Mahendergarh are critically devoid of these amenities thereby widening the gap.

Gender Disparities

Sex ratio is one of the most significant indicators of gender development. The state is characterised with the lowest sex ratio in India. Considerable inter-district variations in the sex-ratio are also noticeable in the state. Fatehabad and Mewat districts possess appreciably high sex ratio as compared to Gurgaon, Sonepat, Jhajjar and Panipat districts. The sex ratio in the state has increased by 1.82 per cent in the state during 2001-2011. Panchkula and Faridabad districts have come forward with an appreciable decadal growth near about five per cent whereas Mahendergarh district has gone aback drastically by recording decadal decline of 2.65 per cent. Inter-district variations are rather high in respect of sex ratio (0-6 age group). Feminine gender is facing hard time as far as participation in economic activities is concerned. The proportion of females, which was already far from the unity, is becoming lesser with time and in 2011 females have made up less than one-fourth of the economically active population of the state. The steep gender gap can be noted in Yamunanagar, Ambala and Faridabad districts whereas it is found lowest in Mahendergarh, Rewari and Bhiwani districts. However, the gender gap has been bridged substantially in the state over time with respect to education and health dimensions whereas the situation is deteriorating as regards to participation in economic activities.

Rural-Urban Disparities

As regards to household amenities, noteworthy rural-urban gaps can be seen in the state. The highest gap is observed in the 'use of LPG/ PNG for cooking' (53.46 per cent) followed by 'latrine within premises' (33.82 per cent) and 'access to safe drinking water' (29.77 per cent). On the contrary, the amenity of 'electricity' has come into view with the lowest rural-urban gap of 9.01 per cent in the state. The district-wise highest rural-urban gap with regard to 'access to safe drinking water' is found in Rohtak (49.76 per cent) whereas the lowest gap can be seen in Sirsa (8.25 per cent) district. The corresponding positions of districts for the other three amenities of electricity, latrine within premises and use of LPG/PNG for cooking are Mewat (29.41 per cent) and Kurukshetra (2.48 per cent); Palwal (50.69 per cent) and Sirsa (8.35 per cent); and Faridabad (58.62 per cent) and Kaithal (39.08 per cent). Keeping in mind the size, location and economic development of the state the prevalence of such high level of rural-urban gaps are in no way convivial.

Remedial Measures: Rays of Hope

- **Revival of Agricultural Sector**: Although Haryana is amongst the most developed states of India as regards to agriculture. But the decreasing input-output ratio in agriculture has turned the people in a pathetic condition characterised with financial crisis and depression. The peasantry class of the state is facing numerous challenges like natural calamities, decreasing productivity, procurement problems, sharp increase in input costs, indebtedness, etc. which are needed to be addressed on priority basis. Agricultural scientists of the state have to toil hard to shift the farmers from traditional agriculture to modern agriculture characterised with crop diversification, dry land farming, increased use of organic fertiliser in place of chemical fertiliser, increased use of disease free high yielding varieties of seeds, etc. The state government has to concentrate on the irrigation projects especially watershed development projects, extension of crop insurance scheme, better marketing facilities, etc. Initiation of agro-processing units in less developed districts can prove an effective tool in reducing regional disparities.

- **Development of Non-farm Sector in Backward Areas:** At present times it is not the primary sector, but secondary and tertiary sectors of economy that contributes a major part of the state GSDP and raised the income level of the population. It has been revealed in the present study that the income dimension has lesser significant correlation with human development index as compared to education and health dimensions. However, the role of economic development cannot be underestimated for sustaining human development. The districts like Gurgaon, Faridabad and Panipat have succeeded to achieve moderate to high HDI only because of high income index. Furthermore, income index has played a decisive role in achieving better HDI ranks by some other districts like Panchkula, Ambala, Rewari, Hisar, etc. On the other hand there are districts like Mahendergarh, Bhiwani, Kaithal, Rohtak, Jhajjar, etc. which have failed to achieve better HDI figure because of poor income index. Keeping in mind the above observations, the state government has to frame policies for economic development especially in the backward districts so as to achieve the targeted level of human development. Policies targeted to growth can sometimes pose danger to environment which in turn may affect human development. For example, development projects like Creation of Special Economic Zone (SEZ), Power Projects, Irrigation Projects, Industrial Hubs, Transport Projects, etc. in the state may degrade the environment if taken up overlooking environmental issues. It must be kept in mind that economic development projects could not cause environment degradation.
- **Employment Generation:** More and effective steps have to be taken by the state government to generate productive employment

especially in the districts with low income index. Rural diversification is an important indicator of the quality of employment and for reducing poverty. Structural changes in agriculture can produce productive employment for rural masses.

- **Increasing Investment on Infrastructure**: There is an urgent need to increase investment on physical and social infrastructure. In addition to public investment, Private Public Partnership (PPP) investment projects must be encouraged especially in power and transport sectors. PPP projects have the potential to improve the quality of human resource by improving health and education to a great extent. The state government has to ensure judicious allocation of funds for all the districts irrespective of socio-economic and political factors.
- **Adoption of Latest Technology:** Man has drastically changed the world in modern times. Credit goes to the latest technological innovations. Green revolution has proved its worth in agriculture development in the state. There is an urgent need to adopt new technology in other spheres such as bio-technology, information and communication technology, etc. as these can play a vital role in reducing regional disparities. Qualitative improvement in education is a prerequisite to take the advantage of new technology.
- **Improvement in Education System:** The educational institutions run by the state government are associated with poor quality education. The numerous instances of poor quality of public education system and flaws of educational policies are highlighted in electronic and print media from time to time. As a result, the children of relatively well-off sections of society are turning towards private educational institutions and a dual education system has emerged between a poor quality public education system and a far better private education system. This undesirable dichotomy in the prevalent education system can be removed by improving the quality of public education system. First of all, the vacant posts of teachers should be filled up immediately and the government has to develop a mechanism in which even the backward and rural areas of the state are provided with teachers in required quantity keeping in mind the ideal student-teacher ratio. Teachers must be provided with better working conditions and their accountability and attendance must be monitored. Experiences all across India have shown that stakeholders i.e. PRIs and parental involvement has enhanced the accountability of both teachers and head of the institutions to a great extent. The government has implemented Right to Education (RTE) Act in the state and provides free education up to eighth standard. But sometimes the books are

not provided to the students even after a reasonable time thereby diverts the attention of students towards regular studies which in turn deteriorates the quality of education and enhance the drop-out rate. The government has to take up the issue seriously and stern action should be taken against the persons responsible for such lapses. One of the important shortcomings in the public education system lies in the fact that the educational policies are framed by the bureaucrats keeping in mind the foreign education system without the active involvement of academicians and neglecting ground realities at local level. Such tendency develops a sense of unresponsiveness among the teachers which in turn adversely affects the teaching-learning environment. In this way the public education system in the state has turned as a science laboratory where new experiments are tested every day. The government must ensure that the educational policies be prepared by the academicians after proper research work and in no way implemented forcefully and hurriedly by the bureaucrats.

- **Efforts for Gender Parity:** There are significant disparities in various spheres of development between males and females in the state. As compared to the national average, critically lower sex ratio and participation rates in economic activities indicate that gender disparities are highly pervasive in the state. The alarming sex ratio in the state has not only grabbed the attention of the government but a number of NGOs and researchers are also investigating the root causes behind it and suggesting remedies. The state government has to take stern action against the people engaged in female foeticide and violating PNDT Act in addition to counter the mindset of people which devalues and degrades the girl child, celebrates the oppression of women by women and justifies female foeticide and infanticide. Participation in economic activities is another gender issue to be addressed seriously. Even while participating in all major activities, women continue to be statistically invisible in the workforce. Although the situation of Haryana is better than its neighbouring state Punjab, yet it is far from satisfactory level. The state government has to take up the issue more seriously as economic independence of females is an effective tool to bridge the gender gap in other social sectors also. For this, there is a need to learn a lesson from the success stories of self help groups run by women in Andhra Pradesh.
- **Revival of Public Health Sector:** The state of public sector health infrastructure is far from satisfactory in Haryana as pointed out in the present study even though the state government has allocated sufficient funds for this sector. Majority of the villages in the state are either devoid of doctor facility or health centre or both. Moreover,

health awareness programmes have not attained desired goals as non-institutional deliveries are prevalent at large scale, prevalence of ante-natal check-ups is quite less and immunisation movement is far from the desired target. It is required from the state government not only to increase allocations in this sector but also to take stern actions to ensure accountability as lack of accountability in the system has emerged as a major problem area. The unnecessary compartmentalisation within health sector has put adverse impact on the efficiency of the health sector and hence, it should work as an integrated whole. Health personnel and infrastructure should be provided as per requirement and must be used to its maximum potential. Unfortunately, the hospitals and health centres itself are not too hygienic to give a message to the people to live in hygienic conditions. Hence, the health institutions should be maintained properly and facilities such as drinking water, sanitation, cleanliness, etc. must be looked after by health personnel. Absenteeism/ vacancy of doctors, especially in rural areas is a big challenge. It not only turns the vast public health system unproductive but also forces patients towards private practitioners. A regular system should be adopted to fill up the vacant posts of doctors. Compulsory rural area service for a certain period should be followed strictly. Moreover, doctors serving in the rural areas must be offered incentives. The posts of doctors should be rationalised effectively by shifting surplus doctors of urban areas to rural areas. Besides, community participation and involvement of Panchayati Raj Institutions (PRIs) can prove an effective tool to keep a check on doctors and paramedical staff.

- **Provision of Basic Amenities in Rural Areas:** It has been observed in the present study that the state of basic amenities such as safe drinking water, electricity, Latrine within premises, LPG/CNG for cooking and health facilities are far from satisfactory level in rural areas. All this resulted in rural-urban migration which turns urban areas overcrowded and the quality of life deteriorates to a great extent in urban areas also. To check the tendency of such rural-urban migration, the state government has to take effective measures to improve the quality of life in rural areas. The former President of India Dr A.P.J. Abdul Kalam put forward the concept of PURA (Provision of Urban Amenities in Rural Areas). PURA proposes that urban infrastructure and services to be provided in rural hubs to create economic opportunities outside of cities. Physical connectivity by providing roads, electronic connectivity by providing communication network, and knowledge connectivity by establishing professional and technical institutions in an integrated way so that economic connectivity will emanate. The central government has been running pilot PURA programmes in several states since 2004. The state government needs to take up the scheme with necessary modifications in the state with commitment.

- **Effective Implementation of Poverty Alleviation Programmes:** Apart from wide-ranging economic policies, poverty alleviation programmes aimed at self-employment and wage labour can help in reducing poverty in the state. Many studies focussing on poverty alleviation programmes have pointed out that the performance of the state has not been satisfactory enough in implementing these programmes in an effective manner and the major chunk of funds released for these programmes is either remained unutilised or drained out in the hands of corrupt people involved in the implementation of such programmes. The official data and the ground realities tell two different stories. Quite often the questions are raised even on the BPL list prepared by the state government to identify the people below poverty line, the beneficiaries of such programmes. It has been observed in the preceding section of the present study that the proportion of BPL population has increased sharply in some of the districts over the period, which raises questions on the viability of BPL survey. In the state like Haryana, there is no need to increase allocations, but the state government is urgently required to concentrate on monitoring and improving delivery systems in poverty alleviation programmes as the scope of improvement is fairly high.

People are always best resource of a nation. The state government should invest in its people keeping in mind the prevalent disparities in income and social sectors because biased development leads to unrest among the unprivileged sections. And no government in a democracy can afford to ignore large sections of the population. Thus, equal opportunities should be provided to the people to participate in their own governance. This is pertinent for reducing exclusion, inequality, social anxiety and to improve overall human development. This is the way on which the state can leap forward to the future to become one of the best performing states in human development.

Appendix Table I

Haryana: Inter-district Per Capita Gross Domestic Product at Constant Prices (1999-00) 2000-01

District/ State	*Per Capita GDP (Rs.)*	*Real PC GDP in PPP ($)*
Ambala	30065	5293
Bhiwani	18141	3193
Faridabad	32577	5735
Fatehabad	26046	4585
Gurgaon	49074	8639
Hisar	26364	4641
Jhajjar	19991	3519
Jind	21433	3773
Kaithal	19381	3412
Karnal	24652	4340
Kurukshetra	21658	3813
Mahendergarh	14897	2622
Panchkula	27788	4892
Panipat	34738	6115
Rewari	26917	4738
Rohtak	21147	3723
Sirsa	25128	4423
Sonepat	21663	3814
Yamunanagar	24514	4315
Haryana	**26562**	**4676**

(Contd.)

(Contd. Appendix Table -I)

Haryana: Inter-district Per Capita Gross Domestic Product at Constant Prices (1999-00) 2008-09

District	*Per Capita GDP (Rs.)*	*Real PC GDP in PPP ($)*
Ambala	49377	3942
Bhiwani	27081	2162
Faridabad	59362	4739
Fatehabad	34487	2753
Gurgaon	107304	8567
Hisar	37840	3021
Jhajjar	33988	2713
Jind	27615	2205
Kaithal	26275	2098
Karnal	37335	2981
Kurukshetra	33759	2695
Mahendergarh	23777	1898
Panchkula	58239	4649
Panipat	68273	5451
Rewari	48835	3899
Rohtak	32791	2618
Sirsa	34947	2790
Sonepat	37354	2982
Yamunanagar	37334	2981
Haryana	**45617**	**3642**

Source: Economic and Statistical Analysis, Govt. of Haryana (For Per Capita GDP) The data of India PC GDP in PPP ($) and (Rs.) is obtained from www.pbplanning.gov.in and tradechakra.com

Note: Real Per Capita GDP has been obtained using the formula: $\frac{\text{India Per Capita GDP in PPP (\$)}}{\text{India Per Capita GDP (Rs.)}} \times \text{District wise GDP}$

Appendix Table II
Demographic Characteristics of Haryana

District/ State	*Sex Ratio 0-6 population*		*Literacy Rate (Persons)*		*Literacy Rate (Males)*		*Literacy Rate (Females)*	
	2001	*2011*	*2001*	*2011*	*2001*	*2011*	*2001*	*2011*
Ambala	782	807	75.3	82.9	82.3	88.5	67.4	76.6
Bhiwani	841	831	67.4	76.7	80.3	87.4	53	64.8
Faridabad	847	842	76.3	83	85.1	89.9	65.5	75.2
Fatehabad	828	845	58	69.1	68.2	78.1	46.5	59.3
Gurgaon	807	826	78.5	84.4	88	90.3	67.5	77.6
Hisar	832	849	64.8	73.2	76.6	82.8	51.1	62.3
Jhajjar	801	774	72.4	80.8	83.3	89.4	59.6	71
Jind	818	835	62.1	72.7	73.8	82.5	48.5	61.6
Kaithal	791	821	59	70.6	69.2	79.3	47.3	60.7
Karnal	809	820	67.7	76.4	76.3	83.7	58	68.3
Kurukshetra	771	817	69.9	76.7	78.1	83.5	60.6	69.2
Mahendergarh	818	778	69.9	78.9	84.7	91.3	54.1	65.3
Mewat	893	903	43.5	56.1	61.2	73	23.9	37.6
Palwal	854	862	59.2	70.3	75.1	82.6	40.8	56.4
Panchkula	829	850	74	83.4	80.9	88.6	65.7	77.5
Panipat	809	833	69.2	77.5	78.5	85.4	58	68.2
Rewari	811	784	75.2	82.2	88.4	92.9	60.8	70.5
Rohtak	799	807	73.7	80.4	83.2	88.4	62.6	71.2
Sirsa	817	852	60.6	70.4	70.1	78.6	49.9	61.2
Sonepat	788	790	72.8	80.8	83.1	89.4	60.7	70.9
Yamunanagar	806	825	71.6	78.9	78.8	85.1	63.4	72
Haryana	**819**	**830**	**67.9**	**76.64**	**78.5**	**85.4**	**55.7**	**66.8**

Source: Census of India 2011, Series 7, Provisional Population Totals

Appendix Table III

Selected Health Indicators of Hayana (2002-04)					
District/ State	*% villages with any Govt. Health Facility*[1]	*% villages With Doctor*[2]	*% of children age 12-35 months Fully Vaccinated*[3]	*% of women received full ante-natal check-ups4*	*% of women who had institutional deliveries*
Ambala	44.3	18.0	92.9	19.2	61.8
Bhiwani	57.9	88.3	47.8	15.6	36.3
Faridabad	65.2	85.4	53.7	6.5	31.2
Fatehabad	70.3	46.5	65.1	7.7	37.9
Gurgaon	57.4	92.8	32.9	10.0	20.4
Hisar	88.0	40.9	63.6	13.9	32.4
Jhajjar	64.6	65.3	68.0	15.4	46.2
Jind	50.2	76.0	62.4	6.6	27.1
Kaithal	76.3	90.1	41.4	13.1	28.4
Karnal	79.1	75.6	73.9	13.2	33.8
Kurukshetra	53.6	19.8	81.7	19.5	50.3
Mahendergarh	63.5	65.4	52.6	7.1	36.8
Panchkula	46.5	79.9	85.7	20.8	45.1
Panipat	81.5	97.4	63.8	13.3	33.9
Rewari	56.5	29.3	65.8	12.7	45.9
Rohtak	86.4	71.2	81.0	19.0	41.9
Sirsa	64.0	70.4	49.1	7.2	33.3
Sonepat	63.0	76.1	55.1	8.8	41.1
Yamunanagar	36.2	77.2	72.0	12.2	31.6
Haryana	**64.0**	**66.4**	**62.9**	**11.8**	**35.1**

Source: IIPS, Mumbai, DLHS-II (2002-04)

(Contd.)

(Contd. Appendix Table -III)

Selected Health Indicators of Hayana (2007-08)				
% villages with any Govt. Health Facility[1]	% villages With Doctor[2]	% of children age 12-35 months Fully Vaccinated[3]	% of women that received full ante-natal check-ups[4]	% of women who had institutional deliveries
37.5	34.4	79.1	17.4	55.4
56.1	12.2	58.4	8.9	35.7
25.0	0.0	46.4	9.3	39.1
68.3	12.2	62.8	9.5	48.6
25.6	16.7	32.3	11.5	28.9
81.1	16.2	55.8	10.4	48.6
71.8	5.1	64.8	16.2	48.0
60.0	27.5	55.4	9.7	42.1
60.0	35.0	72.5	21.1	48.0
40.5	54.1	75.2	16.6	51.3
43.2	54.1	67.8	11.8	64.2
30.2	11.6	67.7	9.1	56.8
28.6	42.9	78.1	19.1	64.3
53.3	46.7	57.0	6.2	39.0
43.9	19.5	67.3	20.6	65.0
78.1	18.8	75.7	27.5	52.8
56.8	21.6	61.3	17.8	53.5
64.9	45.9	73.0	14.9	53.7
12.9	29.0	70.0	20.8	52.3
49.1	**25.8**	**59.6**	**13.2**	**46.8**

Source: IIPS, Mumbai, DLHS-III (2007-08)

Appendix Table IV
District Wise Population and Workers By Sex: 2001

District/State	Population			Main workers		Marginal Workers		Total Workers		
	Males	Females	Total	Males	Females	Males	Females	Males	Females	Total
Ambala	542977	471434	1014411	245559	30089	31073	17800	276632	47889	324521
Bhiwani	758253	666769	1425022	310301	114909	63086	121024	373387	235933	609320
Faridabad	1193063	1001523	2194586	504791	104872	71687	104412	576478	209284	785762
Fatehabad	427862	378296	806158	199817	61806	33042	68310	232859	130116	362975
Gurgaon	886451	773838	1660289	359967	104677	55210	109804	415177	214481	629658
Hisar	830520	706597	1537117	382579	134238	48239	100516	430818	234754	665572
Jhajjar	476475	403597	880072	201164	75044	43645	68862	244809	143906	388715
Jind	642282	547545	1189827	281070	90979	50072	99825	331142	190804	521946
Kaithal	510513	435618	946131	226272	41855	33407	70477	259679	112332	372011
Karnal	683368	590815	1274183	299403	56063	43511	56478	342914	112541	455455
Kurukshetra	442328	383126	825454	205777	44819	20633	37163	226410	81982	308392
Mahendergarh	423578	388943	812521	157295	47409	46006	101154	203301	148563	351864
Panchkula	256939	211472	468411	127013	23340	13110	15181	140123	38521	178644
Panipat	528860	438589	967449	238701	50312	31155	62633	269856	112945	382801
Rewari	403034	362317	765351	159509	45346	40891	87876	200400	133222	333622
Rohtak	509038	431090	940128	216998	71227	34098	48750	251096	119977	371073
Sirsa	593245	523404	1116649	278494	85452	36212	75413	314706	160865	475571
Sonepat	695723	583452	1279175	291032	92417	54418	85164	345450	177581	523031
Yamunanagar	559444	482186	1041630	247262	33466	33027	22778	280289	56244	336533
Haryana	**11363953**	**9780611**	**21144564**	**4933004**	**1308320**	**782522**	**1353620**	**5715526**	**2661940**	**8377466**

Source: Census of India,2001, B01-0600 TABLE

Appendix V

District Wise Population and Workers By Sex: 2011

	Population			Main workers		Marginal Workers		Total Workers		
District/State	Males	Females	Total	Males	Females	Males	Females	Males	Females	Total
Ambala	598703	529647	1128350	282066	37409	38054	14610	320120	52019	372139
Bhiwani	866672	767773	1634445	357937	87738	72741	104590	430678	192328	623006
Faridabad*	1520607	1331834	2852441	611605	100643	106792	69752	718397	170395	888792
Fatehabad	495360	446651	942011	231189	55069	32309	50516	263498	105585	369083
Gurgaon**	1387852	1215843	2603695	576056	115563	81042	62019	657098	177582	834680
Hisar	931562	812369	1743931	420510	110717	67811	92583	488321	203300	691621
Jhajjar	514667	443738	958405	205882	40575	44138	35939	250020	76514	326534
Jind	713006	621146	1334152	313160	72691	55117	82454	368277	155145	523422
Kaithal	571003	503301	1074304	249905	40758	42791	40445	292696	81203	373899
Karnal	797712	707612	1505324	351730	59803	59916	44613	411646	104416	516062
Kurukshetra	510976	453679	964655	244619	41285	23937	26939	268556	68224	336780
Mahendergarh	486665	435423	922088	176687	35715	56248	69934	232935	105649	338584
Panchkula	299679	261614	561293	148695	34136	16170	12478	164865	46614	211479
Panipat	646857	558580	1205437	286740	52276	41927	31375	328667	83651	412318
Rewari	474335	425997	900332	200570	49649	34756	52752	235326	102401	337727
Rohtak	568479	492725	1061204	238995	49954	33651	23367	272646	73321	345967
Sirsa	682582	612607	1295189	330680	68489	38782	64052	369462	132541	502003
Sonepat	781299	668702	1450001	326530	70233	64555	61861	391085	132094	523179
Yamunanagar	646718	567487	1214205	307044	31980	35299	14910	342343	46890	389233
Haryana	**13494734**	**11856728**	**25351462**	**5860600**	**1154683**	**946036**	**955189**	**6806636**	**2109872**	**8916508**

Source: Primary Census Abstract, Haryana 2011

* Including Palwal

** Including Mewat

Appendix Table VI

Proportion of Marriages Below the Legal Age of Marriage (2002-04)		
DISTRICT	*Males*	*Females*
Ambala	12.2	1.6
Bhiwani	32.6	45.1
Faridabad	41.3	33.0
Fatehabad	28.0	23.6
Gurgaon	48.6	49.1
Hisar	25.3	34.5
Jhajjar	19.8	21.9
Jind	34.3	26.6
Kaithal	33.6	31.3
Karnal	25.7	15.6
Kurukshetra	21.0	6.0
Mahendergarh	36.5	42.5
Panchkula	15.8	11.9
Panipat	26.8	29.4
Rewari	23.2	16.5
Rohtak	17.7	26.8
Sirsa	33.8	23.7
Sonepat	21.8	25.8
Yamunanagar	20.7	14.5
Haryana	**29.0**	**27.8**

Source: IIPS, DLHS-II Survey, 2002-04

Proportion of Marriages Below the Legal Age of Marriage (2007-08)		
DISTRICT	*Males*	*Females*
Ambala	14.4	2.9
Bhiwani	31.7	20.7
Faridabad*	23.0	15.3
Fatehabad	23.4	17.2
Gurgaon**	47.7	32.8
Hisar	31.8	25.2
Jhajjar	21.4	14.5
Jind	19.7	20.2
Kaithal	25.5	12.8
Karnal	23.4	10.7
Kurukshetra	20.4	4.4
Mahendergarh	24.1	33.2
Panchkula	17.3	3.4
Panipat	27.2	8.9
Rewari	22.2	14.2
Rohtak	21.4	9.6
Sirsa	31.0	10.1
Sonepat	19.6	4.4
Yamunanagar	16.6	3.8
Haryana	**27.4**	**15.9**

Source: IIPS, DLHS-III Survey, 2007-08
* average value of Faridabad and Palwal
** average value of Gurgaon and Mewat

Bibliography

Census of India, 2001. "A - Series General Population Tables". Directorate of Census Operations, Haryana, Chandigarh.

Census of India, 2001. "B - Series Economic Tables". Directorate of Census Operations, Haryana, Chandigarh.

Census of India, 2001. "HH - Series Household Tables". Directorate of Census Operations, Haryana, Chandigarh.

Census of India, 2001. "Primary Census Abstract, Haryana". Directorate of Census Operations, Haryana, Chandigarh.

Census of India, 2011. "A - Series Provisional Population Tables". Directorate of Census Operations, Haryana, Chandigarh.

Census of India, 2011. "HH - Series Economic Tables". Directorate of Census Operations, Haryana, Chandigarh.

Census of India, 2011. "Primary Census Abstract, Haryana". Directorate of Census Operations, Haryana, Chandigarh.

Dreze, J. and Sen, Amartya. 1995. "India: Economic Development and Social Opportunity". Oxford University Press, New Delhi.

Government of Andhra Pradesh, 2008. "Andhra Pradesh Human Development Report 2007". Centre for Economic and Social Studies, Government of Andhra Pradesh.

Government of Arunachal Pradesh, 2005. "Arunachal Pradesh Human Development Report 2005". Department of Planning, Government of Arunachal Pradesh.

Government of Assam, 2003. "Assam Human Development Report 2003". Government of Assam.

Government of Haryana, 2005. "Haryana's Human Development Report 2005". Haryana Institute of Public Administration (HIPA), Gurgaon.

Government of Haryana, 2010. "Statistical Abstract of Haryana 2008-09". Department of Economic and Statistical Analysis Haryana, Panchkula.

Government of Haryana, 2011. "Economic Survey of Haryana 2010-11". Department of Economic and Statistical Analysis Haryana, Panchkula.

Government of Himachal Pradesh, 2002. "Himachal Pradesh Human Development Report 2002". Government of Himachal Pradesh.

Government of India, 2002. "National Human Development Report 2001". Planning Commission, Government of India.

Government of Karnataka, 1999. "Human Development in Karnataka 1999". Government of Karnataka.

Government of Kerala, 2005. "Kerala Human Development Report 2005". State Planning Board, Government of Kerala.

Government of Maharashtra, 2002. "Human Development Report Maharashtra, 2002". Government of Maharashtra.

Government of Nagaland, 2004. "Nagaland State Human Development Report 2004". Department of Planning and Coordination, Government of Nagaland.

Government of Orissa, 2005. "Orissa Human Development Report 2004". Department of Planning and Coordination, Government of Orissa.

Government of Punjab, 2004. "Human Development Report 2004 Punjab". Government of Punjab.

Government of Rajasthan, 2002. "Rajasthan Human Development Report, 2002". Government of Rajasthan.

Government of Sikkim, 2001. "Sikkim Human Development Report, 2001". Government of Sikkim & Social Science Press, New Delhi.

Government of Tamil Nadu, 2003. "Tamil Nadu Human Development Report, 2003". Government of Tamil Nadu, Social Science Press, New Delhi.

Government of West Bengal, 2004. "West Bengal Human Development Report 2004". Development and Planning Department, Government of West Bengal.

International Institute of Population Sciences, 2002-04. "Reproductive and Child Health: District Level Household Survey- Haryana". International Institute of Population Sciences, Mumbai.

International Institute of Population Sciences, 2007-08. "Reproductive and Child Health: District Level Household and Facility Survey- Haryana". International Institute of Population Sciences, Mumbai.

Joshi, Hemlata, 2003. "Educational Development Index- Rajasthan: Spatio-Temporal Appraisal at Panchayat Samiti/ Block Level (1999-2000)". University Book House (P) Ltd., Jaipur.

Joshi, Hemlata, 2005. "Economic Development Index: Spatio- Temporal & Gender Appraisal at Panchayat Samiti/ Block Level". University Book House (P) Ltd., Jaipur.

Mahatma Gandhi Labour Institute, 2004. "Gujarat State Human Development Report 2004". Mahatma Gandhi Labour Institute, Ahmedabad.

Planning Commission, Government of India, 2009. "Haryana Development Report". Academic Foundation, New Delhi.

Rajput, Pam. "A Situational Analysis of Women and Girls in Haryana". National Commission for Women, New Delhi.

United Nations Development Programme, 2008. "Human Development Report 2007/2008 Fighting Climate Change: Human Solidarity in a divided world". Palgrave Macmillan, New York.

United Nations Development Programme, 2009. "Human Development Report 2009 overcoming barriers: Human mobility and development". Palgrave Macmillan, New York.

Index

F

G

H

I